Camp free in B.C.

EXPLORE, HIKE, FISH, BIKE, PADDLE, RELAX

Field-tested and written by Kathy & Craig Copeland

hiking camping.com

Heading outdoors eventually leads you within.

The first people on earth were hikers and campers. So today, when we walk the earth and bed down on it, we're living in the most primitive, elemental way known to our species. We're returning to a way of life intrinsic to the human experience. We're shedding the burden of millennia of civilization. We're seeking catharsis. We're inviting enlightenment.

hikingcamping.com publishes unique guidebooks – literate, entertaining, opinionated – that ensure you make the most of your precious time outdoors. Our titles cover some of the world's most spectacular wild lands.

To further support the community of hikers and campers, and to connect you with others who share your zeal for wilderness, we created www.hikingcamping.com. Go there to plan your next trip, or to stay inspired between trips. Get advice from people returning from your destination, or share tips from your recent adventure. And please send anything you want to post that will assist or amuse hikers and campers.

To fully benefit from, and contribute to, Camp Free in B.C., visit www.hikingcamping.com and follow this path: Guidebooks> Vehicle Camping>Camp Free in B.C.>Field Reports, or Updates.

nomads@hikingcamping.com **hiking camping**.com

MEMBER

1%

FOR THE
PLANET.

Businesses donating
1% of their sales to the
natural environment
www.onepercentfortheplanet.org

Copyright © 2005 by Kathy and Craig Copeland

First edition, March 1995; Second edition, March 1997
Third edition, updated & revised, June 1999
Fourth edition, updated & revised, May 2005
Fourth edition, updated and reprinted, April 2007

Published in Canada by hikingcamping.com, inc.
P.O. Box 8563, Canmore, Alberta, T1W 2V3 Canada
email: nomads@hikingcamping.com

All photos by the authors.

Maps and production by Angela Lockerbie
email: lockerbie@shaw.ca

Cover and interior design by Matthew Clark
www.subplot.com

Printed in China by Asia Pacific Offset

Library and Archives Canada Cataloguing in Publication

Copeland, Kathy, 1959-
    Camp free in B.C.: explore, hike, fish, bike, paddle, relax
field tested and written by Kathy & Craig Copeland. — 4th ed.

Includes index, contents.   ISBN-13: 978-0-9735099-3-9
                             ISBN-10: 0-9735099-3-7

    1. Camp sites, facilities, etc.—British Columbia—Guidebooks.
2. Camping—British Columbia—Guidebooks. 3. Outdoor recreation—
British Columbia—Guidebooks. 4. British Columbia—Guidebooks.
I. Copeland, Craig, 1955- II. Title.

GV191.46.B75C66 2005   796.54'09711   C2005-902371-6

YOUR SAFETY IS YOUR RESPONSIBILITY

The authors and publisher disclaim liability for any loss or injury to
any person, or damage to any vehicle or property, that could possibly be
attributed to using information in this book.
    Camp Free in B.C. offers suggestions, but you make the decisions. Only
you can assess your vehicle's suitability for exploration. Only you can
assess your competence at navigating unsigned roads and negotiating the
hazards of off-pavement driving. Only you can assess your aptitude for
contending with wilderness and surviving the elements while camping.
This book is not a substitute for skill, common sense or sound judgment.
    The information in this book is as accurate as possible, but not infalli-
ble. Backcountry conditions are always changing. Logging companies
continually build new roads and stop maintaining others. Signs come and
go. You must always be observant and cautious.

Contents

SOUTHERN B.C

Hogsback Lake, Central B.C.

SOUTHERN B.C.
CAMPING REGIONS

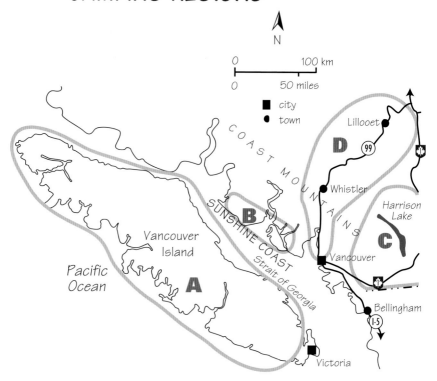

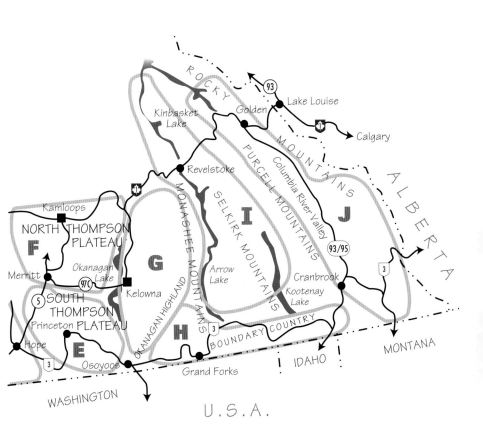

ROCKY MOUNTAINS

Kinbasket Lake

93

Golden

Lake Louise

Calgary

ALBERTA

Revelstoke

PURCELL MOUNTAINS

Columbia River Valley

Kamloops

NORTH THOMPSON PLATEAU

F

SELKIRK MOUNTAINS

MONASHEE MOUNTAINS

I

J

93/95

Merritt

Okanagan Lake

97C

G

Arrow Lake

Cranbrook

3

5

Kelowna

SOUTH THOMPSON PLATEAU

Kootenay Lake

Princeton

OKANAGAN HIGHLAND

H

BOUNDARY COUNTRY

MONTANA

Hope

E

3

Osoyoos

3

Grand Forks

IDAHO

WASHINGTON

U.S.A.

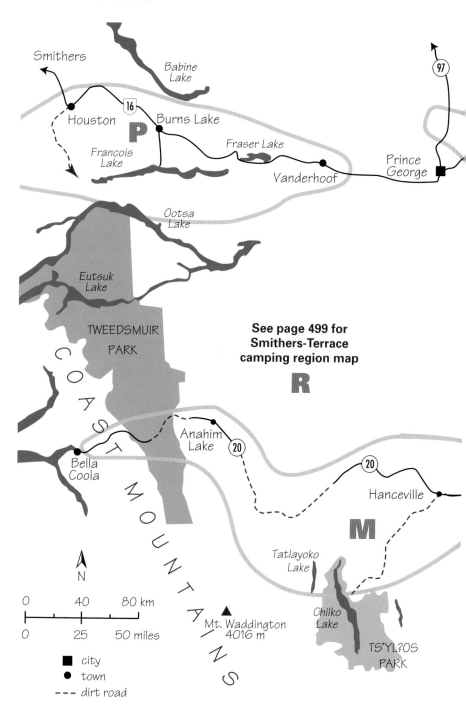

Smithers

Babine Lake

97

Houston

16

Burns Lake

Fraser Lake

P

Francois Lake

Vanderhoof

Prince George

Ootsa Lake

Eutsuk Lake

TWEEDSMUIR PARK

See page 499 for Smithers-Terrace camping region map

R

C O A S T

Anahim Lake

20

20

Bella Coola

Hanceville

M O U N T A I N S

M

Tatlayoko Lake

N

0   40   80 km

0   25   50 miles

Mt. Waddington 4016 m

Chilko Lake

TS'YL?OS PARK

■ city
● town
- - - dirt road

CENTRAL B.C.
CAMPING REGIONS

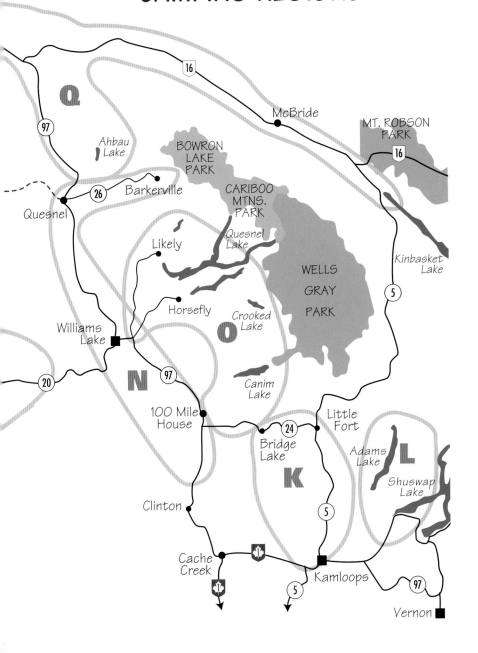

Fraser River Canyon, south of Lillooet

Philosophy, Strategies and Joys of Camping Free

British Columbia has more than 1,150 free campgrounds.

THE ANTIDOTE TO CIVILIZATION

British Columbia has more than 1,300 campgrounds under the stewardship of the Ministry of Tourism, Sport & the Arts. (Abbreviated to MOT elsewhere in this book.) These recreation sites were previously managed by the B.C. Forest Service and were entirely free of charge. Today, 88% of them remain free of charge.

Camp Free in B.C. offers precise directions to the best 430 MOT campgrounds in southern and central British Columbia. They're tucked into immense forests, in the shadows of noble mountains, beside dancing rivers, snuggled up to lakes grand and petite. A few campgrounds are big, organized, groomed, much like provincial parks and nearly as popular. Others are tiny, rough hewn, seldom visited, and almost certain to offer solitude. Many are hidden just a short distance off paved roads. Some are deep in the woods. All are accessible by two-wheel-drive. You can reach them easily and safely in your low-clearance car or your big RV. En route, you'll savour a fresh perspective on the stunning geography of this glorious province. You'll be astonished at where B.C.'s seemingly endless network of backroads can take you. Even with our detailed directions, you'll feel the excitement of discovery.

Nearly all the campgrounds in this book are away from towns and highways, so you'll likely glimpse one of the locals: perhaps an owl or a coyote, maybe a bear or a moose. Even the common sight of a deer or a salmon can thrill and comfort, reminding you that despite the damage done, wilderness still exists and nature is alive and well. That's the joy of free-camping. Not just what you keep in your wallet, but what you take away in your heart.

Camping is CPR for your senses. It opens your eyes to the night sky, with stars so thick they look like clouds. It opens your ears to the music of wind in the trees, water rushing over rocks, or maybe absolute silence. It reacquaints you with the simple, sweet pleasure of not feeling cement under foot, not being confined by fences or walls, not complying with rules, and sometimes not having to look at another human being. It's the antidote to civilization.

And *free* camping is *real* camping. It's an adventure—something sadly missing from most people's lives and impossible to find at commercial campgrounds. Neon signs? Receptions offices? Pop machines? Hook-ups? TV antennas? Where's the adventure in that? It's hard to tell many campgrounds from RV dealerships these days. They're just parking lots. Even provincial-park campgrounds are often within earshot of a roaring highway.

You'll forego conveniences at the campgrounds described *in Camp Free*. None have showers, flush toilets, or even running water. But what most people consider necessities are actually luxuries. Doing without can make you feel more complete. And camping, by definition, means contending

Mitten Lake, Columbia Valley

with the elements—bugs, wind, rain, cold, heat. But if you're prepared and can shrug off minor discomfort, the elements can make you feel more alive. If you go with an open mind and soft heart, *Camp Free* will guide you to a rousing experience. You'll be revitalized, able to calmly slip back into the shackles of civilization with renewed vigor. Your memory, your mental gallery, will be filled with vivid images—sustenance for the soul until your next outing. At the very least, you'll have a story to tell neighbours and co-workers who've never sought adventure beyond the nearest video store.

GET OUT WHILE YOUR CAN

Twenty-five years ago, free-camping was so easy that a guidebook was unnecessary. A short drive from any city would reward you with lots of beautiful places to park where nobody would bother you. But rampant development and population growth have overtaken those of us who would flee. Now you have to drive hours, and still you'll be contending with country homes, resorts, and "no trespassing" or "no overnight camping" signs that make it almost impossible to free-camp—unless you know where to go.

That's why we wrote this book: to describe B.C.'s extensive network of MOT campgrounds, explain exactly where they are and how to get there, and encourage you to enjoy and protect them.

With *Camp Free* in hand, you're now a fully-informed camper. This is the most comprehensive guide to B.C.'s free campgrounds. But get out while you can. Camping is increasingly popular. Most campgrounds are being visited more frequently. Economic pressures have decreased B.C. government budgets. The result: camping in B.C. is not as free as it once was, and that trend could continue.

In 1998, B.C. was gripped by a financial seizure. The provincial government slashed budgets. Recreation in particular was decimated. Attempting to make up the shortfall and continue its services, the Ministry of Forests asked campers to buy an annual camping pass. It cost $27 and entitled a group of up to six people unlimited use of forestry campgrounds throughout the province for an entire year. In theory, it was smart and fair. But the public balked, compliance was poor, and enforcement—by the painfully under-staffed Forest Service—was spotty and half-hearted. The program failed. The government's response was reactionary: "We'll have to close most of the campgrounds." The public squawked louder. In 2003, the Premier, along with Forest Service officials, toured the province and listened to citizens clamor for the recreation program's revival. The people prevailed. The government provided funding to improve forestry campgrounds and keep them open. The funding might be renewed, but don't count on it. The '98 to '03 budget brouhaha wasn't the first time free camping in B.C. has been threatened. Twice before, myopic leaders tried to shortchange or obliterate the recreation budget. Ensure it doesn't happen again. Continue pelting your MLA with pointed reminders: "We want to camp free in B.C.!"

"Got Everything? Okay, let's go."

FREE AND LOW-FEE

Of the 430 campgrounds described here, 350 are free-of-charge year-round. They're either user-maintained, or managed by a volunteer community group or logging company. The other 80 are free-of-charge roughly mid-October through mid-May but charge a low fee mid-May through mid-October. These campgrounds are more popular—due to especially convenient or scenic locations—and therefore require frequent maintenance, hence a nominal, per-site, per-night fee. Seniors and the disabled pay 50% less. The fee covers up to six people per campsite. It helps supplement the cost of removing garbage, pumping pit toilets, maintaining access, ensuring public safety, addressing environmental concerns, and general upkeep. Where necessary, it might fund a patrol to keep the peace, or pay for a repair necessitated by vandalism. Fees are collected by whomever the MOT has authorized to oversee a particular campground. It could be a community organization, First Nations tribe, local government, or independent contractor. Despite the fee, these campgrounds are a bargain compared to commercial or provincial-park campgrounds yet offer a richer camping experience for all the reasons explained above, in *The Antidote to Civilization*.

CAMP FREE NEEDS YOUR HELP

We do our best to collect up-to-date information about all the backroads and campgrounds described in *Camp Free*, but we still need your help. So during your camping trip, if you find any discrepancies between reality and the content of this book, please takes notes, then email nomads@ hikingcamping.com right away. Send us as much detail as possible. Have road junctions, campground conditions, or fees changed? Tell us. We'll immediately post your submission on our website, www.hikingcamping.com, for the benefit of other campers. And we'll include your update in the next printed edition of *Camp Free*. Remember, you're not just contributing to this book. You're making it possible for all of us to continue camping free in B.C. Thank you.

THE MAP IS NOT THE TERRITORY

Free campgrounds are never on paved roads. Signs announcing free campgrounds are rarely on paved roads. Only after you drive onto a backroad might you encounter a sign, typically *way* after. Even many campgrounds are unsigned. That's why *Camp Free* is invaluable.

Researching *Camp Free*, we relied on Forest Service district recreation maps. (They were free-of-charge back then. Due to budget constraints, they're no longer available.) Though helpful, these maps lacked detail. They showed only major junctions, omitting numerous minor ones. They were not topo-

graphical, so ascents, descents, and switchbacks were not indicated. They rarely labeled the roads leading to campgrounds and never specified when to turn off highways. Using these maps, we were reminded: the map is not the territory. And commercially published map books are no better. They too are terribly vague, requiring you to have the skills of an explorer and the instincts of a detective. What we needed were precise directions, written by campers who'd actually driven all the roads and visited all the campgrounds. We realized that's what you'd need, too. So we set about creating the book you now hold in your hands.

A highway sign like this could indicate the logging road you're looking for is just ahead.

With so little information to guide us on our field trips, we were often on edge. "How much farther?" "This can't be the right road." "Think we'll make it?" "No way there's a campground up here." Sometimes we felt like rats in a maze. But you won't. Following *Camp Free's* precise directions, you can relax and enjoy the drive knowing you *are* on the right road, your vehicle *can* make it, and there *is* a campground up there. *Camp Free* is the only resource you can rely on for accurate guidance to most of B.C.'s free campgrounds.

YOU'LL KNOW BEFORE YOU GO

Camp Free not only gives you directions to the campgrounds, it tells you what to expect when you arrive. How's the scenery? Is the area quiet or noisy? What outdoor activities are possible? Now you'll know before you go.

Camp Free even rates each campground. Is it a worthwhile **destination** for an extended stay? Good enough for a **weekend** visit? Or useful only as an **overnight** pullout on your way to someplace else? *Camp Free* goes beyond the facts, offering opinions based on widely-accepted, common-sense criteria.

To help you confidently turn off major highways and forge onto dirt backroads, *Camp Free* states the distance to each campground and the quality of the road. **Easy** means it's a short way and the road is good. **Moderate** means it's 15 to 20 minutes from pavement, or the road is only fair. **Difficult** means it's a long way or the road is poor. Road surfaces, however, change over time—usually for the worse—so make your own assessment before proceeding.

Example of the excellent Ministry of Tourism campgrounds throughout B.C.

Every campground in this book should be accessible in a two-wheel-drive (2WD) low-clearance car. *Camp Free* warns you where conditions could necessitate four-wheel-drive (4WD) or a high-clearance vehicle. *Camp Free* also advises pilots of big rigs (motorhomes, trailers, fifth wheels) if the access road might be troublesome, or the campground too small.

TURN LEFT AT THE BOULDER

"Any chance I'll get lost?" you ask.

Very little. *Camp Free* gives explicit directions that should make sense to you now, and will become perfectly clear en route. "Turn left at the boulder" will be a no-brainer once you're out there, in the shadow of a looming boulder the size of a house.

The forests and ex-forests of B.C. conceal a bird's nest of interlaced dirt roads totaling more than 32,000 kilometers (19,840 miles). With only rudimentary Forest Service maps to work with, the task of unsnarling all the details severely challenged our endurance and sanity. We believe we calculated all our meanderings accurately. We certainly gave it a supreme effort. But it's possible we goofed without knowing.

On the road, if the book seems unclear or you feel uncertain, try to bear with the directions. The description should be adequate to steer you to the campground regardless of a minor error. Look for the stated landmarks. Be intuitive. Poke your nose around the next corner. You'll find it. Remember: free-camping is an adventure. And when you get home, please email your suggested corrections to nomads@hikingcamping.com.

YOU CAN MAKE A DIFFERENCE

The roads to most free campgrounds in B.C. are logging roads. Though logging practices have been irresponsible in the past, keep in mind these campgrounds wouldn't be there, so you probably wouldn't either, if logging companies hadn't built the roads. Ideally, the great wild lands of B.C. would be unscarred, preserved in their original majesty forever. Now the best we can do is get out there and look after what's left. It's a lazy king who never leaves the castle to survey his domain. Just be prepared for disappointment: your forests have been logged rapaciously.

Environmental integrity. Scenic value. Future viability. When you see a clearcut, it's hard to believe any of these were considerations. The good news is that improved forestry practices are helping to sustain our forests and save forestry jobs. But we all need to stand guard. An informed public

One of the thousands of lakes in Central B.C.

is an empowered public. If you don't know or care enough to hold logging companies and the Ministry of Forests responsible for their actions, who will? Just by exploring the backroads, you can make a difference.

GO GIRL!

Many single women are afraid to camp alone. Perhaps you're among them. If so, your fear is understandable. But the following observations and suggestions should help ratchet your fear down to a reasonable level of concern. Because the reality is that you *can* safely enjoy solo camping at MOT campgrounds. If you're drawn to the wilds, go girl! Don't limit yourself to walks in the city park. You'll probably find camping is actually safer. The worst that's likely to befall you is an onslaught of mosquitoes, or a cookie-coveting squirrel.

MOT campgrounds are frequented primarily by couples and families. More travellers from across Canada and even from Europe are also now camping in B.C. They'll all be your neighbours while you're out there. Campers are generally kind, trustworthy, peaceful, likable. They're nature lovers, just like you. Most are happy to converse if you approach them but will otherwise respect your privacy. If you've never camped alone, on your first trip you'll probably make a comforting discovery: you're *not* alone.

When they notice you don't have a companion, other campers—usually a chivalrous, older gentleman—might approach and offer to be of service. "Need help starting that fire?" "Want a hand stringing up your tarp?" Don't assume they're chauvinists who doubt your competence. Such acts are almost always genuinely benevolent. If you welcome assistance, accept the offer. If you decline, be tactful and appreciative.

Common sense dictates that a single woman be cautious and vigilant. But that's true anywhere, not just camping. We all have to be somewhat on guard until we've assessed whatever situation we're entering. Here's how single women can do that at campgrounds:

• When reading *Camp Free* and choosing a campground, note what other campgrounds and towns are nearby and how to reach them. That way you'll already have a plan in case you're later unnerved and decide to move.

• Arrive before nightfall so you can see the campground and other campers. Drive slowly through before picking a campsite. The presence of other women, even in a mixed group, is heartening, because they tend to be a calming influence. Try to camp near them.

• If the campground is empty, and you like solitude, stay. If others arrive after dark, listen and observe intently. Get a sense for who they are and how

Camping gives you time for deep conversation.

you feel about them. Trust your instincts. If the newcomers seem rude or belligerent, if their behaviour puts you on edge, quickly and quietly pack and leave.

• While settling in, talk to your fellow campers. Ask them questions about the lake, the stream, other campgrounds they recommend, anything to get them talking and revealing themselves. Establish a bond with just one couple and you'll relax. They'll probably comment on your solo status. If not, tell them you're on your own. It will heighten their awareness on your behalf. After thoroughly assessing the situation, even if you feel at ease about camping alone, take these precautions:

• Sleep in your vehicle. It's safer than a tent. It will reduce your anxiety and allow you a better night's rest. A van is ideal, because you can move from bed to the driver's seat without exiting. A truck and camper (or shell) is good too. Some cars, particularly wagons, have enough space for a bed if you fold down the rear seat.

• Keep a canister of pepper spray handy but concealed. Its intended use is stopping a charging bear, so you can imagine how effective it would be against a mere human. Cayenne pepper, highly irritating to the nose and eyes, is the active ingredient. Without causing permanent injury, it disables

Drive defensively. You can encounter a speeding logging truck anytime, anywhere.

the aggressor long enough to let you escape. Obviously, it's a last-resort defense. Use it only if you believe you're at serious risk. You can buy pepper spray at outdoor stores. *Counter Assault* is a reputable brand.

During all our years camping in B.C., we've never met anyone scary or suspicious. We've never felt threatened or perceived any danger. That should reassure you. It's inevitable that you'll react negatively to someone. Shabby clothes, a gruff voice, questionable hygiene—something will put you off. But our initial harsh judgments have repeatedly been shattered after a brief conversation reveals a gentle, caring soul beneath the stereotype. We hope your encounters will be equally positive.

HITTING THE DIRT

Inexperienced on backroads? Consider these suggestions before you hit the dirt. A little preparation can increase your confidence and safety.

• Carry more food and water than you think you'll need for your camping trip, in case of emergency. A first-aid kit is also a wise addition.

• Check your vehicle's fuel supply and engine fluid levels before leaving the highway.

- Always drive with your headlights on—even during daylight hours.

- Drive cautiously. You never know who's coming or what's ahead. It's possible the road has been damaged recently by severe weather or other natural hazards.

- Be patient. Keep your speed moderate, unless the road is clearly flat and straight for a long way. Even then, holes or rocks might surprise you.

- Slow down on washboard roads. Go too fast and your dashboard will clack like a player piano. Worse, you could lose traction and slide out of control as your vehicle hops from one ripple to the next.

- Avoid the middle of the road. Always cling to the right side. Even if you haven't seen another vehicle for hours, one could appear at the worst possible moment. On dirt, reduced traction makes vehicles less responsive.

- Never block the road. If you stop, pull far enough off to allow industrial vehicles to pass at high speed.

- Yield to logging trucks or other industrial vehicles. As soon as you see one (a cloud of dust is a sure indicator) pull as far over as possible and let it proceed.

- Obey all posted restrictions. Some active logging roads are closed to the public from 5 a.m. Monday, until 8 p.m. Friday. Don't be tempted to sneak in. The closure is for your own safety. Monster logging trucks are belting down those roads.

- Don't let the logging companies' warning signs scare you off the roads. Except when the area is specifically closed to the public between certain hours, they're just telling you to be aware and drive safely. Sometimes you'll see lots of signs. It can be intimidating. But it doesn't mean you'll be fighting your way upstream against a constant flow of industrial traffic.

Don't let the signs scare you away. Just drive safely.

TWO-WHEELING IT

Driving a low-clearance 2WD car or RV? Don't worry. The roads in this book shouldn't present any serious obstacles. But if you encounter a stretch of rough, challenging road, these suggestions might help.

• Before leaving home, look at your vehicle's underbelly. Get on your knees and really see what's down there. Make note of where you have the least clearance and where you have the most, so you'll know how to straddle rocks.

• When the road looks questionable, it's often the grit of the driver, not the vehicle itself, that determines whether you'll make it. That's not to say you should be bull-headed and plow through come what may. When you assess the road, just be aware of your level of confidence and your capacity for patience.

• Faced with deeply worn tracks on the sides of the road, and a high ridge in the middle that might scrape your underbelly, drive with one tire on the ridge and the other outside the track.

• When there's a deep rut across the road, don't approach it straight on. You might bottom-out. Instead, slice across at an angle, from one side of the road toward the other. That way your tires drop into the rut one at a time, instead of both at once.

• Before you splash through a big mud hole, get out and check how deep it is. Feel with a stick, or drop a large stone in and see what happens. That's a lot easier than getting stuck.

• In mud or sand, don't slow to a crawl. You need momentum. To avoid getting stuck, it's often best to proceed and hope the road surface improves. If you're not stuck yet, but it appears you will be, reverse out immediately. Trying to turn around can land you in a bigger mess. When fishtailing, straighten your vehicle by turning the front wheels in the direction your rear wheels are sliding.

• Know what you're risking. Ask yourself: "How many vehicles have been on the road today?

No need to check this one with a stick.

What's the likelihood of seeing another? How far back is the highway? The last possible telephone? The nearest lived-in-looking house?" Consider your worst-case options before you plunge in. It might sway your decision.

HELP IS ON THE WAY

Concerned about being stranded in the outback? Don't be. Help is probably on the way. Though some roads in this book might seem desolate, they're not. You can usually expect someone to come along within an hour. A few locals and outdoorspeople are always wandering the backcountry. You'll often encounter logging company employees in pickup trucks. If necessary, signal them to stop; you'll find they're friendly and glad to assist. If your vehicle konks out, wave down a logging truck; they all have radios and can call for help.

MEN IN TRUCKS KNOW

Reading *Camp Free* should relieve you of asking anyone for directions. But when you explore backroads other than those described here, you'll probably want to check your bearings with someone. Before you do, a word of caution: assume nothing.

Be very specific when asking for directions. State the names of roads, geographic features, or other landmarks. Be certain you're both talking about the same thing. Rely on your intuition as much as anyone else's opinion. Even a local who should know the area might not. It's alarming how many people are unaware of what's beyond their backyard.

Look for men in trucks. That's not a chauvinistic stereotype, that's reality. Men in trucks usually dispense reliable information. They tend to ply the backroads to earn their living, or at least to hunt and fish. So if you're a man, you're in a truck, and you don't know, you better find out, because here they come.

HOW'S THE ROAD?

Stop four drivers on the same road and you'll get four different impressions of what it's like. Ask "How's the road?" and you'll often hear "It's gravel." Unless you're driving a rugged truck, a 4WD vehicle, or an old beater you don't care about, that's too vague. If you want a detailed road report, ask specific questions. How rough is the road? How steep? How narrow? How muddy? How rocky?

Locals who frequent the backroads are generally quick and direct with their answers. But before you heed anyone's advice, consider the source. Do they seem sensible and mature? Inexperienced and timid? Wild and reckless?

Some four-wheelers are determined to uphold the macho mystique of their off-road rigs. They consider cars an inferior subspecies, little more than go-carts. They would eye ours with disdain and say, "I wouldn't try it in *that*." Then they'd leave us in a cloud of dust, and we'd slowly pick our way through the rocks and potholes until we reached our destination.

Others tried to be open-minded. After scrutinizing our car, one fellow said, "Well, if you go slow, you'll probably make it. But there's a lot of sharp rocks. You better have a good set of spare tires." That sounded like an accurate road-condition summary. And it was. Our car survived, but we hated it and decided you would too, so it's not in the book.

Even when the road looked questionable to us, people were usually encouraging. "Aw, you'll be fine," they said. "Just take 'er easy. Lots of people make it. There's big RVs in there." They were right.

*Many rough access roads like this one are passable in a
2WD car, if the driver is careful and patient.*

With Camp Free *you'll avoid crowded commercial and provincial-park campgrounds.*

Listen to opinions, then decide for yourself. The power to propel you through a difficult patch is probably in your head, regardless of what's under your hood. Technique and determination will take you surprisingly far. And if the road gets too hairy, just turn around. There's always some-place else to explore.

BEYOND CAMP FREE

South of the Trans-Canada Hwy, most campgrounds described in *Camp Free* are within 30 km (18 mi) of a paved road. North of the Trans-Canada, B.C. has a more extensive backroad network, so we describe campgrounds a full day's drive from pavement. Yet the province has hundreds more free camp-grounds not mentioned in *Camp Free*. We know there's a limit to most people's tolerance for dusty, rocky, bouncy backroads. Besides, the final access to some of these remote campgrounds is forbiddingly rough. If you need 4WD and a kidney belt to get there, it's not in the book. But if you have a burly vehicle and a questing mind, keep going beyond where we stopped. You might be gratified by what you find.

GUERILLA CAMPING

It's late. You're tired. You're nowhere near a free, MOT campground. You're also unaware of any commercial campgrounds in the area, but you don't want to pay to camp anyway. And you prefer to avoid hotels.

It's still possible to camp free.

Sniffing out places to free-camp is a skill you can develop. As you become proficient, you'll only pay to camp when you're desperate for a shower. Even then, you can just pay for the shower and camp free elsewhere. Unless the land is fenced off or way too steep, or you absolutely must stop immediately, you probably don't have to pay to camp.

The free-camping spots you find on your own, however, might not be great places to hang around the next morning. They'll likely be adequate only for a night's sleep, nothing more. And it's much easier if you have a vehicle you can sleep in—at least the back of a truck or the bed of a mini-van. It's hard to find places you can safely, comfortably pitch a tent for free.

So what we're really talking about here is creative parking. We call it *guerilla camping*. It's the only way to cope with all the NO CAMPING signs warning you away from public land.

Is there a conspiracy to make us all pay to sleep? It's unwarranted. Campers who pull off the road for a night, whether they sleep in their vehicles or bravely pitch their tents, rarely harm the land or other people. They're just sleeping! If they're allowed to park there all day, why not at night? What's the harm?

Beat the system. Be a guerilla camper. The following questions will help you assess where and when. Just don't violate people's property rights. If you know it's private, don't camp without asking permission. And always respect the land. Never trash it. As a thank-you for a night's sleep, leave it cleaner than you found it.

What are the options? Be open-minded. Use your imagination. How far you must stretch your thinking depends on where you've free-camped before, what you consider safe, and how bold you are. Some people are audacious. They'll camp anywhere it's wide enough to pull a vehicle off the road. But you can also be a stealth camper, cautiously choosing tranquil, secretive locations.

What's your sense of the place? Does it feel inviting, or creepy? Trust your instinct. If it looks clean, you know people don't park there to drink and party. If it makes you feel vulnerable, that feeling will only grow with every noise you hear. You'll lie awake in the dark, straining to detect anything

When you see someone sacked out on the roadside, kindly suggest they buy this book.

suspicious. A passing car will slow down and you'll be on edge until it's gone. That's not a good night's sleep. That's miserable. Find another spot where you can relax.

Is it secluded enough? Before you decide to stay, consider what might awaken you later. Are bright lights shining nearby? What's the noise level? How many cars or pedestrians are passing by? Even if you've pulled off what seems like a little-used road, sit there for ten minutes to gauge the traffic before you settle in for the night; you might be surprised.

Will you harm the land? Guerilla camping isn't crashing your way into places you shouldn't be. It's gliding in at night, then slipping out in the morning, without leaving a trace. Vegetation, even grass, should be left intact. Harm nothing, take nothing, leave nothing. If that's not possible, move on.

Have you tried residential areas? If you can sleep in your vehicle, you might feel safer parked in a town near homes, rather than on a road that's lonely but still close to civilization. Just outside a town, you're within range of malicious teenagers or other suspicious characters, and somewhat defenseless against them. In town, on a quiet, dark, residential street, it's unlikely you'll be hassled, because help is just a horn-honk away.

In a neighbourhood, never intrude on anyone's privacy. Try not to park directly in front of a house. You'll be less obvious beside a field or vacant lot. Ideally you won't be noticed. A resident who peeks out a window should assume you're guests of a neighbour.

Compared to urbanites, people in small towns are generally less jumpy about unfamiliar parked cars. Live and let live seems to be the rural attitude. Plus, small towns have fewer parking restrictions and often no police to enforce them.

Are you arriving late enough so you won't be noticed? At residential streets, university grounds, and hospital or church parking lots, the later you arrive the better your chances of an uninterrupted night. You want to be situated so you're inconspicuous—where it's normal to see a few cars parked overnight, but not many. If you're noticed, it shouldn't occur to anyone that you're sleeping in your vehicle. That means you have to finish cooking and arranging your bed elsewhere, before you park. You'll also have to depart early. By 7:30 a.m. you'll probably attract someone's attention, but at that point it might not matter.

If you're noticed, will anyone care? This is highly subjective. Parked close to anything of obvious importance or value, near any potential object of theft or vandalism, someone will probably care if they notice you. That means they might wake you up and tell you to move, which is always a pain and can be scary. It's better to invest a little more time finding a spot where nobody will care if they suspect you're sacked out.

RESPECT OTHER CAMPERS

Most people live cheek-by-jowl with their neighbors back home. They want a little privacy when they go camping. So don't barge in on someone who already occupies the limited space at a small campground. Make sure there's plenty of room for one more. If you can't leave a buffer between your camp and others, and there's still daylight left to look elsewhere, please go. If it's late and you decide to stay, be as quiet as a lizard. Speak softly. Ready yourself for sleep without commotion.

If you're the captain of a fully-equipped motorhome, please consider the rest of us before firing up your generator. Several times, that wicked racket has forced us to pack and move late at night. Recognize that your generator, though a convenience to you, is a nuisance to others. It shatters what many of us cherish most about camping: peace. Make sure your system is fully charged before you arrive at a campground. If you must run your generator, do it midday when fellow-campers are most active. Everyone will appreciate that.

You don't know B.C. until you've visited its far-flung communities. Camp Free will get you there. Above: the Chilcotin. Below: Kaslo, in the West Kootenay.

Some Neanderthals don't just go camping, they go wild—bellowing at each other, roaring with laughter, blasting stereos, letting their kids rampage. It's rude and obnoxious—night or day. Then there's the couple, inexperienced at backing their trailer into a campsite, who arrives late. The wife shouts directions for fifteen minutes while the husband rocks and rolls the rig. If any of these descriptions sound like you, please be quieter and more considerate.

Because of rowdy, disrespectful campers, a few campgrounds now charge a "keep the peace" fee to employ live-in attendants during summer. They make sure everyone's quiet after 10 p.m. It solves the late-night noise problem but erodes everyone's sense of liberty and burdens you with an expense. Help prevent it from happening elsewhere.

CAMPGROUND DIPLOMACY

What should you do when a raucous family pulls into the campsite next to yours and starts screaming? Or worse, when oblivious adolescents crank up their stereo, intent on partying? (1) Don't assume the noise will stop or the offenders will leave. And don't rely on subtle hints to express your feelings. Be upfront. Talk to them, or the situation and your anger will escalate. (2) Don't shout at them from your site. Walk over and calmly explain the problem. Maybe they were unaware you were bothered. A simple statement might solve it. (3) Kindly but firmly suggest a specific action. Don't be obnoxious, insulting, or demanding; it will only make them defensive. (4) If it's obvious that diplomacy won't work, move—to another campsite farther away, or to another campground if necessary. Yes, it's unfair. But the misery of enduring a joyless day or sleepless night is worse than the hassle of leaving.

BE REVERENT

Reverence is achingly absent from the world today. And if there's anyplace we can and should feel reverent, it's out in nature. Reverence is simply being aware of and respecting life in all its manifestations, including our forests, meadows, rivers and lakes. What you revere, you care for.

It's your responsibility to pick up after yourself at MOT campgrounds. If more campers respect the sites and keep them clean, more of the campgrounds will remain open and free of charge.

If a campground is continually trashed and abused, the B.C. Government will close it or impose camping fees to defray the cost of maintenance. If the user-maintained system fails, you could eventually be slapped with an entry fee at every campground. Most of us can't imagine leaving garbage at a campsite or damaging the already minimal facilities. Please help spread that ethic.

Always carry a few extra garbage bags. If previous campers left anything behind, pick it up. You'll be doing your share of user maintenance. And anyone observing you will see reverence in action.

Whenever trash is left, even in a fire pit, it encourages others to assume they can add to the mess. So take a few minutes to fill up your garbage bag. On your way home, drop it in a dumpster, preferably in a city. Small towns have limited garbage capacity and infrequent pickups.

Anything campers leave behind is trash. Orange and banana peels take years to biodegrade, and animals won't eat them. Cigarette butts are even worse. Smokers have been allowed to assume butts don't qualify as litter. It's time to change that. They give campgrounds a dirty, ravaged look that saddens and disgusts most campers. Never leave your cigarette butts at a campground. It's easy to haul them away with the rest of your trash.

In general, leave as little impact as possible. For example, you'll find more fire rings than are necessary at most campgrounds. If you light a campfire, use an existing ring so you don't further scar the land. Burn only small pieces of deadfall. The foliage is part of the scenery; don't destroy it for fire-wood. Be sure your fire is stone-cold dead before you leave or go to sleep. Also, never wash dishes near a lake or stream. Use a plastic basin, then dump the waste water in thick brush, well away from campsites. Always use biodegradable soap.

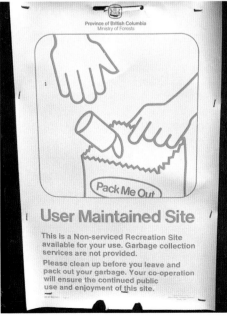

Wouldn't it be refreshing to arrive at a campground and find no evidence anyone had camped there before you? Do it for the next campers. Maybe someone will do it for you.

Always haul out your garbage.

Keep your campsite clean. Food odours attract bears. This one's a grizzly.

PRACTICAL STUFF

This is a how-to-get-there guidebook, not a how-to-do-it manual. You've probably camped many times and know what you need to take on a camping trip. It's not like backpacking, where you can haul only so much and you're a long way from a road. This is *vehicle* camping. You can take whatever you want, or as much as your vehicle can hold. So, if you're not sure, just bring it. The more you camp, the better you'll get at keeping your load light and compact, without forgetting necessities. Until then, this list of practical stuff might be helpful.

• **Water.** Bring plenty. You'll almost never find a potable water source at a free campground.

• **Toilet paper, trowel, plastic bag.** MOT campgrounds are basic, often referred to as *primitive* or *rustic*. Most have outhouses, which might or might not be usually stocked with toilet paper. Bring a spare roll. Unofficial free campgrounds and overnight pullouts have no facilities whatsoever. There you'll need a trowel to bury your poop, and a plastic bag to hold used toilet paper.

Black bear

• **Garbage bags.** Bring one for all your trash, and another to pick up after other campers less considerate than you.

•**Stove, fuel, matches.** Firewood might not be available. Besides, cooking over an open fire is difficult, time consuming and wasteful. Keep extra matches or a lighter in your vehicle.

• **Can Opener.** Ever try to open a can with a rock?

• **Flashlight and extra batteries.** You'll never see Tiki torches lining a cement walkway to a "comfort station" at a free campground. If you let your eyes adjust to the dark, it's surprising how well you can see without a flashlight. But there are times you'll need one.

B.C. STANDS FOR BEAR COUNTRY

The moment you leave any of B.C.'s major cities, you're in bear country. You can encounter a bruin anytime, anywhere—not just on remote hiking trails. Black bears are a common sight on backroads, even on some highways. Grizzly sightings are less frequent but always a possibility.

That doesn't mean bears are lurking behind every bush, stalking you, ready to pounce. They usually avoid human contact. They're generally calm, passive, shy. So don't be bearanoid. Just be careful.

Avoid inviting bears into your camp. Their strongest sense is smell, so never leave food untended. After you eat, keep leftovers sealed in plastic bags and containers, locked in your vehicle. At night, don't even leave your cooler out.

When walking, stay alert and make noise so you won't surprise a bear. Given sufficient warning, they'll usually depart before you see them. If startled, their instinctive response could be aggressive.

If you see a bear, don't look it in the eyes; it might think you're challenging it. Never run. Be still. If you must move, do it in slow motion. Bears are more likely to attack if you flee, and they're fast, much faster than humans. A grizzly can outsprint a racehorse. And it's a myth that bears can't run downhill. They're also capable swimmers. Remember: it's highly unlikely you'll provoke an attack as long as you stay calm, retreat slowly, and make soothing sounds to convey a nonthreatening presence.

What if a bear charges you?

Climbing a tree is an escape option. Some people have saved their lives this way, others have been caught in the process. Despite their ungainly appearance, bears are excellent climbers. To be out of reach of an adult bear, you'd have to climb at least 10 meters (33 feet), something few people are capable of. And you'd probably need to be at least two football fields from the bear to beat it up a tree.

Playing dead is debatable. It used to be the recommended response to a charge, but now some scientists, rangers and surviving victims say it might be better to fight back. It's your call. Every encounter involves different bears, people and circumstances, so the results vary. Even bear behaviour experts cannot suggest one all-purpose response technique. Black bears can be intimidated if you fight back. Grizzlies tend to break off their attack if you remain totally passive. But quickly identifying a bear while under threat requires expertise. Learn more. Read one of the many informative books about safety in bear habitat.

Rating System for Campgrounds and Backroads

Scenery and Recreation

You'll enjoy staying longer at campgrounds with better scenery and more recreation. So that's the basis for these ratings. Just keep higher-rated campgrounds in mind for short stays too, because they're not necessarily farther from pavement.

DESTINATION
You could spend your vacation here. If it's a long drive, it's worth it. The scenery and the campground are wonderful. The recreation is excellent and varied.

WEEKEND
A couple days here might be pleasant, but any longer and you'd want a prettier campground or more impressive scenery. Recreation is available but limited.

OVERNIGHT
Stop here for a convenient place to sleep, but that's it. Don't expect anything special. Something's lacking: either the scenery or the site itself is poor to mediocre.

Note: Nearly all MOT campgrounds have tables, pit toilets, and fire rings. Our descriptions warn you where these are absent. Unofficial, free campgrounds and overnight pullouts have no facilities whatsoever.

Access

At a glance, these ratings tell you the distance to the campground, the quality of the road surfaces, and the patience needed to follow the directions.

EASY
Right under your nose. A wombat could find it. The road is smooth and the distance short—usually less than 10 km (6.2 mi) from pavement.

MODERATE
Just around the corner. In southern B.C., it's probably 10 to 15 km (6.2 to 9.3 mi) from pavement. In central B.C., it's probably 15 to 25 km (9.3 to 15.5 mi) from pavement. There could be a few rough stretches.

DIFFICULT

Back of beyond. You must be patient and adventurous. The navigating is difficult, the roads challenging, the distances longer: up to 25 km (15 mi) from pavement in southern B.C., up to 50 km (31 mi) from pavement in central B.C.

Maps

In the front of this book, you'll find maps of the camping regions. These will help you get oriented. Each chapter begins with a map showing the camp-grounds in that particular region. But even the regional maps are for general reference only. They were simplified to help you easily see where campgrounds are located in relation to each other, and quickly decide which ones are within range. More detailed maps are not necessary, because the driving directions in *Camp Free* are explicit, guiding you with far more precision and accuracy than is possible with any map.

Distance Discrepancies

No vehicle's odometer is perfectly accurate. Every odometer differs slightly. Some are affected by road jostling, or by tires that are not the man-ufacturer's specified size. Others are inherently, appreciably imprecise. So your distances might vary slightly from those in *Camp Free*. Just be looking for the turns or landmarks near the stated distances. If you encounter a dis-crepancy of 0.5 km (0.3 mi) or more, we apologize. That might be an error, in which case we welcome your suggested changes. Please email them to nomads@hikingcaming.com.

Nakusp beach, Upper Arrow Lake

SOUTHERN BRITISH COLUMBIA
from the U.S. border, north to Trans-Canada Hwy 1

Confusing but enticing network of backroads, Sunshine Coast

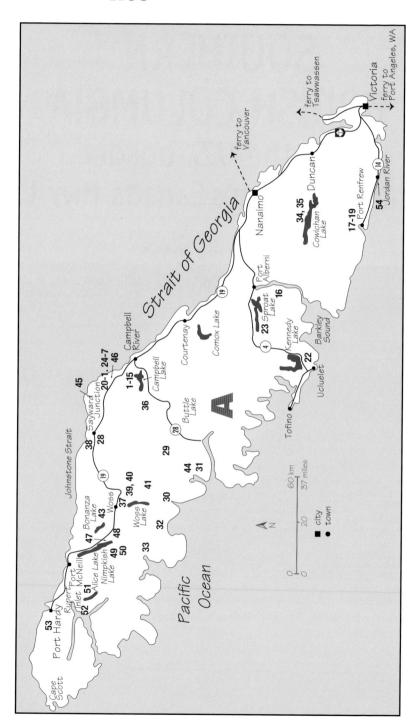

A: Vancouver Island

At the fee campgrounds west of Victoria, charges apply mid-May to October 20. At the fee campgrounds west of Campbell River, charges apply May 1 to September 30.

1-4	Campbell Lake	FREE	30	Leiner River	FREE
6	Campbell Lake	$	31	Cougar Creek	$
7	Dogwood Bay	FREE	32	Resolution Park	$
8	Loon Bay	FREE	33	Fair Harbour	$
9	Fry Lake	FREE	34	Pine Point	$
10	Orchard Meadow	FREE	35	Maple Grove	$
11	Gray Lake	FREE	36	Strathcona Dam	FREE
12	Merrill Lake	FREE	37	Woss Lake	FREE
13	Apple Point	FREE	38	Junction Pool	FREE
14	Brewster Lake	$	39	Lower Klaklakama L	FREE
15	Mohun Lake	FREE	40	Upper Klaklakama L	FREE
16	Arden Creek	FREE	41	Vernon Lake	FREE
17	Fairy Lake	$	42	Naka Creek	FREE
18	San Juan Bridge	$	43	Bonanza Lake	FREE
19	Lizard Lake	$	44	Conuma River	FREE
20	Stella Beach	FREE	45	Bear Creek	FREE
21	Little Bear Bay	FREE	46	Elk Bay	FREE
22	Toquart Bay	$	47	Kinman Creek	FREE
23	Snow Creek	FREE	48	Nimpkish Lake	FREE
24	Pye Lake	FREE	49	Anutz Lake	FREE
25	McCreight Lake	FREE	50	Atluck Lake	FREE
26	Aldergrove	FREE	51	Alice Lake	FREE
27	Sitka Spruce beach	FREE	52	Marble River	FREE
28	Elk Creek	$	53	Georgie Lake	FREE
29	Muchalat Lake	FREE	54	Jordan River	$

Vancouver Island

Scotchbroom, above Saanich Inlet

Long, spectacular lakes here provide a wealth of recreation. It's definitely worth a special trip to visit the campgrounds rated *Destination*. Others don't justify a journey all the way from the Mainland, but they're fine if you're already traveling in the area. There are more pay campgrounds on the island than in any other region of B.C. It's due to the prevalence of vandalism and partying. Fees charged at campgrounds near towns pay for maintenance and caretakers to keep the peace.

Vancouver Island has been clearcut mercilessly. Witnessing this is valuable. It's an inspiration to conserve the world's few remaining ancient forests. Still, cutblocks are not visible from every campground on the Island. Beauty is still abundant and readily available, though not to the same awesome extent as in the Mainland's numerous, world-class mountain ranges.

VICTORIA TO PORT RENFREW

From downtown Vancouver, including the ferry ride to Schwartz Bay, it's about six hours to Port Renfrew. Victoria to Port Renfrew is an easy two-and-a-half hours. From Victoria, head southwest on Hwy 14. Set your trip odometer to 0 in Colwood.

0 km (0 mi)
Starting southwest on Hwy 14 from Colwood, just west of Victoria.

26.1 km (16.2 mi)
Drive through Sooke, at the start of the West Coast Road. Proceed west along the shoreline, enjoying ocean views.

36.7 km (22.8 mi)
Reach Gordon's Beach, a good place to relax in the sun.

39.7 km (24.7 mi)
Cross a bridge and turn left.

48 km (29.8 mi)
Pass French Beach Provincial Park.

56 km (34.8 mi)
Pass the Sandcut trailhead.

58.4 km (36.3 mi)
Arrive at Jordan River campground.

Though little more than a gravel lot, this Western Forest Products campground is very popular. It has a front-row view across Juan de Fuca Strait, to the Olympic Mountains in Washington. You'll be lucky to find a vacant site here in summer. There are water faucets, but you must purify the water for drinking. Sites without tables are beyond the stand of trees, in another big, gravel lot, along the river's mouth.

JORDAN RIVER CAMPGROUND #54
Destination / Easy / $ / year-round
10 drive-up tables, 6 tables in trees for tenters, more campsites
Accessible by motorhomes and 5th-wheels

Continuing west on Hwy 14, passing Jordan River campground.

62.8 km (39 mi)
Pass China Beach Provincial Park.

64.7 km (40.2 mi)
Pass Mystic Beach Trail (logged in the 1940s, planted in '46). Views of the Strait and the Olympics are now limited until Port Renfrew.

78.2 km (48.6 mi)
Attain a sweeping view of coastal forest in various logging stages. The bouncy, serpentine, paved road winds higher onto the hillsides. Several one-lane bridges require caution. You can safely average 50 kph (30 mph).

84.5 km (52.5 mi)
Ascend a hairpin turn.

95.6 km (59.4 mi)
Descend a long hill.

96.6 km (60 mi)
Enter Port Renfrew. Pass a sign for West Coast Trail information.

98.8 km (61.4 mi)
Pass signs for West Coast Trail information and Cowichan Lake. In Port Renfrew, Hwy 14 becomes Parkinson Street. Proceed to the fork and turn right to reach the Trailhead Store, where you can take a shower or do laundry.

PORT RENFREW TO COWICHAN LAKE

Highway 14 ends in Port Renfrew. You'll find more campgrounds northeast, en route to Cowichan Lake. Set your trip odometer to 0 in Port Renfrew, at the sign for Cowichan Lake. Directions from Cowichan Lake southwest to Port Renfrew are on page 47.

East Sooke trail, southeast of Jordan River campground. Print out a map at www.crd.bc.ca/parks.

If you're heading northeast, from Port Renfrew to Cowichan Lake

0 km (0 mi)
Starting on Deering Road, departing Port Renfrew, heading northeast toward Cowichan Lake. Cross a bridge in 300 meters.

0.6 km (0.4 mi)
Continue on the main road for campgrounds. Left enters private property owned by the Pacheenaht Band.

1.6 km (1 mi)
Reach a fork. Go right (northeast).

3.2 km (2 mi)
Turn right. Pass a Timber West sign PUBLIC ROUTE, HARRIS CRK MAINLINE, FAIRY L CAMPSITE 3 KM, LIZARD L CAMPSITE 14 KM, MESACHIE L 52 KM. Mesachie Lake is near the east end of Cowichan Lake, so you can proceed on this road all the way to Hwy 18.

6.5 km (4 mi)
Arrive at Fairy Lake campground.

> Although heavily used, the campground is large enough that a vacant site is likely. The lake itself is pleasant, but the scenery is mediocre. Clearcuts are visible. A sign warns that the area can flood during heavy rain.

FAIRY LAKE CAMPGROUND #17
Weekend / Moderate / $ / May 1 - Oct 20
Elev: 5 m (16 ft) / Lake: 0.8 km (0.5 mi) long, 32 ha
30 campsites, most with tables
Accessible by motorhomes and 5th-wheels

Continuing northeast on the main road, passing Fairy Lake campground.

12 km (7.4 mi)
Go right at the fork, staying on pavement, which soon lapses into rocky, bumpy dirt.

16.3 km (10.1 mi)
Reach a fork. Proceed left (following directions on page 45) for Lizard Lake campground, Mesachie Lake, and Cowichan Lake. Turn right and set your trip odometer to 0 for San Juan campground.

0 km (0 mi)
Starting east, heading for San Juan Bridge campground.

0.3 km (0.2 mi)
Pass Lens Creek trailhead.

2.5 km (1.6 mi)
Go right at the fork, staying on the main road. A yellow sign warns this is a dead-end road. Williams Creek Bridge has been dismantled, but you're not going that far.

4 km (2.5 mi)
Descend a hill to the river.

Lizard Lake

4.5 km (2.8 mi)
Cross the bridge.

4.7 km (2.9 mi)
Arrive at San Juan Bridge campground, on the left. The campsites are above a fine-gravel beach on the river. The shallow, slow water, and smooth, sandy riverbed invite wading. Shade is abundant. A mammoth Sitka Spruce enhances the setting.

SAN JUAN BRIDGE CAMPGROUND #18
Weekend / Moderate / $ / May 1 - Oct 20
5 well-spaced campsites, no tables
Accessible by motorhomes and 5th-wheels

Proceeding left at the 16.3-km (10.1-mile) junction, heading for Lizard Lake campground, Mesachie Lake, and Cowichan Lake.

17.9 km (11.1 mi)
Arrive at Lizard Lake campground.

The small lake has a sandy beach and deep, clear water. It's ringed by forest, but clearcut hillsides are visible beyond. This is a popular campground in summer.

LIZARD LAKE CAMPGROUND #19

Weekend / Moderate / $ / May 1 - Oct 20
Elev: 70 m (230 ft) / Lake: 10 ha
21 campsites with tables, 4 walk-in tentsites with tables
4 picnic tables, wharf
Accessible by motorhomes and 5th-wheels

Continuing north, passing Lizard Lake campground, heading for Mesachie Lake, Cowichan Lake, and Hwy 18.

22.7 km (14.1 mi)
Stay right at the fork. A creek is on your right.

33.5 km (20.8 mi)
Pass a sign COWICHAN LAKE (24 KM) and a blue Fletcher Challenge sign PORT RENFREW (33 KM).

47 km (29.1 mi)
Go right at the fork.

56.3 km (35 mi)
Reach a stop sign in the community of Mesachie Lake. Pavement resumes. Turn right for the town of Lake Cowichan.

If you're heading southwest, from Lake Cowichan to Port Renfrew

Follow Hwy 18 to the 3-way intersection on the east side of the town of Lake Cowichan. Drive 1.1 km (0.7 mi) into town and set your trip odometer to 0 across from Central Park where the South and North Shore roads join. Notice the green highway sign for Mesachie Lake, Honeymoon Bay, and Youbou. Follow the signs straight (southwest) to Mesachie Lake.

0 km (0 mi)
Starting southwest on South Shore Road.

6.5 km (4 mi)
Reach the community of Mesachie Lake.

7 km (4.3 mi)
Pass a sign pointing left PUBLIC ACCESS TO PORT RENFREW 53. Turn left in 100 meters at the flashing yellow light.

Cowichan Lake

For details about the route southwest to Port Renfrew, read the northeast directions in reverse, starting at the 56.3-km (35-mi) point. But the following summary should suffice. Set your trip odometer to 0 at the flashing yellow light in Mesachie Lake. In 9 km (5.5 mi), turn left at the fork. Reach Lizard Lake campground in about 38 km (23.5 mi). About 1.6 km (1 mi) beyond Lizard Lake, go right at a junction; left leads to San Juan Bridge campground. Stay left at the next junction to reach Fairy Lake campground. From Fairy Lake it's 6.5 km (4 mi) to Port Renfrew.

COWICHAN LAKE

East of Cowichan Lake is the scenic Cowichan River. It's worth a detour to admire Skutz Falls. The area offers excellent hiking, swimming and fishing. But free-camping was eliminated here when BC Parks assumed authority over what were previously Forest Service campgrounds.

Cowichan Lake is one of Vancouver Island's largest. It's 31.5 km (19.5 mi) long, 3.5 km (2.2 mi) wide, and covers 6214 hectares. The elevation is 163 m (535 ft). On the north shore are two very large campgrounds: Pine Point and Maple Grove. Maple Grove is more heavily treed and has a fine-gravel beach.

It's possible to reach Cowichan Lake by driving northeast on backroads from Port Renfrew, following directions on page 43. Most people drive west on Hwy 18 from near Duncan, as described here.

If you're heading northwest or southeast, on Hwy 1

From the junction of Hwys 1 and 18, northwest of Duncan, drive Hwy 18 west 26.2 km (16.2 mi) to the 3-way junction and map sign on the east side of Lake Cowichan community. Set your trip odometer to 0.

0 km (0 mi)
Starting west on Hwy 18, heading toward Youbou, from the 3-way junction on the east side of Lake Cowichan community.

4.9 km (3 mi)
Cross a bridge over Meades Creek.

6.4 km (4 mi)
For Pine Point and Maple Grove campgrounds, stay straight (west) on Hwy 18. Proceed through Youbou and beyond the lumber mill. For Spring Beach day-use area on Cowichan Lake, turn left onto Meades Creek Road.

12.8 km (7.9 mi)
Turn left to enter Pine Point campground on Cowichan Lake. Stay straight for Maple Grove campground.

PINE POINT CAMPGROUND #34
Weekend / Easy / $ / May 1 - Oct 20
35 campsites with tables, boat launch
Accessible by motorhomes and 5th-wheel

14.7 km (9.1 mi)
Turn left to enter Maple Grove campground on Cowichan Lake.

MAPLE GROVE CAMPGROUND #35
Weekend / Easy / $ / May 1 - Oct 20
35 campsites with tables, boat launch, fine-gravel beach
Accessible by motorhomes and 5th-wheels

SOUTH OF PORT ALBERNI

South of Port Alberni, the only reasonably accessible primitive campground is Arden Creek, on Alberni Inlet. Even it requires you to travel a jittery road through grim country. The hills were never impressive, but logging has left them looking abused. Reaching the campground is a relief. It's a lovely haven, across the inlet from China Creek Provincial Park.

Arden Creek campground is small, accommodating only very modest RVs. Launching a cartop boat here is easy. And the inlet is often windy—ideal for boardsailing. When the winds die, be prepared for mosquitoes. Shade is plentiful, so this is a comfortable place to relax on a hot summer day. A short trail leads to a picnic site with a panoramic view of the inlet. As for noise, the campsites are well off the logging road, so industrial traffic is not annoying.

If you're heading west on Hwy 4, from Parksville

0 km (0 mi)
Starting west on Hwy 4, departing Hwy 19 southeast of Parksville.

47 km (29.2 mi)
Proceed west, passing the first turnoff to Port Alberni.

51.1 km (31.8 mi)
Turn into Port Alberni and head generally west through the city. At its west edge, pass a marina on the left and cross a cement bridge.

53.8 km (33.4 mi)
Cross a metal bridge over Somass River.

54 km (33.5 mi)
Turn left (south) onto paved Mission Road.

If you're heading east on Hwy 4, from Sproat Lake

Approaching the west side of Port Alberni, turn right (south) onto paved Mission Road. It's 200 meters before Hwy 4 crosses the metal bridge over Somass River. If you miss the turn and cross the bridge, you might have to continue 2.8 km (1.7 mi) east before you can safely turn around at the marina on the right.

For either approach above, now follow the directions below

0 km (0 mi)
Starting south on Mission Road. Immediately bear left.

0.5 km (0.3 mi)
Stay left on pavement. Ignore the right fork signed for Sproat Lake Woodlands Division.

2.1 km (1.3 mi)
Pavement ends.

2.4 km (1.5 mi)
Reach a fork. Go right and ascend. Follow the sign for Maktush and Nahmint lakes.

2.9 km (1.8 mi)
Go left at the fork. Pass more signs for Maktush Lake and Sproat Lake Woodlands.

6 km (3.7 mi)
Turn left. Summit Road is right. The road improves, with fewer big, sharp rocks.

10.3 km (6.4 mi)
Go left at the junction. On the other side of the bridge, bear left again.

16.9 km (10.5 mi)
The road now parallels Alberni Inlet.

20.8 km (12.9 mi)
The road veers left. Turn left to enter Arden Creek campground.

ARDEN CREEK CAMPGROUND #16
Weekend / Difficult / Free
4 tables, cartop boat launch
Accessible by small motorhomes but not trailers

WEST OF PORT ALBERNI

West of Port Alberni, Hwy 4 parallels the north side of Sproat Lake, then briefly follows the north bank of Taylor River. The gravel riverbank and lakeshore are prime spawning habitat for Coho and Sockeye salmon. Sproat Lake's campground is at Snow Creek, near the lake's west end, on the south shore.

After crossing the Taylor River bridge, Hwy 4 turns southwest. It winds through the MacKenzie Range and eventually passes Kennedy Lake. Southeast of the lake is a huge campground on Toquart Bay.

Beyond Kennedy Lake, Hwy 4 reaches a T-junction near the coast: turn right (northwest) for Pacific Rim National Park and Tofino, left (south) for Ucluelet or Port Albion. There are no cheap campgrounds in either direction. That's unfortunate, because the Park and Tofino are very popular destinations.

Directions for driving Hwy 4 from the coast to Port Alberni are on page 53.

Alberni Inlet, from Arden Creek campground

If you're heading west on Hwy 4, from Port Alberni

0 km (0 mi)
Starting west on Hwy 4, from the west edge of Port Alberni. Set your trip odometer to 0 on the low cement bridge just past the marina. Follow signs for Sproat Lake.

40.6 km (25.2 mi)
After crossing the Taylor River bridge, proceed straight (west) on Hwy 4 (following directions on page 52) to reach Toquart Bay campground. For Snow Creek campground on Sproat Lake, turn left onto South Taylor Main FS road and set your trip odometer to 0.

0 km (0 mi)
Starting east on South Taylor Main FS road, departing Hwy 4 just south of the Taylor River bridge.

0.6 km (0.4 mi)
Bear left at the junction.

5 km (3.1 mi)
Reach a junction. Bear right (east) before the bridge and continue on South Taylor Main FS road.

9.7 km (6 mi)
Turn left to enter Snow Creek campground on Sproat Lake. A few campsites are in the open. Others are less appealing, off the lake, in scrubby trees.

Snow Creek campground on Sproat Lake

SNOW CREEK CAMPGROUND #23
Weekend / Easy / Free
Elev: 29 m (95 ft) / Lake: 23.3 km (14.5 mi) long
1.2 km (0.8 mi) average width, 4233 ha
2 tables, 7 campsites, rocky beach, rough boat launch
Accessible by small motorhomes and trailers

Continuing west on Hwy 4, passing the 40.6-km (25.2-mi) turnoff to Snow Creek campground and winding through the MacKenzie Range.

79.7 km (49.5 mi)
Turn left and set your trip odometer to 0 for Toquart Bay campground. This turnoff is 12.5 km (7.8 mi) northeast of the Tofino - Ucluelet Junction.

0 km (0 mi)
Starting east on Toquart Bay Road, departing Hwy 4.

4.2 km (2.6 mi)
Pass a brown signpost indicating Toquart Bay is straight ahead.

6.3 km (3.9 mi)
Stay straight, passing a right fork.

8 km (5 mi)
Pass Maggie Lake on the right.

16.1 km (10 mi)
Pass an **overnight pullout** on the right. It's treed and secluded, with a boat launch, log wharf, and room for three vehicles. Just beyond, Toquart Bay Road crosses a bridge.

16.3 km (10.1 mi)
Arrive at Toquart Bay campground. Ocean kayaking and fishing are popular here. Expect a crowd. The campground is a huge, level clearing with room for 100 vehicles. A few campsites are treed, most are exposed, about 15 are on the waterfront.

TOQUART BAY CAMPGROUND #22
Destination / Moderate / $ / mid-May to late Oct
28 tables, log pier, cement boat launch
Accessible by motorhomes and 5th-wheels

Continuing southwest on Hwy 4, passing the 79.7-km (49.5-mi) turnoff to Toquart Bay campground.

If you're heading northeast on Hwy 4, from the coast

0 km (0 mi)
Starting northeast on Hwy 4, from Tofino - Ucluelet Junction, heading for Toquart Bay campground, Snow Creek campground on Sproat Lake, or Port Alberni.

12.5 km (7.8 mi)
Turn right (following directions on page 52) for Toquart Bay campground.

51.6 km (32.1 mi)
After winding through the MacKenzie Range, Hwy 4 crosses the Taylor River bridge and proceeds west to Port Alberni. Just before the Taylor River bridge, turn right onto South Taylor Main FS road (following directions on page 51) for Snow Creek campground on Sproat Lake.

92.2 km (57.3 mi)
Arrive in Port Alberni, near the marina.

WEST OF CAMPBELL RIVER

The hills just west of the town of Campbell River are splashed with lakes. Cozied up to their shores are a couple dozen MOT campgrounds. Of the dozen or so described here, nearly half are on Campbell Lake. It's sprawling: 18 km (11.2 mi) long, up to 7.5 km (4.7 mi) wide, covering 2147 hectares, at 178 m (585 ft) elevation. But you don't need a boat or even a fishing rod to enjoy it. Just dive in. The clear, comfortably-cool water is a swimmer's

Toquart Bay campground

delight. Other campgrounds described here are on smaller lakes just west and north of Campbell Lake. The entire area is popular, so solitude is elusive, but there seems to be enough campgrounds to comfortably absorb all the campers.

You have a choice of access routes. This one is the most direct. It starts on the west edge of Campbell River, heads generally west along the north shore of Campbell Lake, then loops back east to intersect Hwy 19 about 14.8 km (9.2 mi) northwest of town. Excluded from the loop route description, however, is Strathcona Dam campground. Though it's near the loop, the easiest access is directly off Hwy 28, farther west from Campbell River. So Strathcona Dam campground is described separately, on the bottom of page 59.

If you're heading north or south, on Hwy 19

Set your trip odometer to 0 at the junction of Hwys 19 and 28. Drive west on Hwy 28. After crossing the river, enter Elk Falls Park at 1.6 km (1 mi). At 4.4 km (2.7 mi) turn right, following the sign for Loveland Bay Park, and reset your trip odometer to 0. Hwy 28 proceeds left (southwest) to Strathcona Park, Gold River, and the coast.

0 km (0 mi)
Starting northwest toward Loveland Bay Park, departing Hwy 28.

0.5 km (0.3 mi)
Cross above the Campbell River at John Hart Dam. Curve left around John Hart Lake. Follow the paved road until the next junction.

2 km (1.2 mi)
Turn left onto gravel at the brown sign LOVELAND BAY PROVINCIAL PARK 10.5 KM.

3 km (1.8 mi)
Go left at the fork signed for Snowden Forest and Campbell Lake. Continue on well-graded gravel.

9.8 km (6.1 mi)
Proceed straight (west) for most of the area's campgrounds. Turn left (south) for Big Bay campground on Campbell Lake.

BIG BAY CAMPGROUND #1
Weekend / Easy / Free
10 tables, gravel beach
Accessible by small motorhomes and trailers

12.7 km (7.9 mi)
Pass Loveland Bay Provincial Park.

13.1 km (8.1 mi)
Turn sharply left (south) onto Sayward FS road. Pass a sign for Snowden Demonstration Forest. (What a laughable concept. How about a Demonstration Ancient Forest? That wouldn't need a sign. The awesome giants themselves would stop everyone in their tracks.)

15.6 km (9.7 mi)
Proceed on the main road for most of the area's campgrounds. Right soon leads to Gosling Lake campground, on the left.

GOSLING LAKE CAMPGROUND #3
Weekend / Easy / Free
Elev: 225 m (738 ft) / Lake: 3 km (1.9 mi) long, 69.5 ha
4 tables, small float
Accessible by small motorhomes and trailers

18.4 km (11.4 mi)
Proceed on the main road for most of the area's campgrounds. Turn left to reach Gosling Bay campground in 0.5 km (0.3 mi). It has a beautiful, rocky beach, and a grand view across the widest part of Campbell Lake.

GOSLING BAY CAMPGROUND #2
Destination / Easy / Free
7 tables, rough boat launch
Accessible by motorhomes and 5th-wheels

19.3 km (12 mi)
Proceed on the main road for most of the area's campgrounds. Left descends to fully-treed Fir Grove campground on Campbell Lake.

FIR GROVE CAMPGROUND #4
Weekend / Moderate / Free
3 tables, rocky beach
Accessible by small motorhomes and trailers

22.2 km (13.8 mi)
Proceed on the main road for more campgrounds. Turn left for Campbell Lake campground. It has grassy areas, plentiful shade, and a view of the mainland Coast Mountains.

CAMPBELL LAKE CAMPGROUND #6
Destination / Moderate / $ / May 1 – Sept 30
20 tables, rocky beach
Accessible by motorhomes and 5th-wheels

23 km (14.3 mi)
Proceed on the main road for more campgrounds. Turn left for Dogwood Bay campground. It's less appealing than others on Campbell Lake, because the campsites are grouped closely at a circular pullout.

DOGWOOD BAY CAMPGROUND #7
Weekend / Moderate / Free
3 tables, 4 campsites, boat launch, sand/gravel beach
Accessible by motorhomes and 5th-wheels

24 km (14.9 mi)
Proceed on the main road for more campgrounds. Turn left for Loon Bay campground on Campbell Lake.

Campbell Lake

LOON BAY CAMPGROUND #8
Weekend / Moderate / Free
10 campsites, sandy beach at low water
Accessible by motorhomes and 5th-wheels

26.5 (16.4 mi)
Proceed on the main road for more campgrounds. Turn left for Fry Lake campground.

FRY LAKE CAMPGROUND #9
Weekend / Moderate / Free
Elev: 170 m (558 ft) / Lake: 68 ha
5 tables, beach, rough boat launch
Inaccessible by motorhomes and trailers

27 km (16.8 mi)
Proceed on the main road for more campgrounds. Turn left for Orchard Meadow campground on Fry Lake. After descending, go right to find intimate campsites on a narrow arm.

ORCHARD MEADOW CAMPGROUND #10
Weekend / Moderate / Free
6 tables, many more campsites, boat launch
Accessible by motorhomes and 5th-wheels

~

28.3 km (17.5 mi)
Reach a junction. Proceed straight (north) on the main road.

30.3 km (18.8 mi)
Proceed on the main road for more campgrounds. Turn left to reach Gray
Lake campground in 300 meters. The sites are cramped.

GRAY LAKE CAMPGROUND #11
Weekend / Difficult (due only to distance) / Free
Elev: 170 m (558 ft) / Lake: 4 km (2.5 mi) long, 55 ha
5 tables, boat launch
Not suitable for motorhomes and 5th-wheels

~

31 km (19.2 mi) to 33 km (20.5 mi)
Watch left for two campgrounds. Brittany Bay campground ($), on Gray
Lake, has three tables. Brewster Camp campground ($), on the channel
between Gray and Brewster Lakes, has seven tables.

33.6 km (20.9 mi)
Reach a junction. Go straight onto a wide main road, staying on the east side of
Brewster Lake. Apple Point campground is on the shore, beside the road.

APPLE POINT CAMPGROUND #13
Weekend / Difficult (due only to distance) / Free
Elev: 213 m (700 ft) / Lake: 5.3 km (3.3 mi) long, 480 ha
6 tables, boat launch
Accessible by motorhomes and 5th-wheels

~

39.4 km (24.5 mi)
Proceed east on the main road for Hwy 19. Turn left to enter Mohun Lake
campground.

Enjoy the art and science of stone skipping.

MOHUN LAKE CAMPGROUND #15
Weekend / Difficult (due only to distance) / Free
Elev: 198 m (650 ft) / Lake: 9.5 km (6 mi) long, 612 ha
2 tables, cement boat launch
Accessible by motorhomes and 5th-wheels

41 km (25.5 mi)
Proceed east on the main road for Hwy 19. Left leads north to Morton Lake
Provincial Park.

51 km (31.5 mi)
Reach Hwy 19, at the Mac Blo Menzies Bay Division. Campbell River is
right (southeast). Turn left for campgrounds northwest of Campbell River.

For Strathcona Dam, now follow the directions below

From the junction of Hwys 19 and 28, drive Hwy 28 west, then southwest. In
29 km (18 mi) turn right (north) onto Strathcona Dam Road to reach the BC-
Hydro-managed campground in 4 km (2.5 mi). It's below the dam retaining
Upper Campbell Lake, at the southwest tip of Lower Campbell Lake.

Vancouver Island harbours are certifiably picturesque.

STRATHCONA DAM CAMPGROUND #36
Weekend / Easy / Free
11 tables, small beach, boat launch, garbage cans
Accessible by motorhomes and 5th-wheels

WEST OF STRATHCONA PARK

From the junction of Hwys 19 and 28, on the west edge of the town of Campbell River, Hwy 28 heads generally southwest all the way to the coast. It reaches Strathcona Provincial Park in about 50 km (31 mi), the village of Gold River in about 90 km (56 mi), and finally the west end of Muchalat Inlet in about 105 km (65 mi). The Lions manage a campground ($) in **Gold River**. The well-separated sites are in trees, beside the river.

Past Gold River and beyond the scope of this book are four primitive campgrounds reached via remote logging roads. If the following brief descriptions intrigue you, and you're willing to drive the entire width of Vancouver Island for an adventurous camping experience, find a recreation map and hither forth. These campgrounds are 2WD accessible and able to accommodate big RVs. Three are free. A fee is charged at Cougar Creek.

Near the north end of Tahsis Inlet, about 60 km (37 mi) beyond Gold River, is the farthest of these campgrounds: Leiner River campground #30. It's treed, near a swimming hole, has room for up to ten vehicles, and it's free.

Conuma River campground #44 is a small campground on the riverbank near the north end of Tlupana Inlet. You can watch black bears feeding on salmon here each fall.

The biggest of these campgrounds is Cougar Creek campground #31, on the east side of Tlupana Inlet. It has a float, gravel boat launch, extensive docks, and room for up to 50 vehicles. On a map, the location looks lonely. It's not. Expect to see a fleet of RVs here in summer. The fee is levied June 1 to September 30.

On the east end of Muchalat Lake, about 16 km (10 mi) northwest of Gold River, is the nearest of these campgrounds: Muchalat Lake campground #29. It's free, has a float, boat launch, gravel and sand beaches, and 37 individual sites. The lake is 6.5 km (4 mi) long and covers 531 hectares, at 200 m (656 ft) elevation.

NORTHWEST OF CAMPBELL RIVER

The country northwest of Campbell River is exciting. More mountainous than the area around Campbell Lake, it looks wilder, despite all the second-growth forest. Many campgrounds here feel secluded yet are easily and quickly reached.

McCreight Lake is rated *Destination*. The well-spaced campsites are in lush forest, on a bench above the rocky shore. Scramble down to the clear water for a refreshing swim. The lake is just the right size, and the setting beautiful enough, that canoeists can enjoy exploring it all. McCreight is 5 km (3 mi) long, 0.8 km (0.5 mi) wide, and covers 275 hectares.

Past McCreight is another *Destination* campground: Little Bear Bay. Though small and usually crowded, the location is idyllic. From here, boaters can venture into Johnstone Strait and numerous channels.

South of Little Bear Bay is Elk Bay campground, also on **Johnstone Strait.** It's described separately, on page 65, because the direct access is different than for campgrounds en route to Little Bear Bay.

If you're heading northwest on Hwy 19, from Campbell River

From the junction of Hwys 19 and 28, drive Hwy 19 northwest 41 km (25.5 mi). Turn right (north) onto Rock Bay Road and set your trip odometer to 0. (It's 3.4 km / 2.1 mi past Pye Lake West FS road, and 200 meters before the bridge over Amor De Cosmos Creek.)

If you're heading southeast on Hwy 19, from Sayward Junction

From Sayward Junction, drive Hwy 19 southeast 24 km (15 mi). Turn left (north) onto Rock Bay Road and set your trip odometer to 0. (It's 200 meters past the bridge over Amor De Cosmos Creek.)

For either approach above, now follow the directions below

0 km (0 mi)
Starting north on Rock Bay Road, departing Hwy 19. Expect potholes all the way to Rock Bay on Johnstone Strait.

3 km (1.8 mi)
Reach a pullout on the left. A short path leads to Sitka Spruce Beach campground.

> For tenters only, this small campground is on a beach at the south end of McCreight Lake. The view north is stirring. Behind the beach is a lovely hemlock-and-cedar forest.

SITKA SPRUCE BEACH CAMPGROUND #27
Destination / Easy / Free
Several campsites for tenters only, sandy beach, no tables
Footpath accessible by all vehicles

Continuing north on the main road, passing the pullout for Sitka Spruce Beach campground.

3.3 km (2 mi)
Proceed straight (north) for campgrounds at McCreight Lake, Bear Creek, Pye Lake, Stella Lake, Little Bear Bay, and for Rock Bay. Turn left for Aldergrove campground.

> Near the south end of McCreight Lake, this tiny, treed campground is on an old, logging railroad grade. The lake is not visible from the campsites, but a trail leads to a sandy beach.

ALDERGROVE CAMPGROUND #26
Weekend / Easy / Free
2 tables, trail to sandy beach
Accessible by small motorhomes and trailers

Continuing north on the main road, passing the turnoff to Aldergrove campground.

4 km (2.4 mi)
Proceed straight (northeast) for campgrounds at Bear Creek, Pye Lake, Stella Lake, Little Bear Bay, and for Rock Bay. Turn left to enter McCreight Lake campground.

McCREIGHT LAKE CAMPGROUND #25
Destination / Easy / Free
2 tables, 3 well-spaced campsites, rough boat launch
Accessible by small motorhomes and trailers

~

Continuing northeast on the main road, passing the turnoff to McCreight Lake campground.

7.8 km (4.8 mi)
Proceed right (northeast) for campgrounds at Pye Lake, Stella Lake, Little Bear Bay, and for Rock Bay. Turn left (north) onto Bear Bite Road to reach Bear Creek campground, on the left, in about 5 km (3.1 mi).

BEAR CREEK CAMPGROUND #45
Weekend / Moderate / Free
5 tables
Inaccessible by motorhomes and trailers

~

Continuing northeast on the main road, passing the turnoff to Bear Creek campground.

9 km (5.6 mi)
Proceed straight (east) for campgrounds at Stella Lake and Little Bear Bay, and for Rock Bay. Right (south) leads to Pye Lake campground in a couple kilometers. It's also accessible from Hwy 19, via Pye Lake West FS road, 3.4 km (2.1 mi) east of Rock Bay Road. Both approaches are rough.

PYE LAKE CAMPGROUND #24
Weekend / Moderate / Free
Elev: 150 m (492 ft) / Lake: 4 km (2.5 mi) long, 370 ha
4 tables, small beach
Inaccessible by motorhomes and 5th-wheels

~

Continuing east on the main road, passing the turnoff to Pye Lake campground.

11.3 km (7 mi) and 13 km (8.1 mi)
Proceed straight.

14.1 km (8.7 mi)
Proceed straight (northeast) for Little Bear Bay campground and Rock Bay.
Turn right (southeast) to reach Stella Beach campground in about 5 km (3.1 mi),
and Stella Bay campground just beyond.

Both campgrounds are on Stella Lake, at 150 m (392 ft) elevation. The
lake is 6 km (3.7 mi) long and covers 422 hectares. These campgrounds
are also accessible en route to Elk Bay campground (page 65).

STELLA BEACH CAMPGROUND #20a
Weekend / Moderate / Free
10 tables, sandy beach, boat launch
Accessible by small motorhomes and trailers

STELLA BAY CAMPGROUND #20b
Weekend / Moderate / Free
2 tables, small sandy beach, boat launch
Too small for motorhomes and trailers

*Continuing northeast on the main road, passing the turnoff to the Stella Lake
campgrounds.*

16.7 km (10.4 mi)
Reach a junction. Turn left and descend toward the fish hatchery for Little
Bear Bay campground. (Right, then left at 18.2 km / 11.3 mi, quickly leads
to a commercial campground and small marina on Rock Bay.)

17.5 km (10.9 mi)
Go right to enter Little Bear Bay campground. A river flows into Johnstone
Strait here. The setting is beautiful. The campground is often full.

LITTLE BEAR BAY CAMPGROUND #21
Destination / Moderate / Free
10 tables, grassy area, rough boat launch, short trail to waterfall
Accessible by small motorhomes and trailers

Rock Bay on Johnstone Strait, near Little Bear Bay campground

For Elk Bay, now follow the directions below

From the junction of Hwys 19 and 28, drive Hwy 19 northwest 32.8 km (20.3 mi). Or, from Sayward Junction, drive Hwy 19 southeast 32.2 km (20 mi). From either approach turn northeast onto Elk Bay Road and set your trip odometer to 0. At 11.3 km (7 mi) reach a T-junction. Left (northwest) soon passes the Stella Lake campgrounds, and later intersects Rock Bay Road. Turn right (southeast). At 14.5 km (9 mi) reach the Elk Bay log dump and turn right (south). At 15.2 km (9.4 mi) reach the main Elk Bay campground. A smaller, second camping area is 0.4 km (0.25 mi) farther, across the creek.

ELK BAY CAMPGROUND #46
Weekend / Moderate / Free
7 tables, rough boat launch
Accessible by small motorhomes and trailers

NORTHWEST OF SAYWARD JUNCTION

Sayward Junction is on Hwy 19, about midway between Campbell River and Woss. A road leads north from here to the village of Sayward, on Johnstone Strait, where there are private campgrounds.

A couple minutes northwest of Sayward Junction, just off Hwy 19, is Elk Creek campground. It's very handy for a night's sleep but has little appeal in daylight.

Near where Hwy 19 veers southwest toward Woss, you can head north on a logging road to two more campgrounds. The first, Junction Pool, is by the confluence of Adam and Eve rivers. Beyond is Naka Creek, on Johnstone Strait.

If you're heading northwest on Hwy 19, from Sayward Junction

0 km (0 mi)
Starting northwest on Hwy 19 from Sayward Junction. You'll see signs here for camping and whale watching at Robson Bight.

0.5 km (0.3 mi)
Proceed northwest on Hwy 19 for Woss, or Junction Pool and Naka Creek campgrounds. Turn left (south) for Elk Creek campground. It's directly across from a white sign AIRCRAFT PATROLLED. It's also 200 meters before Lower Elk Creek bridge.

Just 0.3 km (0.2 mi) off pavement, the campsites are deep in trees, without views. The creek is often just a dribble.

ELK CREEK CAMPGROUND #28
Overnight / Easy / $ / May 1 - Sept 30
10 tables
Accessible by small motorhomes and trailers

Continuing northwest on Hwy 19, passing the turnoff to Elk Creek campground. Cross the Adam River bridge, proceed beneath the underpass and descend the 3-lane hill.

32 km (19.8 mi)
Proceed southwest on Hwy 19 for Woss. For Junction Pool and Naka Creek campgrounds, turn right (north) onto South Main road and set your trip odometer to 0 at the huge log sign EVE RIVER DIVISION.

0 km (0 mi)
Starting north on South Main, heading for Junction Pool and Naka Creek campgrounds. Cross two small bridged creeks, pass fish farm tanks on the right, and reach a fork. There's a bridge to the left. Go right here on East Main road. Follow it to a stop sign, where you turn left and descend. Cross a bridge over Eve River. Junction Pool campground is a few minutes farther, on the right, near the confluence of Adam and Eve rivers, about 15 km (9.3 mi) from Hwy 19.

JUNCTION POOL CAMPGROUND #38
Weekend / Moderate / Free
10 tables
Accessible by motorhomes and 5th-wheels

Continuing north on the main road, passing Junction Pool campground.

Soon skirt the Mac Blo mechanical shop. A few minutes farther, turn onto Naka Main road. Follow it generally northwest to reach Naka Creek campground in about 20 minutes. It's on Johnstone Strait, near Naka Creek logging camp.

NAKA CREEK CAMPGROUND #42
Weekend / Difficult (due only to distance) / Free
7 tables
Accessible by small motorhomes and trailers

If you're heading east on Hwy 19, from Woss

0 km (0 mi)
Starting east on Hwy 19 from the Woss turnoff. Set your trip odometer to 0.

35 km (21.7 mi)
Proceed east on Hwy 19 for Elk Creek campground near Sayward Junction. For Junction Pool and Naka Creek campgrounds, turn left (north) onto South Main road and set your trip odometer to 0 at the huge log sign EVE RIVER DIVISION. Directions continue at the top of this page.

66.6 km (41.3 mi)
Turn right (south) for Elk Creek campground. It's 200 meters past Lower Elk Creek bridge. It's also directly across from a white sign AIRCRAFT PATROLLED. The campground is just 0.3 km (0.2 mi) off pavement. Read page 66 for details.

67.1 km (41.6 mi)
Reach Sayward Junction. Proceed southeast on Hwy 19 (following directions on page 62) for campgrounds northwest of Campbell River.

SOUTH OF WOSS

To be precise, only Woss Lake campground is directly south of the community of Woss. The other three campgrounds described here are slightly east, but all are in the same area, south of Hwy 19.

Woss Lake campground is big, on a sheltered cove with a sandy beach and a float. Swimmers love it. Pleasant enough to be rated *Weekend*, it's also close enough to the highway to be convenient for overnight use.

Two small campgrounds are on **Klaklakama Lake**—one at the north (lower) end, the other at the south (upper) end. Both are quickly and easily reached from the highway, and neither is special, so they're rated *Overnight*. But they could be enjoyable for a weekend.

Well south of Klaklakama Lake is another, much larger campground at the north end of Vernon Lake, where you might not be so pressed by other campers.

If you're heading west on Hwy 19, from Sayward Junction

For Klaklakama Lake, turn left (south) off Hwy 19 about 55.7 km (34.6 mi) west of Sayward Junction. This is also the signed west access for Schoen Lake Provincial Park.

For Woss Lake, turn left (south) off Hwy 19 about 66.7 km (41.4 mi) west of Sayward Junction. The turn is signed for the community of Woss.

The distance on Hwy 19 between the turnoffs for Klaklakama and Woss lakes is about 11 km (6.8 mi).

If you're heading southeast on Hwy 19, from Port McNeill

For Woss Lake, turn right (south) off Hwy 19 about 64.7 km (40 mi) southeast of Port McNeill. The turn is signed for the community of Woss.

For Klaklakama Lake, turn right (south) off Hwy 19 about 75.7 km (47 mi) southeast of Port McNeill. This is also the signed west access for Schoen Lake Provincial Park. The distance on Hwy 19 between the turnoffs for Woss and Klaklakama lakes is about 11 km (6.8 mi).

For KLAKLAKAMA LAKE, now follow the directions below

0 km (0 mi)
Starting south, departing Hwy 19. Set your trip odometer to 0.

0.3 km (0.2 mi)
Go right at the wide Y-junction. Left leads to Schoen Lake Park. Soon cross a bridge and curve right.

1 km (0.6 mi)
Reach a fork. Stay left on the main road.

2.6 km (1.6 mi)
Bear right (south) for Upper Klaklakama Lake campground. Turn left (east) to reach Lower Klaklakama Lake campground in about 1.1 km (0.7 mi), on the right.

> Scruffy, second-growth forest offers little shade here. You can swim from the rocky beach. The lake itself is pleasant, but the clearcut hills are unsightly. Two campsites are on the shore.

LOWER KLAKLAKAMA LAKE CAMPGROUND #39
Overnight / Easy / Free
Elev: 293 m (535 ft) / Lake: 4.3 km (2.6 mi) long, 255 ha
5 tables, rocky beach
Accessible by small motorhomes and trailers

Continuing south from the 2.6-km (1.6-mi) junction, passing the turnoff to Lower Klaklakama Lake campground.

7 km (4.3 mi)
Reach Upper Klaklakama Lake campground.

Views of clearcuts are worse here than at the lower campground, but the campsites are more private. Three are on the shore. Also, several huge trees are still standing—a reminder that Vancouver Island was once covered by glorious, ancient monarchs.

UPPER KLAKLAKAMA LAKE CAMPGROUND #40
Overnight / Easy / Free
Elev: 293 m (535 ft) / Lake: 4.3 km (2.6 mi) long, 255 ha
4 tables, sandy beach, boat launch
Accessible by small motorhomes and trailers

Continuing south from Upper Klaklakama Lake campground.

About 16 km (9.9 mi) beyond Upper Klaklakama Lake campground is a much larger campground at the north end of Vernon Lake. Get there by proceeding generally south on the main road. Immediately after crossing a bridge over Nimpkish River, reach a junction. Turn right (northwest). After the road curves south again, bear left at the next major junction and continue south, soon reaching the lake.

VERNON LAKE CAMPGROUND #41
Weekend / Moderate / Free
Elev: 221 m (725 ft) / Lake: 7 km (4.3 mi) long, 802 ha
20 tables, boat launch
Accessible by motorhomes and 5th-wheels

For WOSS LAKE, now follow the directions below

0 km (0 mi)
Starting south, departing Hwy 19. Set your trip odometer to 0.

0.7 km (0.4 mi)
Cross railroad tracks.

1.1 km (0.7 mi)
Cross railroad tracks again and immediately curve right. Turn left on S. Railway Avenue. Cross the bridge and go right. (Just after the bridge, left follows the Nimpkish River Valley about 22 km / 13.6 mi to Vernon Lake campground—described on page 70.)

4.3 km (2.7 mi)
Fork left.

4.6 km (2.9 mi)
Fork right to enter Woss Lake campground. A sheltered cove, a float, and a sandy beach make this a great place to swim. The campsites are close together, near the north end of the lake. Clearcuts glare at you across the cove.

WOSS LAKE CAMPGROUND #37
Weekend / Easy / Free
Elev: 150 m (492 ft) / Lake: 16.2 km (10 mi) long
1 km (0.6 mi) wide, 1378 ha
20 tables, sandy beach, boat launch
Accessible by motorhomes and 5th-wheels

WOSS TO PORT MCNEILL

Several superior campgrounds are located on inviting lakes very close to Hwy 19 between Woss and Port McNeill.

Bonanza Lake (10.5 km / 6.5 mi long) is longer than McCreight Lake, but shorter than Woss Lake or giant Nimpkish Lake (25.5 km / 15.8 mi long). The large, pleasant campground on Bonanza Lake's south shore is rated *Destination*. It has a spacious, sandy beach where you can swim and enjoy a grand view. The campsites are in cedar-and-hemlock forest. There are two ways to access Bonanza Lake. The south approach, described here, takes only about 15 minutes on good road. The north approach, from Telegraph Cove, passes two small primitive campgrounds (Ida Lake and Bonanza North), but it's longer and the road rougher.

Just south of Nimpkish Lake is small **Anutz Lake.** On its south shore is a large, open, grassy campground provided by Western Forest Products. Atluck Lake

Nimpkish Lake

(5.8 km / 3.6 mi long), south of Anutz, is about the same size as Klaklakama Lake. The campground at its north end is small and partially treed. Beyond Atluck, a logging road continues way south to two campgrounds (described on page 75) near isolated settlements on West Coast inlets.

Nimpkish Lake, beneath sweeping mountainsides, is stunning. It has two *Destination*-rated campgrounds a short way off the highway. Both are ideal for a convenient overnight stop or a multi-day retreat. Strong, dependable winds make this a fine boardsailing lake. You can also just sit on the beach and lose yourself in the exciting scenery.

Kinman Creek campground is in forest, high above Nimpkish Lake. You can reach the shore by walking about a kilometer down a wide gravel path. A benefit of the campground's distance from the lake is that the stony beach feels wild. The campground itself is provincial-park quality. It was thoughtfully planned and is well maintained. Campsites are comfortably spaced among tall trees.

Nimpkish Lake campground, as the name suggests, is right on the lake. Most of the campsites are along the shore and have lakeviews. It's grassy here, with a treed hillside behind. The sites offer less privacy than those at Kinman, and they're exposed to the lake's frequently strong winds, but the scenery compensates.

If you're heading northwest on Hwy 19, from Woss

For Bonanza Lake, turn right (east) off Hwy 19 just south of the Steele Creek bridge, about 21.5 km (13.3 mi) northwest of Woss.

For Anutz and Atluck lakes, turn left (west) off Hwy 19 just north of the Steele Creek bridge, about 21.7 km (13.5 mi) northwest of Woss. The turnoff is signed for Zeballos.

For Kinman Creek and Nimpkish Lake, turn left (west) off Hwy 19 about 30.5 km (18.9 mi) northwest of Woss.

If you're heading southeast on Hwy 19, from Port McNeill

For Kinman Creek and Nimpkish Lake, turn right (west) off Hwy 19 about 34.2 km (21.2 mi) southeast of Port McNeill.

For Anutz and Atluck lakes, turn right (west) off Hwy 19 just north of the Steele Creek bridge, about 43 km (26.7 mi) southeast of Port McNeill. The turnoff is signed for Zeballos.

For Bonanza Lake, turn left (east) off Hwy 19 just south of the Steele Creek bridge, about 43.2 km (26.8 mi) southeast of Port McNeill.

For BONANZA LAKE, now follow the directions below

0 km (0 mi)
Starting east, departing Hwy 19. Set your trip odometer to 0. Cross railroad tracks and curve right. Do not drive left over the railroad trestle bridge. Ignore the right fork.

1.5 km (0.9 mi)
Bear left. At subsequent minor forks, stay straight on the main road. The trees here are about 35 years old—mere infants. The lower half of the mountain slopes have been logged and replanted the entire length of the valley.

13.7 km (8.5 mi)
Bonanza Lake is visible.

15.3 km (9.5 mi)
Bear left and cross the Bonanza River bridge.

16 km (9.9 mi)
Just before a Forest Fire Hazard sign, turn left and descend for Bonanza Lake campground. The main road continues north along Bonanza Lake's east shore, passing tiny Bonanza Lake North campground and small Ida Lake campground en route to Telegraph Cove.

16.3 km (10.1 mi)
Arrive at Bonanza Lake campground.

BONANZA LAKE SOUTH CAMPGROUND #43
Destination / Moderate / Free
Elev: 267 m (876 ft) / Lake: 10.5 km (6.5 mi) long
1.3 km (0.8 mi) wide, 896 ha
10 tables, sandy beach, rough boat launch
Accessible by small motorhomes and trailers

For ANUTZ and ATLUCK LAKES, now follow the directions below

0 km (0 mi)
Starting west, departing Hwy 19. Set your trip odometer to 0. The road immediately bends northwest, paralleling the highway.

1.3 km (0.8 mi)
Bear left on the main road. Proceed straight at the next two minor forks.

2 km (1.2 mi)
Cross a high bridge over Nimpkish River.

2.4 km (1.5 mi)
Stay straight.

2.8 km (1.7 mi)
Go right.

3.1 km (1.9 mi)
Reach a junction. Turn right (north) for Anutz Lake campground. Directions continue on page 75. Turn left (south) for Atluck Lake campground or to continue way south to remote campgrounds on two West Coast inlets.

Atluck Lake campground is about 10 km (6.2 mi) beyond the 3.1-km (1.9-mi) junction. Stay on the main road, then turn right (west) just north of Wolfe Lake, where the main road proceeds south to Zeballos. Shortly after crossing Atluck Creek, stay straight where right returns north to Anutz Lake. Soon reach the campground on Atluck Lake's north shore.

ATLUCK LAKE CAMPGROUND #50
Weekend / Moderate / Free
Elev: 134 m (440 ft) / Lake: 5.8 km (3.6 mi) long, 278 ha
5 tables, gravel beach
Accessible by small motorhomes and trailers

Continuing south on the main road to Zeballos, passing the turnoff to Atluck Lake campground.

After crossing the boundary between the Port McNeill and Campbell River FS districts, the main road eventually reaches Zeballos. From there you can proceed northwest to Fair Harbour. Both are isolated settlements on West Coast inlets, and both have government campgrounds nearby: Resolution Park campground #32 and Fair Harbour campground #33. At Fair Harbour a fee is charged May 1 to Sept 30. It has 15 tables, a boat launch, and a nearby government dock. Resolution Park is free. It has 12 tables, a cobble beach, a boat launch, a float, and a freshwater source.

Turning right (north) at the 3.1-km (1.9-mi) junction, heading for Anutz Lake campground.

5.8 km (3.6 mi)
Fork right.

6.4 km (4 mi)
Fork left.

6.6 km (4.1 mi)
Go right and descend.

6.8 km (4.2 mi)
Arrive at Anutz Lake campground.

ANUTZ LAKE CAMPGROUND #49
Overnight / Easy / Free
Elev: 300 m (984 ft) / Lake: 1.5 km (0.9 mi) long, 87 ha
14 tables around a large field
Accessible by motorhomes and 5th-wheels

**For KINMAN CREEK and NIMPKISH LAKE,
now follow the directions below**

0 km (0 mi)
Starting west, departing Hwy 19. Set your trip odometer to 0. There's an old gas station here.

100 meters
Proceed straight for Nimpkish Lake campground. Turn right across from the gas station, immediately cross railroad tracks, then descend to reach Kinman Creek campground at 1.3 km (0.8 mi). A map sign indicates all the campsites.

KINMAN CREEK CAMPGROUND #47
Destination / Easy / Free
Elev: 70 m (230 ft) / Lake: 25.5 km (15.8 mi) long, 3680 ha
24 tables, 6 walk-in tent sites, trail to lake
Accessible by motorhomes and 5th-wheels

Proceeding straight at the gas station, passing the turnoff to Kinman Creek campground.

0.3 km (0.2 mi)
Turn left at the T-junction.

0.8 km (0.5 mi)
Go right, then immediately stay left at another fork.

1 km (0.6 mi)
Ignore the left fork. Stay straight, proceeding downhill.

1.5 km (0.9 mi)
Arrive at Nimpkish Lake campground.

NIMPKISH LAKE CAMPGROUND #48
Destination / Easy / Free
Elev: 20 m (65 ft) / Lake: 25.5 km (15.8 mi) long
2 km (1.2 mi) wide, 3680 ha
20 tables, short trail to a point
Accessible by motorhomes and 5th-wheels

SOUTHWEST OF PORT MCNEILL

Most of the campgrounds southwest of Port McNeill are small and remote. The two described here are big. The first is very convenient, the second is reasonably so.

Marble River campground is provincial-park quality. Reached via paved road, it's on a playful, spirited river, at the north end of Alice Lake, in a wonderful, forested setting. Several campsites line the riverbank. Others are well away from the campground road, with privacy created by trees and bushes. The river is audible at most sites, even if it's not visible. Shade is abundant. Large, grassy areas at many sites are great for pitching your tent on, or curling your toes in. This is as attractive as any campground in B.C. Expect mosquitoes in summer.

Find your own paradise.

Alice Lake campground has a rough, wild atmosphere—totally unlike the intimate, manicured Marble River campground. It's not a long drive off pavement, but the claustrophobic access road feels like Alice in Wonderland's rabbit hole. The final approach has light branches arching overhead that might scrape the tops of big rigs. This is an open strip-camp, where RVs line up close together on the stone beach. Drift-logs have blown ashore and piled up here. The strong winds that often whip across this exciting lake keep the bugs down.

If you're heading northwest on Hwy 19, from Port McNeill

Set your trip odometer to 0 at the turnoff to Port McNeill. Drive 20 km (12.5 mi) northwest, then turn left (south) onto Port Alice Road and reset your trip odometer to 0. There's a map sign here.

If you're heading southeast on Hwy 19, from Port Hardy

Set your trip odometer to 0 at the sign WELCOME TO PORT HARDY with the cavorting bears on it. This is also the turnoff for the ferry terminal. Drive 16.4 km (10.2 mi) southeast, then turn right (south) onto Port Alice Road and reset your trip odometer to 0. There's a map sign here.

For either approach above, now follow the directions below

0 km (0 mi)
Starting south on paved Port Alice Road, departing Hwy 19. Stay left on the main road.

10.6 km (6.6 mi)
For Marble River campground, proceed straight (southwest) where a logging road crosses the highway. Commercial campgrounds on Rupert Inlet are right (northwest). Turn left (south) and reset your trip odometer to 0 for Alice Lake campground. Directions continue below.

14.6 km (9.1 mi)
Cross Marble River bridge. You'll see picnic tables for day use on the right, in grass beside the bridge. Immediately after the bridge, turn right and follow the dirt road past the big WFP sign.

15.3 km (9.5 mi)
Reach a fork. Right descends to forested riverside campsites in 100 meters. Left leads to grassy campsites.

MARBLE RIVER CAMPGROUND #52
Destination / Easy / Free
30 campsites, most with tables
Accessible by motorhomes and 5th-wheels

Turning left (south), departing Port Alice Road at the 10.6-km (6.6 mi) junction described above, heading for Alice Lake campground.

0 km (0 mi)
Starting south on Alice Lake Main FS road.

1.2 km (0.7 mi)
Stay right at the fork.

8.2 km (5.1 mi)
Stay right. In 100 meters, go right again onto a narrower road. Trees arch overhead.

12 km (7.4 mi)
Reach Alice Lake.

13.2 km (8.2 mi)
Arrive at Alice Lake campground.

ALICE LAKE CAMPGROUNDS #51
Weekend / Moderate / Free
Elev: 56 m (185 ft) / Lake: 14.3 km (8.8 mi) long, 1074 ha
12 campsites, no tables
Accessible by motorhomes and 5th-wheels

NORTH OF PORT HARDY

A free campground closest to Port Hardy, and the only one north of it, is on the east end of Georgie Lake, about a 20-minute drive from the ferry terminal. The area has been violently logged. Thankfully, no clearcuts are visible from the lake. Boaters might enjoy it here, but the campground lacks appeal. A 3-km (1.9-mi) hiking trail leads to Songhees Lake.

Bound for **Cape Scott**, at the northwest tip of Vancouver Island? Georgie Lake is a possible overnight refuge, but it's out of the way. Hepler Creek campground, near the southwest shore of Nahwitti Lake, is beside the road to Cape Scott.

0 km (0 mi)
Set your trip odometer to 0 at the WELCOME TO PORT HARDY sign with the cavorting bears on it. This is also the turnoff for the ferry terminal.

1.3 km (0.8 mi)
Pass the turnoff to Coal Harbour.

2.1 km (1.3 mi)
Turn left (west) toward Cape Scott.

4.7 km (2.9 mi)
Pavement ends.

9.2 km (5.7 mi)
Reach a junction. Bear right (north) for Georgie Lake campground and cross a small, narrow bridge. Left (west) proceeds across the island, passing Nahwitti Lake campground (12 campsites with tables) in ancient forest, on the southwest shore of Nahwitti Lake, grazing Holberg Inlet, and eventually reaching Cape Scott Provincial Park on the west coast.

14.8 km (9.2 mi)
Fork right to quickly reach Georgie Lake campground.

GEORGIE LAKE CAMPGROUND #53
Overnight / Moderate / Free
Elev: 218 m (715 ft) / Lake: 8.8 km (5.4 mi) long, 486 ha
4 tables, sandy beach, boat launch, short hiking trail
Accessible by small motorhomes and trailers

B: Sunshine Coast

At the fee campgrounds, charges apply year-round.
Dinner Rock camp is gated and closed from September 16 to April 30.

3	Klein Lake	$
4	Khartoum Lake	FREE
5	Lois Lake	FREE
8	Nanton Lake	FREE
12	Dodd Lake	FREE
29	Dinner Rock	$

Sunshine Coast

Jervis Inlet, between Earls Cove and Saltery Bay

The Sunshine Coast has high, rugged mountains and luxuriant forests, ocean inlets and long, mysterious lakes. The continental clash of rock and water is dramatic, often soul-stirring.

This stretch of coast north of Vancouver seems a long way from civilization, yet the journey is short: two brief ferry rides and a couple hours of driving will bring you to Lund, the northern terminus of Hwy 101.

Between Langdale and Earls Cove, the only convenient free campground is at Klein Lake, near Earls Cove. But there are many more inland from Powell River, which is about midway between Saltery Bay and Lund.

LANGDALE TO EARLS COVE

Klein Lake campground, though handy, is not scenic. If it's your only stop between Langdale and Earls Cove, you won't fully appreciate this section of the Sunshine Coast. So visit some of the many regional and provincial parks along the way. **Smugglers Cove,** for example, has a small network of short trails allowing you to easily wander around an idyllic coastal nook. It's reached via Brooks Road, just northwest of Halfmoon Bay, or about 19.8 km (12.3 mi) northwest of Sechelt.

For more excitement, drive 3.8 km (2.4 mi) beyond the Klein Lake turnoff, toward Egmont, then walk the 4-km (2.5-mi) trail to **Skookumchuck Narrows.** You'll witness the sea surging through an impressive tidal bore. The constantly energized water is also a good place to observe seastars.

If you're heading northwest on Hwy 101, from Langdale

From Langdale ferry terminal, drive Hwy 101 generally northwest about 83 km (51.5 mi) to a junction 1 km (0.6 mi) before Earls Cove ferry terminal. Turn right (northeast) toward Egmont and reset your trip odometer to 0.

If you're heading southeast on Hwy 101, from Earls Cove

From Earls Cove ferry terminal, drive Hwy 101 southeast 1 km (0.6 mi), then turn left (northeast) toward Egmont and reset your trip odometer to 0.

For either approach above, now follow the directions below

0 km (0 mi)
Starting northeast toward Egmont, departing Hwy 101.

1.7 km (1.1 mi)
Turn right (southeast) onto North Lake FS road.

3 km (1.9 mi)
After passing cottages and nearing the end of North Lake, bear right for Klein Lake.

4.9 km (3 mi)
Arrive at Klein Lake campground. Go right or left to campsites. The road circles the lake.

KLEIN LAKE CAMPGROUND #3
Overnight / Easy / $ / year-round
Elev: almost sea level / Lake: 1.5 km (0.9 mi) long, 35 ha
19 tables, cartop boat launch (electric motors only)
Accessible by small motorhomes and trailers

Klein Lake campground

SALTERY BAY TO POWELL RIVER

Midway between Saltery Bay and Powell River, if you turn north off Hwy 101 you can quickly reach **Lois Lake** campground or continue to campgrounds at **Khartoum, Nanton and Dodd lakes.** All have a wild, lonely atmosphere that campers find relaxing yet revitalizing. These long lakes are part of the **Powell Forest Canoe Route** (PFCR)—a good alternative to the much busier Bowron Lakes circuit farther north in B.C. For a grand view of the area, including the Strait of Georgia, hike the short but rigorous trail to the summit of Tin Hat Mountain. The trailhead is near Nanton Lake. Directions are on page 86.

The access described below, via Stillwater Main FS road, is restricted due to logging operations. It's open to public travel on weekends, holidays, and between 8 p.m. and 5 a.m. weekdays.

For direct, unrestricted access to Lois Lake campground, turn north off Hwy 101 onto Canoe Main FS road. It's a few minutes east of Stillwater Main FS road and the steel bridge over Lois River. Canoe Main is also a better road than Branch 41 described on the next page.

If you're heading west on Hwy 101, from Saltery Bay

From Saltery Bay ferry terminal, drive Hwy 101 west 11.5 km (7.1 mi). Turn right (north) just before the steel bridge over Lois River and reset your trip odometer to 0.

If you're heading southeast on Hwy 101, from Powell River

From the east edge of the town of Powell River, drive Hwy 101 generally southeast 14.5 km (9 mi). Turn left (north) just after the steel bridge over Lois River and reset your trip odometer to 0.

For either approach above, now follow the directions below

0 km (0 mi)
Starting north on Stillwater Main FS road, departing Hwy 101.

1.1 km (0.7 mi)
Reach a junction. Continue left for campgrounds at Khartoum, Nanton and Dodd lakes. Turn right onto Branch 41 and reset your trip odometer to 0 for Lois Lake campground.

0 km (0 mi)
Turning right onto Branch 41, heading for Lois Lake campground. The road is rough but passable in a 2WD car.

3.6 km (2.2 mi)
Reach a junction. Turn left and descend.

4.5 km (2.8 mi)
Curve right.

4.7 km (2.9 mi)
Arrive at Lois Lake campground.

LOIS LAKE CAMPGROUND #5
Destination / Easy / Free
Elev: 131 m (430 ft) / Lake: 14 km (8.7 mi) long, 2252 ha
8 tables, 3 walk-in tent sites, cartop boat launch
Accessible by small motorhomes and trailers

~

Continuing left at the 1.1-km (0.7-mi) junction, heading for Khartoum, Nanton and Dodd lakes, passing the turnoff to Lois Lake campground.

1.7 km (1.1 mi)
Stay right.

Lois Lake campground

3.9 km (2.4 mi) and 5.2 km (3.2 mi)
Proceed straight on the main road.

6.7 km (4.1 mi) and 8.5 km (5.3 mi)
Pass overnight pullouts beside Lois Lake.

12.3 km (7.6 mi)
Reach a fork. Continue left for campgrounds on Nanton and Dodd lakes.
Turn right and set your trip odometer to 0 for Khartoum Lake campground.

0 km (0 mi)
Turning right, heading for Khartoum Lake campground.

7.4 km (4.6 mi)
Proceed through a fish farm on Lois Lake.

10 km (6.2 mi)
The road is narrow, steep, rocky, but passable in a 2WD car.

15.1 km (9.4 mi)
Turn right for the sharp descent to Khartoum Lake campground. If
you're high on a cliff with a clear view of the lake way below, you've
gone about 2.3 km (1.4 mi) too far; turn back. This viewpoint, however,
is worth walking or driving to from the campground. It enables you to
appreciate the lake's dramatic, mountain-valley setting. As for the
campsites, several are in the open, along the shore; others are among
beautiful trees; one is next to a loud creek.

KHARTOUM LAKE CAMPGROUND #4
Destination / Moderate / Free
Elev: 131 m (430 ft) / Lake: 6.8 km (4.2 mi) long, 436 ha
6 tables, boat launch
Accessible by small motorhomes and trailers

Continuing left at the 12.3-km (7.6-mi) fork, heading for Nanton and Dodd lakes, passing the turnoff to Khartoum Lake campground.

13.1 km (8.1 mi)
Stay right on Goat Lake Main FS road.

17.5 km (10.9 mi)
Tin Hat Mountain is visible ahead.

18.8 km (11.7 mi)
Reach a junction. Go right, onto the wider road, for Nanton and Dodd lakes. (Left ascends to the Tin Hat Mountain trailhead. It's about 450 meters past tiny Spring Lake. Start hiking on the old logging road that forks right. In about two hours, follow a faint trail left to the rocky summit.)

20 km (12.4 mi)
Proceed straight (north) for Dodd Lake campground. Turn right and descend to reach Nanton Lake campground in 200 meters. Mountains are visible across the lake. A couple campsites are on the shore; most are in trees.

NANTON LAKE CAMPGROUND #8
Weekend / Moderate / Free
Elev: 175 m (575 ft) / Lake: 1.3 km (0.8 mi) long, 129 ha
13 tables, boat launch
Accessible by small motorhomes and trailers

Continuing north, passing the turnoff to Nanton Lake campground.

25.2 km (15.6 mi)
Turn right for Dodd Lake campground. It's a pretty lake among beautiful mountains.

DODD LAKE CAMPGROUND #12
Weekend / Moderate / Free
Elev: 210 m (670 ft) / Lake: 6.4 km (4 mi) long, 704 ha
12 tables, boat launch
Accessible by small motorhomes and trailers

Khartoum Lake

NORTH OF POWELL RIVER

The Sunshine Coast ends north of Powell River. Paved road extends only as far as Lund and Okeover Inlet. Other than nearby Okeover Arm Provincial Park, camping on the ocean is limited to Dinner Rock, on the Malaspina Strait, just southeast of Lund. Dinner Rock is preferable. It's well manicured, with several campsites directly above the sea. You can launch a cartop boat here.

From the Petro Canada station on the north edge of the town of Powell River, drive Hwy 101 northwest 15.8 km (9.8 mi). Or, from the turnoff to Okeover Inlet, drive Hwy 101 southeast 1.3 km (0.8 mi). From either approach, turn west onto the rough, steeply descending access road. The campground is 1.6 km (1 mi) off pavement. Don't try it in a big RV; others have required tow-truck rescue. Okeover Provincial Park is 1.3 km (0.8 mi) northwest. Boaters embark here for Desolation Sound Marine Park.

DINNER ROCK CAMPGROUND #29
Destination / Easy / $ / open May 1 to Sept 15
12 tables, cartop boat launch, picnic sites
Inaccessible by motorhomes and trailers

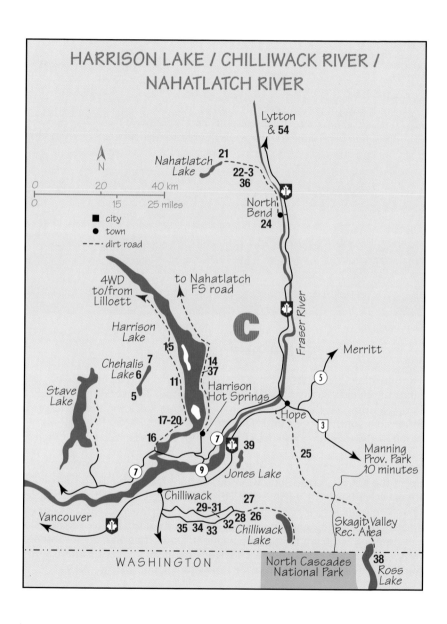

HARRISON LAKE / CHILLIWACK RIVER / NAHATLATCH RIVER

Lytton
& **54**

N

Nahatlatch **21**
Lake   **22-3**
        36

0   20   40 km
0   15   25 miles

■ city
● town
--- dirt road

North
Bend •
        24

4WD
to/from
Lilloett

to Nahatlatch
FS road

Harrison
Lake

Chehalis **7**
Lake **6**

Stave
Lake

1 5

14
37

11

5

Harrison
Hot Springs

Fraser River

Merritt

5

Hope

3

17-20

16

7

39

25

Manning
Prov. Park
10 minutes

7

9

Jones Lake

Chilliwack

Vancouver

27

29-31

28 **26**

35 **34** **33** **32**

Chilliwack
Lake

Skagit Valley
Rec. Area

WASHINGTON

North Cascades
National Park

38

Ross
Lake

C. Harrison Lake / Chilliwack River / Nahatlatch River

The fee campgrounds in the Chilliwack and Nahatlatch river valleys are open year-round, and charges are levied year-round. Throughout the rest of the region, the enhanced, fee campgrounds are usually open mid-May through the long September weekend, plus Thanksgiving and Easter weekends. Outside those dates, entry is barred by lock and gate. You can, however, still camp there by phoning the site operator and requesting a key. The phone numbers are listed on www.for.gov.bc.ca/dck/recreation/recs.html. In addition to the camping fee, expect to pay a refundable security deposit—your promise not to trash or vandalize the campground.

5	Chehalis Lake South	FREE	25	Eaton Creek	FREE
6	Skwellepil Creek	$	26	Riverside	$
7	Chehalis Lake North	$	27	Foley Lake	FREE
11	Wood Lake	$	28	Camp Foley	$
14	Cogburn Beach	FREE	29	Chipmunk Peninsula	$
15	Twenty Mile Bay	$	30	Rapids	FREE
16	Chehalis River	$	31	Eagles Roost	FREE
17	Grace Lake	$	33	Thurston Meadows	$
18	Wolf Lake	$	34	Allison Pool	$
19	Weaver Lake	$	35	Tamihi Creek	$
20	Francis Lake	FREE	36	Nahatlatch River	$
21	Log Creek	$	37	Bear Creek	FREE
22	Fir Flat	$	38	Hozomeen	FREE
23	Apocynum	$	39	Jones Lake	FREE
24	Scuzzy Creek	FREE	54	Botanie Lake	FREE

Harrison Lake
Chilliwack River
Nahatlatch River

B.C.'s southwest corner has a great diversity of campgrounds. Many are clustered around Harrison Lake and its outlet, Chehalis River. Another group is sprinkled along Chilliwack River, upstream toward Chilliwack Lake. What they all have in common is proximity to the metropolitan sprawl of Vancouver and its pressure valve—Trans-Canada Hwy 1—which vents a burst of urban steam every weekend, when all the wage slaves flee the city in search of sanity. The result is a lot of frequently full campgrounds, sometimes the insanity of a wild, beer-drenched party, and once in a while the perversion of a torched outhouse or chopped-up campsite table. The Forest Service does a commendable job of coping despite limited means. Thanks to them, your camping experience here is likely to be safe and enjoyable. The campgrounds along Nahatlatch River and at Botanie Lake are farther from Vancouver and therefore more popular with true outdoorspeople, who are usually quiet, versus noisy yahoos.

CHEHALIS LAKE

Chehalis Lake is in a valley between Harrison and Stave lakes. Access is long and can be rough depending on the current level of industrial traffic. Motorhomes, 5th-wheels and trailers might suffer here. Public travel is prohibited weekdays 6 a.m. to 6 p.m. due to logging. But if you're driving a rugged vehicle, and you're indifferent to clearcuts, maybe you'll enjoy one of the three substantial campgrounds on Chehalis Lake. The following brief directions should be adequate for experienced explorers.

Coast Mountains, above Fraser Valley

If you're heading east or west on Hwy 7

Drive to Harrison Mills. Turn north onto Morris Valley Road. In 0.5 km (0.3 mi) turn left onto Chehalis FS road and follow it generally north. Above and west of Chehalis River, the road angles northwest. After crossing the bridge over Statlu Creek, proceed generally north to reach the south end of Chehalis Lake, about 21 km (13 mi) from Harrison Mills. The road continues north, following the lake's west shore. Turnoffs to the other campgrounds are about 31 km (19 mi) and 34 km (21 mi) from Harrison Mills.

Chehalis South campground #5 is on the lake's south shore. It's a medium-size, forested campground: 13 campsites without tables.

Skwellepil Creek campground #6 is about two-thirds of the way up the lake's west shore. The final approach is a steep, rugged descent, possibly requiring 4WD. It's a large, forested campground with a gravel beach. It has only 15 tables, but room for about 40 vehicles. You can launch a cartop boat here. There's also an upland overflow camping area—handy if the main campground is full or too noisy for you.

Chehalis Lake North campground #7 is on the lake's north shore. It's a large, forested campground with 30 tables. The beach has no vehicle access, but there is a gravel boat launch.

CHEHALIS RIVER & HARRISON LAKE

Harrison Lake is 60 km (37 mi) long and up to 7.5 km (4.7 mi) wide. Backroads head north, up the west and east shores. The driving is tedious. Most visitors don't venture beyond the tourist town of Harrison Hot Springs—on the south shore, reached via paved Hwy 9. That's far enough to appreciate the lake's magnitude and beauty.

Chehalis River campground, en route to Harrison Lake's west shore, is the most attractive and easily accessible in the area. The only drive-in campground actually on the west shore of Harrison Lake is halfway up the lake, at Twenty Mile Bay. Within easier reach are both of Harrison Lake's east-shore campgrounds: Bear Creek ($) and Cogburn Beach (free). They're about 18 km (11.2 mi) beyond where pavement ends. Bear Creek is popular with boardsailors. The Cogburn Beach campsites are for tenters only, in a stand of ancient trees.

Even if you're not camping, Chehalis River and Harrison Lake are good destinations for a scenic drive. En route, Hwy 7 plies the lush, pastoral Fraser Valley and grants views of monstrous Mt. Cheam and the Border Peaks. Come here in early October, and you'll also see salmon in Weaver Creek and the spawning channel near the lake's southwest arm.

Harrison Lake and the Coast Mountains

If you're heading east on Hwy 7, from Vancouver

Drive Hwy 7 to Harrison Mills. Turn left (north) onto Morris Valley Road and set your trip odometer to 0.

If you're heading east or west, on Trans-Canada Hwy 1

Between Chilliwack and Hope (36 km / 22.3 mi southwest of Hope), take Exit 135 signed for Bridal Falls, Agassiz, and Harrison Hot Springs. Head north and cross the Fraser River. Turn left (west) on Hwy 7. Proceed straight (west) where Hwy 9 goes right (north) to Harrison Hot Springs. Cross a huge metal bridge over Harrison River (good salmon viewing here in October). About 21 km (13 mi) from Hwy 1, reach Harrison Mills. Turn right (north) onto Morris Valley Road and set your trip odometer to 0.

For either approach above, now follow the directions below

0 km (0 mi)
Starting north on Morris Valley Road, departing Hwy 7 at Harrison Mills. You'll see signs for Hemlock Valley Recreation Area, Chehalis River Hatchery (6 km), and Weaver Creek Spawning Channel (12 km).

0.5 km (0.3 mi)
Proceed straight, on pavement, toward Hemlock Valley and Harrison Lake. Left is Chehalis FS road leading to Chehalis Lake. Directions continue on page 92.

5.8 km (3.6 mi)
Stay straight for Harrison Lake and campgrounds at Weaver, Wolf, Grace and Wood lakes. Turn right to reach the first and largest Chehalis River campground in 0.3 km (0.2 mi). The campsites are well-spaced in forest, near the wide, shallow river.

CHEHALIS RIVER CAMPGROUND #16
Weekend / Easy / $ / year-round
40 tables, sandy beach
Accessible by motorhomes and 5th-wheels

Continuing north on Morris Valley Road, passing the turnoff to Chehalis River campground.

6 km (3.7 mi)
Proceed over the steel bridge for Harrison Lake and campgrounds at Weaver, Wolf, Grace and Wood lakes. Before the bridge, turn left to reach the second Chehalis River campground. Smaller and less attractive than the first one, it has five tables.

6.1 km (3.8 mi)
Cross the steel bridge and stay straight for Harrison Lake and campgrounds at Weaver, Wolf, Grace and Wood lakes. Immediately after the bridge, turn left for the third Chehalis River campground. This one's the smallest and least appealing, but if the others are full you'll find three tables here.

6.8 km (4.2 mi)
Reach a junction. Stay straight on Morris Valley Road.

7.9 km (4.9 mi)
Go straight through the junction, toward Weaver Creek Spawning Channel. Left leads to Hemlock Ski Area.

10.9 km (6.8 mi)
Pavement ends.

11.4 km (7.1 mi)
Cross a bridge and arrive at the spawning channel. If the salmon are running, check out the action in Weaver Creek. The road begins ascending.

13 km (8.1 mi)
Proceed on Harrison West FS road for Harrison Lake and campgrounds at Wolf, Grace and Wood lakes. Left is a rough, steep road leading about 5 km (3.1 mi) to Weaver Lake campground. It's passable but challenging in a 2WD car. High clearance is helpful; 4WD is preferable. A 6.2-km (3.8-mi) hiking trail circles the small lake.

WEAVER LAKE CAMPGROUND #19
Weekend / Difficult / $ / mid-May to early Sept
Elev: 255 m (836 ft) / Lake: 1.7 km (1.1 mi) long, 78 ha
16 tables, hiking trail
Inaccessible by motorhomes and trailers

Continuing east on Harrison West FS road, passing the turnoff to Weaver Lake campground.

13.2 km (8.2 mi)
Arrive at Wolf Lake campground. Proceed on Harrison West FS road for Harrison Lake and campgrounds at Grace and Wood lakes.

Wolf Lake is tiny, surrounded by forest. Power boats are prohibited. Campsites are near the road. One has a lakeview.

WOLF LAKE CAMPGROUND #18
Overnight / Easy / $ / mid-May to early Sept
Elev: 91 m (298 ft) / Lake: 2 ha
3 tables, short trail to lake
Accessible by small motorhomes and trailers

Continuing north on Harrison West FS road, passing Wolf Lake campground.

13.4 km (8.3 mi)
Reach the turnoff for Grace Lake campground. Proceed on Harrison West FS road for Wood Lake campground and Harrison Lake.

The Grace Lake access road is narrow, with insufficient room for big rigs to turn around. In 150 meters fork right. Arrive at the campground in another 300 meters. The lake is in a steep-sided, forested bowl that feels secluded. The campsites are too high above the shore for lakeviews. Yet the campground is superior to the one at Wolf Lake and should be quieter. Power boats are prohibited.

GRACE LAKE CAMPGROUND #17
Overnight / Easy / $ / mid-May to early Sept
Elev: 100 m (328 ft) / Lake: 4.5 ha
2 tables, steep trail to lake
Inaccessible by motorhomes and trailers

∿

Continuing north on Harrison West FS road, passing the turnoff to Grace Lake campground.

17 km (10.5 mi)
Reach a high viewpoint above Harrison Lake. Having ascended, the road now levels as it continues north.

19.6 km (12.2 mi)
Proceed on Harrison West FS road for Wood Lake campground. Sharp left ascends to Francis Lake campground #20. It's a small campground on a tiny lake, accessible only by 4WD.

25.4 km (15.7 mi)
Cross a bridged creek.

28.7 km (17.8 mi)
Pass Harrison West - Simms Cr FS road on the left.

30.3 km (18.8 mi)
Cross a bridged creek. Pass Harrison West - Walian Cr FS road on the left.

32.4 km (20.1 mi)
Reach a junction. Go right, then bear left at the fork to arrive at Wood Lake campground. (Continue on the main road another 150 meters for the turnoff to more campsites on the other side of Wood Lake.)

A view of the distant, glacier-clad Pemberton Mountains is insufficient reward for driving this far. Consider camping at Wood Lake only if you're exploring much farther north.

WOOD LAKE CAMPGROUND #11
Weekend / Difficult (due only to distance) / $ / mid-May to early Sept
Elev: 152 m (500 ft) / Lake: 5 ha
8 tables, 10 campsites
Not recommended for motorhomes and trailers

∿

Local colour, B.C. backroads

Harrison West FS road continues north, following the west shore of Harrison Lake. At about the lake's midpoint is Twenty Mile Bay campground #15. *It's a medium-size, forested campground with a cartop boat launch. Nearby is a rough emergency airstrip for light aircraft.*

HARRISON LAKE EAST SHORE

It's a beautiful drive from Harrison Hot Springs up the east shore of Harrison Lake. Unlike the west shore road, this one initially hugs the water's edge. A massive glacier is visible far north. Opportunities to camp free are limited to Bear Creek, and a small, tenters-only campground at Cogburn Beach. The alternative is to pay to camp at Sasquatch Provincial Park, above the lake's southeast corner.

If you're heading east or west, on Trans-Canada Hwy 1

Between Chilliwack and Hope (36 km / 22.3 mi southwest of Hope), take Exit 135 signed for Bridal Falls, Agassiz, and Harrison Hot Springs. Head north and cross the Fraser River. Turn left (west) on Hwy 7. Soon turn right (north) onto Hwy 9. Follow it to Harrison Hot Springs, on Harrison Lake's south shore, about 16 km (9.9 mi) from Hwy 1. At the T-junction in town, set your trip odometer 0 and turn right onto the road following the lake's east shore, heading for Sasquatch Provincial Park.

0 km (0 mi)
Starting northeast from the T-junction in Harrison Hot Springs. The roller-coaster road is paved until Sasquatch Park.

6.3 km (3.9 mi)
Reach a junction. Go right, toward Sasquatch Park and Hicks Lake. Left leads to a day-use area.

7.4 km (4.6 mi)
Reach a junction. Go left onto Harrison East FS road for Bear Creek and Cogburn Beach campgrounds.

22 km (13.6 mi)
Reach Bear Creek campground on Harrison Lake. Proceed north for Cogburn Beach campground.

BEAR CREEK CAMPGROUND #37
Weekend / Difficult (due only to distance) / Free
10 tables, gravel beach
Accessible by small motorhomes and trailers

Continuing north on Harrison East FS road, passing Bear Creek campground.

25 km (15.5 mi)
Reach Cogburn Beach campground on Harrison Lake.

For tenters only, the campsites are in a stand of ancient trees beside the lake. They're reached via short trail (about a 6-minute walk) descending from the road. Vehicles are prohibited on the beach. A small mill and booming-ground are nearby.

COGBURN BEACH CAMPGROUND #14
Weekend / Difficult (due only to distance) / Free
4 tentsites with tables, gravel beach
Parking accessible by all vehicles

CHILLIWACK RIVER

On Trans-Canada Hwy 1, about 105 km (65 mi) east of downtown Vancouver, is the town of Chilliwack. South of town is the Chilliwack River, flowing from Chilliwack Lake farther east. The **North Cascade mountains** rise abruptly along the U.S. border here, creating an impressive backdrop. It's an inviting area, well worth a weekend or more. Recreation opportunities—

Chilliwack River, from Eagles Roost campground

hiking, kayaking, boating, fishing—are abundant. MOT campgrounds are numerous and easy to access. Proximity to Vancouver, however, ensures a constant flow of campers. Don't come here seeking solitude.

If you're heading east or west, on Trans-Canada Hwy 1

Take Exit 119A signed for Sardis and Cultus Lake. Drive south on Vedder Road, past fast-food restaurants and gas stations in the town of Chilliwack. About 5.5 km (3.4 mi) from Hwy 1, reach a three-way junction at the metal bridge over Chilliwack River. Set your trip odometer to 0 and turn left (southeast) just before the bridge. Follow the sign for Chilliwack Lake Provincial Park (42 km).

0 km (0 mi)
Starting southeast along the north side of Chilliwack River, from the three-way junction at the metal bridge.

9.7 km (6 mi)
Proceed straight on the main road where Slesse Park Road forks left.

10 km (6.2 mi)
Pass a treed pullout near the river.

10.5 km (6.5 mi)
After crossing a bridge to the south side of Chilliwack River, proceed east on the main road for more campgrounds. Turn right (south) onto Chilliwack - Liumchen Creek FS road to reach Tamihi Creek campground in 0.4 km (0.2 mi). Bear right and cross Tamihi Creek bridge; don't fork left up Chilliwack - Tamihi Cr FS road.

This is a large, provincial-park quality campground, in a healthy, deciduous forest. Many campsites are beside the lovely creek. A city-park atmosphere can prevail here when it's crowded, which is often.

TAMIHI CREEK CAMPGROUND #35
Weekend / Easy / $ / year-round
30 tables, day-use area
Accessible by small motorhomes and trailers

Continuing east on the main road, passing the turnoff to Tamihi Creek campground, following the south side of Chilliwack River.

14 km (8.7 mi)
Proceed east on the main road for more campgrounds. Turn left for the short descent to Allison Pool campground on Chilliwack River.

ALLISON POOL CAMPGROUND #34
Weekend / Easy / $ / March 15 – Oct 15
4 well-spaced tables
Too small for motorhomes and trailers

Continuing east on the main road, passing the turnoff to Allison Pool campground, following the south side of Chilliwack River.

17.4 km (10.8 mi)
Proceed east on the main road for more campgrounds. Turn left to enter Thurston Meadows campground on Chilliwack River. The campsites ring a clearing.

THURSTON MEADOWS CAMPGROUND #33
Weekend / Easy / $ / year-round
14 tables
Accessible by motorhomes and 5th-wheels

Continuing east on the main road, passing the turnoff to Thurston Meadow campground, following the south side of Chilliwack River.

27.2 km (16.9 mi)
Cross a bridge to Chilliwack River's north side. Proceed east on the main road for Riverside campground and Chilliwack Lake. Turn left (between the bridge and Foley Creek FS road) for Camp Foley. After turning, double back toward the river.

Camp Foley is a big pullout with lush trees on two sides. It's next to Chilliwack River but also beside the road. Passing vehicles are audible.

CAMP FOLEY CAMPGROUND #28
Overnight / Easy / $ / mid-May to early Sept
3 tables, 5 campsites
Accessible by small motorhomes

Continuing east on the main road, passing the turnoff to Camp Foley.

27.4 km (17 mi)
Proceed east on the main road for Riverside campground and Chilliwack Lake. For more campgrounds on the north side of Chilliwack River, turn left (north) onto Foley Creek FS road (just past Camp Foley) and set your trip odometer to 0. Directions continue in the middle of the next page.

28.8 km (17.9 mi)
Pavement ends.

30.1 km (19 mi)
Proceed east on the main road for Chilliwack Lake. Turn right to enter Riverside campground on Chilliwack River.

The campsites are well-spaced among Douglas firs. Little sunlight penetrates the forest. The road is nearby, but the river helps muffle noise.

RIVERSIDE CAMPGROUND #26
Weekend / Easy / $ / mid-May to early Sept
11 campsites
Accessible by small motorhomes / difficult for trailers

Continuing east on the main road, passing the turnoff to Riverside campground.

40.4 km (25.1 mi)
Stay straight for Chilliwack Lake. Left quickly reaches the Lindeman, Greendrop and Flora lakes trailhead.

41 km (25.4 mi)
Arrive at Chilliwack Lake Provincial Park.

*Turning left (north) onto **Foley Creek FS road**, departing paved Chilliwack River road at 27.4 km (17 mi). Set your trip odometer to 0.*

0 km (0 mi)
Starting north on Foley Creek FS road, heading for Chipmunk Peninsula, Rapids and Eagles Roost campgrounds. All are on Chilliwack River's north bank.

2.1 km (1.3 mi)
Cross a bridge over Foley Creek and turn left (southwest).

4 km (2.5 mi)
Proceed straight (southwest) where Chipmunk Creek FS road forks right (north).

4.5 km (2.8 mi)
Proceed southwest on the main road for Rapids and Eagles Roost campgrounds. Turn left to enter Chipmunk Peninsula campground on Chilliwack River.

The sites at this provincial-park-quality campground are among ancient evergreens. The atmosphere is enhanced by the revitalizing sound of river rapids. This is a popular starting point for motorcycle and ATV riders, because nearby trails are open to off-road riding. If you're not here to ride, you won't enjoy the noise on weekends.

CHIPMUNK PENINSULA CAMPGROUND #29
Destination / Easy / $ / mid-May to early Sept
14 tables, nearby motorcycle trails
Accessible by motorhomes and 5th-wheels

Continuing southwest on the main road, passing the turnoff to Chipmunk Peninsula campground, following the north side of Chilliwack River.

6.8 km (4.2 mi)
Pass Mt. Thurston FS road.

7.3 km (4.5 mi)
Proceed southwest on the main road for Eagles Roost campground. Turn left to enter Rapids campground on Chilliwack River.

As the name suggests, roaring rapids are the entertainment here. A big, sloping rock serves as grandstand. The river is too swift for swimming or even wading. ATVers also use this as a basecamp.

RAPIDS CAMPGROUND #30
Weekend / Easy / Free
4 campsites
Too small for motorhomes and trailers

8.1 km (5mi)
Turn left to enter Eagles Roost campground near deep pools and roaring whitewater along Chilliwack River. See photo on page 99.

EAGLES ROOST CAMPGROUND #31
Weekend / Easy / Free
1 table, 2 campsites
Too small for motorhomes and trailers

NEAR HOPE

The North Cascade Mountains loom south of Hope and Trans-Canada Hwy 1. Free campgrounds await you in two of the valleys that pierce this mighty range.

BC Hydro manages a large campground at the north end of **Jones Lake**. It's only 10 km (6.2 mi) off the highway but is rated moderate because the road is steep with sharp switchbacks. It's challenging for even small motorhomes and trailers, but 2WD cars can make it easily if slowly. Dramatic peaks rise south of the lake. In fall, brilliantly-coloured deciduous trees compensate for unsightly low water-levels that time of year.

The small campground at Eaton Creek is en route to huge **Ross Lake**. The campsites are on a bench above the road, allowing you to appreciate Silverhope Creek valley's fine scenery and exuberant fall colours. The entry road is short, but steep and rough. When dry, it's passable in a 2WD car. Even the smallest motorhomes and trailers will struggle. This is a good basecamp for hikers. Several trails climb into the surrounding mountains. The Eaton Lake trail begins near the campground. It gains 880 m (2886 ft) in 6.5 km (4 mi), ending at the alpine lake that feeds Eaton Creek.

About 47 km (29 mi) south of Eaton Creek campground is Ross Lake. It sounds like a long way to drive on dirt, but the road's good, and the destination is compelling: Hozomeen campground, just across the U.S. border, at the north end of Ross Lake. The lake extends south 32.3 km (20 mi) into Washington State. The campground is expansive, and there's currently no fee. Recreation opportunities are rife. Boaters, anglers and hikers will easily entertain themselves. Plop-and-admire-the-scenery campers will be smiling too.

In Washington, Ross Lake is visible from Hwy 20, but the shore is roadless. The only way to reach it is by hiking, or portaging a canoe. So vehicle access to Ross Lake is a B.C. exclusive. As for the border crossing—no worries. It's very relaxed. You're unlikely to be questioned.

Hozomeen campground is in cool, dense forest, but some campsites have lakeviews. A choice of boat launches will please the weekend admiral. "Winnebago Flats," just before Hozomeen, is an open area where RV pilots can land even the biggest rigs. Ross Lake, fed by mountain streams, is not "full pool" until about July 1. In spring, the water level is kept low to allow for snowmelt.

A 6-km (3.7-mi) trail climbs 350 m (1150 ft) from near Ross Lake to much smaller Hozomeen Lake beneath the sky-spearing twin pinnacles of Hozomeen Mountain. It's an excellent dayhike. For details, inquire at the Ross Lake ranger station.

Silverhope Creek valley, en route to Eaton Creek and Ross Lake campgrounds

If you're heading east or west, on Trans-Canada Hwy 1

For Jones Lake, take Exit 153 signed for Laidlaw and Jones Lake. The exit is 18.7 km (11.6 mi) northeast of Harrison Hot Springs Exit 135, or 17.3 km (10.7 mi) west of Hope. Set your trip odometer to 0.

For Eaton Creek and Ross Lake, take Exit 168 signed for Flood - Hope Rd and Silverhope Creek. The exit is 32.7 km (20.3 mi) northeast of Harrison Hot Springs Exit 135, or 3.2 km (2 mi) west of Hope. Set your trip odometer to 0. (Coming from the west, the 0 point is 0.5 km / 0.3 mi off the highway.)

For JONES LAKE, now follow the directions below

0 km (0 mi)
Starting on Laidlaw Road, departing Hwy 1.

0.8 km (0.5 mi)
Cross a bridge over Jones Creek and immediately veer right. Ascend steeply. Proceed south on Jones Lake FS road, ignoring forks.

4 km (2.5 mi)
The road levels. The grade is easy the rest of the way.

8.5 km (5.3 mi)
Reach a junction. Stay straight on Jones Lake FS road to reach Jones Main campground #39 in 1.5 km (0.9 mi). Or fork right (southeast) on Jones Lake West FS road to reach the Jones West campground in about the same distance.

10 km (6.2 mi)
Arrive at Jones Lake campground, at the northwest end of the lake, north of Wahleach Dam, with campsites on the west and east sides of Boulder Creek. There's a large parking lot east of the creek.

Jones West is on a peninsula immediately south of the dam. East of the dam are 22 campsites between the lakeshore and Boulder Creek. Just south of the creek are 3 more sites, a small beach and a grassy landing. West of the dam are 11 campsites.

The Jones Reservoir area was used by the STO:LO First Nation as a rest stop en route to summer hunting grounds. In 1995, STO:LO elders blessed the area for the enjoyment of all people.

JONES LAKE MAIN CAMPGROUND #39a
Weekend / Moderate / Free, maintained May 1 – Oct 15
Lake: 5 km (3.1 mi) long, 1 km (0.6 mi) wide, 133 ha
37 tables, cartop boat launch, potable water well with handpump
Accessible by small motorhomes and trailers

JONES LAKE WEST CAMPGROUND #39b
Weekend / Moderate / Free, maintained May 1 – Oct 15
Lake: 5 km (3.1 mi) long, 1 km (0.6 mi) wide, 133 ha
18 tables, cartop boat launch, no drinking water
Accessible by small motorhomes and trailers

Hozomeen campground on Ross Lake

For EATON CREEK AND ROSS LAKE,
now follow the directions below

0 km (0 mi)
Starting on Flood - Hope Road, departing Hwy 1.

0.3 km (0.2 mi)
Turn south onto Silver Skagit Road. Pass a sign for Silver Lake and Hozomeen campground.

2.6 km (1.6 mi)
Pavement ends.

6.6 km (4.1 mi)
Reach a junction. Bear left and continue south toward Skagit Valley and Ross Lake. Right leads to Silver Lake's west shore in 1 km (0.6 mi).

17.2 km (10.7 mi)
Turn left and ascend to enter Eaton Creek campground. Proceed on the main road to reach Ross Lake, the U.S. border, and Hozomeen Campground.

EATON CREEK CAMPGROUND #25
Weekend / Easy / Free
3 tables, hiking trail to Eaton Lake
Not suitable for motorhomes and trailers

Continuing generally southeast on the main road, passing the turnoff to Eaton Creek campground.

64.5 km (40 mi)
Nearing road's end, pass the B.C. Parks Ross Lake Campground. Fork left where right leads to the **International Point day-use area.** Pass the Canadian warden office, cross the border, enter Ross Lake National Recreation Area, and pass the American ranger station (an A-frame cabin). Rangers are on duty May through late October.

65.5 km (40.6 mi)
Reach "Winnebago Flats" camping area for RVs just before Hozomeen campground on Ross Lake. A sign directs you left to the Hozomeen Lake trail near an old cabin, 3 km (1.8 mi) from the ranger station. You'll find faucets with potable water there.

HOZOMEEN CAMPGROUND #38
Destination / Difficult (due only to distance) / Free
Elev: 518 m (1700 ft) / Lake: 34 km (21 mi) long
120 campsites, many with tables
3 boat launches (2 cement, 1 gravel)
Accessible by motorhomes and 5th-wheels

ABOVE FRASER RIVER CANYON

Within a half-hour drive of Hwy 1 in Fraser River Canyon, you'll find several campgrounds. Access them from the towns of Lytton and Boston Bar. The **Nahatlatch River Valley** holds a few cheaper Ministry of Tourism campgrounds, and many provincial-park campgrounds. You have a choice of camping beside whitewater, or in a shady lakeside forest.

The Nahatlatch River is 85 km (53 mi) long, and drains a mountainous, 130,000-hectare watershed. The river flows into the Fraser River and provides migration and spawning habitat for several species of salmon, as well as rainbow trout and bull trout. Farther up-valley is a string of lakes (bring your canoe) fed by streams tumbling down from the wild, remote Upper Stein Wilderness.

Native art, Fraser Canyon

The river's fury makes swimming unthinkable, but just sitting beside it has a cooling effect. Make reservations for REO whitewater-rafting on the Nahatlatch (www.reorafting.com). You'll pass their lodge en route to the campgrounds.

All four MOT river campgrounds are small. The road is passable in a 2WD car. Only Fir Flat, Log Creek, and the park's Squakum Creek campgrounds can accommodate motorhomes and trailers.

The Nahatlatch is a beautiful, mountain-bound valley. Competent kayakers and experienced hikers will enjoy staying here longer than just a weekend. The elevation is roughly 305 m (1000 ft), so the area is usually accessible in early spring.

Drive or bike a couple kilometers beyond Squakum Creek campground to High Bench Lookout. You'll attain grand vistas of the lakes in the upper valley, and the surrounding mountains. Proceed 13 km (8 mi) farther to short trails leading to waterfalls.

If you find the Nahatlatch campgrounds crowded, try **Scuzzy Creek.** Though nearby, it's less popular. Small motorhomes and trailers can get there if they have the power to surmount the steep road. Directions are on page 114.

Just above Lytton, the slopes of **Botanie Mountain** are a dazzling wild-flower garden in spring. Hiking to the lookout site on the minor summit is a rewarding challenge, but the steep trail ascends 1425 m (4674 ft) in 8.8 km (5.5 mi), and it's heat-stroke hot here in summer. East of the mountain is tiny Botanie Lake, on a Native reserve. The small campground near its shore is accessible by all vehicles. Directions are on page 115.

NAHATLATCH RIVER

From the Fraser River bridge in Hope, drive Trans-Canada Hwy 1 north about 65 km (40 mi). Or, from Lytton, drive Hwy 1 south 45 km (30 mi). From either approach, exit Hwy 1 by turning west at the village of **Boston Bar.** Set your trip odometer to 0 midway across the Fraser River bridge.

For NAHATLATCH RIVER, now follow the directions below

0 km (0 mi)
Midway across the Fraser River bridge. On the west bank, cross railroad tracks and follow the paved West Side Road north through the village of North Bend.

7.7 km (4.8 mi)
Pavement ends.

10.7 km (6.6 mi)
Bear left at the fork. Soon rejoin the main road after skirting a ranch.

13.7 km (8.5 mi)
Bear right on the main road for campgrounds on the north bank of Nahat-latch River. Fork left onto Powderpuff Main FS road for the south bank Nahatlatch River campground.

About 2.5 km (1.6 mi) up the Powderpuff Main, fork right. Proceed upstream, generally northwest, another 10 minutes to the campground at road's end, where a bridge used to span the river.

NAHATLATCH RIVER CAMPGROUND #36
Weekend / Moderate / $ / year-round
6 tables
Too small for motorhomes and trailers

Nahatlatch River

Bearing right on the main road at the 13.7-km (8.5-mi) fork, passing the turnoff to the south bank Nahatlatch River campground.

15.4 km (9.5 mi)
Cross a narrow bridge over Nahatlatch River, which roars through a chasm here.

16.6 km (10.2 mi)
After passing the left fork to REO's whitewater rafting base, pass a fork ascending right. Proceed northwest on the main road, following the Nahatlatch River upstream.

16.8 km (10.3 mi)
Proceed on the main road where Nahatlatch FS road ascends right—a worthwhile detour leading to **Fraser Canyon viewpoints** (see photo on page 114) and Nahatlatch Lookout. If wet, the soft, silty surface might require 4WD. When dry, low-clearance 2WD vehicles can go 16 km (10 mi) without difficulty, though the steep ascent at 8 km (5 mi) will strain a small motor.

18.4 km (11.4 mi)
Proceed west on the main road for Fir Flat and Log Creek campgrounds. Turn left to enter Apocynum campground on Nahatlatch River. The access road ends abruptly at the riverbank in 0.4 km (0.2 mi), so approach slowly.

APOCYNUM CAMPGROUND #23
Weekend / Moderate / $ / year-round
7 tables
Too small for motorhomes and trailers

Continuing west on the main road, passing the turnoff to Apocynum campground.

19.9 km (12.3 mi)
Proceed west on the main road for Log Creek campground. Left is Fir Flat campground on Nahatlatch River. There's just enough shade here to create a welcome refuge in this hot, dry valley.

FIR FLAT CAMPGROUND #22
Weekend / Moderate / $ / year-round
3 tables
Accessible by small motorhomes and trailers

Continuing west on the main road, passing Fir Flat campground.

25.3 km (15.7 mi)
Proceed west on the main road, passing a right fork near Log Creek.

25.4 km (15.8 mi)
Turn left to enter Log Creek campground on Nahatlatch River.

LOG CREEK CAMPGROUND #21
Weekend / Difficult / $ / year-round
4 tables
Accessible by small motorhomes and trailers

Continuing west on the main road, passing Log Creek campground.

26 km (16.1 mi)
Reach the junction with Kookpi Creek FS road, which leads left to a bridge over the Nahatlatch River. Stay straight, on the north side of the river, for pricey provincial-park lakeside campgrounds in the upper valley.

Upper Nahatlatch Valley

26.5 km (16.4 mi)
Arrive at Francis Lake campground. It's on a small lake, where the water flows into the river.

28.2 km (17.5 mi)
Arrive at Hannah Lake campground. There's only one table and no privacy from the road.

29 km (18 mi)
Arrive at Hannah Lake Ranger Station campsite. The cabin here is open to the public, first come, first served. Don't count on it being available.

31.9 km (19.8 mi)
Arrive at Nahatlatch Lake campground. All three campsites have tables and are on the lake, which is actually a broad river at this point. There's a view up the lake, toward the peaks.

33.3 km (20.6 mi)
Arrive at Salmon Beach campground. It offers plentiful shade, two tables beside the lake, and a view of snowy mountains.

Fraser Canyon, from Nahatlatch FS road

36 km (22.3 mi)
After passing a rough boat launch, arrive at Squakum Creek campground. Drive 0.5 km (0.3 mi) down a rough, rutty road. There are 11 shady campsites with fire rings. It's a good spot if you enjoy the stillness of a lake more than the energy of a river. The mountain view is excellent.

37.5 km (23.3 mi)
From **High Bench Lookout** you can see the upper reaches of Nahatlatch Valley.

SCUZZY CREEK

Drive Trans-Canada Hwy 1 north about 65 km (40 mi) from the Fraser River bridge in Hope, or south 45 km (30 mi) from Lytton. Turn west off Hwy 1 at the village of **Boston Bar** and set your trip odometer to 0 midway across the Fraser River bridge. It's about 13 km (8 mi) to Scuzzy Creek.

After crossing railroad tracks on the Fraser's west bank, turn left (south) where right (north) enters the village of North Bend. Proceed straight (south) on Scuzzy Creek FS road, following the Fraser River. The road soon veers northwest, away form the river. It climbs steeply, staying north of Scuzzy Creek. After the terrain levels, cross the bridge to the creek's south bank, then bear right (southwest). The campground is about eight minutes farther, on the right.

SCUZZY CREEK CAMPGROUND #24
Weekend / Moderate / Free
6 tables
Accessible by small motorhomes & trailers

BOTANIE LAKE

Drive to Lytton, where Hwys 1 and 12 intersect. Follow Hwy 12 across the Thompson River bridge just north of town. About 0.5 km (0.3 mi) north of the bridge, turn right (northeast) onto Botanie Valley Road.

0 km (0 mi)
Departing Hwy 12, starting northeast on Botanie Valley Road.

6.8 km (4.2 mi)
Proceed north on Botanie Valley Road for Botanie Lake campground. Fork left onto Botanie Mountain Lookout Road for the trailhead.

17 km (10.5 mi)
Arrive at Botanie Lake campground, 300 meters from the south shore.

BOTANIE LAKE CAMPGROUND #54
Weekend / Moderate (due only to distance) / Free
Elev: 1115 m (3657 ft) / Lake: 12.5 ha
3 tables / Accessible by motorhomes and 5th-wheels

Balsamroot flourish in June, on dry, sunny hillsides.

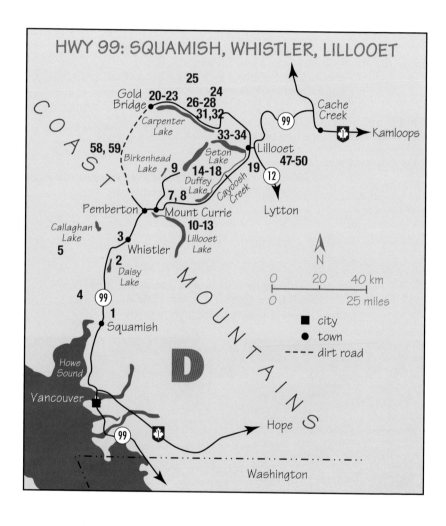

HWY 99: SQUAMISH, WHISTLER, LILLOOET

D: Hwy 99—Squamish, Whistler, Lillooet

At the fee campgrounds, charges apply May 1 to October 15.

1	Cat Lake	$	18	Cinnamon	FREE
2	Cal-Cheak	$	19	Seton Dam	FREE
3	Alexander Falls	FREE	20	Tyaughton Lake	FREE
4	Lower Squamish R	FREE	21	Gun Lake South	FREE
5	Upper Squamish R	FREE	22	Gun Creek	FREE
7	Owl Creek	$	23	Mowson Pond	FREE
8	Spetch Creek	FREE	24	Yalakom	FREE
9	Blackwater Lake	FREE	25	Beaverdam Creek	FREE
10	Strawberry Point	$	26	Carol Lake	FREE
11	Twin One Creek	$	27	Marshall Creek	FREE
12	Lizzie Bay	$	28	Marshall Lake N.	FREE
13	Driftwood Bay	$	32	Jones Creek	FREE
14	Cayoosh Creek	FREE	33	Mission Dam	FREE
15	Roger Creek	FREE	34	Carpenter Lake	FREE
16	Gott Creek	FREE	47-50	Kwotlenemo Lake	$
17	Cottonwood	FREE			

Bighorn sheep

Hwy 99–Squamish, Whistler, Lillooet

SQUAMISH TO WHISTLER

Looking for the nearest cheap or free campgrounds north of Vancouver? Exploring the massive mountains and fierce rivers of B.C.'s southern Coast Range? Want to enjoy Whistler on the cheap? The campgrounds described here will serve you well. They're listed from south to north, according to their turnoff points from Hwy 99.

On the **Squamish River** are a couple small, primitive campgrounds without tables. They're up the scenic Squamish Valley Road, north-northwest of Squamish. The first is only 1.3 km (0.8 mi) off pavement, about 25 minutes from Hwy 99. The second is 27 km (16.7 mi) beyond where pavement ends and takes about an hour to reach from Hwy 99.

If you don't mind walking the 1-km (0.6-mi) access trail, the tenters-only campground at tiny **Cat Lake** (page 121) is conveniently located for an easy, overnight stop. The turnoff, just north of Alice Lake Provincial Park, is a mere 15-minute drive north of Squamish. The parking area is only 3 km (1.9 mi) east of Hwy 99.

Callaghan Creek flows into Cheakamus River about 5.5 km (3.4 mi) southwest of Whistler. You'll find three Cal-Cheak Confluence campgrounds here (page 121). The first is just 200 meters east of Hwy 99. The others are only a few minutes farther. Lush forest, roaring water, and a hiking trail to Brandywine Falls are the attractions.

A tenters-only campground is perched above thundering Alexander Falls (page 124). It's west of Whistler but is reached by turning off Hwy 99 about

The Tantalus Range, en route to Squamish River campgrounds

5 km (3.1 mi) southwest of Whistler. The turnoff is nearly across the highway from the turnoff for Cal-Cheak Confluence. The road to Alexander Falls grants views of mountains that most people, speeding between Vancouver and Whistler, never see. Continue driving past the falls to reach photogenic **Callaghan Lake,** ringed by rugged peaks, a glacier, and a waterfall. There's a small, free, BC Parks camping area there. Bring your canoe, or scramble around the lakeshore. Driving back to the highway, you'll see the Black Tusk east across the valley.

SQUAMISH RIVER

If you're heading north on Hwy 99, from Vancouver

From the Horseshoe Bay exit just north of Vancouver, drive Hwy 99 north 54.4 km (33.7 mi), then turn left (west) onto Squamish Valley Road (across from the Alice Lake Provincial Park turnoff). Set your trip odometer to 0.

If you're heading south on Hwy 99, from Whistler

From Brandywine Falls Provincial Park, drive Hwy 99 south 31.6 km (19.6 mi), then turn right (west) onto Squamish Valley Road (across from the Alice Lake Provincial Park turnoff). Set your trip odometer to 0.

For either approach above, now follow the directions below

0 km (0 mi)
Starting west on Squamish Valley Road, departing Hwy 99.

2 km (1.3 mi)
Stay straight (north). Left leads back to Squamish.

3.7 km (2.3 mi)
Cross a bridge over Cheakamus River. At the junction 100 meters beyond, stay left (northwest) on Squamish Valley Road. Proceed through Native reserve.

23 km (14.3 mi)
Pavement ends.

24.2 km (15 mi)
Proceed straight (north) for upper Squamish River campground. Quickly reach the first Squamish River campground by turning left (west) here, crossing the Squamish River bridge, then immediately turning right. It's on the west bank.

SQUAMISH RIVER CAMPGROUND #17
Weekend / Easy / Free
3 campsites without tables, beneath cottonwoods
Accessible by small motorhomes and trailers

Continuing north on Squamish River Road, passing the turnoff to the first Squamish River campground.

26.5 km (16.4 mi)
Pass a powerhouse and cross a bridged creek.

27.3 km (16.9 mi)
Pass High Falls Creek trailhead on the right. It begins 100 meters past the creek and should be signed. The trail stays left / northwest of the creek and soon climbs a rocky bluff. For details about this premier hike, and others in the area, read *Where Locals Hike in Southwest B.C.* Visit www.hikingcamping.com to check availability.

31.5 km (19.5 mi)
Stay straight and cross a bridge.

43 km (26.7 mi)
Bear left on the main road.

50 km (31 mi)
Reach upper Squamish River campground on the left. It's on the east bank, near the confluence of the Squamish and Elaho rivers, just past a Mile 37 sign, about 0.4 km (0.25 mi) before Elaho River FS road forks left (west).

UPPER SQUAMISH RIVER CAMPGROUND #18
Weekend / Difficult (due only to distance) / Free
3 campsites without tables
Accessible by small motorhomes and trailers

CAT LAKE

If you're heading north on Hwy 99, from Vancouver

From the Horseshoe Bay exit just north of Vancouver, drive Hwy 99 north about 61 km (37.8 mi), then turn right (east) onto Brohm FS road (the first right after Alice Lake Provincial Park). Set your trip odometer to 0.

If you're heading south on Hwy 99, from Whistler

From Brandywine Falls Provincial Park, drive Hwy 99 south about 25 km (15.5 mi), then turn left (east) onto Brohm FS road. Set your trip odometer to 0.

For either approach above, now follow the directions below

Follow Brohm FS road. Stay right. Reach a gate at about 3 km (1.9 mi). Park there and walk about 1 km (0.6 mi) to the tenters-only campground on the shore of Cat Lake.

CAT LAKE CAMPGROUND #1
Weekend / Easy / $ / May 1 – Oct 15
Elev: 330 m (1082 ft) / Lake: 6 ha
10 walk-in tentsites with tables
Parking accessible by all vehicles

CAL-CHEAK CONFLUENCE

If you're heading north on Hwy 99, from Vancouver

From the Horseshoe Bay exit just north of Vancouver, drive Hwy 99 north about 90 km (55.8 mi), then turn right (southeast) onto Daisy Lake FS road (4 km / 2.5 mi past Brandywine Falls Provincial Park, and just past Callaghan Creek bridge). Set your trip odometer to 0.

If you're heading south on Hwy 99, from Whistler

From Whistler, at Village Gate Blvd. (where there's a traffic light and WEL-COME TO WHISTLER sign), drive Hwy 99 south 5.5 km (3.4 mi), then turn left (southeast) onto Daisy Lake FS road just before Callaghan Creek bridge. Set your trip odometer to 0.

For either approach above, now follow the directions below

0 km (0 mi)
Starting southeast on Daisy Lake FS road, departing Hwy 99.

200 meters
Turn right for the first Cal-Cheak camping area. The campsites ring a cleared cul de sac near the highway.

CAL-CHEAK CONFLUENCE CAMPGROUND #3a
Overnight / Easy / $ / May 1 – Oct 15
5 tables near Callaghan Creek
Accessible by motorhomes and 5th-wheels

Continuing southeast on Daisy Lake FS road, passing the first Cal-Cheak camping area.

0.5 km (0.3 mi)
Proceed right (south) for the third Cal-Cheak camping area and the day-use site. Turn left to reach the second Cal-Cheak camping area in 0.3 km (0.2 mi).

CAL-CHEAK CONFLUENCE CAMPGROUND #3b
Weekend / Easy / $ / May 1 – Oct 15
9 tables near Cheakamus River
Accessible by small motorhomes and trailers

Continuing south on Daisy Lake FS road, passing the turnoff to the second Cal-Cheak camping area.

0.8 km (0.5 mi)
Proceed straight (south) for the Cal-Cheak day-use site. Turn right for the third Cal-Cheak camping area.

CAL-CHEAK CONFLUENCE CAMPGROUND #3c
Weekend / Easy / $ / May 1 – Oct 15
8 tables near Callaghan Creek
Accessible by small motorhomes and trailers

Settled in at Cal-Cheak Confluence campground

Continuing south on Daisy Lake FS road, passing the third Cal-Cheak camping area.

0.9 km (0.6 mi)
Reach the Cal-Cheak day-use site, near the powerline structure and the confluence of Callaghan Creek and Cheakamus River. Walk across the suspension bridge to begin the 4-km (2.5-mi) hike to Brandywine Falls.

ALEXANDER FALLS

If you're heading north on Hwy 99, from Vancouver

From the Horseshoe Bay exit just north of Vancouver, drive Hwy 99 north about 90.5 km (56 mi), then turn left (northwest) onto Callaghan Lake FS road (300 meters past Callaghan Creek bridge). Set your trip odometer to 0.

If you're heading south on Hwy 99, from Whistler

From Whistler, at Village Gate Blvd. (where there's a traffic light and WELCOME TO WHISTLER sign), drive Hwy 99 south 5 km (3 mi), then turn right (northwest) onto Callaghan Lake FS road (300 meters before Callaghan Creek bridge). Set your trip odometer to 0.

For either approach above, now follow the directions below

0 km (0 mi)
Starting northwest on Callaghan Lake FS road, departing Hwy 99. The road is stony and rough. Drive through a recovery area and see a clearcut hillside to the west.

9 km (5.5 mi)
Reach a junction. Less than 200 meters beyond, on the left, is Alexander Falls campground. It's for tenters only.

ALEXANDER FALLS CAMPGROUND #4
Overnight / Moderate / Free
5 tentsites with tables
Parking accessible by all vehicles.

Continuing north on Callaghan Lake FS road, passing Alexander Falls campground, heading for Callaghan Lake.

9.2 km (5.7 mi)
Cross a bridged creek, pass a huge pullout / viewpoint, and ascend.

9.5 km (5.9 mi)
Proceed northwest on Callaghan Lake FS road for Callaghan Lake. The right fork leads to Madely Lake.

17.7 km (11 mi)
Reach Callaghan Lake campground at 1204 m (3950 ft). Though administered by BC Parks, the camping area is unimproved and remains free-of-charge. Close to the lake, it accommodates several vehicles and perhaps five tents.

NORTHEAST OF PEMBERTON

The crowd stops at Whistler. But the B.C. Coast Mountains keep marching north. So do the campgrounds. Turn off Hwy 99 at the town of Mount Currie. The road is paved nearly to its end at **Birkenhead Lake Provincial Park.** The lake is a beauty: 6 km (3.7 mi) long, boldly guarded by Birkenhead Peak and its sentinel siblings along the ridge. A short trail allows you to appreciate the ancient forest gracing the lake's north shore.

En route to Birkenhead Lake are three campgrounds. The first is on Owl Creek, where it flows into Birkenhead River, not far from Hwy 99 and Mount Currie. A choice of campsites (creekside, riverside, clearing, forest) and a variety of hiking trails nearby (read *Done in a Day: Whistler*, described on page 537) earn Owl a *Destination* rating. It has room for all but behemoth RVs.

Owl Creek campground

The second campground is just up the road, at Spetch Creek. Rated *Weekend*, Spetch is smaller and less scenic than Owl, but it feels more secluded, which some people prefer. The entry road and campsites accommodate nothing larger than trucks with campers.

Just outside Birkenhead Park is an *Overnight* campground on tiny, lackluster Blackwater Lake. It's next to the road, so small motorhomes and trailers can squeeze in, but the only attraction here is avoiding the cost of provincial-park camping.

If you're heading east on Hwy 99, from Pemberton

From the edge of Pemberton (at the junction by the Petro Canada gas station) drive Hwy 99 east 7.1 km (4.4 mi) to Mount Currie, then reset your trip odometer to 0.

If you're heading southwest on Hwy 99, from Lillooet

From Joffre Lakes Recreation Area parking lot, drive Hwy 99 southwest 23.5 km (14.6 mi) to Mount Currie, then reset your trip odometer to 0.

For either approach above, now follow the directions below

0 km (0 mi)
Starting north, from the 3-way intersection in Mount Currie, heading toward D'Arcy and Birkenhead Lake Provincial Park.

4.6 km (2.8 mi)
Cross a bridge over Owl Creek. Proceed straight (north) for campgrounds at Spetch Creek and Blackwater Lake. Turn right (under the lines from a small power station) for Owl Creek campground.

> In 0.3 km (0.2 mi) cross railroad tracks. Fork right for campsites on Owl Creek, left for camping areas near Birkenhead River. Big RVs should go left, where there's room to turn around. The mixed forest provides plentiful shade. The Cayoosh Range rises abruptly to the east. The confluence of two romping streams keeps campers entertained.

OWL CREEK CAMPGROUND #7
Destination / Easy / $ / May 1 – Oct 15
13 tables
Accessible by motorhomes and trailers

Continuing north, passing the turnoff to Owl Creek campground.

6.6 km (4.1 mi)
Look for possible **overnight pullouts** after crossing the bridge over Birkenhead River.

12.2 km (7.6 mi)
Turn right to arrive at Spetch Creek campground in 0.3 km (0.2 mi). It's not as open or spacious as Owl Creek campground.

SPETCH CREEK CAMPGROUND #8
Weekend / Easy / Free
6 secluded campsites with tables, near the creek
Inaccessible by motorhomes and trailers

Continuing north, passing the turnoff to Spetch Creek campground.

34.6 km (21.5 mi)
Reach a junction. Turn left (northwest) for Blackwater campground and Birkenhead Lake Provincial Park. Straight (northeast) soon reaches D'Arcy, at the southwest end of Anderson Lake.

36 km (22.3 mi)
Pavement ends. Cross a bridge over Blackwater Creek.

43 km (26.7 mi)
Proceed straight (west) for Birkenhead Lake Provincial Park. Turn left to enter Blackwater Lake campground.

NORTHEAST OF PEMBERTON **127**

Because this campground lacks charm, few campers stop here and none stay long, so it's usually quiet. The lake is tiny. The campsites are private, huddled in a horseshoe of brush and trees. The convenient location allows you to enjoy the grandeur of Birkenhead Lake without paying to stay at the huge provincial park campground.

BLACKWATER LAKE CAMPGROUND #9
Overnight / Easy / Free
Elev: 770 m (2525 ft) / Lake: 15 ha
3 tables, 6 campsites
Accessible by small motorhomes and trailers

Continuing west, passing Blackwater Lake campground.

50.2 km (31.1 mi)
Arrive at Birkenhead Lake Provincial Park. In addition to a sprawling campground, it has a day-use area, sandy beach, large expanse of grass, and lakeshore hiking trail among ancient trees.

LILLOOET LAKE

Hikers bound for the Upper Stein Wilderness, or a dayhike to Joffre Lakes, have the convenient option of a pre- or post-trip refuge at any of four campgrounds on Lillooet Lake. But you don't have to go beyond Lillooet Lake to find enjoyment. The campgrounds on its east shore, south of Hwy 99, are themselves worthy goals. Two are rated *Destination*: Strawberry Point (walk-in tentsites only) and Lizzie Bay. At 195 m (640 ft) elevation, Lillooet Lake is 24 km (15 mi) long and covers 3220 hectares.

If you're heading east on Hwy 99, from Pemberton

From the 3-way junction in Mount Currie, drive Hwy 99 east 10.3 km (6.4 mi), then turn right (southeast) onto In-SHUCK-ch FS road (where the highway begins climbing, before the winter closure gate and sign for Lillooet). Reset your trip odometer to 0.

If you're heading southwest on Hwy 99, from Lillooet

From Joffre Lakes Recreation Area parking lot, drive Hwy 99 southwest 13.2 km (8.2 mi), then turn left (southeast) onto In-SHUCK-ch FS road (just after the winter closure gate, at the bottom of the steep hill). Reset your trip odometer to 0.

Lillooet Lake, from Driftwood Bay campground

For either approach above, now follow the directions below

0 km (0 mi)
Starting southeast on In-SHUCK-ch FS road, following the northeast shore of Lillooet Lake.

6.8 km (4.2 mi)
Reach the parking area for Strawberry Point tenters-only campground, on the right.

It's a five-minute walk down to this peaceful little campground on Lillooet Lake. The scenery across the lake includes a glacier. An abundance of driftwood encourages playful creativity. If you have a campfire, use an existing fire ring; don't further mar the beach.

STRAWBERRY POINT CAMPGROUND #10
Destination / Easy / $ / May 1 – Oct 15
2 walk-in tentsites with tables, gravel beach
Parking accessible by all vehicles

Continuing southeast on the main road, passing Strawberry Point campground.

9.4 km (5.8 mi)
Proceed straight (southeast) on the main road for more campgrounds on Lillooet Lake. Twin One Creek Haul Road forks left and ascends.

10 km (6.2 mi)
Proceed straight (southeast) on the main road for more campgrounds on Lillooet Lake. Turn right to descend to Twin One Creek campground on Lillooet Lake. A couple campsites are in the open, beside the lake. Others are in trees.

TWIN ONE CREEK CAMPGROUND #11
Overnight / Moderate / $ / May 1 – Oct 15
5 tables, boat launch
Accessible by small motorhomes and trailers

Continuing southeast on the main road, passing the turnoff to Twin One Creek campground.

11.6 km (7.2 mi)
Pass a lodge and commercial campground.

15.8 km (9.8 mi)
Pass a KM 16 sign. Look for a campsite on the right, in trees, at the end of Lizzie Bay. It has one table, a beach and a boat launch.

16 km (9.9 mi)
Proceed straight (south) on the main road for Driftwood Bay campground. Turn right and descend to reach Lizzie Bay campground in 300 meters.

This is Lillooet Lake's best campground. The campsites are well spaced, surrounded by trees, on the waterfront, with views north up the lake. Only one campsite has a sandy beach on this rocky shore.

LIZZIE BAY CAMPGROUND #12
Destination / Moderate / $ / May 1 – Oct 15
9 tables, level tentsites
Accessible by small motorhomes and trailers

Continuing south on the main road, passing the turnoff to Lizzie Bay campground.

16.6 km (10.3 mi)
Proceed straight (south) on the main road for Driftwood Bay campground. Left (southeast) on Douglas-Lizzie Cr Branch FS road leads to the **Stein Divide trailhead** in 11 km (6.8 mi). Hikers must now park at the beginning of the Lizzie road and walk the entire distance to Lizzie Lake. The road was washed out in several places and will not be repaired. At periods of high runoff, it's dangerous to attempt one of the unbridged crossings.

17.7 km (11 mi)
Turn right and descend to reach Driftwood Bay campground in 200 meters.

DRIFTWOOD BAY CAMPGROUND #13
Weekend / Moderate / $ / May 1 – Oct 15
3 tables
Accessible by small motorhomes and trailers

~

LILLOOET LAKE TO LILLOOET

Between Lillooet Lake and the town of Lillooet, Hwy 99 plies the valley that cradles Duffey Lake. Most people blast through here. There are two good reasons not to: (1) a surprising number of free campgrounds, all just off the pavement; and (2) engaging scenery.

At the valley's southwest end are glacier-capped peaks. After passing Duffey Lake, the highway meanders along delightful Cayoosh Creek and crosses several one-lane wooden bridges built when a slower pace of travel allowed greater appreciation of the land. Farther northeast, the highway works through a deep, rugged canyon, hugging the cliffsides then careening into the town of Lillooet, on the Fraser River.

Beautiful year-round, this stretch of Hwy 99 is especially pleasing in October, when fall colours are intense. But it can be chilly here then, even when sunny.

If you're heading east on Hwy 99, from Pemberton

From the edge of Pemberton (at the junction by the Petro Canada gas station) drive Hwy 99 east 17.3 km (10.7 mi). You'll pass through Mount Currie, then cross the narrow, north arm of Lillooet Lake. Just before the winter closure gate and sign for Lillooet (where In-SHUCK-ch FS road forks right / southeast along Lillooet Lake, and the highway begins climbing) reset your trip odometer to 0.

0 km (0 mi)
Proceeding northeast on Hwy 99, from the north end of Lillooet Lake.

13.2 km (8.2 mi)
Pass Joffre Lakes Recreation Area on the right. The two-hour hike to Upper Joffre Lake, beneath Matier Glacier and Joffre Peak, is spectacular. For details, read *Done in a Day: Whistler*, described on page 537.

32.8 km (20.4 mi)
At the northeast end of **Duffey Lake** is a stupendous view. There's no vehicle camping at this provincial park.

Campsite view of Cayoosh Creek

45.2 km (28.1 mi)
Turn left, just before the bridge, to enter Cayoosh Creek campground. Treed campsites line the creek. In the late 1800s, eager prospectors churned Cayoosh Creek seeking their fortunes in gold.

CAYOOSH CREEK CAMPGROUND #3
Weekend / Easy / Free
6 tables
Accessible by small motorhomes and trailers

49.4 km (30.7 mi)
Turn right to enter Roger Creek campground. Roger Creek campground is
on Cayoosh Creek. The namesake creek flows into Cayoosh farther northeast. This is the first of two Roger Creek camping areas. The sites here face
dense forest and feel private, but by October they're shaded until 11:30 a.m.

ROGER CREEK CAMPGROUND #4a
Weekend / Easy / Free
4 tables
Accessible by small motorhomes and trailers

49.9 km (30.9 mi)
Turn right to enter the second Roger Creek camping area. It's more open, so
it's sunnier and easier for big rigs to enter and turn around in.

ROGER CREEK CAMPGROUND #4b
Weekend / Easy / Free
4 tables, 5 campsites
Accessible by motorhomes and 5th-wheels

51.5 km (32 mi)
Turn left to enter Gott Creek campground, at the confluence of Cayoosh
and Gott Creeks.

GOTT CREEK CAMPGROUND #5
Overnight / Easy / Free
2 tables
Too small for motorhomes and trailers

58.9 km (36.6 mi)
Turn left to enter Cottonwood campground, just before Downton Creek FS
road forks left.

The campsites are well spaced, beneath thin pines and tall cottonwoods, near the creek but not on it. Big RVs should camp only in the
first clearing, where there are no tables.

COTTONWOOD CAMPGROUND #6
Weekend / Easy / Free
7 tables
Accessible by motorhomes and 5th-wheels

Cayoosh Creek, from near Cottonwood campground

62.5 km (38.8 mi)
Turn left to enter Cinnamon campground.

This is the most developed of the Cayoosh Creek campgrounds. It's a pretty spot, with a view of a dry, rugged mountainside. A couple campsites are on the creek.

CINNAMON CAMPGROUND #7
Weekend / Easy / Free
12 tables
Accessible by motorhomes and 5th-wheels

77.8 km (48.3 mi)
Turn right to enter Seton Dam campground, near Lillooet.

This huge, well-maintained campground is provided by BC Hydro. Across the highway is Seton Reservoir (22 km / 13.6 mi long, covering 2475 hectares) where you'll find a beach, boat launch, and day-use area. Compared to Cayoosh Creek valley, it's much warmer here due to lower elevation (236 m / 774 ft) and greater sun exposure. Watch for mountain goats performing anti-gravity stunts on the sheer cliffs across the valley.

SETON DAM CAMPGROUND #57
Weekend / Easy / Free
45 campsites, 32 tables, garbage cans, free firewood
Accessible by motorhomes and 5th-wheels

82.1 km (51 mi)
Arrive at the junction of Hwys 99 and 12 in Lillooet, on the Fraser River's west bank.

If you're heading southwest on Hwy 99, from Lillooet

0 km (0 mi)
Starting southwest on Hwy 99 from the junction of Hwys 99 and 12 in Lillooet, on the Fraser River's west bank.

4.3 km (2.7 mi)
Turn left to enter Seton Dam campground. The highway begins ascending steeply through the canyon, toward Duffey Lake.

19.6 km (12.2 mi)
Turn right to enter Cinnamon campground, described on page 133.

23.2 km (14.4 mi)
Turn right to enter Cottonwood campground, described on page 133.

30.6 km (19 mi)
Turn right to enter Gott Creek campground, described on page 132.

32.7 km (20.3 mi)
Turn left to enter Roger Creek campground, described on page 132.

37 km (22.9 mi)
Turn right, just after the bridge, to enter Cayoosh Creek campground, described on page 131.

68.9 km (42.7 mi)
Pass Joffre Lakes Recreation Area on the left.

82.1 km (51 mi)
Proceed straight (west) on Hwy 99 for Mount Currie, Pemberton, Whistler, Squamish and Vancouver. Turn left (southeast) onto In-SHUCK-ch FS road for campgrounds on Lillooet Lake. Directions continue on page 127.

Seton Dam campground, outside Lillooet

EAST OF LILLOOET

Fountain Ridge forms the east wall of Fraser River canyon near Lillooet. Just over the ridge is **Kwotlenemo Lake** (also called Fountain Lake) in Fountain Valley. Clustered around the lake are a couple campgrounds set in large pines and Douglas fir. Forested mountains rise 245 m (800 ft) to 305 m (1000 ft) above the valley floor. You can launch a small boat on the lake, but only electric motors are allowed.

Blue skies prevail here, so Fountain Valley is a good spring camping destination for Lower Mainlanders seeking to escape West Coast drizzle. If you're travelling through Fraser River canyon in summer, where soaring temperatures can be oppressive, you'll find Fountain Valley slightly cooler because it's 500 m (1640 ft) higher.

Though it's possible to drive Hwy 12 north 39.5 km (24.5 mi) to the southern end of the Fountain Valley road, that end is very narrow and rough. So instead, continue to the Fraser River bridge, east of Lillooet. Drive Hwy 99 northeast 14 km (8.7 mi) to the signed turnoff. Then follow directions on page 136 from the second 0-km point under "The northern approach, from Hwy 99."

Kwotlenemo Lake South campground is large and very open. It has 20 tables and accommodates motorhomes and 5th-wheels.

Kwotlenemo Lake West campground is small and quiet. It has only 2 tables and is accessible by nothing bigger than trucks with campers.

Kwotlenemo Lake East campground is small (just 2 tables) but not quiet. It's on the main road, near private cabins. It's also on a hillside, so access is limited to vehicles no larger than trucks with campers.

Kwotlenemo Lake North campground has 10 tables, is very open and therefore accessible by all vehicles. Camping is allowed, but this is primarily a day-use area.

The northern approach, from Hwy 99

0 km (0 mi)
Driving west on Hwy 99, from the junction of Hwys 97 and 99 (11 km / 6.8 mi northwest of Cache Creek).

27 km (16.7 mi)
Pass through Marble Canyon Provincial Park, and the hamlet of Pavilion soon after.

60 km (37.2 mi)
After many tight curves in Fraser Canyon, the highway passes under a railroad overpass, and makes a tight curve right.

60.8 km (37.7 mi)
The road flattens out. A sign warns of the Fountain Valley turn. At 61.3 km (38 mi) turn left onto paved Fountain Valley Road. Set your odometer to 0.

0 km (0 mi) Turning onto Fountain Valley Road. After passing the village, the road ascends through pines.

10 km (6.2 mi) Pass a house.

10.7 km (6.6 mi), go right 100 m / 110 yd to enter Kwotlenomo Lake North campground. This end of the lake has many huge cottonwood trees. There's a fence along the side. The first two campsites are in view of a house, but you can find a private spot tucked in the bushes and trees farther along the lakeshore. This site might become only a day-use area.

KWOTLENEMO LAKE NORTH CAMPGROUND #47
Weekend / Easy / $ / May 17 to Oct 31
7 campsites, several with tables
Accessible by motorhomes and 5th-wheels

Firewood artist creates masterpiece at Seton Dam campground.

11.1 km (68.8 mi)
Kwotlenomo Lake East campground with three campsites is on the right, immediately below the road, in trees, and just before homes.

11.6 km (7.2 mi)
The largest campground is on the right at the south end of the lake. It has a large grassy area and beautiful, large pines and Douglas fir. You can choose campsites in the open with a lake view or tucked away in forest. As the spur road loops back into the woods, the forest is scruffier and less attractive. 300 meters back, a narrow road ascends the hillside to more campsites.

KWOTLENEMO LAKE SOUTH CAMPGROUND #49
Weekend / Easy / $ / May 17 to Oct 31
20 campsites
Elev: 910 m (2985 ft) / Lake: 35 ha
Accessible by motorhomes and 5th-wheels

Continuing south from this last campground, the main road soon starts a descent out of the valley, paralleling Cinquefoil Creek. At 25 km (15.5 mi) the road is only one-lane on a steep slope, with a dropoff on the outside. At

25.6 km (16 mi) there's a layby for passing and a few more passing spots in the next 0.5 km (0.3 mi). At 27.6 km (17 mi) reach Hwy 12 above the deep Fraser River Canyon. Go right for Lillooet in 23 km (14.3 mi). Be careful in 5 km (3 mi). The highway might still be one-lane where a rockslide damaged it.

CARPENTER LAKE

Carpenter Lake is a sinuous blue swath about a 45-minute drive west-northwest of Lillooet. You can choose from more than a dozen free campgrounds here. One is a big, well-maintained, BC Hydro campground, on the lake's north shore. The rest are smaller, primitive campgrounds, mostly on tiny satellite lakes just north of Carpenter.

At 654 m (2145 ft) elevation, Carpenter Lake is 57 km (35 mi) long and covers 4625 hectares. The surrounding mountains are dry, scattered with pines and firs. The sun seems to be a constant fixture in the perpetually blue sky. In summer, prepare to broil. But Carpenter Lake is a springtime haven for anyone seeking to escape the gray and damp that clings to areas farther west.

Northwest of Carpenter Lake is the Southern Chilcotin—premier backpacking country distinguished by wondrous red-and-mauve soil and vast meadowed slopes. (See photo on page 139.) For details about an exquisite alpine circuit, read *Where Locals Hike in Southwest B.C.* Visit www.hikingcamping.com to check availability.

0 km (0 mi)
From the middle of the Fraser River bridge, just west of the junction of Hwys 99 and 12, continue to the river's west bank. Left is Hwy 99 to Whistler. Turn right and ascend into Lillooet, following signs for Gold Bridge. Cross railroad tracks and turn right (north) onto Main Street. Fill up with gas before leaving town.

2.9 km (1.8 mi)
Turn left, following the green highway sign SHALATH 69 KM, GOLD BRIDGE 101 KM.

9 km (5.6 mi)
Cross a bridge over the narrow Bridge River chasm, just up from Fraser Canyon.

9.3 km (5.8 mi)
Stay straight on the main, paved road, passing Pavillion Road that cuts sharply back right. Also soon pass Slok FS road on the right.

18 km (11.2 mi)
Pavement ends, but the road is well-graded gravel. Later it alternates with sections of pavement.

Overlooking Cinnabar Basin, in the Southern Chilcotin mountains

33.8 km (21 mi)
Reach a signed junction. For Carpenter Lake and Gold Bridge, bear left and descend a spectacular canyon to the Yalakom River bridge. For Yalakom and Beaverdam campgrounds, bear right, reset your trip odometer to 0, and proceed northwest on Yalakom FS road.

0 km (0 mi)
Proceeding northwest on Yalakom FS road, from the 33.8-km (21-mi) junction.

8.5 km (5.3 mi)
Reach Yalakom campground, on Yalakom River's east bank, just before the next bridge over the river. The tight valley limits sun exposure.

YALAKOM CAMPGROUND #8
Weekend / Moderate / Free
3 tables
Accessible by motorhomes and 5th-wheels

Continuing northwest on Yalakom FS road, passing Yalakom campground.

22.5 km (14 mi)

Reach Beaverdam campground, on the left. It's just before the bridge over Beaverdam Creek, near its confluence with Yalakom River. There's another camping area across the bridge. The valley is broader and sunnier here than at Yalakom campground.

BEAVERDAM CREEK CAMPGROUND #9
Weekend / Difficult (due only to distance) / Free
6 tables
Accessible by motorhomes and 5th-wheels

Continuing left at the 33.8-km (21-mi) junction, heading for Carpenter Lake and Gold Bridge.

35.4 km (22 mi)

Cross the Yalakom River bridge. You're now in a deep, narrow canyon. Pavement ends in 10 km (6 mi).

50 km (31 mi)

Proceed straight (west) for Carpenter Lake. Turn left and descend to reach Mission Dam campground in 0.4 km (0.25 mi).

Though it's beneath the dam, where scenery is nil, this campground is big and open, ideal for large groups.

MISSION DAM CAMPGROUND #33
Overnight / Difficult (due only to distance) / Free
3 tables
Accessible by motorhomes and 5th-wheels

Continuing west on the main road, passing the turnoff to Mission Dam campground.

50.9 km (31.6 mi)

Reach a junction at the dam. Proceed right (west) for most Carpenter Lake area campgrounds. Turn left onto Mission Mtn. road, cross the dam and go through the tunnel to reach Carpenter Lake campground #34 in 1.6 km (1 mi). It's tiny (2 tables), across the road from the lake, not recommended.

72 km (44.6 mi)

Turn left (just after crossing the bridge) for Jones Creek campground. Bear right and descend parallel to the highway, ignoring the left forks. After 0.4 km (0.25 mi), a former gravel pit near the lake affords room for several vehicles.

Beyond the narrow access road is overgrown with bushes and trees. Because it's well off the main road, this is a special campground on Carpenter Lake. The forest is pretty, with lots of aspen. A couple more campsites, including one on the creek, are beyond those with tables.

JONES CREEK CAMPGROUND #32
Destination / Difficult (due only to distance) / Free
3 tables, more campsites
Accessible by small motorhomes and trailers

Continuing west on the main road, passing the turnoff to Jones Creek campground.

72.2 km (44.8 mi)
Reach a junction. For more Carpenter Lake area campgrounds and Gold Bridge, bear left (west) on the main road. For campgrounds on Carol Lake, Marshall Creek and Marshall Lake, turn right, reset your trip odometer to 0, and ascend northwest.

0 km (0 mi)
Starting northwest from the 72.2-km (44.8-mi) junction.

3 km (1.9 mi)
Proceed straight (northwest) for campgrounds on Marshall Creek and Lake. Turn right (northeast) to reach the campground on tiny Carol Lake in 0.7 km (0.4 mi).

CAROL LAKE CAMPGROUND #10
Weekend / Difficult (due only to distance) / Free
8 tables
Accessible by motorhomes and 5th-wheels

Continuing straight (northwest) passing the turnoff to Carol Lake campground.

11.7 km (7.3 mi)
Proceed straight (northwest) for Marshall Lake North campground. Turn left to enter Marshall Creek campground, near the lake outlet.

MARSHALL CREEK CAMPGROUND #11
Weekend / Difficult (due only to distance) / Free
3 tables
Inaccessible by motorhomes and trailers

Continuing straight (northwest), passing the turnoff to Marshall Creek campground.

12 km (7.4 mi)
Reach a fork. Turn left onto rougher Marshall Lake Road. The main road continues right.

16.5 km (10.2 mi)
Arrive at Marshall Lake North campground on the west side of the lake's north end, near private cabins. It's larger and more open than Marshall Creek campground.

MARSHALL LAKE NORTH CAMPGROUND #12
Weekend / Difficult (due only to distance) / Free
Lake: 65 ha
7 tables, beach, cartop boat launch
Accessible by small motorhomes and trailers

Continuing west on the main road along Carpenter Lake, from the 72.2-km (44.8-mi) junction.

95.8 km (59.4 mi)
Reach Tyax Junction. For Gun Creek campground on Carpenter Lake, Gold Bridge, and Gun Lake South campground, bear left and follow the main road southwest along Carpenter Lake. For campgrounds on Mowson Pond and Tyaughton Lake, turn right, reset your trip odometer to 0, and ascend steeply northwest.

0 km (0 mi)
Starting northwest from the 95.8-km (59.4-mi) junction.

2 km (1.2 mi)
Reach Mowson Pond campground, at the top of the rise, on the left. The surrounding mountains are visible.

MOWSON POND CAMPGROUND #19
Weekend / Difficult (due only to distance) / Free
Elev: 796 m (2611 ft) / Lake: 23 ha
8 well-spaced campsites with tables
Accessible by small motorhomes and trailers

Tyaughton Lake

Continuing northwest, passing Mowson Pond campground.

3.5 km (2.2 mi)
Reach a junction. For Friburg campground on Tyaughton Lake, proceed northwest, following signs for Tyax Lodge.

6 km (3.6 mi)
Pass a road veering left, then reach a fork. Curve left and descend on the main road, passing Hornal Road on the right.

8.2 km (5.1 mi)
Turn right to enter Friburg campground on beautiful Tyaughton Lake. Tyax Lodge is just beyond. If you get tired of primitive camping, the lodge's camping fee includes use of their recreation room, sauna, showers, and lounge.

FRIBURG CAMPGROUND #20
Destination / Difficult (due only to distance) / Free
Elev: 1036 m (3400 ft) / Lake: 90 ha
4 tables, boat launch
Accessible by small motorhomes and trailers

Continuing southwest on the main road along Carpenter Lake, from Tyax Junction at 95.8 km (59.4 mi).

99.5 km (61.8 mi)
Proceed straight (southwest) on the main road for Gold Bridge and Gun Lake South campground. Turn left to enter BC Hydro's Gun Creek campground on Carpenter Lake.

GUN CREEK CAMPGROUND #18
Weekend / Difficult (due only to distance) / Free
13 tables, garbage cans, maintained mid-May to Oct
Accessible by motorhomes and 5th-wheels

Continuing southwest on the main road along Carpenter Lake, passing the turnoff to Gun Creek campground.

107.5 km (66.7 mi)
Reach a junction near the southwest end of Carpenter Lake. Left, across Bridge River, is the community of Gold Bridge. Straight (toward Gun Lake), then left in 250 meters onto Gwyneth Lake Road (signed for Pemberton) leads southwest onto Hurley River FS road. Rough but passable in a 2WD car, it connects the Bridge River Road from Lillooet to Pemberton Valley. Set your trip odometer to 0 and follow the directions below to quickly reach the free campground on cottage-crowded Gun Lake.

0 km (0 mi)
Proceeding straight at the 107.5-km (66.7-mi) junction (near the southwest end of Carpenter Lake), heading for Gun Lake. In 250 meters stay straight on pavement.

1.3 km (0.8 mi)
Go left on Gun Lake Road West.

2 km (1.2 mi)
Pass Downton Lake. Mt. Sloan is visible southwest.

Carpenter Lake, from Gun Creek campground

5.7 km (3.5 mi) and 6.8 km (4.2 mi)
Bear left.

10.2 km (6.3 mi)
Reach Gun Lake South campground, in trees on a bench above the lake. About 200 cottages ring the shore, so don't expect a wilderness experience. There's a cement boat launch at the lake's south end.

GUN LAKE SOUTH CAMPGROUND #17
Weekend / Difficult (due only to distance) / Free
Elev: 888 m (2913 ft) / Lake: 572 ha
6 tables
Accessible by small motorhomes and trailers

CARPENTER LAKE TO PEMBERTON

Hurley River FS road offers a 60-km (37.2-mi) shortcut between Carpenter Lake and the paved Pemberton Valley Road. Though rough, 2WD cars can handle it. Just go slowly—which you'll want to do anyway, especially at the south end, where the road is worst and the scenery best.

On both sides of **Pemberton Valley**, peaks rise 2010 m (6600 ft). While coaxing your vehicle up the switchbacks, you can stare at the Pemberton Icefield and the peaks marching northwest along the Upper Lillooet River toward Meager Mountain.

If you're heading south, from Carpenter Lake

From the junction at the southwest end of Carpenter Lake (where the community of Gold Bridge is left across Bridge River), go straight toward Gun Lake. In 250 meters, turn left (south) onto Gwyneth Lake Road (signed for Pemberton) and set your trip odometer to 0. It leads southwest onto Hurley River FS road (rough but passable in a 2WD car).

After 60 km (37.2 mi), intersect Pemberton Valley Road after crossing the bridge over Lillooet River. Turn left (southeast) to reach Hwy 99 at Pemberton in about 25 km (15.5 mi).

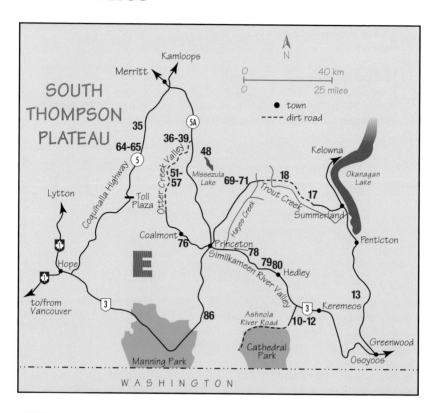

Hedley, Similkameen River Valley

E: South Thompson Plateau

At the fee campgrounds, charges apply mid-May through September 30 or mid-October. In the Princeton to Summerland area (69-71), charges apply May 1 through October 15. Along the Old Hedley Road, charges apply April 1 through October 31.

10	Red Bridge	$
11	Tunnel Mtn	$
12	Horseshoe Canyon	$
13	Burnell Lake	FREE
17	Trout Creek Crossing	FREE
18	Thirsk Lake	FREE
35	Gillis Lake	FREE
36	Shea Lake	$
37	Tahla Lake	$
38	Boss Lake	$
39	Davis Lake	$
48	Missezula Lake	FREE
51-57	Plateau Lakes	FREE to $
64	Murray Lake North	FREE
65	Murray Lake South	FREE
69	Chain Lake West	$
70	Link Lake	$
71	Osprey Lake	$
76	Granite Creek	$
78	Dewdney	FREE
79	Old Hedley Road West	$
80	Old Hedley Road East	$
86	Copper Creek	$

South Thompson Plateau

Most people living elsewhere in the province have just three vague images of the South Thompson Plateau. Cement. Fruit. Forest. The cement is in the form of the monster highways: the Coquihalla and the Okanagan Connector. The fruit comes from orchards around Keremeos. The forest would be Manning Provincial Park. What else is here? Much more. You'll find it's best appreciated not by aiming for a particular destination, but by roaming with a broad goal in mind: to sample B.C.'s marvelous multiplicity.

Work-stressed, caffeine-buzzed Vancouverites needing a couple day's decompression usually look no farther than the nearby and obvious. That includes Manning Park, which is why it gets frenetic there on summer weekends and offers little respite unless you hike one of the more challenging trails. So drive another hour east, into the **Tulameen River valley**, northwest of Princeton. Pitch your tent at spacious Granite Creek campground (page 150), far from the annoying whine of highway traffic, yet just off pavement.

Up for more adventure? Explore the **Plateau Lakes** (page 154). About mid-way between Princeton and Merritt, the plateau is splattered with lakes and campgrounds. Bring your mountain bike and cruise the spiderweb of roads. Or come simply for tranquility. Listen to loons calling and aspen leaves fluttering, instead of boom boxes shattering the peace as often happens at highway-side campgrounds.

Or, if quiet doesn't relax you, head to Keremeos, drive south toward Cathedral Provincial Park, and settle in at one of the Ashnola River campgrounds (page 169). The roaring whitewater can be like audio-therapy, drowning out

Canoeing the Similkameen River

the superficial chatter of your conscious mind, soothing you into a state of deep serenity, allowing the wellspring of your subconscious to bubble-up new insight and understanding.

MANNING PARK TO PRINCETON

Well south of Princeton, just northeast of Manning Provincial Park, Copper Creek flows into the Similkameen River. Near the confluence is a cheap campground—the only one on this stretch of Hwy 3. Though small and within earshot of the highway, it's very convenient, barely off pavement. The approach, however, is tricky, because the access road departs the highway at a hairpin turn. Be careful.

If you're heading northeast on Hwy 3, from Manning Park

Set your trip odometer to 0 at Manning Park Lodge. Drive Hwy 3 northeast 24 km (15 mi) then turn right, off the highway, just after it descends into a hairpin turn and crosses Copper Creek. There's a dirt pullout here. Descend to quickly reach Copper Creek campground on the right. If you're still on the highway at Sunday Summit, you've gone too far. Turn around and drive back 6.7 km (4.2 mi).

If you're heading south on Hwy 3, from Princeton

Set your trip odometer to 0 in Princeton, at the Petro Canada station by the blue bridge over the Similkameen River. Drive Hwy 3 south. At 35 km (21.7 mi) reach 1232-m (4041-ft) Sunday Summit. At 41.7 km (25.8 mi) turn left, off the highway, just before it crosses Copper Creek and ascends out of a hairpin turn. There's a dirt pullout here. Descend to quickly reach Copper Creek campground on the right.

COPPER CREEK CAMPGROUND #86
Overnight / Easy / $ / mid-July to mid-Oct
4 tables
Accessible by small motorhomes and trailers

PRINCETON TO TULAMEEN

The Tulameen River flows into the Similkameen River at Princeton. A paved road follows the Tulameen west, then northwest through a pretty valley to the village of Coalmont. Just beyond is the village of Tulameen, near Otter Lake. There used to be another, much larger settlement here: Granite Creek. In the 1880s, during its prime as a gold-mining town, it comprised more than 200 buildings. You can mingle with the ghosts of Granite Creek at the campground that today bears its name. Ponderosa pines and a big, grassy clearing create an inviting atmosphere. It's on the Tulameen River, next to Granite Creek, just outside Coalmont.

0 km (0 mi)
Starting northwest on Bridge Street in Princeton, departing Hwy 3 at the Petro Canada station by the blue bridge over the Similkameen River. Set your trip odometer to 0 and follow the sign for Hwy 5A. Proceed through the historic downtown, cross a bridge over the Tulameen River, and reach a T-intersection. Turn left, following the sign for Coalmont (18 km) and Tulameen (25 km). The small, curvy road parallels the river, then ascends through a canyon.

20 km (12.4 mi)
Reach Coalmont and the historic hotel established in 1912. For Tulameen (9 km / 5.6 mi farther), Otter Lake, and the Plateau Lakes, proceed straight (northwest). Directions continue on page 152. For Granite Creek campground turn left (south) and cross a bridge over the Tulameen River.

21.6 km (13.4 mi)
Go left for Granite Creek campground. Right eventually leads to Lodestone Lake campground #75 and Wells Lake campground #84. Both lakes are tiny. So are the campgrounds. Access requires 4WD.

Thalia Lake

21.7 km (13.5 mi)
Cross a bridge over Granite Creek, then turn left to reach the campground.

GRANITE CREEK CAMPGROUND #76
Weekend / Easy / $ / mid-April to mid-Oct
15 tables & more campsites
Accessible by motorhomes and 5th-wheels

TULAMEEN TO PLATEAU LAKES

The Plateau Lakes are about midway between Princeton and Merritt. The shortest, easiest access is via Hwy 5A. That description begins on page 154 and includes more details about the plateau, campgrounds, and driving conditions. If you're an explorer, you might prefer the backroad access described

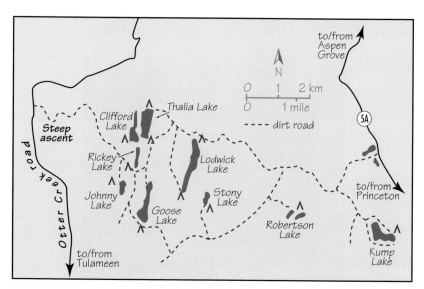

here. It's longer, and the final approach is a rough, steep, 275-m (900-ft) ascent—too much for big RVs. But it's more interesting and adventurous.

With about 16 tiny lakes, 11 small campgrounds, and a snarly network of roads, driving the plateau is potentially confusing. You're unlikely to get lost, but you might have to backtrack. Don't go unless you have the patience and curiosity to be a happy wanderer. This route description is general, follows only the main road (obvious once you're on top of the 1050-m / 3444-ft plateau), and includes only easy-to-find campgrounds.

From Princeton, drive 20 km (12.4 mi) to Coalmont and pass the turnoff to Granite Creek campground. Continue northwest on the main, paved road, following the directions below.

29 km (18 mi)
Reach the village of Tulameen. Just beyond is Otter Lake Provincial Park. Proceed north, along the west shore of Otter Lake.

40.1 km (24.9 mi)
Pavement ends.

58.6 km (36.3 mi)
Straight (north) soon passes beneath a Kettle Valley Railway trestle, then heads northeast, eventually intersecting Hwy 5A south of Aspen Grove. For the Plateau Lakes, turn right (east) onto narrow Youngsberg Road, near a small wooden bridge, just before the KM 22 sign. The road is rough, steep and rutted as it ascends through an old clearcut. But it should be passable in a 2WD car. Stay on the main road.

67.8 km (42 mi)
Fork left.

68.4 km (42.4 mi)
Reach Rickey Lake campground #51, described on page 157.

68.6 km (42.5 mi)
Straight continues across the plateau. Right leads to Goose Lake South campground #55 in just over 1 km (0.6 mi). It's described on page 156.

Drying the tent after a rainy night

69.2 km (42.9 mi)
Right continues across the plateau. Turn left to enter Thalia Lake South campground #54, described on page 156.

71.2 km (44.1 mi)
Straight continues across the plateau. Turn right to quickly reach Lodwick Lake North campground #56, described on page 156.

81.8 km (50.7 mi)
Intersect Hwy 5A. Turn left (north) to reach Hwy 5 at Merritt in about 44 km (27.3 mi). Turn right (south) to reach Hwy 3 at Princeton in about 39 km (24.2 mi).

PLATEAU LAKES VIA HWY 5A

The Plateau Lakes are about midway between Princeton and Merritt. The shortest, easiest access, via Hwy 5A, is described here. If you're an explorer, you might prefer the longer, rougher, but more interesting and adventurous backroad access (page 151).

With about 16 tiny lakes, 11 small campgrounds, and a snarly network of roads, driving the plateau is potentially confusing. You're unlikely to get lost, but you might have to backtrack. Don't go unless you have the patience and curiosity to be a happy wanderer. This route description follows only the main road (obvious once you're on top of the plateau) and includes only easy-to-find campgrounds. The map on page 152 will help you find the rest.

Unless recent, heavy rains have turned the roads to slop, a low-clearance 2WD car will get you to most Plateau Lakes, but not all. Even the main road is too narrow for big RVs. Some spurs are little more than a pair of tracks. Before venturing off the main road, consider how your vehicle will fare if conditions deteriorate.

Enough warnings. Now for some encouragement. The plateau, at 1050 m (3444 ft) elevation, is scenic. Aspen lighten the evergreen forest. Meadows welcome in the sunshine. The small campgrounds are intimate. You might end up with one all to yourself. And driving on the plateau can be a joy. During dry weather, wheeling along the soft, gracefully winding roads might remind you of those miniature cars on set tracks at amusement parks that thrilled you as a child. Go slowly. Stay lighthearted. You'll love it.

If you're heading north on Hwy 5A, from Princeton

Drive Hwy 5A about 39 km (24.2 mi) north of Hwy 3 at Princeton, then turn left (west). Set your trip odometer to 0.

Daisies

If you're heading south on Hwy 5A, from Merritt

Drive Hwy 5A about 44 km (27.3 mi) south of Hwy 5 at Merritt, then turn right (west). Set your trip odometer to 0.

For either approach above, now follow the directions below

0 km (0 mi)
Starting west on Pike Mtn. FS road, departing Hwy 5A near a small lake.

1 km (0.6 mi)
Stay straight, passing A&P Guest Ranch on the right.

1.9 km (1.2 mi)
Reach a triangular junction and go right. Follow the sign for W H Ranch. Pass Robertson Lake Road on the left.

3.9 km (2.4 mi)
Reach another triangular junction and go left. See more signs for W H Ranch.

4.3 km (2.7 mi)
Fork right.

7.6 km (4.7 mi)
Pass an overnight pullout next to a meadowy hill.

9.2 km (5.7 mi)
Reach another triangular junction. Straight continues across the plateau. Turn sharply left to quickly reach Lodwick Lake North campground. If you're lucky, you might hear the loons in a yodeling frenzy.

LODWICK LAKE NORTH CAMPGROUND #56
Weekend / Moderate / Free
3 tables
Inaccessible by motorhomes and trailers

Continuing generally west on the main road, passing the turnoff to Lodwick Lake North campground.

11.8 km (7.3 mi)
Reach a fork. Left continues across the plateau. Turn right to enter Thalia Lake campground. It's set in aspen and pines. Nearby glades are bright with wildflowers in early summer.

THALIA LAKE SOUTH CAMPGROUND #54
Weekend / Moderate / Free
Elev: 1052 m (3450 ft) / Lake: 19 ha
8 tables
Inaccessible by motorhomes and trailers

Continuing generally south on the main road, passing the turnoff to Thalia Lake South campground.

12.4 km (7.7 mi)
Straight continues across the plateau. Turn left to reach Goose Lake campground in just over 1 km (0.6 mi).

GOOSE LAKE SOUTH CAMPGROUND #55
Weekend / Moderate / Free
Elev: 1036 m (3400 ft) / Lake: 13.5 ha
8 tables
Inaccessible by motorhomes and trailers

Continuing generally west on the main road, passing the turnoff to Goose Lake South campground.

12.6 km (7.8 mi)
Reach Rickey Lake campground on the right, beside the main road. There are two grassy areas near the shore. The lake is cluttered with cattails and deadfall.

RICKEY LAKE CAMPGROUND #51
Weekend / Moderate / Free
3 tables
Inaccessible by motorhomes and trailers

Continuing generally northwest on the main road, passing Rickey Lake campground, then descending the rough road on the plateau's west side.

22.4 km (13.9 mi)
Reach a T-junction in Otter Creek valley. Turn left (south) to reach Tulameen in another 29.6 km (18.4 mi), Coalmont in 38.6 km (23.9 mi), and Princeton in 58.6 km (36.3 mi).

PRINCETON TO MERRITT

Hwy 5A links Princeton and Merritt. At about the midpoint, west of the highway, are the Plateau Lakes campgrounds, described on page 152. East of the highway is Missezula Lake campground, described here. Other campgrounds between Princeton and Merritt are farther from the highway, have rough access, or both, but the turnoffs to several are also listed here.

If you're heading north on Hwy 5A, from Princeton

0 km (0 mi)
Starting northwest on Bridge Street in Princeton, departing Hwy 3 at the Petro Canada station by the blue bridge over the Similkameen River. Set your trip odometer to 0 and follow the sign for Hwy 5A. Turn right onto Tapton Ave., signed for Merritt.

1 km (0.6 mi)
After crossing a bridge over the Tulameen River, reach a junction. Right is the Old Hedley Road and the Princeton-Summerland Road. Bear left (north) onto Hwy 5A, toward Merritt (90 km).

9.3 km (5.8 mi)
Pass Summers Creek Road on the right. Follow it north (bearing right at about 8.5 km / 5.3 mi) to reach Rampart Lake campground #68 (free) at

about 14.7 km (9.1 mi). There are two small camping areas on this minor lake; the first should be 2WD accessible.

31.7 km (19.7 mi)
Pass the north end of Allison Lake.

35.6 km (22.1 mi)
Pass Hornet Lake FS road on the right. This is the rough access to three small campgrounds on dinky lakes. The first, Loosemore Lake campground #62 (free), is about 3.2 km (2 mi) off pavement, has four campsites, and should be 2WD accessible. Just beyond, requiring 4WD, are Deadman Lake South campground #63 (5 campsites) and Prosser Lake campground #61 (2 campsites free).

37.8 km (23.5 mi)
Pass Gulliford Lake Rest Area.

39 km (24.2 mi)
Turn left (west) onto Pike Mtn. FS road for the Plateau Lakes campgrounds. Directions continue on page 154.

48.8 km (30.3 mi)
Pass a yellow sign warning of trucks entering the highway.

49.1 km (30.5 mi)
Turn right (southeast) onto Dillard Creek FS road for Missezula Lake campground. Directions continue on page 159.

60.1 km (37.3 mi)
Reach Aspen Grove and pass Connector Hwy 97C, which leads east to the Okanagan.

83.1 km (51.5 mi)
Intersect Hwy 5 at the Merritt Interchange.

If you're heading south on Hwy 5A, from Merritt

0 km (0 mi)
Starting south on Hwy 5A, from the junction with Hwy 5 at the Merritt Interchange. Set your trip odometer to 0.

23 km (14.3 mi)
Reach Aspen Grove and pass Connector Hwy 97C, which leads east to the Okanagan.

34 km (21.1 mi)
Turn left (southeast) onto Dillard Creek FS road for Missezula Lake campground. Directions continue on page 159.

44.1 km (27.3 mi)
Turn right (west) onto Pike Mtn. FS road for the Plateau Lakes campgrounds. Directions continue on page 154.

45.3 km (28.1 mi)
Pass Gulliford Lake Rest Area.

47.5 km (29.5 mi)
Pass Hornet Lake FS road on the left. This is the rough access to three small campgrounds on dinky lakes. The first, Loosemore Lake campground #62, is about 3.2 km (2 mi) off pavement, has four campsites, and should be 2WD accessible. Just beyond, requiring 4WD, are Deadman Lake South campground #63 (5 campsites) and Prosser Lake campground #61 (2 campsites). Both are free.

51.4 km (31.9 mi)
Pass the north end of Allison Lake.

73.8 km (45.8 mi)
Pass Summers Creek Road on the left. Follow it north (bearing right at about 8.5 km / 5.3 mi) to reach Rampart Lake campground #68 at about 14.7 km (9.1 mi). There are two small camping areas on this minor lake; the first should be 2WD accessible.

82.1 km (50.9 mi)
Reach a junction in Princeton. Left is the Old Hedley Road and the Princeton-Summerland Road. Turn right, cross a bridge over the Tulameen River, and continue through town.

83.1 km (51.5 mi)
Intersect Hwy 3. Turn left for Hedley and Keremeos. Turn right for Manning Provincial Park.

For MISSEZULA LAKE, now follow the directions below.

0 km (0 mi)
Starting southeast on Dillard Creek FS road, departing Hwy 5A.

1.6 km (1 mi)
Stay straight at the fork. The wide road passes through unimpressive forest.

4.2 km (2.6 mi)
Reach a fork. Stay left on Dillard Creek FS road.

6.7 km (4.2 mi)
Reach a fork. Go right for Missezula Lake. Left (north) is a 4WD road to Bluey Lake campground #40. It's free.

7.6 km (4.7 mi)
Reach a fork. Go right for Missezula Lake. Left (north) is a rough road to Loon Lake and eventually Connector Hwy 97C.

9.7 km (6 mi)
Turn right and descend to reach Missezula Lake campground, at the lake's north end.

MISSEZULA LAKE CAMPGROUND #48
Weekend / Moderate / Free
Elev: 1052 m (3450 ft) / Lake: 6.2 km (3.8 mi) long, 241 ha
8 tables, boat launch
Accessible by small motorhomes and trailers

Continue to Loon Lake Exit on Connector Hwy 97C by turning right when leaving Missezula campground. In about 2.4 km (1.5 mi), turn left (northeast) onto Dillard-Galena Creek FS road. En route to the highway, pass Buck Lake campground #46.

PRINCETON TO SUMMERLAND

Don't come here in search of a quiet, lonely campsite. Much of the land is settled. Private cabins crowd the lakes. The biggest campground, on Chain Lake, is often a hive of activity. Yet the terrain through this corridor is scenically substandard for beautiful British Columbia. Driving Princeton - Summerland Road, however, is an enjoyable alternative to the major highways. The generally smooth gravel surface allows comfortable cruising. And, unlike the highways, this backroad has several very convenient, inexpensive campgrounds along the way

If you're heading east, from Princeton to Summerland

In Princeton, drive northwest on Bridge Street. It departs Hwy 3 at the Petro Canada station by the blue bridge over the Similkameen River. Follow the sign for Hwy 5A. Turn right onto Tapton Avenue, signed for Merritt. Cross a bridge over the Tulameen River and reach a junction. Left (north) is Hwy 5A. Turn right onto Old Hedley Road and set your trip odometer to 0.

0 km (0 mi)
Starting on Old Hedley Road in Princeton.

0.3 km (0.2 mi)
Turn left (north) onto Princeton - Summerland Road, signed for Osprey Lake.

36.6 km (22.6 mi)
Reach Chain Lake West campground, beside the road, on the right.

Camping in B.C. sometimes feels like you're the owner of a private lake.

CHAIN LAKE WEST CAMPGROUND #69
Weekend / Difficult (due only to distance) / $ / late April to Oct 10
Elev: 1036 m (3400 ft) / Lake: 42 ha
20 tables, boat launch
Accessible by motorhomes and 5th-wheels

Continuing northeast on the main road, passing Chain Lake West campground.

41.6 km (25.7 mi)
Stay straight (east) on the main road for Summerland. Turn right (south) onto Agur Road to reach Link Lake campground in 0.8 km (0.5 mi).

This small lake and campground have little appeal. Private cabins are nearby. The access road loops around the lake, back to the main road.

LINK LAKE CAMPGROUND #70
Overnight / Difficult (due only to distance) / $ / late April to Oct 10
Elev: 1100 m (3608 ft) / Lake: 15 ha
3 tables, more campsites, boat launch
Accessible by small motorhomes and trailers

Continuing east on the main road, passing the turnoff to Link Lake campground.

42.4 km (26.3 mi)
Pass Link Lake Road, on the right. To access Link Lake campground this way, immediately go left, then right at the junction. At the fork with Osprey Lake on the left, go right on the main road. Pass the boat launch. Go right at the T-junction. After reaching the campground, you can rejoin the main road just beyond.

43.8 km (27.2 mi)
Stay straight (east) on the main road for Summerland. Turn right to enter Osprey Lake campground.

The densely forested hillside here is prettier than the scenery at Link Lake. The campground is far enough below the main road that noise is minimal.

OSPREY LAKE CAMPGROUND #71
Overnight / Difficult (due only to distance) / $ / May 1 – Oct 15
Elev: 1082 m (3550 ft) / Lake: 39 ha
5 campsites with tables, rough boat launch
Accessible by small motorhomes and trailers

Continuing east on the main road, passing the turnoff to Osprey Lake campground.

46.6 km (28.8 mi)
Reach a junction. Stay straight (east) on the main road for Summerland. Trout Creek FS road forks left (northeast) eventually accessing Okanagan Connector Hwy 97C and several campgrounds en route.

52 km (32.3 mi)
Reach a junction. Bear right (east) on the main road for Summerland.

52.8 km (32.8 mi)
Reach Thirsk Lake campground, beside the road, on the right. Irrigation drops the water level significantly in summer.

THIRSK LAKE CAMPGROUND #18
Overnight / Difficult (due only to distance) / Free
Elev: 1020 m (3346 ft) / Lake: 59 ha
5 tables, beach
Accessible by small motorhomes and trailers

Old Hedley Road campsite above Similkameen River

Continuing east on the main road, passing Thirsk Lake campground.

53.1 km (33 mi)
Pass more Thirsk Lake campsites.

70.5 km (43.8 mi)
Stay straight (southeast) on the main road for Summerland. Turn left for Trout Creek Crossing campground, just before a bridge and switchback.

Set in pines and cottonwoods, beside the rushing creek, this small, intimate campground is delightful. But it's often ignored, because most campers prefer lakes.

TROUT CREEK CROSSING CAMPGROUND #17
Weekend / Difficult (due only to distance) / Free
4 tables, 3 campsites
Too small for motorhomes and trailers

Continuing southeast on the main road, passing the turnoff to Trout Creek Crossing campground.

82 km (50.8 mi)
Pass a viewpoint overlooking Okanagan Valley to the east.

82.8 km (51.3 mi)
Pavement resumes.

84.3 km (52.3 mi)
Stay straight (southeast) for Summerland. Fish Lake Road forks left (north) to Darke Lake Provincial Park.

90.3 km (56 mi)
Reach a junction. Go left and curve downhill.

94 km (58.3 mi)
Arrive at the junction of Prairie Valley and Victoria Roads, at Giant's Head in Summerland. Continue east on Prairie Valley Road, toward Okanagan Lake.

94.4 km (58.5 mi)
Proceed through the 4-way intersection, on Prairie Valley Road.

95.3 km (59.2 mi)
Intersect Hwy 97, by the IGA shopping centre. Turn left for Peachland and Kelowna. Turn right for Penticton.

If you're heading west, from Summerland to Princeton

Driving the first 11 km (6.8 mi) west from Summerland is worthwhile just for the scenery. The road ascends a lovely, cultivated valley above Okanagan Lake. The rest of the way to Princeton isn't special, but it's an enjoyable alternative to the major highways. And you can camp cheap en route. Read page 160 for details. The following route description is general.

Summerland is beside Hwy 97, south of Peachland, north of Penticton, near the southwest shore of Okanagan Lake. Begin this backroad drive to Princeton by heading west on Prairie Valley Road. It departs Hwy 97 at the IGA shopping centre, 5.4 km (3.3 mi) south of Sun Oka Beach Provincial Park.

0 km (0 mi)
Starting west on Prairie Valley Road in Summerland, departing Hwy 97 at the IGA shopping centre.

0.9 km (0.5 mi)
Reach a 4-way intersection. Proceed left on Prairie Valley Road.

1.3 km (0.8 mi)
Reach a junction with Victoria Road. Stay straight on Prairie Valley Road, toward Rutherford Farms.

2.4 km (1.5 mi)
Begin ascending.

4.6 km (2.9 mi)
Curve right.

5 km (3 mi)
Go left on Bathfield Road. Follow the yellow line on the pavement. At the white signs outlined in red, curve right.

10.9 km and 11 km (6.8 mi)
Stay straight on the main road, signed for Osprey Lake and Princeton.

12.5 km (7.8 mi)
Pavement ends.

17.6 km (10.9 mi)
Stay straight.

24.7 km (15.3 mi)
Turn right for Trout Creek Crossing campground, just after a bridge and switchback. Read page 163 for details.

42.5 km (26.4 mi)
Reach Thirsk Lake campground, beside the road, on the left. Read page 162 for details.

51.5 km (32 mi)
Turn left for Osprey Lake campground. Read page 162 for details.

53.7 km (33.3 mi)
Turn left for Link Lake Campground. Read page 161 for details.

58.7 km (36.4 mi)
Reach Chain Lake West campground, beside the road, on the left. Read page 161 for details.

95.3 km (59.2 mi)
Intersect Old Hedley Road, in Princeton. Go right 300 meters, then turn left to proceed through town and reach Hwy 3.

PRINCETON TO HEDLEY

Travelling between Princeton and Hedley, you can take your pick: water, pavement, or dirt. The **Similkameen River** is a boating playground, a delicious sight in such dry, hot country. Hwy 3 follows the river's south bank for most of this short stretch. Along the river's north bank is Old Hedley Road. Initially paved, it soon lapses into a dusty track. But it offers you three campgrounds on the sparkling river. Dewdney is the only free one; the others charge a nominal fee.

The Old Hedley Road campgrounds are unremarkable. They afford no privacy from fellow campers or passing vehicles. Highway traffic is audible despite the river's throaty attempts to muffle it. Still, rafters, canoeists and fisherfolk who want to launch their boats or wet their lines will find these campgrounds convenient and useful.

If you're heading southeast, from Princeton to Hedley

In Princeton, drive northwest on Bridge Street. It departs Hwy 3 at the Petro Canada station by the blue bridge over the Similkameen River. Follow the sign for Hwy 5A. Turn right onto Tapton Avenue, signed for Merritt. Cross a bridge over the Tulameen River and reach a junction. Left (north) is Hwy 5A. Turn right onto Old Hedley Road. It follows the Similkameen River's north bank, rejoining Hwy 3 in about 35 km (21.7 mi). Reach Dewdney campground #78 in about 7 km (4.3 mi). Reach Old Hedley Road West campground #79 and Old Hedley Road East campground #80 just before rejoining Hwy 3. All are on the right, above the riverbank. All have tables. Dewdney is small. Old Hedley West is big, with room for motorhomes and trailers. Old Hedley East is medium size.

If you're heading northwest, from Hedley to Princeton

From Hedley, drive Hwy 3 northwest 6.5 km (4 mi). Just before a bridge over the Similkameen River, turn right onto Old Hedley Road. It follows the river's north bank, reaching Princeton in about 35 km (21.7 mi). Reach Old Hedley Road East campground #80 and Old Hedley Road West campground #79 shortly after departing the highway. Reach Dewdney campground #78 in about 28 km (17.4 mi). All are on the left, above the riverbank. All have tables. Old Hedley East is medium size. Old Hedley West is big, with room for motorhomes and trailers. Dewdney is small.

Glacier Lake, Cathedral Provincial Park

NEAR KEREMEOS

With Hwy 3 in pursuit, the Similkameen River rushes southeast from Princeton, past Hedley and Keremeos. A tributary, the Ashnola River, races down from mountainous **Cathedral Provincial Park,** flowing north into the Similkameen just west of Keremeos. A backroad departs Hwy 3 and follows the Ashnola upstream, where you'll find four MOT campgrounds (3 are $), plus two BC Parks campgrounds (currently free) that are used mostly by backpackers heading to or from the Cathedral lakes. The campgrounds are within sight and sound of the lusty Ashnola, making them very conducive to a couple days of R & R. Except for the Lakeview trailhead, they're all accessible by motorhomes.

Keremeos is dry, sunny, orchard country, so the Ashnola River's lower canyon has a comfortable camping climate from April until November. The Cathedral lakes, however, are high above at 2100 m (6888 ft), where it can snow even in summer. Hiking to the lakes is a steep grunt. The trail gains 1200 m (3936 ft) in 14 km (8.7 mi). And the ascent is worse than the numbers indicate, because there's no scenery en route to fuel motivation. But the heavenly alpine country in the Park's core area is a generous reward. Allow at least three days. For details, read *Hiking from here to WOW: North Cascades*, described on page 538. If your preferred method of payment is a credit card, instead of sweat, you can ride a jeep up to the lakes. For prices, departure times, and reservations, phone Cathedral Lakes Resort: 1-888-255-4453. Visit their website at www.cathedral-lakes-lodge.com. Directions to the parking lot for the resort's private jeep road are included here.

If you're heading east or west on Hwy 3, near Keremeos

The Ashnola River road departs Hwy 3 at the west edge of Keremeos, or 66 km (40.5 mi) southeast of Princeton. Turn south at the sign for Cathedral Lakes Provincial Park. Immediately cross the Similkameen River. Set your trip odometer to 0 on the bridge.

For ASHNOLA RIVER, now follow the directions below

0 km (0 mi)
Starting west on the red bridge over the Similkameen River, heading for Ashnola River and Cathedral Park.

12.2 km (7.6 mi)
Turn left to enter Red Bridge campground. It's set in good shade trees beside the Ashnola River. A beautiful pool invites swimming but requires caution.

RED BRIDGE CAMPGROUND #10
Weekend / Easy / $ / May 15 to Oct 31
12 campsites with tables
Accessible by motorhomes and 5th-wheels

Continuing south on the main road, to more campgrounds and Cathedral Lakes trailhead.

13.6 km (8.4 mi)
Turn left to enter Tunnel Mtn campground #11 ($). It has only four campsites and little shade.

14.8 km (9.2 mi)
Turn left to enter Horseshoe Canyon campground #12 ($). It has five campsites and big Douglas fir and cottonwoods.

15.5 km (9.6 mi)
Reach a junction at the Ewart Creek bridge. Bear right (west). You're now in Cathedral Park. In 3 km (1.8 mi) farther, there's a park kiosk on the right.

21.5 km (13.3 mi)
Pass Cathedral Lakes Resort base parking lot, on the left, just over the bridge. The resort is high in the mountains, at Quiniscoe Lake. Their private jeep road begins here.

Ashnola River campsite

23.2 km (14.4 mi)
The signed Cathedral Lake (Lakeview) trailhead and campground are left. Descend the rough road 0.6 km (0.4 mi) to road's end at 900 m (2952 ft).

BC Parks administers the campground, which is likely still free. Overnight parking is permitted for self-contained units. The tenting walk-in campsites (no fire rings or tables), within 20 m/yd of the parking lot, are along the Ashnola River, downstream from the footbridge.

Continuing west on the main road, passing the turnoff to Lakeview trailhead.

25.7 km (16 mi)
Reach BC Parks' Buckhorn campground with several tables and a few fire rings.

38 km (23.5 mi)
Reach Cathedral Park's Wall Creek trailhead, on the left. Just before the trailhead there might still be a free campground in a grassy clearing, with room for about five vehicles.

KEREMEOS TO OLIVER

Dependably clear skies make **Kobau Observatory,** southeast of Keremeos, one of Canada's prime stargazing sites. A decent gravel road (with sections of severe washboard) climbs to the 1874-m (6147-ft) summit of Mt. Kobau. Camping is no longer permitted here, but there's a 5-km (3-mi) hiking trail network. Earthgazing is enjoyable here too. The view encompasses Similkameen River valley (west and northwest), Okanagan Falls (north), and Washington's Okanagan country (south). Motorhomes or trucks pulling trailers can handle the ascent if they have brawny engines.

About a 15-minute drive northwest of Oliver is small **Burnell Lake.** Locals call it Sawmill Lake. The campground here is convenient for a brief overnight stay, accessible by motorhomes and trailers, and attractive for fly fishing. The lake has a reputation for lunker rainbow trout. Catch-and-release rules apply.

For MT. KOBAU, now follow the directions below

Drive Hwy 3 northwest 11.2 km (6.9 mi) from the junction of Hwys 3 and 97 in Osoyoos. Or drive Hwy 3 south then northeast 23 km (14.3 mi) from the junction of Hwy 3 and the road south out of Cawston. From either approach, turn northwest onto Mt. Kobau Road. It departs Hwy 3 near the pass. Follow the serpentine, gravel road 19.8 km (12.3 mi) to the observatory on the summit.

~

For BURNELL LAKE, now follow the directions below

0 km (0 mi)
Leaving Hwy 97, from downtown Oliver, head west on 350 Avenue.

3.9 km (2.4 mi)
Turn right (north) onto White Lake Road.

8 km (5 mi)
Watch for a sign SAWMILL LAKE. The road passes through private property and there are numerous forks. Stay on the slightly larger main road, which is usually the left branch.

11.8 km (7.3 mi)
Reach Burnell (Sawmill) Lake campground on the south end of the lake. The lake is at a fairly low elevation, so the water warms up quite quickly in the hot Okanagan sun. Forested hills surround the lake.

BURNELL LAKE CAMPGROUND #13
Weekend / Easy / Free
6 tables, rough boat launch
Elev: 762 m (2500 ft)
Accessible by motorhomes and trailers

~~~

HOPE TO MERRITT

Coquihalla Hwy 5 is B.C.'s only toll highway. It's the straighter, smoother, faster alternative to a circuitous stretch of Trans-Canada Hwy 1. The southern segment, between Hope and Merritt, climbs through the husky Cascade Mountains. Farther inland the topography goes slack and the forests wither, but the scenery is impressively vast the entire way. Equally awesome is the highway itself. Observant travellers marvel at snow sheds, diversion trenches, avalanche dams, and dozens of bridges and overpasses crossing roads, rivers and railways. The Coquihalla is a monument to engineering prowess. It also defines the west side of the South Thompson Plateau, where all the campgrounds described here are reached by turning off the highway at well signed, easy-to-see exits.

Murray Lake is a narrow, unremarkable, water-filled gap in the woods. Yet opulent cabins belly-up to the east shore. The access road is rough—passable in a 2WD car but problematic for big RVs. Approaching the lake, beware of potholes the size of kiddy pools. Avoid Murray Lake after heavy rain, when the road can be a muddy morass. Of the two campgrounds here, the one on the north shore is bigger and better.

Gillis Lake is in a tight bowl. Forest rises abruptly from the shore. The campground is on a treed bench well below the main road. Some campers will enjoy hunkering down in this tiny pocket, others will feel squeezed. The approach road poses no difficulties. Small RVs can access Gillis Lake campground, but motorhomes and trailers will find Boss and Davis lakes much bigger and more accommodating.

Shea, Tahla, Boss and Davis lakes are small and close together. Their attendant campgrounds range in size from peewee to jumbo. It's easy to check them all out, then settle in at your favourite. Variety of choice and relatively easy access make this the most attractive camping area near Hwy 5 between Hope and Merritt. Shea and Tahla are fine for small motorhomes and trailers. Boss and Davis accommodate land yachts. But beware of mud in early season.

If you're heading northeast on Hwy 5 from Hope

0 km (0 mi)
Starting northeast on Hwy 5 from the junction of Hwys 3 and 5, just east of Hope. Set your trip odometer to 0.

50 km (31 mi)
Proceed through the toll plaza near 1240-m (4067-ft) Coquihalla Pass.

63 km (39 mi)
Reach the Juliet Exit. Proceed northeast for more campgrounds en route to Merritt. Turn off the highway here for Murray Lake campgrounds. Directions continue on page 173.

80 km (50 mi)
Reach the Coldwater Exit (Kingsvale Interchange). Proceed northeast for Merritt. Turn off the highway here for Gillis Lake campground (directions continue on page 173), and for campgrounds at Shea, Tahla, Boss and Davis lakes. Directions continue on page 174.

110 km (68 mi)
Reach the junction of Hwys 5 and 5A, at the Merritt Interchange.

If you're heading southwest on Hwy 5 from Merritt

0 km (0 mi)
Starting southwest from the junction of Hwys 5 and 5A, at the Merritt Interchange. Set your trip odometer to 0.

30 km (19 mi)
Reach the Coldwater Exit (Kingsvale Interchange). Proceed southwest for Murray Lake campgrounds and for Hope. Turn off the highway here for Gillis Lake campground (directions continue on page 173), and for campgrounds at Shea, Tahla, Boss and Davis lakes (directions continue on page 174).

47 km (29 mi)
Reach the Juliet Exit. Proceed southwest for Hope. Turn off the highway here for Murray Lake campgrounds. Directions continue on next page.

60 km (37 mi)
Proceed through the toll plaza near 1240-m (4067-ft) Coquihalla Pass.

110 km (68 mi)
Reach the junction of Hwys 5 and 3, just east of Hope.

For MURRAY LAKE, now follow the directions below

0 km (0 mi)
After departing Hwy 5 at the Juliet Exit, go straight toward the hill. Set your trip odometer to 0 and turn right after the big cattle guard. Head north on Maka-Murray FS road. Stay left, above the canyon on your right.

0.9 km (0.5 mi)
Proceed through a hairpin turn and climb steeply.

5 km (3 mi)
Turn left to enter Murray Lake South campground. Or continue to the larger, more attractive campground on the north shore.

MURRAY LAKE SOUTH CAMPGROUND #65
Weekend / Difficult / Free
Elev: 1143 m (3750 ft) / Lake: 2 km (1.2 mi) long, 25 ha
3 tables
Inaccessible by motorhomes and trailers

~

6.9 km (4.3 mi)
Turn left to enter Murray Lake North campground. It has a small, mucky beach and a view down the forest-enclosed lake.

MURRAY LAKE NORTH CAMPGROUND #64
Weekend / Difficult / Free
10 tables, level grassy area for tents, boat launch
Inaccessible by motorhomes and trailers

~

For GILLIS LAKE, now follow the directions below

0 km (0 mi)
After departing Hwy 5 at the Coldwater Exit (Kingsvale Interchange), set your trip odometer to 0 and head north on the paved road paralleling the highway's west side.

2.6 km (1.6 mi)
In Kingsvale, turn left before the railway overpass. Cross the bridge then go left on Maka - Murray FS road.

6.5 km (4 mi)
Begin ascending.

7.1 km (4.4 mi)
Bear left at the fork.

7.9 km (4.9 mi)
Gillis Lake is visible below. Left is the first and longer of the campground's two entrances. It descends steeply then skirts the shore to reach the campground in 1 km (0.6 mi). Proceed straight on the main road for the second, shorter entrance.

8.9 km (5.6 mi)
Turn left for the second, shorter entrance to Gillis Lake campground.

GILLIS LAKE CAMPGROUND #35

Weekend / Moderate / Free
Elev: 1143 m (3750 ft) / Lake: 19 ha
6 tables, rough boat launch, crude dock, level ground for tents
Too small for motorhomes and trailers

~

For SHEA, TAHLA, BOSS and DAVIS LAKES, now follow the directions below

After departing Hwy 5 at the Coldwater Exit (Kingsvale Interchange), head north on the paved road paralleling the highway's west side. At 2.6 km (1.6 mi), in Kingsvale, proceed straight beneath the railway overpass. Shortly beyond, turn right (east) onto unpaved Kane Valley Road. Follow it about 10 km (6.2 mi), then turn right (southeast) onto Voght Valley Road and set your trip odometer to 0. Kane Valley Road continues northeast, passing campgrounds at Harmon and Kane lakes (page 186) en route to Hwy 5A.

0 km (0 mi)
Starting southeast on Voght Valley Road.

5.3 km (3.3 mi)
Proceed south on Voght Valley Road for campgrounds at Tahla, Boss and Davis lakes. Turn left (northeast) onto Shea Lake FS road to reach Shea Lake campground in 2 km (1.2 mi).

SHEA LAKE CAMPGROUND #36

Weekend / Moderate / $ / early May to mid-Oct
5 tables, boat launch
Accessible by small motorhomes and trailers

~

6.5 km (4 mi)
Proceed south on Voght Valley Road for Boss and Davis lakes. Turn right to enter Tahla Lake campground. It's not on the shore.

TAHLA LAKE CAMPGROUND #37
Weekend / Moderate / $ / early May to mid-Oct
3 tables
Accessible by small motorhomes and trailers

7.1 km (4.4 mi)
Proceed south on Voght Valley Road for Davis Lake. Turn right to enter Boss Lake campground.

BOSS LAKE CAMPGROUND #38
Weekend / Moderate / $ / early May to mid-Oct
15 tables, boat launch
Accessible by motorhomes and 5th-wheels

9.5 km (5.9 mi)
Turn right to enter Davis Lake campground.

DAVIS LAKE CAMPGROUND #39
Weekend / Moderate / $ / early May to mid-Oct
55 tables, boat launch
Accessible by motorhomes and 5th-wheels

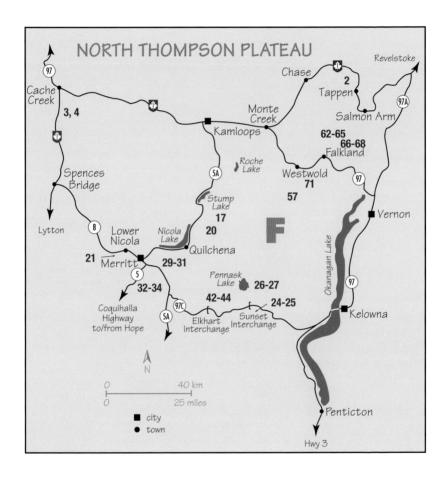

F: North Thompson Plateau

At the fee campgrounds, charges apply May 1 to October 15.

2	Skimikin Lakes	$	33	Harmon Lake West	$
3	Willard Lake	FREE	34	Harmon Lake East	$
4	Barnes Lake	FREE	42	Bob's Lake	FREE
17	Peter Hope Lake	$	43	Island Lake	FREE
20	Glimpse Lake	$	44	Elkhart Lake	FREE
21	N'Kwala	FREE	57	Woods Lake	FREE
24	MacDonald Lake	FREE	62	Charcoal Creek	FREE
25	Brenda Lake	FREE	63	Chase Creek	FREE
26	Pinnacle Lake	FREE	64	Pillar Lake	FREE
27	Hatheume Lake	FREE	65	Joyce Lake	FREE
29	Marquart Lake	$	66	Spa Lake	FREE
30	Lundbom Lake West	$	67	Arthur Lake	FREE
31	Lundbom Lake East	$	68	Bolean Lake	FREE
32	Kane Lake	$	71	Pinaus Lake	FREE

North Thompson Plateau

Autumn colours, near Bolean Lake

Aspen, ponderosa pines and other conifers cloak much of this region. The rest is grassland. An all-you-can-eat smorgasbord for cows. Some of the nation's largest cattle ranches sprawl across the rolling hills and gentle valleys near Nicola, Quilchena, and Douglas Lake. A gaggle of this industry's hapless victims, loitering on a backroad, will occasionally slow your progress to a crawl. They'll stare at you for minutes with uncomprehending eyes, then suddenly bolt—stiff-legged and scared. You'll be aware of their presence even when they're not in sight: cattle mementos collage many campgrounds.

The lakes, marshes and springs of the plateau, especially along Hwy 5A between Merritt and Kamloops, are optimal nesting grounds for thousands of waterfowl. In addition to the ducks that delight kids playing on shorelines, look for larger, more elegant species: trumpeter swans, Canada geese, snow geese, and great blue herons. The habitat that attracts birds also nurtures moose. Though huge, these homely creatures are shy. You'll be lucky to see one.

At many plateau lakes, the horizon is not serrated. It's a level line of trees. This gives the land a pre-Columbus appearance, a flatness that some people find dull compared to the magnanimous mountains of B.C.'s Coast Range, Kootenays, or Rockies. But camped beside a plateau lake, you'll have a unique perspective. The sky is a blue dome, filling your field of vision. The earth is just a sliver. It seems you're on top of the world.

Many free campgrounds and many low-fee sites are strewn throughout the region. You'll find as much variety in campground size, quality and accessibility here as elsewhere in the province. A choice of easy-to-reach campgrounds along Hwys 5A and 97 invites you to venture off the major thoroughfares, slow down, and explore.

NEAR CACHE CREEK

Trans-Canada Hwy 1 turns abruptly at Cache Creek, creating a right angle. From an abstract perspective, it resembles an open nut cracker. The nut is the town of Ashcroft. Nearby are free campgrounds at Willard and Barnes lakes. Both are convenient to Hwy 1, accessed via paved road, and easily reached by any vehicle, so they're heavily used. But late some night while driving across the province, you too might appreciate how handy they are. You can be there in 15 minutes from Ashcroft. The surrounding grassland is scattered with pines. Think of it as a vast openness, rather than emptiness.

If you're heading south on Hwy 1, from Cache Creek

From the junction of Hwys 1 and 97 at Cache Creek, drive Hwy 1 south 4.2 km (2.6 mi). Turn left (southeast) at the north access to Ashcroft. Proceed 6.2 km (3.8 mi) into town. Set your trip odometer to 0 on the northwest side of the Thompson River bridge.

If you're heading north on Hwy 1, from Spences Bridge

From Spences Bridge, drive Hwy 1 north about 39 km (24 mi). Turn right (east) at the south access to Ashcroft. Proceed 5 km (3.1 mi) into town. Set your trip odometer to 0 on the northwest side of the Thompson River bridge.

For either approach above, now follow the directions below

0 km (0 mi)
Starting southwest on Hwy 97C, leaving Ashcroft and crossing the Thompson River bridge.

7.8 km (4.8 mi)
After heading generally south, the highway jogs north.

9.2 km (5.7 mi)
Where the highway veers south again, turn left (north) onto paved Barnes Lake Road.

10 km (6.2 mi)
Reach Willard Lake campground on the south shore. Proceed north for Barnes Lake.

WILLARD LAKE CAMPGROUNDS #3
Weekend / Easy / Free
Elev: 700 m (2296 ft)
2 campsites without tables, cartop boat launch
Accessible by small motorhomes and trailers

11.1 km (6.9 mi)
Reach the sound end of Barnes Lake.

12.8 km (7.9 mi)
Arrive at Barnes Lake campground on the northwest shore.

BARNES LAKE CAMPGROUNDS #4
Weekend / Easy / Free
Elev: 687 m (2253 ft)
8 tables, boat launch
Accessible by motorhomes and 5-wheels

Nicola River, from N'Kwala campground

NORTHWEST OF MERRITT

N'Kwala. Nicola. The latter is obviously an English speaker's version of the Native place name. The only easy-to-reach campground northwest of Merritt still bears the original name: N'Kwala. It's on the Nicola River, just off paved Hwy 8, which links Trans-Canada Hwy 1 at Spences Bridge with Hwys 97C, 5 and 5A at Merritt.

The other free campgrounds in this general area are much harder to reach— way north of Hwy 8. It's a tediously long backroad journey made confusing by extensive recent logging. Those who persist can choose from nearly a dozen tiny campgrounds on small lakes reputed to offer good fishing. The final access to most is rough. We've included only the initial directions to **Tyner Lake**.

If you're heading northwest on Hwy 97C, from Merritt

0 km (0 mi)
Starting northwest on Hwy 97C, from the junction of Hwys 5 and 97C at the Merritt Interchange near the Tourist Info Centre.

4 km (2.5 mi)
Follow signs for Spences Bridge, Logan Lake and Cache Creek.

9 km (5.6 mi)
Proceed west on Hwy 8 for N'Kwala campground and Spences Bridge.
Hwy 97C forks right (north) to Logan Lake, Ashcroft, and Cache Creek on
Trans-Canada Hwy 1.

12.6 km (7.8 mi)
Proceed west on Hwy 8 through Lower Nicola to reach N'Kwala campground and Spences Bridge.

Turn right (north) onto initially-paved Aberdeen Road for Tyner Lake
campground #11. Set your trip odometer to 0. At the 14-km (8.7-mi) junction,
turn left (northwest) to reach Tyner Lake at about 20 km (12.4 mi).

26.2 km (16.2 mi)
Proceed northwest on Hwy 8 for Spences Bridge. Turn left (south) to enter
N'Kwala campground on the Nicola River. It's before a cement barrier and
an abrupt curve north. Two big, dark boulders mark the entry road.

N'KWALA CAMPGROUND #21
Weekend / Easy / Free
9 tables / Accessible by small motorhomes and trailers

Continuing northwest on Hwy 8, passing the turnoff to N'Kwala campground.

69 km (42.8)
Reach Spences Bridge and Trans-Canada Hwy 1.

If you're heading southeast on Hwy 8, from Spences Bridge

0 km (0 mi)
Starting southeast on Hwy 8, from Spences Bridge and Trans-Canada Hwy 1.

42.8 km (26.5 mi)
Proceed southeast on Hwy 8 for Merritt. Turn right (south) to enter
N'Kwala campground on the Nicola River, described above. It's by a
cement barrier, immediately after an abrupt curve east. Two big, dark boulders
mark the entry road.

56.3 km (34.9)
Proceed southeast on Hwy 8 through Lower Nicola to reach Merritt.

60 km (37.2 mi)
Proceed southeast for Merritt. Hwy 97C forks left (north) to Logan Lake,
Ashcroft, and Cache Creek on Trans-Canada Hwy 1.

65 km (40.3 mi)
Arrive in Merritt.

69 km (42.8 mi)
Reach the junction of Hwys 97C and 5 at the Merritt Interchange near the Tourist Info Centre.

EAST AND SOUTH OF MERRITT

The campgrounds at **Marquart and Lundbom lakes** are a short drive east of Merritt and only a few kilometers off pavement. They're very convenient for a brief overnight stay. Though both lakes are small, Lundbom is bigger, has two spacious campgrounds, and offers a choice of treed or open campsites. The Marquart setting is barren.

If you want to settle in for a couple days near Merritt, look south of town, where campgrounds at **Kane and Harmon lakes** offer a prettier mixture of grassland, aspen, and ponderosa pines; a more intimate camping atmosphere; a short interpretive trail; and the Kane Valley cross-country ski trails—a 37-km (23-mi) network available to equestrians and mountain bikers in summer. These campgrounds are slightly farther off pavement than Marquart and Lundbom, but the Kane Valley Road is smoother. Cows can be a nuisance here—a reminder that this isn't wilderness. At least they're wandering, instead of imprisoned in factory farms.

If you're heading east on Hwy 5A, from Merritt

0 km (0 mi)
Starting east on Hwy 5A, from the junction with Hwy 5 at the Merritt Interchange. The highway soon bends southeast.

9.4 km (5.8 mi)
Proceed south on Hwy 5A for Kane and Harmon lakes. Turn left (east) near a cattleguard, reset your trip odometer to 0, and follow the directions on page 185 for **Marquart and Lundbom lakes.**

14.3 km (8.9 mi)
Pass a sign announcing the turn for Kane Valley.

14.5 km (9 mi)
Proceed south on Hwy 5A to reach Hwy 97C or Princeton. Turn right (west) at the top of the rise, reset your trip odometer to 0, and follow the directions at the bottom of page 185 for **Kane and Harmon lakes.**

23 km (14.3 mi)
Reach the junction with Hwy 97C, which leads east to the Okanagan. Hwy 5A continues south to Princeton and Hwy 3.

Harmon Lake, in Kane Valley, south of Merritt

If you're heading north on Hwy 5A, from Hwy 97C

0 km (0 mi)
Starting north on Hwy 5A, from the junction with Hwy 97C near Aspen Grove.

8.5 km (5.3 mi)
Proceed north on Hwy 5A for Marquart and Lundbom Lakes. Turn left (west), reset your trip odometer to 0, and follow the directions at the bottom of page 185 for **Kane and Harmon lakes.**

13.6 km (8.4 mi)
Proceed north on Hwy 5A for Merritt. Turn right (east) near a cattleguard, reset your trip odometer to 0, and follow the directions on page 185 for **Marquart and Lundbom lakes.**

23 km (14.3 mi)
Reach the junction with Hwy 5 at the Merritt Interchange.

For MARQUART and LUNDBOM LAKES,
now follow the directions below

0 km (0 mi)
Starting east, departing Hwy 5A. Quickly reach a junction and go left on the rough road through rolling grassland. Pass the day-use area on Marquart Lake's southwest shore.

2.7 km (1.7 mi)
Reach Marquart Lake campground, on the northeast shore. The lake is shallow; the campground shadeless.

MARQUART LAKE EAST CAMPGROUND #29
Overnight / Easy / $ / May 1 to Oct 15
Elev: 1123 m (3683 ft) / Lake: 22 ha
6 tables, boat launch
Accessible by small motorhomes and trailers

4.7 km (2.9 mi)
Reach Lundbom Lake West campground, spread around the southwest shore.

LUNDBOM LAKE WEST CAMPGROUND #30
Weekend / Easy / $ / May 1 to Oct 15
Elev: 1128 m (3700 ft) / Lake: 49 ha
35 tables, boat launch, horse corral
Accessible by motorhomes and 5th-wheels

5.7 km (3.5 mi)
Reach Lundbom Lake East campground, spread around the northeast shore.

LUNDBOM LAKE EAST CAMPGROUND #31
Weekend / Easy / $ / May 1 to Oct 15
Elev: 1128 m (3700 ft) / Lake: 49 ha
14 tables, boat launch
Accessible by motorhomes and 5th-wheels

For KANE and HARMON LAKES, now follow the directions below

0 km (0 mi)
Starting west, departing Hwy 5A. The road soon bends southwest and continues in that general direction until past the campgrounds.

Fall foliage

3.7 km (2.3 mi)
Bear right on the main road. Pass several tiny lakes.

9 km (5.6 mi)
Reach Kane Lake campground on the left.

KANE LAKE CAMPGROUND #32
Weekend / Easy / $ / May 1 to Oct 15
Elev: 1100 m (3608 ft) / Lake: 8 ha
5 tables, open grassy area
Accessible by motorhomes and trailers

9.2 km (5.7 mi)
Reach Harmon Lake West campground on the left.

HARMON LAKE WEST CAMPGROUND #33
Weekend / Easy / $ / May 1 to Oct 15
Elev: 1120 m (3675 ft) / Lake: 27 ha
6 tables / Accessible by motorhomes and trailers

9.8 km (6.1 mi)
Turn left just before the cattleguard to reach Harmon Lake East campground in about 200 meters.

HARMON LAKE EAST CAMPGROUND #34
Weekend / Easy / $ / May 1 to Oct 15
Elev: 1120 m (3675 ft) / Lake: 27 ha
18 tables / Accessible by motorhomes and 5th-wheels

~

11.9 km (7.4 mi)
Pass Englishmen Lake. Proceed southwest on Kane Valley Road to reach Coquihalla Hwy 5 at the Coldwater Exit (Kingsvale Interchange). En route, Voght Valley Road forks left (southeast) to campgrounds at Shea, Tahla, Boss and Davis lakes, described on page 175.

~

MERRITT TO KAMLOOPS

Lakes, like a string of sausages, line the bottom of a sweeping valley between Merritt and Kamloops. The land is vast and open, as if the earth is baring itself to the sky. It feels lonely. Looks like cowboys should be riding the range. And they do. This is cattle country. Huge ranches lay claim to the grassland. Driving here on Hwy 5A is a peaceful alternative to the more hectic Trans-Canada Hwy 1 or Coquihalla Hwy 5. You can't cruise quite as fast, but the blacktop is straight enough to let you make good time—unless you exit eastward to visit the area's large, lakeside campgrounds. They're not far from pavement, close enough for a brief overnight stay, via access roads that even big RVs can handle.

Glimpse Lake has a cabin community, and campgrounds on its south and north shores. It's a pretty lake. A few stately Douglas firs add elegance to the surrounding forest. But enough people come here to get away from it all that it often feels they've brought it all with them.

Peter Hope Lake is attractive though unremarkable. The campground is pleasant. Bring your own shade in summer; the setting is only lightly treed. Kids can play in the lumpy grass, and a meadowy forest across the road. As at many lakes throughout the province, there's a fishing lodge here. It might give you a smug chuckle to think that most of what the lodge guests are paying for, you're enjoying for a nominal fee.

If you're heading northeast on Hwy 5A, from Merritt

0 km (0 mi)
Starting northeast on Hwy 5A, from the junction with Hwy 5, just north of Merritt.

8.4 km (5.2 mi)
Proceed through Nicola.

20.5 km (12.7 mi)
Proceed through Quilchena.

25.5 km (15.8 mi)
Proceed north on Hwy 5A for Peter Hope Lake campground and Kamloops. Turn right (east) onto Douglas Lake Road and reset your trip odometer to 0 for the Glimpse Lake campgrounds. Directions continue on page 190. Beyond Douglas Lake, the road heads northeast, eventually intersecting Hwy 97 at Westwold.

31.4 km (19.5 mi)
Pass Nicola Lake rest area.

42.2 km (26.2 mi)
Proceed north on Hwy 5A for Kamloops. Turn right (east) onto Peter Hope Road and reset your trip odometer to 0 for Peter Hope Lake campground. Directions continue at the bottom of page 190.

49.8 km (30.9 mi)
Pass Stump Lake rest area.

68.1 km (42.2 mi)
Proceed north on Hwy 5A for Kamloops. Just past Trapp Lake, turn right (east) for Roche Lake Provincial Park.

74.1 km (45.9 mi)
Pass Shumway Lake on the right.

91.8 km (56.9 mi)
Intersect Trans-Canada Hwy 1 at Kamloops.

If you're heading south on Hwy 5A, from Kamloops

0 km (0 mi)
Starting south on Hwy 5A, from Trans-Canada Hwy 1 at Kamloops.

17.7 km (11 mi)
Pass Shumway Lake on the left.

B.C. stands for Boating Country.

23.7 km (14.7 mi)
Proceed south on Hwy 5A for campgrounds at Peter Hope and Glimpse lakes, and for Merritt. Turn left (east) for Roche Lake Provincial Park.

37.4 km (23.2 mi)
Stump Lake is visible.

42 km (26 mi)
Pass Stump Lake rest area.

49.6 km (30.8 mi)
Proceed south on Hwy 5A for the Glimpse Lake campgrounds and for Merritt. Turn left (east) onto Peter Hope Road and reset your trip odometer to 0 for Peter Hope Lake campground. Directions continue at the bottom of page 190.

60.4 km (37.4 mi)
Pass Nicola Lake rest area.

66.3 km (41.1 mi)
Proceed south on Hwy 5A for Merritt. Turn left (east) onto Douglas Lake Road and reset your trip odometer to 0 for the Glimpse Lake campgrounds; directions continue on the next page. Beyond Douglas Lake, the road heads northeast, eventually intersecting Hwy 97 at Westwold.

71.3 km (44.2 mi)
Proceed through Quilchena.

83.4 km (51.7 mi)
Proceed through Nicola.

91.8 km (56.9 mi)
Intersect Hwy 5 just north of Merritt.

For GLIMPSE LAKE, now follow the directions below

0 km (0 mi)
Starting east on Douglas Lake Road, departing Hwy 5A.

8 km (5 mi)
Proceed straight (southeast) for Douglas Lake. Just beyond the power station, turn left (east) onto Lauder Creek FS road. It soon bends northeast and continues in that general direction all the way to Glimpse Lake.

23 km (14.3 mi)
Reach the west end of 93.5-hectare Glimpse Lake. The campgrounds are on the south and north shores, at 950 m (3116 ft) elevation.

GLIMPSE LAKE SOUTH CAMPGROUND #20
Weekend / Moderate / $ / May 1 to Oct 1
7 tables / Inaccessible by motorhomes and trailers

GLIMPSE LAKE NORTH CAMPGROUND #19
Weekend / Moderate / $ / May 1 to Oct 1
11 tables / Accessible by small motorhomes and trailer

For PETER HOPE LAKE, now follow the directions below

0 km (0 mi)
Starting east on Peter Hope Road, departing Hwy 5A.

6.5 km (4 mi)
Bear left on the main road.

7.6 km (4.7 mi)
Arrive at Peter Hope Lake campground. The first camping area has a few tables in an open, grassy clearing on the shore. The main campground is 200 meters farther, on the reedy side of the lake.

PETER HOPE LAKE CAMPGROUND #17
Weekend / Easy / $ / May 1 – Oct 15
1082 m (3550 ft) / Lake: 116 ha
16 tables, boat launch
Accessible by motorhomes and 5th-wheels

~

The road continuing along Peter Hope Lake's east shore soon forks. Left (northeast) is 4WD access to Plateau Lake campground. Right (south) is 4WD access to the Glimpse Lake campgrounds (described on page 190).

OKANAGAN CONNECTOR HWY 97C

Hwy 97C, between Merritt and Okanagan Lake, is an efficient but despotic structure, rigidly commanding motorists to travel nonstop. But there are a few exits. Use them to escape. They quickly access several campgrounds at higher elevations (about 1525 m / 5000 ft) where even the hottest summer day is comfortably cool.

The Elkhart Interchange accesses campgrounds at **Bob's and Island lakes.** The Sunset Interchange accesses campgrounds at **Brenda and MacDonald lakes.**

Consider the tiny campground at puny Bob's Lake for only a brief overnight stay. The others are small or medium-size campgrounds on pretty, forested lakes, where a couple days of relaxation might be enjoyable. All are quickly reached via good backroads that won't alarm RV pilots.

If you're heading east on Hwy 97C, from Hwy 5A

0 km (0 mi)
Starting east on Hwy 97C, departing Hwy 5A near Aspen Grove, southeast of Merritt.

27.7 km (17.2 mi)
Reach the Elkhart Interchange. Proceed east on Hwy 97C for campgrounds at Pinnacle, Hatheume, Brenda or MacDonald lakes, or for the Okanagan. Exit the highway here for campgrounds at Bob's and Island lakes. Directions continue on page 192.

39.5 km (24.5 mi)
Reach the Sunset Interchange. Proceed east on Hwy 97C for the Okanagan. Exit the highway here for campgrounds at Pinnacle and Hatheume lakes (directions continue on page 195), or Brenda and MacDonald lakes (directions continue on page 195).

48.7 km (30.2 mi)
Proceed east over 1728-m (5668-ft) Pennask Summit.

82 km (50.8 mi)
Intersect Hwy 97 on the west side of Okanagan Lake. Turn left (north) for Kelowna. Turn right (south) for Peachland, Summerland or Penticton.

If you're heading west on Hwy 97C, from the Okanagan

0 km (0 mi)
Starting west on Hwy 97C from the west side of Okanagan Lake, departing Hwy 97 between Peachland and Westbank.

33.3 km (20.7 mi)
Proceed west over 1728-m (5668-ft) Pennask Summit. Pennask Lake is visible north.

42.5 km (26.4 mi)
Reach the Sunset Interchange. Proceed west on Hwy 97C for campgrounds at Bob's and Island lakes, or for Hwy 5A. Exit the highway here for campgrounds at Pinnacle and Hatheume lakes (directions continue on page 193), or Brenda and MacDonald lakes (directions continue on page 195).

54.3 km (33.7 mi)
Reach the Elkhart Interchange. Proceed west on Hwy 97C to reach Hwy 5A. Exit the highway here for campgrounds at Bob's and Island lakes. Directions continue below.

82 km (50.8 mi)
Intersect Hwy 5A near Aspen Grove. Turn right (north) for Merritt. Turn left (south) for Princeton.

For BOB'S and ISLAND LAKES, now follow the directions below

From the eastbound exit, turn left (north) and go under the highway, then reset your trip odometer to 0. From the westbound exit, ignore the first right fork, descend toward the tunnel, then turn right (north) and reset your trip odometer to 0.

0 km (0 mi)
Starting north on Bob's Lake Pit Road.

5 km (3.3 mi)
Pass an unnamed lake on the right.

5.7 km (3.5 mi)
Proceed straight for Island Lake. Turn right to enter Bob's Lake campground. It's convenient for a brief overnight stay, but the lake is just a pond in the woods.

BOB'S LAKE CAMPGROUND #42
Overnight / Easy / Free
Elev: 1524 m (5000 ft) / Lake: 5 ha
2 tables / Accessible by small motorhomes and trailers

Continuing on the main road, passing the turnoff to Bob's Lake campground.

7.2 km (4.5 mi)
Pass the turnoff to Paradise Lake.

7.5 km (4.7 mi)
Go left at the four-way junction.

7.7 km (4.8 mi)
Turn left to enter Island Lake campground. This is a larger, prettier lake than Bob's. The campsites here are much more appealing.

ISLAND LAKE CAMPGROUND #43
Weekend / Easy / Free
Elev: 1524 m (5000 ft)
5 tables, boat launch / Accessible by small motorhomes and trailers

For PINNACLE and HATHEUME LAKES,
now follow the directions below

From the eastbound exit, proceed straight (east) and reset your trip odometer to 0 where left (north) goes under the highway. From the westbound exit, turn left (south), go under the highway, then turn left (east) at the T-junction and reset your trip odometer to 0.

0 km (0 mi)
Starting east on the frontage road paralleling the south side of the highway.

5 km (3.1 mi)
Go left at the junction.

6.1 km (3.8 mi)
Curve left.

6.4 km (4 mi)
Bear right.

6.8 km (4.2 mi)
Reach a T-junction. Right (south) on Sunset FS road leads to Brenda and MacDonald lakes (page 195). For Pinnacle and Hatheume lakes, turn left (northeast) on Bear FS road and go under the highway.

9.3 km (5.8 mi)
Go right.

13.7 km (8.5 mi)
Proceed straight where Pennask FS road forks left.

14.2 km (8.8 mi)
Proceed straight where a rough road forks left to reach Pennask Lake Recreation Area in 6 km (3.7 mi).

19 km (11.8 mi)
Turn left at the junction.

21.3 km (13.2 mi)
Proceed right for Hatheume Lake. Turn left to quickly reach Pinnacle Lake campground.

PINNACLE LAKE CAMPGROUND #26
Weekend / Moderate / Free
Elev: 1433 m (4700 ft) / Lake: 10.5 ha
5 tables, boat launch
Accessible by small motorhomes and trailers

Continuing on the main road, passing the turnoff to Pinnacle Lake campground.

22.2 km (13.8 mi)
Fork right.

22.9 km (14.2 mi)
Arrive at Hatheume Lake campground.

HATHEUME LAKE CAMPGROUND #27
Weekend / Moderate / Free
Elev: 1402 m (4600 ft) / Lake: 106 ha
14 tables, 1 walk-in tent site, boat launch
Accessible by motorhomes and 5th-wheels

For BRENDA and MACDONALD LAKES,
now follow the directions below

Follow the directions for Pinnacle and Hatheume lakes (page 193) as far as the T-junction at 6.8 km (4.2 mi), then turn right (south) on Sunset FS road and continue following the directions below.

11.8 km (7.3 mi)
Reach a junction. Turn left (northeast) onto Brenda FS road.

13.5 km (8.4 mi)
Reach a junction. Stay straight on the main road.

14 km (8.7 mi)
Proceed straight for MacDonald Lake. Turn left to reach Brenda Lake campground.

BRENDA LAKE CAMPGROUND #25
Weekend / Easy / Free
Elev: 1707 m (5600 ft) / Lake: 20 ha
5 tables, cartop boat launch
Accessible by small motorhomes and trailers

Continuing on the main road, passing the turnoff to Brenda Lake campground.

14.8 km (9.2 mi)
Reach a junction and turn left. Soon bear right at the fork to reach MacDonald Lake campground.

MACDONALD LAKE CAMPGROUND #24
Weekend / Easy / Free
Elev: 1707 m (5600 ft) / Lake: 11 ha
5 tables, cartop boat launch
Accessible by small motorhomes and trailers

SOUTHWEST OF SALMON ARM

Between Kamloops and Salmon Arm, Trans-Canada Hwy 1 drunkenly wanders north and bumps into Shuswap Lake. At Monte Creek, just east of Kamloops, Hwy 1 loses touch with its equally inebriated little buddy, Hwy 97, which veers southeast, waking up the towns of Monte Lake, Westwold and Falkland before smacking into the Okanagan just north of Vernon. The campgrounds described here are south and north of Hwy 97.

Funky RV at Pinaus Lake campground

You can pinpoint the area on maps by looking southwest of Salmon Arm. It's picturesque ranching country. A good place for a leisurely, exploratory drive.

(1) Woods Lake is south of Westwold. **Pinaus Lake** is southeast. (Ah, go ahead. Enjoy the bawdy pronunciation.) Both lakes are handsome, bearded with forest. Pinaus is larger. A rocky escarpment high on the treed slope opposite the campground adds interest to the view. The Woods campsites are more comfortably spaced, however, and the access road is better. The final few kilometers to Pinaus are narrow, rough, and can be dangerously muddy. A high-clearance vehicle is preferable. After heavy rain, 4WD might be necessary. Big RVs (motorhomes, trucks pulling trailers) should opt for Woods.

(2) Bolean, Arthur and Spa lakes (page 199) are on a 1525-m (5000-ft) plateau northeast of Falkland. All are small (about 1.6 km / 1 mi long), peaceful, and laced with forest. Bring a fishing rod, a good book, or your meditation cushion. These campgrounds are fine for an overnight stop and a peaceful morning, but none has a setting likely to keep you entertained. Bolean is a steep, 30-minute drive from Hwy 97. The narrow, bumpy road has sections of washboard. Your 2WD car will make it—in first gear much of the way. Big RVs (motorhomes, trucks pulling trailers) need after burners to surmount the ascent. There are pullouts for passing, and viewpoints overlooking the Salmon River valley.

(3) Joyce and Pillar lakes (page 201) are on the good gravel road linking Falkland (Hwy 97) with Chase (Hwy 1). Pillar is a small lake. Joyce is extra small. Both have campgrounds that are little more than day-use pullouts. They'll suffice for an overnight stop only if you arrive late and leave early. The same is true of the campground at Chase Creek. The only inviting campground along here is at Charcoal Creek, where you can get well off the road, into a creekside clearing, but it's too small for motorhomes and trailers.

(1) WOODS AND PINAUS LAKES

If you're heading southeast on Hwy 97 from Monte Creek

From Trans-Canada Hwy 1 at Monte Creek, drive Hwy 97 southeast. At 30.2 km (18.7 mi) pass Westwold School on the right. At 32.2 km (20 mi) turn right (south) onto Ingram Creek FS road and reset your trip odometer to 0.

If you're heading west on Hwy 97 from Falkland

From the junction with Falkland-Chase Road (near the Falkland store and pub) drive Hwy 97 west 13.4 km (8.3 mi), then turn left (south) onto Ingram Creek FS road and reset your trip odometer to 0.

For either approach above, now follow the directions below

0 km (0 mi)
Starting south on Ingram Creek FS road, departing Hwy 97.

6.4 km (4 mi)
Reach a junction. Proceed right (southwest) for Woods Lake. Directions continue on page 198. For Pinaus Lake, turn left (northeast) and reset your trip odometer to 0.

0 km (0 mi)
Starting left (northeast) for Pinaus Lake.

2.4 km (1.5 mi) and 2.7 km (1.7 mi)
Bear left.

3.9 km (2.4 mi)
Fork left.

6.7 km (4.2 mi)
Go right at the T-junction. The road deteriorates.

7.2 km (4.5 mi)
Stay straight and begin descending.

9.3 km (5.8 mi)
Bear left where right descends to a resort. Beware of mud. The road narrows on a high slope.

9.9 km (6.1 mi)
Pinaus Lake is visible.

12.1 km (7.5 mi)
Turn right and descend to reach Pinaus Lake campground in 200 meters. Pass a couple individual campsites. Bear left to reach the main campground in another 200 meters. Beware of further mud.

PINAUS LAKE CAMPGROUND #71
Weekend / Difficult / Free
Elev: 1006 m (3300 ft) / Lake: 3.3 km (2 mi) long, 162 ha
5 tables, 7 campsites, gravel boat launch
Inaccessible by motorhomes and trailers

Continuing southwest at the 6.4-km (4-mi) junction, passing the turnoff to Pinaus Lake campground.

10.2 km (6.3 mi), 11.3 km (7 mi), and 11.4 km (7.1 mi)
Fork right.

15.3 km (9.5 mi)
Stay straight on the main road. Ignore a minor right fork.

15.6 km (9.7 mi)
Proceed under the powerline.

15.8 km (9.8 mi)
Bear right and ascend north, beneath the powerline.

16.5 km (10.2 mi)
Re-enter forest.

18.2 km (11.3 mi)
Reach Woods Lake. The first campsite is on the right.

18.7 km (11.6 mi)
Pass more campsites.

19.5 km (12.1 mi)
Arrive at the main Woods Lake campground.

Bolean Lake

WOODS LAKE CAMPGROUND #57
Weekend / Moderate / Free
Elev: 1151 m (3775 ft) / Lake: 27 ha
6 tables, boat launch
Accessible by small motorhomes and trailers

(2) BOLEAN, ARTHUR & SPA LAKES

If you find a vacant campsite at Bolean Lake, stay there. Arthur Lake is pretty, but the campsites are at the weedy end and have a limited view. Endure the rough road to Spa Lake only in search of solitude.

If you're heading southeast on Hwy 97, from Monte Creek

From Trans-Canada Hwy 1 at Monte Creek, drive Hwy 97 southeast about 47 km (29 mi). Just east of Falkland, turn left (north) onto Silvernails Road and reset your trip odometer to 0.

If you're heading northwest on Hwy 97, from near Vernon

From the junction of Hwys 97 and 97A (about 9 km north of Vernon) drive Hwy 97 northwest about 29 km (18 mi). Just before Falkland, turn right (north) onto Silvernails Road and reset your trip odometer to 0.

For either approach above, now follow the directions below

0 km (0 mi)
Starting north on Silvernails Road, departing Hwy 97.

0.3 km (0.2 mi)
Turn left onto Ord Road. The lakes are above the hill visible ahead. The gravel road switchbacks steeply.

8.9 km (5.5 mi)
Reach a junction and proceed on the main road. Shortly after, fork left for Bolean Lake campground. Directions continue at the bottom of this page. Stay straight and reset your trip odometer to 0 for Arthur and Spa lakes.

> **0 km (0 mi)**
> Proceeding straight on the main road, heading for Arthur and Spa lakes.
>
> **2.9 km (1.8 mi)**
> Reach a junction. Go right, on the higher road, for Arthur Lake. Left is the rough road (4WD recommended) to Spa Lake campground #66.
>
> **4.2 km (2.6 mi)**
> Turn right
>
> **4.9 km (3 mi)**
> Arrive at Arthur Lake campground.

ARTHUR LAKE CAMPGROUND #67
Weekend / Difficult / Free
Elev: 1563 m (5127 ft) / Lake: 76 ha
1 table, many campsites, rough boat launch
Inaccessible by motorhomes and trailers

Continuing left, shortly after the 8.9-km (5.5-mi) junction, where straight leads to Arthur and Spa lakes.

9.2 km (5.7 mi)
Reach Bolean Lake Lodge. Go left.

9.7 km (6 mi)
Arrive at Bolean Lake campground.

BOLEAN LAKE CAMPGROUND #68
Weekend / Moderate / Free
Elev: 1437 m (4713 ft) / Lake: 71 ha
4 tables, 5 campsites, rough boat launch
Accessible by small motorhomes and trailers

(3) FALKLAND-CHASE ROAD

If you're heading southeast on Hwy 97, from Monte Creek

From Trans-Canada Hwy 1 at Monte Creek, drive Hwy 97 southeast about 45.6 km (28.3 mi) to Falkland. Turn left (north) onto Falkland-Chase Road and reset your trip odometer to 0.

If you're heading northwest on Hwy 97, from near Vernon

From the junction of Hwys 97 and 97A (about 9 km north of Vernon) drive Hwy 97 northwest about 30.4 km (18.8 mi) to Falkland. Turn right (north) onto Falkland-Chase Road and reset your trip odometer to 0.

For either approach above, now follow the directions below

0 km (0 mi)
Starting north on Falkland-Chase Road. It's paved to Pillar Lake.

7.2 km (4.5 mi)
Stay straight. Pass a sign stating the distance to Chase: 43 km.

10.1 km (6.3 mi)
Reach Joyce Lake day-use area / overnight pullout, on the left, just after crossing the small bridge over Bolean Creek.

The first site has room for a tent, in trees, away from the road. The second site is 100 meters farther, at a large pullout near the lake.

JOYCE LAKE CAMPGROUND #65
Overnight / Easy / Free
Elev: 853 m (2800 ft) / Lake: 6.5 ha
2 tables, boat launch
Accessible by motorhomes and 5th-wheels

Continuing north on Falkland-Chase Road, passing Joyce Lake.

13 km (8 mi)
Pillar Lake is visible on the left.

13.4 km (8.3 mi)
Reach Pillar Lake day-use area / overnight pullout, on the left, below the road. Across the road, a short trail leads to the pillar —a geologic curiosity.

PILLAR LAKE CAMPGROUND #64
Overnight / Easy / Free
Elev: 853 m (2800 ft) / Lake: 38 ha
boat launch / Accessible by motorhomes and 5th-wheels

Continuing north on Falkland-Chase Road, passing Pillar Lake.

15.8 km (9.8 mi)
Reach Chase Creek campground, on the right, just before a small bridge.

CHASE CREEK CAMPGROUND #63
Overnight / Easy / Free
3 roadside campsites
Too small for motorhomes and trailers

Continuing north on Falkland-Chase Road, passing Chase Creek campground.

19.8 km (12.3 mi)
Reach Charcoal Creek campground, on the right. About 50 meters behind the roadside campsite are several more sites in a creekside meadow wedged between low hills.

CHARCOAL CREEK CAMPGROUND #62
Weekend / Moderate / Free
3 tables, level tent sites
Too small for motorhomes and trailers

Continuing north on Falkland-Chase Road, passing Charcoal Creek campground.

39.5 km (24.5 mi)
Reach a junction. Left intersects Hwy 1 at Chase in 10 km (6.2 mi). Right, then right at the next junction, leads generally east 19 km (11.8 mi) to Skimikin Lakes campground (described below) before intersecting Hwy 1 at Tappen.

NEAR SALMON ARM

Skimikin Lakes campground, just northwest of Salmon Arm, is a rarity: reached via paved road, a short distance from the Trans-Canada. You can also get there on a well-maintained backroad via bucolic Turtle Valley. Each of the two small lakes has a camping area. The scenery isn't beautiful, but the atmosphere can be soothing. Choose from campsites in grassy clearings, or among pines, alders and aspen. The area is open enough to accommodate land yachts.

The paved access to Skimikin Lakes, if you're heading east on Hwy 1

From Chase, drive Trans-Canada Hwy 1 (northeast along Shuswap Lake, then south) 35 km (21.7 mi). Turn right (northwest) onto Tappen Valley Road, signed for Turtle Valley. It's across from the lumber mill at Tappen Bay. Reset your trip odometer to 0.

The paved access to Skimikin Lakes, if you're heading west on Hwy 1

From the Salmon River bridge, on the west edge of Salmon Arm, drive Trans-Canada Hwy 1 north 10.8 km (6.7 mi). Turn left (northwest) onto Tappen Valley Road, signed for Turtle Valley. It's across from the lumber mill at Tappen Bay. Reset your trip odometer to 0.

For either approach above, now follow the directions below

0 km (0 mi)
Starting northwest on Tappen Valley Road, departing Hwy 1.

4 km (2.5 mi)
Turn left (west) at the junction.

10.1 km (6.3 mi)
Turn left (south) to enter the first Skimikin Lakes campground, on the south lake. Big RVs will find room here in a large clearing.

10.8 km (6.7 mi)
Turn left (south) to enter the second Skimikin Lakes campground, on the north lake. Choose from campsites up to the right in trees, or ahead on an open point.

SKIMIKIN LAKES CAMPGROUND #3
Weekend / Easy / $ / mid-May to mid-October
Elev: 525 m (1722 ft) / Lake: 11 ha
6 tables, 20 campsites
Accessible by motorhomes and 5th-wheels

The backroad access to Skimikin Lakes, if you're heading east on Hwy 1

From the rest area beside Chase Creek, near the north entrance to Chase, drive Trans-Canada Hwy 1 northeast. At 9.1 km (5.6 mi) pass a BC Parks sign for Roderick Haig-Brown. Get in the right turn lane. At 9.4 km (5.8 mi) turn right (south) following the sign for North Shuswap Resort Area, Adams Lake, and Squilax-Anglemont Rd. Reset your trip odometer to 0.

0 km (0 mi)
Starting south, departing Hwy 1.

0.3 km (0.2 mi)
Fork left onto Turtle Valley Road for Skimikin Lakes campground. Right crosses Hwy 1 on an overpass and leads to excellent campgrounds on Adams Lake. Read about those on page 370. Pavement soon ends.

3.7 km (2.3 mi)
Pass a sign WELCOME TO TURTLE VALLEY.

6 km (3.7 mi)
Fork left. Chum Lake is right.

7.3 km (4.5 mi) and 9.3 km (5.8 mi)
Stay straight, following signs for Tappen.

10 km (6.2 mi)
Bear left on the main road. In the next 8.2 km (5.1 mi) stay straight, ignoring right forks.

18.3 km (11.3 mi)
Turn right (south) to enter the first Skimikin Lakes campground.

19 km (11.7 mi)
Turn right (south) to enter the second Skimikin Lakes campground.

25.1 km (15.6 mi)
Turn right (east) at the junction.

29.1 km (18 mi)
Intersect Hwy 1, across from the lumber mill at Tappen Bay. Turn right (south) for Salmon Arm. Turn left (north) for Kamloops.

Explore B.C.'s beautiful backroads.

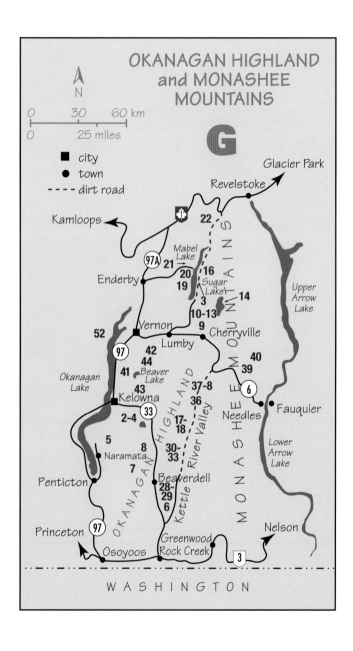

OKANAGAN HIGHLAND and MONASHEE MOUNTAINS

N

0   30   60 km

0   25 miles

■ city
● town
---- dirt road

Glacier Park

Revelstoke

Kamloops

22

Mabel Lake

97A 21

20   16
19   Sugar Lake

3   14

10-13

Enderby

MONASHEE MOUNTAINS

Upper Arrow Lake

Vernon   9   Cherryville

52   Lumby

97   42
44   40
41   Beaver Lake   39

Okanagan Lake

43   37-8   6
36   Needles   Fauquier

Kelowna

2-4   33   17-18   River Valley

5   8   30-33   Lower Arrow Lake

Naramata   7   Beaverdell

Penticton   28-29   Kettle

6

97   Nelson

Princeton   Greenwood   3

Osoyoos   Rock Creek

OKANAGAN HIGHLAND

W A S H I N G T O N

G: Okanagan Highland and Monashee Mountains

At the fee campgrounds southeast of Kelowna, charges apply mid-May through October 31. Northeast of Vernon, fees at Sugar Lake campgrounds apply April 1 to October 31; at Mabel Lake, May 1 to September 30.

2	Browne Lake	FREE		22	Noisy Creek	$
3	Hydraulic Lake	$		28	Canyon Flats	FREE
4	Minnow Lake	$		29	Canyon Creek	FREE
5	Chute Lake	FREE		30	Thone Lake	FREE
6	Taurus Lake	FREE		31	Kettle Bench	FREE
7	Saunier Lake	FREE		32	Kettle Canyon	FREE
8	Arlington Lakes	$		33	State Creek	FREE
9	Cherryville	FREE		36	Nevertouch Lake	FREE
10-13	Sugar Lake	$		37	Sandy Bend	FREE
14	Sugar Creek	$		38	Kettle River	FREE
15	Cascade South	FREE		39	Monashee-Kettle R	FREE
16	Cottonwood Bay	$		40	Holmes Lake	FREE
17	Lassie Lake	FREE		41	Beaver Lake	FREE
18	Cup Lake	FREE		42	Doreen Lake	FREE
19	Hidden Lake	$		43	Postill Lake	FREE
20	Cooke Creek	$		44	Island Lake	FREE
21	Dale Lake	FREE		52	Okanagan Lake	$

Okanagan Highland and Monashee Mountains

Kettle Valley Railway trestle that spanned Myra Canyon, before the August 2003 Okanagan Mountain fire

Every summer, after enduring perpetual cold and damp elsewhere in the province, wave upon wave of British Columbians rolls into the sunny Okanagan Valley seeking resuscitation of the senses. Like hypothermic shipwreck survivors, they wash onto the beaches of **Okanagan Lake.** It's an inland sea measuring 125 km (78 mi) long, 2 to 5 km (1.2 to 3.1 mi) wide, up to 550 m (1805 ft) deep, and covering 35,008 hectares. That much water is difficult to cool, which contributes to a dreamy climate, which supports thriving orchards and vineyards. Among people who shovel snow all winter, the Okanagan Valley's mythic Mediterranean image is understandable.

As a result of its popularity and subsequent development, the Okanagan Valley has undergone a rapid character shift—from rural to urban. Finding an unofficial free campsite here used to be easy. Now you have to be a crafty stealth-camper to pull it off. That's no fun. And there's just one cheap MOT campground on Okanagan Lake. But many more are nearby, above and east of the valley, in the **Okanagan Highland.**

If you're unfamiliar with the region, *highland* might suggest Scottish moors carpeted with blazing-green grass. Give your head a shake. Most of the Okanagan Highland is dry forest. Unsightly clearcuts are prevalent. The remaining trees look emaciated. They're nothing like the proud Ponderosa pines and stately Doug firs closer to Okanagan Lake. And here, *high* simply refers to relative elevation. The highland is really just a 1310-m (4300-ft) plateau. It's way above the Okanagan Valley, but it's not impressively mountainous. To complete this accurate but dull picture, the highland lakes are small, mere birdbaths compared to Okanagan Lake. Yet the highland offers campers a cool refuge from the valley heat. Driving to some, you'll gain a panoramic perspective on the celebrated lake and valley below. Several campgrounds are near Hwy 33, which traverses the highland. And a few highland campgrounds accommodate behemoth RVs.

East of the Okanagan Highland is **Kettle River Valley,** at about 720 m (2360 ft) elevation. You'll find eleven MOT campgrounds here, several on a healthy river with glorious swimming holes. The south end of the valley is actually Boundary Country. It's described in this Okanagan chapter because of the RV-passable backroad access departing Hwy 33 at Beaverdell, reaching more highland lakes campgrounds along the way.

East of Enderby, the topography is more rambunctious, the climate wetter, the vegetation lusher. Cedars and hemlocks rise among the deciduous trees. An irresistible camping destination here is 35-km (21.7-mi) long **Mabel Lake,** in a trough scooped by an ice-age glacier. Noisy Creek campground, on the lake's northwest shore, is provincial-park quality. It has plenty of room for big RVs but the final approach is a steep descent. On the southeast shore is Cascade South campground, where you can walk in and pitch your tent on a sandy beach. Another RV-accessible campground is farther up the east shore, at Cottonwood Bay.

Hwy 6 links Vernon with **Lower Arrow Lake.** En route it swoops through the **Monashee Mountains.** Turn north at Cherryville to reach lovely **Sugar Lake,** in a verdant bowl at the foot of the Monashees. The lake is ringed by several MOT campgrounds ranging in size from dwarf to giant. One is provincial-park quality and easily absorbs big RVs. Hwy 6 also obliges travellers in need of a quick, easy overnight stop, offering convenient camprounds on the Shuswap River near Cherryville, and the Kettle River farther southeast.

OKANAGAN LAKE

Don't count on finding a vacant site at Okanagan Lake's lone cheap campground. This is a great place to camp: shady pines, pocket beaches scattered along the shore, water lapping at your feet, and the ever-enticing possibility of a refreshing plunge. The campground is on the lake's quiet northwest shore, with a more comfortable buffer from pavement than you'll find at the pricier provincial parks. Access is via the paved Westside Road.

If you're heading north on Hwy 97, from Vernon

From Vernon, drive Hwy 97 north about 9 km (5.6 mi) to the junction with Hwy 97A near the north end of Swan Lake. Proceed east on Hwy 97 another 5.7 km (3.5 mi), then turn left (southwest) onto Westside Road and reset your trip odometer to 0. It's 1 km (0.6 mi) past O'Keefe Ranch. It's signed for Westshore, Killiney and Fintry.

If you're heading south on Hwy 97A, from Enderby

From Enderby, drive Hwy 97A south to the junction with Hwy 97 near the north end of Swan Lake. Turn right (east) onto Hwy 97, proceed 5.7 km (3.5 mi), then turn left (southwest) onto Westside Road and reset your trip odometer to 0. It's 1 km (0.6 mi) past O'Keefe Ranch. It's signed for Westshore, Killiney and Fintry.

If you're heading southeast on Hwy 97, from Hwy 1

From Trans-Canada Hwy 1 at Monte Creek, drive Hwy 97 generally southeast about 70 km (43 mi), then turn right (southwest) onto Westside Road and reset your trip odometer to 0. It's signed for Westshore, Killiney and Fintry. It's just before O'Keefe Ranch and well before the junction with Hwy 97A.

For any approach above, now follow the directions below

0 km (0 mi)
Starting southwest on Westside Road.

18.3 km (11.3 mi)
After cresting a rise and attaining a viewpoint, turn left (across from Sugarloaf Mtn. Road) and descend to reach Okanagan Lake campground in 1 km (0.6 mi).

OKANAGAN LAKE CAMPGROUND #52
Destination / Easy / $ / mid-May to Oct 31
Elev: 342 m (1122 ft)
30 campsites, 17 tables, boat launch
Accessible by small motorhomes and trailers

ABOVE OKANAGAN VALLEY

Pastel palaces crawling up every hillside. Visually dominant highways. Traffic. The Okanagan Valley resembles Southern California. But the B.C. bush is not far away. Head for the hills east of the valley. Aim for one of these campgrounds.

Small (1 km / 0.6 mi long) **Chute Lake** has always been an underwhelming sight. Now, it is surrounded by burned forest. The Okanagan Mountain Fire (August 2003), on the east side of the northern half of Okanagan Lake, swept up here. Ten of the sixteen wooden trestles of the famous Kettle Valley Railway between Chute Lake and Myra Canyon were destroyed. The provincial and federal governments spent $13.5 million to reconstruct the historic Kettle Valley railway trestles.

Over time, the unsightly scene will rebound more vigourous than it was. That's the gift of fire: robust, dynamic renewal. A richer, more diverse understory springs back. Flowers proliferate. Burgeoning grass and shrubs attract wildlife.

The access to Chute Lake, from Penticton, through Naramata, is a tour of picture-perfect orchard and vineyard country overlooking Okanagan Lake. And Chute Lake campground, accessible by small motorhomes and trailers, is an ideal base for exploring the historic Kettle Valley Railway (KVR).

In terms of size and scenery, **Postill Lake** (page 213) is typical of others in the Okanagan Highland. But the campground is tiny, cramped, unlevel, without tables. Just maneuvering a truck is difficult here, so don't bring your motorhome or trailer. Until this campground is upgraded, think of it as merely a parking area with a cartop boat launch. Be aware that the lake level fluctuates; this is a domestic water supply.

East of Hwy 97, about halfway between Vernon and Kelowna, is a cluster of highland lakes. You'll find more than 20 campgrounds here. The three easiest to reach are **Beaver (Swalwell) Lake, Island Lake,** and **Doreen Lake** (page 214). They have room for big RVs. Rough access, possibly requiring 4WD, precludes most of the other nearby campgrounds from this book. Be aware that the Beaver and Island lake levels fluctuate; they supply domestic water. Returning to Winfield from Beaver Lake, cyclists can enjoy a wicked downhill ride with aerial views of the Okanagan Valley. All you need is an agreeable companion to drive your vehicle while you ride your bike.

CHUTE LAKE

If you're heading north or south on Hwy 97 to Penticton

Exit Hwy 97 at the north end of Penticton, following the CITY CENTRE sign onto Westminster Avenue. It leads northeast toward Okanagan Lake's south shore. Follow signs for Naramata. Angle left onto Front Street. It soon intersects Lakeshore Drive (west) and Vancouver Avenue (east) at the waterfront. Turn right onto Vancouver Avenue. Where it becomes Lower Bench Road, set your trip odometer to 0 and continue following signs for Naramata.

0 km (0 mi)
Starting on Lower Bench Road in Penticton.

1.7 km (1.1 mi), 2.8 km (1.7 mi), and 3.1 km (1.9 mi)
Curve left.

4 km (2.5 mi)
Proceed on Naramata Road.

13 km (8.1 mi)
Bear right and ascend. Robinson Road descends left.

13.5 km (8.4 mi)
Proceed straight on the main road, leaving the vineyards, entering ponderosa-pine and sage country overlooking Okanagan Lake. Smethurst Road, ascending right, leads to a KVR trailhead. From there, the abandoned railbed climbs 915 m (3000 ft) and passes through two tunnels.

20 km (12.4 mi)
Fork right onto Chute Lake Road. Pavement ends.

23 km (14.3 mi)
Go right. The road narrows.

25 km (15.5 mi)
Go right. Left leads to Okanagan Mountain Park in 1.6 km (1 mi).

27.3 km (16.9 mi)
Stay straight.

28.2 km (17.5 mi)
Stay straight. The road levels.

30 km (18.6 mi)
Bear left.

30.7 km (19 mi)
Go right to reach Chute Lake campground, on the south shore. Chute Lake Resort is straight ahead, on the west shore. The road north along the west shore, is the KVR railbed leading to Myra Canyon.

30.9 km (19.2 mi)
Reach a 4-way intersection. Proceed straight onto Elinor Lake FS road, then immediately bear right.

31.1 km (19.3 mi)
Turn sharply left to arrive at Chute Lake campground in 100 meters.

CHUTE LAKE CAMPGROUND #5
Weekend / Moderate / Free
Elev: 1180 m (3870 ft) / Lake: 3 ha
4 well-spaced tables, boat launch
Accessible by small motorhomes and trailers

POSTILL LAKE

If you're heading north on Hwy 97, from Kelowna

From Hwy 33 in Kelowna, drive Hwy 97 north 4.1 km (2.5 mi). Where Sexsmith goes left (west), turn right (east) onto Old Vernon Road. Continue 7.4 km (4.6 mi), curving north, then turn right (northeast) onto Postill Drive and set your trip odometer to 0.

If you're heading south on Hwy 97, from Winfield

Drive Hwy 97 south to the community of Postill, just past Ellison Lake. Turn left (east) onto Old Vernon Road and set your trip odometer to 0. It's signed for Postill Lake Lodge (19 km). Soon enter the community of Ellison. At 1.1 km (0.7 mi) turn right at Ellison Market. At 1.3 km (0.8 mi) turn left (northeast) onto Postill Drive and reset your trip odometer to 0.

For either approach above, now follow the directions below

0 km (0 mi)
Starting northeast on Postill Drive.

1.2 km (0.7 mi)
Turn left onto Post Lake Road

2.5 km (1.6 mi)
Go left onto gravel.

3.3 km (2 mi)
Cross a bridge

6.1 km (3.8 mi)
Proceed straight.

7.9 km (4.9 mi) and 8.4 km (5.2 mi)
Pass overnight pullouts.

10.8 km (6.7 mi)
Bear right. The road levels.

12.2 km (7.6 mi) and 13.2 km (8.2 mi)
Bear right.

16 km (10 mi)
Proceed straight.

17.3 km (10.7 mi)
Go right. The road deteriorates.

17.5 km (10.8 mi)
Arrive at Postill Lake campground.

POSTILL LAKE CAMPGROUND #43
Overnight / Moderate / Free
Elev: 1326 m (4350 ft) / Lake: 2 km (1.2 mi) long, 70 ha
2 campsites, no tables, cartop boat launch
Inaccessible by motorhomes and trailers

BEAVER, ISLAND and DOREEN LAKES

If you're driving Hwy 97 south, from Vernon or north from Kelowna

Drive Hwy 97 to the town of Winfield. Turn east onto Beaver Lake Road, signed for Beaver Lake (17 km) and Dee Lake (26 km). There's a Turbo gas station here. It's just north of Voyageur RV Center, just south of Winfield Industrial Park. Set your trip odometer to 0.

Fall foliage

0 km (0 mi)
Starting east on Beaver Lake Road. Cross railroad tracks and proceed straight.

8.5 km (5.3 mi)
Pavement ends. The road is wide and well-graded.

15.6 km (9.7 mi)
Go left at the junction. Follow the sign for Dee Lake. Ignore the right fork to Beaver Lake Resort.

18.4 km (11.4 mi)
Proceed straight (northeast) for campgrounds at Island and Doreen lakes. Turn right (south) to quickly reach Beaver Lake campground.

BEAVER LAKE CAMPGROUND #41
Weekend / Moderate / Free
Elev: 1348 m (4420 ft) / Lake: 4 km (2.5 mi) long, 305 ha
11 tables, 2 laveview campsites, boat launch
Accessible by motorhomes and 5th-wheels

Continuing northeast on the main road, passing the turnoff to Beaver Lake campground.

24.3 km (15.1 mi)
Proceed straight (northeast) for Doreen Lake campground. Turn right to enter Island Lake campground.

ISLAND LAKE CAMPGROUND #44
Weekend / Moderate / Free
Elev: 1524 m (5000 ft) / Lake: 1.5 km (0.9 mi) long, 45 ha
7 tables, boat launch
Accessible by motorhomes and 5th-wheels

Continuing northeast on the main road, passing the turnoff to Island Lake campground. Proceed on the main road as it veers southeast.

28.5 km (17.7 mi)
Reach Doreen Lake campground, on the south shore.

DOREEN LAKE CAMPGROUND #42
Weekend / Moderate / Free
Lake: 1.8 km (1.1 mi) long, 60 ha
20 campsites, 10 tables, boat launch
Accessible by motorhomes and 5th-wheels

KELOWNA TO ROCK CREEK

Access these campgrounds from Hwy 33. Most are not far from pavement. After reading the brief descriptions below and choosing your destination, check where to turn off the highway. Then turn to the page indicated for route details. Read page 218 for directions heading north on Hwy 33, from Hwy 3 at Rock Creek.

Hydraulic Lake is 5 km (3 mi) off Hwy 33. **Minnow (McCulloch) Lake** is just beyond. Both campgrounds are handy for a brief overnight stop, but a longer stay can be enjoyable. Small RVs will find sufficient room. Locals refer to the entire reservoir system as McCulloch Lake—the name of a Kettle Valley Railway engineer. The KVR grazes Hydraulic Lake, so this is a good base for exploring (on foot or mountainbike) the abandoned railbed and trestle bridges. The campground at small Browne Lake is north of Hydraulic, on a rough access road unsuitable for big RVs.

Arlington Lakes are 3.4 km (2.1 mi) off Hwy 33. Campsites on both sides of the south lake are accessible by small motorhomes and trailers. The lake and setting are unremarkable. Other than convenience, the attraction here is the nearby KVR.

Beaverdell Creek FS road departs Hwy 33 at Beaverdell, about 81 km (50 mi) southeast of Kelowna. Follow it northeast to access campgrounds at several more highland lakes. Some will accommodate RVs. From there, you can descend into **Kettle River Valley,** passing excellent riverside campgrounds south on Kettle River Road. Rejoin Hwy 33 at Westbridge. The other Kettle River Valley access is from Hwy 3 at Rock Creek, between Osoyoos and Greenwood. Starting at Rock Creek, more than 30 km (18.6 mi) of Kettle River Road is paved. It's virtually level, has a wide shoulder, and traffic is minimal, making it ideal for road cycling.

Saunier Lake is 6 km (3.7 mi) from Hwy 33. The lake is small (just 3 hectares) and marshy, but it's pretty. The lonely atmosphere is soothing. With luck, you'll have the tiny campground all to yourself. It's not big enough for motorhomes or trailers.

If you're heading southeast on Hwy 33, from Kelowna

0 km (0 mi)
Starting east on Hwy 33, departing Hwy 97 in Kelowna.

23.3 km (14.4 mi)
Cross a bridged creek at the community of Three Forks.

33.5 km (20.8 mi)
Pass the road to Big White ski area, on the left.

35.3 km (22 mi)
Reach the highway's 1265-m (4150-ft) summit.

40 km (24.8 mi)
Proceed south on Hwy 33 for more campgrounds. Turn right (west) near a large pullout and reset your trip odometer to 0 for campgrounds at Hydraulic, Minnow and Browne lakes. Directions continue on page 220.

56 km (34.7 mi)
Pass through a shallow canyon.

58 km (36 mi)
Proceed south on Hwy 33 for more campgrounds. Turn right (west) and reset your trip odometer to 0 for Arlington Lakes campground. Directions continue at the bottom of page 221.

73.7 km (46 mi)
Proceed south through the community of Carmi.

80.6 km (50 mi)
Proceed south on Hwy 33 for more campgrounds. Turn left (northeast) onto Beaverdell Creek Road and reset your trip odometer to 0 for highland lakes campgrounds on the backroad to Kettle River Valley. Directions continue on page 222.

82 km (50.8 mi)
Pass the Beaverdell Hotel.

89 km (55.2 mi)
Proceed south on Hwy 33 for more campgrounds. Turn right (west) onto Tuzo Creek FS road and reset your trip odometer to 0 for Saunier Lake campground. Directions continue on page 224.

98.6 km (61.1 mi)
Proceed south on Hwy 33 for more campgrounds. Turn left (northeast) onto Taurus Lake FS road to reach Taurus Lake campground in 8.3 km (5.1 mi). This is the shortest access, but it's unsuitable for big rigs. The campground, and the RV-passable access from Kettle River Road, are described on page 226.

115.3 km (71.5 mi)
Reach the community of Westbridge. Proceed south on Hwy 33 to intersect Hwy 3. Turn sharply left (northeast) onto paved Kettle Valley Road and reset your trip odometer to 0 for the Kettle River campgrounds. Directions continue on page 226.

129 km (80 mi)
Intersect Hwy 3 at Rock Creek. Turn left (east) for Greenwood. Turn right (west) for Osoyoos.

If you're heading north on Hwy 33, from Hwy 3 at Rock Creek

0 km (0 mi)
Starting north on Hwy 33, departing Hwy 3 at Rock Creek.

13.7 km (8.5 mi)
Reach the community of Westbridge. Proceed north on Hwy 33 for numerous campgrounds. Turn right (northeast) onto paved Kettle Valley Road and reset your trip odometer to 0 for the Kettle River campgrounds. Directions continue on page 226.

30.4 km (18.8 mi)
Proceed north on Hwy 33 for more campgrounds. Turn right (northeast) onto Taurus Lake FS road to reach Taurus Lake campground in 8.3 km (5.1 mi).

Osoyoos Lake

This is the shortest access, but it's unsuitable for big rigs. The campground, and the RV-passable access from Kettle River Road, are described on page 226.

40 km (24.8 mi)
Proceed north on Hwy 33 for more campgrounds. Turn left (west) onto Tuzo Creek FS road and reset your trip odometer to 0 for Saunier Lake campground. Directions continue on page 224.

47 km (29.1 mi)
Pass the Beaverdell Hotel.

48.4 km (30 mi)
Proceed north on Hwy 33 for more campgrounds. Turn right (northeast) onto Beaverdell Creek Road and reset your trip odometer to 0 for highland lakes campgrounds on the backroad to Kettle River Valley. Directions continue on page 222.

55.3 km (34.3 mi)
Proceed north through the community of Carmi.

71 km (44 mi)
Proceed north on Hwy 33 for more campgrounds. Turn left (west) and reset your trip odometer to 0 for Arlington Lakes campground. Directions continue on page 221.

89 km (55.2 mi)
Proceed north on Hwy 33 for Kelowna. Turn left (west) near a large pullout and reset your trip odometer to 0 for campgrounds at Hydraulic, Minnow and Browne lakes. Directions continue below.

93.7 km (58.1 mi)
Reach the highway's 1265-m (4150-ft) summit.

95.5 km (59.2 mi)
Pass the road to Big White ski area, on the right.

105.7 km (65.5 mi)
Cross a bridged creek at the community of Three Forks.

108 km (67 mi)
Proceed west on Hwy 33 for Kelowna.

129 km (80 mi)
Intersect Hwy 97 in Kelowna.

~~

For HYDRAULIC, MINNOW and BROWNE LAKES,
now follow the directions below

0 km (0 mi)
Starting west on McCulloch Road, departing Hwy 33.

0.8 km (0.5 mi)
Proceed straight at the junction. Follow the sign for McCulloch Lake Resort.

4.5 km (2.7 mi)
Turn left (south) and cross the KVR railbed for Hydraulic and Minnow lakes. Proceed straight (northwest) and reset your trip odometer to 0 for Browne Lake.

> **0 km (0 mi)**
> Continuing northwest on McCulloch Road, passing the turnoff to Hydraulic and Minnow lakes.
>
> **3 km (1.9 mi)**
> Turn right (east) onto rough Browne Lake FS road. It heads northeast, then veers north along the west shore of Long Meadow Lake.

6.6 km (4.1 mi)
Reach Browne Lake campground.

BROWNE LAKE CAMPGROUND #2
Weekend / Moderate / Free
5 tables, cartop boat launch
Inaccessible by motorhomes and trailers

Turning left (south) at the 4.5-km (2.7-mi) junction, heading for Hydraulic and Minnow lakes.

5 km (3 mi)
Reach Hydraulic Lake campground.

HYDRAULIC LAKE CAMPGROUND #3
Weekend / Easy / $ / mid-May to Oct 31
Elev: 1257 m (4123 ft) / Lake: 2.5 km (1.6 mi) long, 286 ha
25 campsites, many with tables, cartop boat launch
Accessible by small motorhomes and trailers

Continuing south through Hydraulic Lake campground. Slow down. The road deteriorates.

6 km (3.7 mi)
Reach Minnow Lake campground. It's on the channel between Minnow and Hydraulic lakes.

MINNOW (McCULLOCH) LAKE CAMPGROUND #4
Weekend / Easy / $ / mid-May to Oct 31
22 campsites, many with tables
Accessible by small motorhomes and trailers

For ARLINGTON LAKES, now follow the directions below

0 km (0 mi)
Starting west, departing Hwy 33.

2.9 km (1.8 mi)
Fork right or left to quickly reach Arlington Lakes campground. Campsites are on both sides of the south lake.

ARLINGTON LAKES CAMPGROUND #8
Weekend / Easy / $ / June 20 to Sept 15
Elev: 1052 m (3450 ft) / South lake: 7 ha
12 tables, cartop boat launch
Accessible by small motorhomes and trailers

～

For MORE HIGHLAND LAKES, now follow the directions below

0 km (0 mi)
Starting northeast on Beaverdell Creek Road, departing Hwy 33 just north of the Beaverdell Hotel.

5.6 km (3.5 mi)
Bear right where Wallace Lake FS road forks left. Proceed generally east on the main Beaverdell-State FS road. Ignore Sago Creek FS road on the left.

10.6 km (6.6 mi)
Stay right on the main road.

11.2 km (6.9 mi)
Stay left on the main road where Crouse FS road forks right.

13.8 km (8.6 mi), 14.5 km (9 mi), and 17.7 km (11 mi)
Proceed straight (north-northeast) on the main road.

18 km (11.2 mi)
Reach Sago Creek campground.

> This is a handy place for a brief overnight stay, but it's beside the road, with no buffer from passing vehicles. A trail leads east 1 km (0.6 mi) to a walk-in campsite at Lower Collier Lake, then continues 0.5 km (0.3 mi) southeast to another walk-in campsite at Upper Collier Lake.

SAGO CREEK CAMPGROUND
Overnight / Moderate / Free
3 tables
Accessible by motorhomes and 5th-wheels

～

Continuing north-northeast on the main road, passing Sago Creek campground.

20.2 km (12.5 mi)
Bear right on the main road. Proceed through clearcuts.

23.8 km (14.8 mi)
Proceed straight, ignoring a right fork.

24.4 km (15.1 mi)
Reach a stop sign at a 3-way junction. Proceed straight (east) on State Creek FS road to descend into Kettle River Valley; directions continue on page 224. Turn left (north) onto Lassie Lake FS road and reset your trip odometer to 0 for campgrounds at Cup and Lassie lakes.

0 km (0 mi)
Starting north and ascending on Lassie Lake FS road.

3.4 km (2.1 mi)
Proceed north on Lassie Lake FS road, passing a right fork signed for State Creek.

5.3 km (3.3 mi)
Bear right to quickly reach tiny Cup Lake campground on the right. The entry road rejoins the main road in 100 meters. This is a pretty lake, with an island.

CUP LAKE CAMPGROUND #18
Weekend / Difficult (due only to distance) / Free
Elev: 1295 m (4248 ft) / Lake: 9 ha
2 well-spaced tables, rough boat launch, small dock
Accessible by small motorhomes and trailers

~

Continuing north on Lassie Lake FS road, passing Cup Lake campground.

8.4 km (5.2 mi)
Reach a junction and a map-sign indicating campsites and trails in the area. Turn right and descend to reach Lassie Lake campground in 100 meters. The entry road gets very muddy when wet. Pass a lone table, then proceed left for more campsites on the west shore.

LASSIE LAKE CAMPGROUND #17
Weekend / Difficult (due only to distance) / Free
Elev: 1295 m (4248 ft) / Lake: 36 ha
7 tables, rough boat launch, 2 docks
Accessible by small motorhomes and trailers

~

Continuing east on State Creek FS road, from the 24.4-km (15.1-mi) junction, passing Lassie Lake FS road on the left.

25.6 km (15.9 mi)
Proceed straight at the triangular junction. Pass Lower State FS road on the left.

31 km (19.2 mi)
Curve left.

31.5 km (19.5 mi)
Intersect Kettle River Road, across from a barn in Kettle River Valley. Reset your trip odometer to 0. Turn left (north), following directions on page 228 from the 44.6-km (27.7-mi) point, for campgrounds in the upper Kettle River Valley. Turn right (south), following directions below, to reach campgrounds in the lower Kettle River Valley before intersecting Hwy 33 at Westbridge in 44.6 km (27.7 mi).

For SAUNIER LAKE, now follow the directions below

0 km (0 mi)
Starting west on Tuzo Creek FS road. Proceed northwest through a narrow valley. The forest is a pleasing mix of cottonwoods, aspen and larch. Beware of rocks on the road that fall from the steep hillside on the right.

6.1 km (3.8 mi)
Reach Saunier Lake campground on the left, just before the bridged outlet stream. A short trail leads south to a tiny, potable spring.

SAUNIER LAKE CAMPGROUND #7
Weekend / Easy / Free
2 tables
Too small for motorhomes and trailers

For KETTLE RIVER VALLEY, now follow the directions below

If you're heading south on Kettle River Road, from State Creek

0 km (0 mi)
Starting south on Kettle River Road, from the junction with State Creek FS road at the bottom of page 228.

3.7 km (2.3 mi)
Proceed south on Kettle River Road for more campgrounds and to reach Hwy 33. Turn left for Kettle Canyon campground, described on page 228.

Swimming hole at Kettle Canyon campground

5.2 km (3.2 mi)
Proceed south on Kettle River Road for more campgrounds and to reach
Hwy 33. Turn left for Kettle Bench campground, described on page 228.

6.5 km (4 mi)
Proceed south on Kettle River Road.

12.8 km (7.9 mi)
Pavement begins. Proceed south on Kettle River Road, passing Fourth of
July Creek FS road on the right.

13 km (8.1 mi)
Proceed south on Kettle River Road for more campgrounds and to reach
Hwy 33. Turn left for Canyon Creek campground, described on page 227.

14 km (8.7 mi)
Proceed south on Kettle River Road for more campgrounds and to reach
Hwy 33. Turn left for Canyon Flats campground, described on page 227.

17.4 km (10.8 mi)
Proceed south on Kettle River Road for one more campground and to reach
Hwy 33. Turn left for Thone Lake campground, described on page 226.

30.6 km (19 mi)
Proceed south on Kettle River Road to reach Hwy 33. Turn right for Taurus Lake campground, described below.

44.6 km (27.7 mi)
Intersect Hwy 33 and reach the community of Westbridge, at the bridge over West Kettle River. Right (northwest) leads to Kelowna. Proceed south for Hwy 3.

51.7 km (32.1 mi)
Pass Kettle River Provincial Park on the left.

58.2 km (36.1 mi)
Intersect Hwy 3. Turn right (west) for Osoyoos. Turn left (east) for Greenwood.

If you're heading north on Kettle River Road, from Westbridge

0 km (0 mi)
Starting north on Kettle River Road, departing Hwy 33 at the community of Westbridge.

14 km (8.7 mi)
Proceed north on Kettle River Road for more campgrounds. Turn left onto Ouellette Creek FS road and follow it generally northwest to reach Taurus Lake campground in about 10 km (6.2 mi). Campsites are on the east and west shores of the tiny lake.

TAURUS LAKE CAMPGROUND #6
Weekend / Moderate / Free
9 tables, cartop boat launch
Accessible by small motorhomes and trailers

Continuing north on Kettle River Road, passing the turnoff to Taurus Lake.

27.2 km (16.9 mi)
Proceed north on Kettle River Road for more campgrounds. Turn right onto Thone Lake - Lost Horse Creek FS road, cross a bridge over the Kettle River, and immediately turn left (northeast) to reach Thone Lake campground in about 14 km (8.7 mi). Campsites are on the south and northwest shores of the tiny lake.

THONE LAKE CAMPGROUND #30
Weekend / Moderate / Free
7 tables, cartop boat launch
Accessible by motorhomes and 5th-wheels

Continuing north on Kettle River Road, passing the turnoff to Thone Lake.

30.6 km (19 mi)
Proceed north on Kettle River Road for more campgrounds. Turn right to reach Canyon Flats campground in 200 meters.

Two campsites are on the riverbank. Others are wide, flat, grassy, surrounded by forest. There's a swimming hole here, and a sandy beach just downstream.

CANYON FLATS CAMPGROUND #28
Weekend / Easy / Free
7 campsites, 2 tables / Accessible by motorhomes and 5th-wheels

Continuing north on Kettle River Road, passing the turnoff to Canyon Flats campground.

31.6 km (19.6 mi)
Proceed north on Kettle River Road for more campgrounds. Turn right (just before Fourth of July Creek FS road forks left) to quickly reach Canyon Creek campground.

This stretch of river is slow and quiet, so you won't be lulled to sleep by water music. But there's a big swimming hole here and a sandy beach.

CANYON CREEK CAMPGROUND #29
Weekend / Easy / Free
2 tables / Accessible by small motorhomes and trailers

Continuing north on Kettle River Road, passing the turnoff to Canyon Creek campground.

31.8 km (19.7 mi)
Pavement ends.

38.1 km (23.6 mi)
Proceed north on Kettle River Road.

39.4 km (24.4 mi)
Proceed north on Kettle River Road for more campgrounds. Turn right to quickly reach Kettle Bench campground.

This is a spacious, grassy, riverside clearing. There's a swimming hole here, and a sandy beach just downstream.

KETTLE BENCH CAMPGROUND #31
Weekend / Easy / Free
2 tables / Accessible by small motorhomes and trailers

Continuing north on Kettle River Road, passing the turnoff to Kettle Bench.

41 km (25.4 mi)
Proceed north on Kettle River Road for more campgrounds. Turn right to quickly reach Kettle Canyon campground.

This steep-sided canyon harbours huge swimming holes, a small waterfall, and large, flat rocks for lounging. The riverside campsites are treed.

KETTLE CANYON CAMPGROUND #32
Weekend / Easy / Free
3 tables / Accessible by small motorhomes and trailers

Continuing north on Kettle River Road, passing the turnoff to Kettle Canyon campground.

44.6 km (27.7 mi)
Reach a junction across from a barn. Proceed north on Kettle River Road for campgrounds in the upper Kettle River Valley. Turn left (west) onto State Creek FS road and reset your trip odometer to 0 for highland lakes campgrounds on the backroad access to Hwy 33 at Beaverdell. Directions continue on page 230.

46.8 km (29 mi)
Proceed north on Kettle River Road for more campgrounds. Reach State Creek campground on the right.

STATE CREEK CAMPGROUND #33
Overnight / Easy / Free
4 campsites, 2 tables
Accessible by motorhomes and 5th-wheels

Continuing north on Kettle River Road, passing State Creek campground. Proceed through Christian Valley. Pass FS roads forking right and left.

66 km (41 mi)
Pass Copperkettle Lake trailhead on the left. The 3-km (1.9-mi) trail ascends to a campsite on the tiny lake.

68 km (42.2 mi)
Proceed north on Kettle River Road for more campgrounds. Reach Damfino Creek campground on the right. One campsite is on each side of the creek, near its confluence with Kettle River.

DAMFINO CREEK CAMPGROUND #35
Weekend / Moderate / Free
3 tables / Accessible by motorhomes and 5th-wheels

Continuing north on Kettle River Road, passing Damfino Creek campground.

68.2 km (42.3 mi)
Proceed north on Kettle River Road for more campgrounds. Turn left onto Nevertouch FS road and follow it generally northwest then northeast to reach Nevertouch Lake campground in about 14 km (8.7 mi). Campsites are on the north shore.

NEVERTOUCH LAKE CAMPGROUND #36
Weekend / Difficult (due only to distance) / Free
10 tables, cartop boat launch
Accessible by motorhomes and 5th-wheels

Continuing north on Kettle River Road, passing the turnoff to Nevertouch Lake campground.

79.5 km (49.3 mi)
Proceed north on Kettle River Road for one more campground. Reach Sandy Bend campground on the right.

SANDY BEND CAMPGROUND #37
Weekend / Difficult (due only to distance) / Free
2 tables, swimming hole, sandy beach
Accessible by small motorhomes and trailers

Continuing northeast on Kettle River Road, passing Sandy Bend campground.

80 km (49.6 mi)
Reach Kettle River crossing campground on the right. Campsites are on both sides of the bridge.

KETTLE RIVER CROSSING CAMPGROUND #38
Weekend / Difficult (due only to distance) / Free
1 table, grassy area / Accessible by small motorhomes and trailers

**If you're heading west on the backroad to Hwy 33,
from Kettle River Valley**

0 km (0 mi)
Starting west on State Creek FS road, departing Kettle River Road at 44.6 km (27.7 mi), across from a barn. Begin ascending.

0.5 km (0.3 mi)
Curve right.

5.9 km (3.7 mi)
Stay left.

7.1 km (4.4 mi)
Reach a 3-way junction. Proceed straight (west) on the main Beaverdell-State FS road for Hwy 33 at Beaverdell. Turn right (north) onto Lassie Lake FS road and reset your trip odometer to 0 for campgrounds at Cup and Lassie lakes. Directions continue on page 223.

7.7 km (4.8 mi)
Proceed west on the main road.

11.3 km (7 mi)
Bear left (south) on the main road.

13.5 km (8.4 mi)
Reach Sago Creek campground, beside the road. Read page 222 for details.

13.8 km (8.6 mi), 17 km (10.5 mi), and 17.7 km (11 mi)
Proceed straight (south-southwest) on the main road.

20.3 km (12.6 mi)
Stay right on the main road.

20.9 km (13 mi)
Stay left on the main road.

Shuswap River, from Cooke Creek campground

26 km (16.1 mi)
Curve left (south) on the main road where Wallace Lake FS road forks right.

31.5 km (19.6 mi)
Intersect Hwy 33, just north of the Beaverdell Hotel. Turn right (north) for Kelowna. Turn left (south) for Kettle Valley Road at Westbridge, or Hwy 3 at Rock Creek.

ENDERBY TO MABEL LAKE

Enderby is on Hwy 97A, about midway between Okanagan Lake and Shuswap Lake. Travelling east to Mabel Lake, your choice of campgrounds ranges from puny to colossal. You can take your pick of settings, too: pond, river or lake. The area even offers you a selection of lake sizes: medium or XXL.

Hidden Lake is about a 20-minute drive from Enderby. It's surrounded by low hills and a forest peppered with cedars. Though not memorably scenic, it's very accommodating, with about 45 campsites in three separate camping areas, good boat launches, and room for big rigs. A few minutes east of

Hidden Lake is much smaller **Baird Lake**. It has two, small, separate camping areas. Check it out if you can't find peace at Hidden Lake.

Cooke Creek is about a 15-minute drive from Enderby, on pavement the whole way. The campground is a lovely, tranquil, shady haven where the creek flows into Shuswap River. Big rigs will find adequate space. The slow-moving river allows easy canoeing. Come here in fall to watch surging salmon.

Dale Lake is about a 20-minute drive from Enderby. It's north of Cooke Creek campground, in a group of dinky, shallow, marshy lakes. Ponds, really. The others are Elbow, Grassy and Spruce lakes. All have small camp-grounds with insufficient room for motorhomes or trailers. Dale has the best access and is the one you'll reach first. The road deteriorates beyond.

Noisy Creek helps keep massive Mabel Lake's fluid level topped up. It gurgles into the lake at the far northwest shore. The sprawling campground here is provincial-park quality. The view is world class. And in mid-summer, it seems the whole world has heard about this place. Expect a crowd. It was one of the first Forest Service campgrounds to have a per-night camping fee to help defray the cost of increased maintenance. But it's worth it. A short loop trail, the creek, broad beaches and pretty forest give you more to appreciate than at most campgrounds. The water's warm enough for a plunge in summer. The peninsula between the two camping areas offers a grand perspective on the lake.

A minor drawback: beachcombing bovines; better keep your sandals on. The major drawback: overpopularity; try to come before the long May weekend, or after mid-September. Noisy is about an hour's drive from Enderby. The final approach is a steep descent. Exiting, the stiff ascent could bully a weakling motorhome or trailer-tugger into backing down.

0 km (0 mi)
Starting east on Cliff Avenue, departing Hwy 97 in Enderby. Follow the sign for North Mabel Lake (37 km).

0.3 km (0.2 mi)
Cross a bridge over Shuswap River.

0.6 km (0.4 mi)
Proceed straight.

8.1 km (5.1 mi)
Cross a bridge over Brash Creek.

9.4 km (5.8 mi)
Pass Ashton General Store and curve right.

9.6 km (5.9 mi)
Reach a junction. Bear left (east) for Cooke Creek, Dale Lake, and Noisy Creek (Mabel Lake). Directions continue on page 234. Turn right (south) and reset your trip odometer to 0 for Hidden Lake.

0 km (0 mi)
Starting south, heading for Hidden Lake.

1.2 km (0.7 mi)
Cross a bridge over Shuswap River and bear left.

5.8 km (3.6 mi)
Reach a junction. Turn left. Pavement ends. Proceed east.

13.4 km (8.3 mi), 15 km (9.3 mi), and 15.9 km (9.9 mi)
Stay straight.

16.7 km (10.4 mi)
Bear right. Pass a KM 11 sign.

17.6 km (10.9 mi)
Bear left.

18.4 km (11.4 mi)
Hidden Lake is visible.

18.8 km (11.7 mi)
Arrive at Hidden Lake. Camping areas are on the southwest, southeast, and north shores.

HIDDEN LAKE CAMPGROUND #19
Weekend / Moderate / $ / May 1 to Sept 30
Elev: 655 m (2150 ft) / Lake: 2.2 km (1.4 mi) long, 131 ha
45 campsites, many with tables, boat launch
Accessible by motorhomes and 5th-wheels

Fork right (east), departing Hidden Lake's east shore road, to quickly reach tiny Baird Lake. The north and south shores each have one campsite.

BAIRD LAKE CAMPGROUND
Weekend / Moderate / $ / May 1 to Sept 30
Lake: 9 ha / 2 tables, cartop boat launch
Inaccessible by motorhomes and trailers

Continuing east at the 9.6-km (5.9-mi) junction, heading for Cooke Creek, Dale Lake, and Noisy Creek (Mabel Lake).

23 km (14.3 mi)
Cross a bridge over Fall Creek.

26.1 km (16.2 mi)
Proceed east on pavement for Noisy Creek (Mabel Lake). Turn left (north) onto Cooke Creek FS road to reach small Dale Lake campground in 4 km (2.5 mi)—it's just beyond the creek crossing, on the right fork. Turn right (south) to reach Cooke Creek campground on Shuswap River, 200 meters off pavement.

COOKE CREEK CAMPGROUND #20
Weekend / Easy / $ / May 1 to Sept 30
11 tables, boat launch / Accessible by motorhomes and 5th-wheels

Continuing east on pavement, passing the turnoffs to Dale Lake and Cooke Creek campgrounds.

30.6 km (19 mi)
Turn left onto Three Valley - Mabel FS road and reset your trip odometer to 0 for Noisy Creek campground on Mabel Lake's northwest shore. East on pavement is the short, direct route to Mabel Lake's west shore.

0 km (0 mi)
Turning left onto Three Valley - Mabel FS road.

11.9 km (7.4 mi)
Proceed straight and cross a small bridge.

13.7 km (8.5 mi)
Fork right. Beware of cattle.

20 km (12.4 mi)
Cross another small bridge.

21 km (13 mi)
Fork right. Begin the long, steep, final descent.

26.1 km (16.2 mi)
Arrive at Noisy Creek campground on Mabel Lake. Fork right or left for campsites.

Noisy Creek campground on Mabel Lake

NOISY CREEK CAMPGROUND #22

Destination / Difficult (due only to distance) / $ / May 1 to Sept 30
Elev: 393 m (1290 ft)
Lake: 35 km (21.7 mi) long, 2.2 km (1.4 mi) wide, 5942 ha
87 campsites, most with tables, 5 tent sites, cement boat launch
sandy beach, hiking trail
Accessible by motorhomes and 5th-wheels

~

VERNON TO LOWER ARROW LAKE

From Vernon, Hwy 6 plies pastoral valleys cradled by forested slopes, then gradually climbs through the Monashee Mountains before plummeting to Lower Arrow Lake. Standing between the Okanagan and Kootenay regions, the rounded Monashee peaks are indistinct. But the range is so lonesome, it feels wilder than some that are more photogenic. On a sunny, summer day, driving the highway as it spasms through the mountains southeast of Cherryville can be exhilarating.

If your direction of travel is flexible, drive Hwy 6 east. The scenery builds in that direction, climaxing with a view of Lower Arrow Lake—762 m (2500 ft) below. The Selkirk Mountains leap from the far shore and swagger off to the eastern horizon.

Two campgrounds on the east shore of **Mabel Lake** are your invitation to turn north off Hwy 6 at Lumby. Much of the way is paved. The lake is a whopper: 34.5 km (21.4 mi) long, 2.2 km (1.4 mi) wide, covering 5942 hectares. The elevation is 393 m (1290 ft). The setting is dramatic. Several walk-in campsites on the southeast shore allow you to pitch your tent in relative seclusion, and perhaps be monarch of your own beach for a day. Much farther north is Cottonwood Bay campground, accessible by big rigs if you can endure the paint-shaker effect for that distance.

Sugar Lake—12 km (7.5 mi) long, 4 km (2.5 mi) wide, covering 2130 hectares—is smaller than Mabel. But it's still big, and comparably beautiful. The elevation is slightly higher: 595 m (1952 ft). On the west shore are three tiny campgrounds, plus a huge one where even a converted school-bus can lumber in and out. On the east shore is a medium-size campground suitable for small motorhomes and trailers. Some campsites are treed, others are in the open. A few choice parcels of real estate have lake and mountain views. The pebble beaches allow your body to comfortably absorb all the harmful rays your brain will permit. When you're toasted on both sides, chill down in the lake.

Several campgrounds are located along the Kettle River, southwest of where Hwy 6 crosses Monashee Summit. The first two—Sandy Bend and

Kettle River—are close together, about a 15-minute drive off pavement. Bruer Creek has a swimming hole. Kettle has a large grassy area. The well-maintained backroad continues south into Kettle River Valley, described below at 83 km.

If Hwy 6 is simply part of your route between A and B, and a night's sleep is all you ask, a detour isn't necessary. Try Cherryville campground on **Shuswap River,** or Monashee-Kettle River campground near Monashee Summit. Considering how convenient they are, all both are surprisingly agreeable.

Remember that camping in the vicinity of Hwy 6, especially farther east toward Lower Arrow Lake, you'll be sharing the forest with bears. Black bears are prevalent. And the Monashee Mountains are grizzly bear habitat. Read *B.C. Stands for Bear Country* on page 33.

If you're heading southeast on Hwy 6, from Vernon

0 km (0 mi)
Starting east on Hwy 6, departing Hwy 97 at the east edge of Vernon, just before Polson Place Mall.

24.5 km (15.2 mi)
Reach Lumby. Proceed east on Hwy 6 for Sugar Lake and Lower Arrow Lake. Turn left (north) for Mabel Lake's east shore campgrounds. Directions continue on page 239.

49 km (30.4 mi)
Pass a sign stating the Monashee turnoff is 2 km ahead.

51 km (31.6 mi)
Reach Cherryville. Proceed southeast on Hwy 6 for Lower Arrow Lake. Turn left (northeast) onto Sugar Lake Road for campgrounds on Shuswap River and Sugar Lake. Directions continue on page 241.

83 km (51 mi)
Proceed southeast on Hwy 6 for Lower Arrow Lake. Turn right (south) onto Kettle River FS road and follow it southwest to reach Sandy Bend campground (just before a bridge) in about 13 km (8.1 mi). Just beyond (across the bridge, then left) is Kettle River campground. Together they have about 6 campsites. The road continues south 98 km (60 mi) through Kettle River Valley (bottom of page 224) to Hwy 33, passing more campgrounds en route.

89 km (55.2 mi)
Cross 1241-m (4070-ft) Monashee Summit. Lost Lake Rest Area is on the right. Proceed southeast on Hwy 6 for Lower Arrow Lake. Turn left (north) onto Keefer Lake Road for campgrounds on Kettle River and Holmes Lake. Directions continue on page 243.

Lower Arrow Lake ferry links Needles and Fauquier.

130.1 km (80.7 mi)
Proceed southeast on Hwy 6 to quickly reach Lower Arrow Lake. Turn left (north) onto Whatshan Lake FS road (following directions on page 269 in the Arrow and Kootenay Lakes chapter) to reach Whatshan Lake campgrounds on the north end in about 26 km (16 mi).

134.5 km (83.4 mi)
Reach Needles, on the west shore of Lower Arrow Lake. A free ferry crosses the lake to Fauquier, where Hwy 6 continues north along the east shore to Nakusp.

If you're heading northwest on Hwy 6, from Arrow Lake

0 km (0 mi)
Resuming on Hwy 6 from Needles, after disembarking the Lower Arrow Lake ferry on the west shore.

4.4 km (2.7 mi)
Proceed west on Hwy 6 for Sugar Lake, Mabel Lake, and Vernon. Turn right (north) onto Whatshan Lake FS road (following directions on page 269 in the Arrow and Kootenay Lakes chapter) to reach Whatshan Lake campgrounds on the north end in about 26 km (16 mi).

45.5 km (28.2 mi)
Cross 1241-m (4070-ft) Monashee Summit. Lost Lake Rest Area is on the left. Proceed west on Hwy 6 for Sugar Lake, Mabel Lake, and Vernon. Turn right (north) onto Keefer Lake Road for campgrounds on Kettle River and Holmes Lake. Directions continue on page 243.

51.5 km (31.9 mi)
Proceed northwest on Hwy 6 for Sugar Lake, Mabel Lake, and Vernon. Turn left (south) onto Kettle River FS road for Sandy Bend and Kettle River campgrounds. Directions continue on page 237 at the 83-km point.

83.5 km (51.8 mi)
Reach Cherryville. Proceed west on Hwy 6 for Mabel Lake and Vernon. Turn right (northeast) onto Sugar Lake Road for campgrounds on Shuswap River and Sugar Lake. Directions continue on page 241.

110 km (68.2 mi)
Reach Lumby. Proceed west on Hwy 6 for Vernon. Turn right (north) for Mabel Lake's east shore campgrounds. Directions continue below.

134.5 km (83.4 mi)
Intersect Hwy 97 at the east edge of Vernon, just after Polson Place Mall.

For MABEL LAKE'S EAST SHORE, now follow the directions below

0 km (0 mi)
Starting north, departing Hwy 6 in Lumby. Follow signs for Mabel Lake.

17 km (10.5 mi)
Proceed on the main road past Shuswap Falls.

28 km (17.4 mi)
Pavement ends. Proceed north on Mabel Lake FS road.

35 km (21.7 mi)
Mabel Lake is visible.

38 km (23.6 mi)
Pass Mabel Lake Provincial Park.

42.5 km (26.4 mi)
Reach trails on the left leading to Cascade South walk-in tent sites on Mabel Lake. They start near a sharp bend in the road. The first (south) site is a couple minutes from the road; others are a bit farther.

Sugar Lake

CASCADE SOUTH CAMPGROUND #15
Weekend / Moderate / Free
3 walk-in tent sites, good beaches
Parking accessible by all vehicles

Continuing north on Mabel Lake FS road, passing Cascade South walk-in tent sites.

43.2 km (26.8 mi)
Reach a trail on the right leading to Cascade Falls. It's about a 10-minute ascent to the picnic table at the falls.

43.5 km (27 mi)
Reach a trail on the left leading to another Mabel Lake walk-in tent site.

55.3 km (34.3 mi)
Turn left and descend to quickly reach Cottonwood Bay campground on Mabel Lake. Mabel Lake FS road continues generally north, passing campgrounds at Wap Lake and Frog Falls (described on page 263) shortly before intersecting Trans-Canada Hwy 1 at Three Valley Gap in about 55 km (34 mi).

COTTONWOOD BAY CAMPGROUND #16

Destination / Difficult (due only to distance) / $ / May 1 – Sept 30
10 tables, 20 campsites, sandy beach, cartop boat launch
Accessible by motorhomes and 5th-wheels

~

**For SHUSWAP RIVER and SUGAR LAKE,
now follow the directions below**

0 km (0 mi)
Starting (northeast) on Sugar Lake Road, departing Hwy 6 at Cherryville.

2.6 km (1.6 mi)
Cross a bridge over Cherry Creek.

5.5 km (3.4 mi)
Proceed northeast for Sugar Lake. Turn left to reach Cherryville campground in 0.5 km (0.3 mi). It's a grassy clearing in forest, beside Shuswap River.

CHERRYVILLE CAMPGROUND #9

Overnight / Easy / Free
2 tables, many more campsites
Accessible by small motorhomes and trailers

~

Continuing northeast on Sugar Lake Road, passing the turnoff to Cherryville campground.

13.2 km (8.2 mi)
Pavement ends.

16.3 km (10.1 mi)
Reach a junction near the south end of Sugar Lake. Proceed left for several campgrounds on the west shore. Turn right onto Kate Creek FS road and reset your trip odometer to 0 for Sugar Creek campground on the lake's east shore.

0 km (0 mi)
Starting east on Kate Creek FS road. Soon cross the bridge over Outlet Creek, then bear left and head north. After paralleling Sugar Lake's southeast shore, the road veers east again.

12 km (7.4 mi)
Cross the bridge over Sitkum Creek, then bear left (west).

14 km (8.7 mi)
Fork left to quickly reach Sugar Creek campground. Fork right and
ascend about 3 km (1.7 mi) to a trailhead just past Sugar Creek. From
there you can hike about 7 km to either the summit of Sugar Mountain
or a campsite at Kate Lake.

SUGAR CREEK CAMPGROUND #14
Destination / Moderate / $ / April 1 – Oct 31
10 campsites, a few tables, cartop boat launch, good beach
Accessible by small motorhomes and trailers

*Continuing left at the 16.3-km (10.1-mi) junction, passing the turnoff to Sugar
Creek campground.*

16.8 km (10.4 mi)
Go left, following the sign for Monashee Provincial Park. Pass a commercial
fishing camp on the right.

17.4 km (10.8 mi)
Go right at the junction.

18.2 km (11.3 mi)
Proceed north along the west shore for more campgrounds. Turn right to
enter Sugar 1-Mile campground.

SUGAR 1-MILE CAMPGROUND #10
Weekend / Easy / $ / April 1 – Oct 31
1 table, cartop boat launch
Accessible by small motorhomes and trailers

20.1 km (12.5 mi)
Proceed north along the west shore for two small campgrounds. Turn right
to enter Sugar 2-Mile campground.

SUGAR 2-MILE CAMPGROUND #11
Destination / Easy / $ / April 1 – Oct 31
20 tables, many more campsites, tent sites, boat launch
Accessible by motorhomes and 5th-wheels

21.7 km (13.5 mi)
Proceed north along the west shore for another small campground. Turn
right to enter Sugar 3-Mile campground.

SUGAR 3-MILE CAMPGROUND #12
Weekend / Easy / $ / April 1 – Oct 31
1 table, creeklet, cartop boat launch
Accessible by small motorhomes and trailers

22.5 km (14 mi)
Proceed north for Monashee Provincial Park trailhead. Turn right to enter
Sugar 3½-Mile campground.

SUGAR 3½-MILE CAMPGROUND #13
Weekend / Easy / $ / April 1 – Oct 31
1 table, creeklet, cartop boat launch
Accessible by small motorhomes and trailers

**For KETTLE RIVER and HOLMES LAKE,
now follow the directions below**

0 km (0 mi)
Starting north on Keefer Lake Road, departing Hwy 6.

1 km (0.6 mi)
Reach Monashee Kettle River campground on the left, just after crossing a
bridge to the river's northwest bank.

MONASHEE KETTLE RIVER CAMPGROUND #39
Overnight / Easy / Free
1 table, 2 campsites, grassy area for tents
Accessible by motorhomes and 5th-wheels

Keefer Lake Road continues generally northeast, following the river about
another 15 km (9.3 mi) to its source at Keefer Lake. Fork left at the lake's
west end, then proceed east along the north shore. A few minutes beyond
Keefer Lake is a free campground on smaller Holmes Lakes.

HOLMES LAKE CAMPGROUND #40
Weekend / Moderate / Free
Lake: 34 ha
4 campsites, a couple tables
Inaccessible by motorhomes and trailers

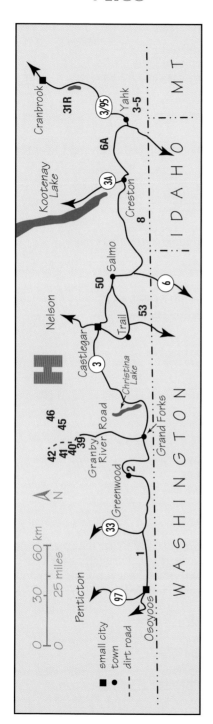

H: Boundary Country

Boundary Country

Boundary Lake

In its east-west journey along the Canada-U.S. boundary, Hwy 3 ricochets north and south like a cartoon bullet. Between Cranbrook in the east, Osoyoos in the west, it travels up and down passes, in and out of valleys, offering numerous access points for campgrounds.

Read the brief campground descriptions below. After choosing your destination, check where to turn off the highway. Then turn to the page indicated for route details.

Near Bridesville is a small, little-used campground on **Jolly Creek.** It's in a lush, lumpy meadow, wedged in a ravine, beneath rolling mountains. Trees are few. There's sufficient space for small motorhomes and trailers. Tenters will appreciate all the grass if they can find a level patch. You'll see wild rose here in spring; golden larches in fall.

Departing Hwy 3 at Rock Creek, Hwy 33 heads north, accessing **Kettle River Valley** at Westbridge. The Kettle River has excellent riverside campgrounds and enticing swimming holes. Though the Kettle is in Boundary

Country, we describe it with the rest of Hwy 33, in the Okanagan Highland and Monashee Mountains chapter (page 226).

The community of **Greenwood** has a low-fee campground. The charming town is well worth a stop even if you don't camp. It flourished during an 1890s mining boom. Many historic buildings have been restored. If you prefer lonelier camping, but want to stay near Greenwood, a ten-minute drive east into the hills will bring you to a mediocre campground at **Providence (Marshall) Lake**. The road is paved much of the way, but motorhomes and trailers will struggle on the steep ascent, only to be thwarted by the final, rough approach.

North of Grand Forks is the beautiful **Granby River valley**. The hilly terrain is a crazy quilt of meadows, forest, and rock outcroppings. Road cyclists should take advantage of the paved road probing the valley for more than 40 km (25 mi). Granby-Burrell and Bluejoint Creek campgrounds have enough space for small motorhomes and trailers. Up valley are more campgrounds. At road's end, hikers can venture north into Granby Provincial Park. A 4.5-km (2.8-mi) riverside trail through hemlock-and-cedar forest pierces the park boundary then forges 8 km (5 mi) deeper.

Southeast of Trail, the Pend-d'Oreille River loops into B.C. for just 24 km (15 mi). Canadians seized the opportunity, damming the river before it joins the Columbia and escapes back into the U.S. The result is called **Pend d'Oreille Reservoir**. In a meadow beside the dam is Buckley campground, managed by BC Hydro. Like all their campgrounds, this one is smartly organized, well maintained, roomy enough for big RVs, and free to the public.

The campground on sparkling, clear **Erie Creek** is about a ten-minute drive west of Salmo. Though its in mixed forest, a clearcut hillside is visible. Two individual, treed campsites offer privacy from the main camping area. Space is inadequate for motorhomes and trailers. The creek bank has sandy beaches. The area's roadside berry bushes offer fruitful picking in season.

Boundary Lake is in a narrow mountain basin just inside Canada, southeast of Stagleap Park. The campground has several sites on the lakeshore and accommodates motorhomes and 5th-wheels. The forest has enough big trees to be admirable. Come here to fish, canoe or swim. It gets buggy, so bring your anti-insect arsenal.

Between Creston and Yahk is a campground in **Goat River Canyon**. It's spacious enough to lay out the welcome mat for your small motorhome or trailer. The forest is open, but there's little to look at. From the campsites, you can't even see the river, though it's audible. The deep pool by the bridge is a swimmer's delight. There's also a short trail along the riverbank.

Wood lilies

The campgrounds along gentle **Hawkins Creek,** just outside Yahk, are handy for cross-province travellers. Access is quick and easy. Stop here overnight, or just to rest your road-weary brain. The campsites are suitable for only the smallest motorhomes and trailers.

Monroe Lake is a very convenient campground: south of Cranbrook, just off the highway, near the provincial park at the north end of Moyie Lake. Space is adequate for small motorhomes and trailers. The access road is even paved. But the lake is small, private cabins are nearby, and the area is busy, so don't expect a wilderness experience.

If you're heading east on Hwy 3, between Osoyoos and Cranbrook

For **Jolly Creek,** drive Hwy 3 east 2.7 km (1.7 mi) from the hamlet of Bridesville. Turn left (north) just before Rock Creek Canyon bridge and reset your trip odometer to 0. Directions continue on page 249.

For **Greenwood,** drive Hwy 3 east 22 km (13.6 mi) from the village of Rock Creek at the junction of Hwys 3 and 33. For **Providence Lake,** turn right (east) onto Greenwood Road (in the business district) and reset your trip odometer to 0. Directions continue on page 250.

For **Granby River valley,** drive Hwy 3 east of Greenwood to Grand Forks. Just after crossing the Granby River bridge, turn left (north) onto Granby Road and reset your trip odometer to 0. Directions continue on page 251.

For **Pend d'Oreille Reservoir,** drive Hwy 3 northeast of Christina Lake to Castlegar, then Hwy 22 south to Trail, then Hwy 3B southeast to Waneta Junction, and finally Hwy 22A south. Just north of Waneta, turn left (southeast) onto Seven Mile Dam road. Directions continue on page 254.

For **Erie Creek,** drive Hwy 3 east of Castlegar. Proceed 7 km (4.3 mi) past the Hwy 3B junction. Just after crossing the small bridge over Erie Creek, turn left (north) onto Second Relief Road and reset your trip odometer to 0. Directions continue on page 254.

For **Boundary Lake,** drive Hwy 3 east of Salmo. Proceed 16.2 km (10 mi) beyond Kootenay Pass summit in Stagleap Provincial Park. Turn sharp right (southwest) onto Maryland Creek FS road and reset your trip odometer to 0. Directions continue on page 255.

For **Goat River Canyon,** drive Hwy 3 east 21 km (13 mi) from Hwy 3A at the north end of Creston. Turn left (north) onto Leadville Road at the café in Kitchener. Reset your trip odometer to 0. Directions continue on page 256.

For **Hawkins Creek,** drive Hwy 3 northeast 1 km (0.6 mi) from Yahk Provincial Park. Immediately after crossing the bridge over Moyie River, turn right (southeast) onto Yahk Meadow Creek Road and reset your trip odometer to 0. Directions continue on page 256.

For **Monroe Lake** drive Hwy 3 north 12.5 km (7.8 mi) from the community of Moyie. Turn left (southwest) onto Monroe Lake Road (signed for Moyie Lake Provincial Park) and reset your trip odometer to 0. Directions continue on page 257.

If you're heading west on Hwy 3, between Cranbrook and Osoyoos

For **Monroe Lake** drive Hwy 3 southwest 17 km (10.5 mi) from the Travel Info Centre on the southwest edge of Cranbrook. Turn right (southwest) onto Monroe Lake Road (signed for Moyie Lake Provincial Park) and reset your trip odometer to 0. Directions continue on page 257.

For **Hawkins Creek,** drive Hwy 3 southwest 32.5 km (20 mi) from the community of Moyie. Just before the bridge over Moyie River, turn left (southeast) onto Yahk Meadow Creek Road and reset your trip odometer to 0. Directions continue on page 256.

For **Goat River Canyon,** drive Hwy 3 west 19.5 km (12.1 mi) from Hwy 95 just southwest of Yahk. Turn right (north) onto Leadville Road at the café in Kitchener. Reset your trip odometer to 0. Directions continue on page 256.

For **Boundary Lake,** drive Hwy 3 west from Hwy 3A at the north end of Creston. At 4.2 km (2.6 mi) cross the Kootenay River bridge. At 22 km (13.6 mi) pass a rest area on the left. At 28.7 km (17.8 mi) turn left (southwest) onto Maryland Creek FS road and reset your trip odometer to 0. Directions continue on page 255.

For **Erie Creek,** drive Hwy 3 west 3.6 km (2.2 mi) from Salmo. Just before the small bridge over Erie Creek, turn right (north) onto Second Relief Road and reset your trip odometer to 0. Directions continue on page 254.

For **Pend d'Oreille Reservoir,** drive Hwy 3 west of Salmo, then Hwy 3B southwest to Waneta Junction, and finally Hwy 22A south. Just north of Waneta, turn left (southeast) onto Seven Mile Dam road. Directions continue on page 254.

For **Granby River valley,** drive Hwy 3 west of Christina Lake to Grand Forks. Just before crossing the Granby River bridge, turn right (north) onto Granby Road and reset your trip odometer to 0. Directions continue on page 251.

For **Greenwood,** drive Hwy 3 west of Grand Forks. For **Providence Lake,** turn left (east) onto Greenwood Road (in the business district) and reset your trip odometer to 0. Directions continue on page 250.

For **Jolly Creek,** drive Hwy 3 west 12.7 km (7.9 mi) from the village of Rock Creek at the junction of Hwys 3 and 33. Turn right (north) just after Rock Creek Canyon bridge and reset your trip odometer to 0. Directions continue below.

For JOLLY CREEK, now follow the directions below

0 km (0 mi)
Starting north on the road signed for Mt. Baldy Ski Area, departing Hwy 3 just west of Rock Creek Canyon bridge.

1.7 km (1.1 mi)
Turn right onto Canyon Road and descend to the canyon floor.

2.5 km (1.6 mi)
Turn right to enter Jolly Creek campground, across from an historic cabin. The site is actually on Rock Creek. Jolly Creek is farther up towards Little Fish lake.

Settlers' cabin near Jolly Creek

JOLLY CREEK CAMPGROUND #1
Weekend / Easy / Free
3 tables
Accessible by small motorhomes and trailers

For PROVIDENCE LAKE, now follow the directions below

0 km (0 mi)
Starting east on Greenwood Street, departing Hwy 3 in Greenwood. Pass the historic post office and ascend.

6.8 km (4.2 mi)
Pavement ends.

7.7 km (4.8 mi) and 8.2 km (5.1 mi)
Turn left.

8.4 km (5.2 mi)
Reach a clearing beside Providence Lake. Skirt the west shore on a rough, potentially very muddy road to reach the small campground across the lake.

8.6 km (5.3 mi)
Arrive at Providence Lake campground.

PROVIDENCE LAKE CAMPGROUND #2
Overnight / Easy / Free
Elev: 1386 m (4546 ft) / Lake: 5.5 ha
2 tables, cooking shelter
Inaccessible by motorhomes and trailers

For GRANBY RIVER VALLEY, now follow the directions below

0 km (0 mi)
Starting north on North Fork Road, departing Hwy 3 in Grand Forks, just
east of the Granby River bridge.

16.2 km (10 mi)
Reach a junction. Turn right and proceed north, up valley, along Granby
River's east bank.

44.3 km (27.5 mi)
Pavement ends. Turn left onto Granby River FS road and cross Burrell
Creek bridge. Granby-Burrell campground is immediately on the left, at the
river/creek confluence. Proceed northwest, along the river's east bank, to
reach four more campgrounds en route to Granby Provincial Park. Just
beyond Burrell Creek bridge, turn right (north) onto Burrell Creek FS road
and reset your trip odometer to 0 for two more campgrounds.

A rocky bluff called Bunch Grass Hill is visible from the campground.
There's a deep swimming hole beneath the bridge.

GRANBY - BURRELL CAMPGROUND #39
Weekend / Easy / Free
2 tables, grassy tent sites
Accessible by small motorhomes and trailers

*Turning right (north) onto Burrell Creek FS road, just beyond Granby-Burrell
campground.*

0 km (0 mi)
Starting north on Burrell Creek FS road, soon following the west bank of
Burrell Creek.

7 km (4.3 mi)
Bear left onto Franklin Mine road, staying on the creek's west bank. Burrell
Creek FS road goes right, crossing a bridge to the east bank. It continues

northeast, eventually reaching Edgewood, on Lower Arrow Lake. From there, a paved road leads north to Hwy 6 and the Needles - Fauquier ferry.

11 km (6.8 mi)
Reach Bluejoint Creek campground on the right.

BLUEJOINT CREEK CAMPGROUND #45
Overnight / Moderate / Free
1 table, grassy area
Accessible by small motorhomes and trailers

14.5 km (9 mi)
Reach St. Annes Meadow campground on the right.

ST. ANNES MEADOW CAMPGROUND #46
Overnight / Moderate / Free
2 tables / Inaccessible by motorhomes and trailers

Continuing northwest on Granby River FS road, passing Granby-Burrell campground and Burrell Creek FS road.

49.4 km (30.6 mi)
Proceed north on Granby River FS road for three more campgrounds and the provincial park. Fork left and descend to reach tiny Gable Creek campground in 1.5 km (0.9 mi). It's on the Granby River, near the confluence with Gable Creek. Even in summer, it's shaded here by mid afternoon.

GABLE CREEK CAMPGROUND #40
Weekend / Easy / Free
1 table / Accessible by small motorhomes and trailers

Continuing north on Granby River FS road, passing the turnoff to Gable Creek campground.

59.3 km (36.8 mi)
Proceed north on Granby River FS road for one more campground (4WD access only) and the provincial park. Fork left to reach two campgrounds on Granby River's west bank.

Descend, cross a bridge over Granby River, and reach a T-junction. Turn left (south) to reach small Eight Mile Flats campground #41 in

Confluence of Granby River and Burrell Creek

about 3 km (1.9 mi). Turn right (north), then right at the next junction, to reach large Howe Creek campground #42 in about 3 km (1.9 mi).

Continuing north on Granby River FS road, passing the turnoff to Eight Mile Flats and Howe Creek campgrounds.

61 km (37.8 mi)
Reach a junction. Bear right for the 2WD-accessible provincial park trailhead. Left is a rough 4WD road fording Howe Creek—only possible in summer, when the water's low. Beyond the ford, bear left and proceed north to reach small Traverse Creek campground #44, at the actual provincial-park trailhead, in about 4 km (2.5 mi).

61.5 km (38.1 mi)
Turn left, cross the Howe Creek bridge, and look for a signed trail on the left. Park here to begin hiking to the provincial park. In about 1 km (0.6 mi) the trail intersects a small road. Follow it left. Soon join the road that fords Howe Creek. Bear right and proceed north to reach small Traverse Creek campground #44, at the actual provincial-park trailhead, in about 4 km (2.5 mi).

For PEND d'OREILLE RESERVOIR, now follow the directions below

0 km (0 mi)
Starting south on Hwy 22A, departing Hwy 3B at Waneta Junction.

6.3 km (3.9 mi)
Turn left (southeast) onto Seven Mile Dam Road.

19.3 km (12 mi)
Pass Seven Mile Dam.

20.5 km (12.7 mi)
Reach Buckley campground, on the right.

BUCKLEY CAMPGROUND #53

Weekend / Easy / Free, open May 1 – Sept 30
22 campsites with tables and fire rings, beach, grassy area
designated wheelchair accessible campsites and pit toilets
gravel boat launch, 60 meters of boarding floats, garbage cans
free firewood, drinking water
Accessible by motorhomes and 5th-wheels

For ERIE CREEK, now follow the directions below

0 km (0 mi)
Starting north on Second Relief Road, departing Hwy 3. Pavement ends in 200 meters.

0.8 km (0.5 mi)
Go left onto Erie Creek FS road.

7 km (4.3 mi)
Fork left.

8.5 km (5.3 mi)
Bear left and descend into the valley.

10 km (6.2 mi)
Turn left and cross Erie Creek. The campground is on the right, just after the bridge.

ERIE CREEK CAMPGROUND #50

Weekend / Easy / Free
5 tables
Too small for motorhomes and trailers

For BOUNDARY LAKE, now follow the directions below

0 km (0 mi)
Starting southwest on Maryland Creek FS road, departing Hwy 3. It drops below the highway, across from Jordan's historic log cabin.

1.1 km (0.7 mi)
Cross a bridge over Summer Creek.

2.7 km (1.7 mi)
Go right at the junction and ascend steeply.

6.9 km (4.3 mi)
Go right at the junction.

9.1 km (5.6 mi)
Stay right on the main road. It levels out in a meadow. Proceed through an upper valley and descend gradually.

13.7 km (8.5 mi)
Fork left.

13.9 km (8.6 mi)
Stay straight on the main road.

16.7 km (10.4 mi)
Bear left on the main road.

17.7 km (11 mi)
Boundary Lake is visible below to the right.

18 km (11.2 mi)
Turn sharply right and descend.

18.2 km (11.3 mi)
Arrive at Boundary Lake campground. Go either way to reach campsites.

BOUNDARY LAKE CAMPGROUND #8

Weekend / Moderate / Free
Elev: 1220 m (4000 ft) / Lake: 25 ha
11 tables, 3 wharves, small beach
Accessible by motorhomes and 5th-wheels

For GOAT RIVER CANYON, now follow the directions below

0 km (0 mi)
Starting north on Leadville Road, departing Hwy 3 at Kitchener.

0.5 km (0.3 mi)
Cross a bridge over Meadow Creek. Immediately after, stay straight on the main road.

7.4 km (4.6 mi)
Proceed straight on the main road. Anchor Creek FS road forks right.

8.1 km (5 mi)
Stay left. Leadville Creek FS road forks right.

10.9 km (6.8 mi)
Cross a wooden bridge over a deep swimming hole on Goat River.

11 km (6.8 mi)
Turn left (south) just before another bridge. This final approach is narrow, but the road is good.

11.7 km (7.3 mi)
Arrive at Goat River Canyon campground.

GOAT RIVER CANYON CAMPGROUND #6
Weekend / Easy / Free
7 tables
Accessible by small motorhomes and trailers

For HAWKINS CREEK, now follow the directions below

0 km (0 mi)
Starting southeast on Yahk Meadow Creek Road, departing Hwy 3 at Yahk. In 100 meters proceed straight where River Avenue forks right. Pavement ends 0.7 km (0.4 mi) beyond.

3.8 km (2.4 mi)
Reach Hawkins Creek campground #5, on the right. It has 4 tables. For more campgrounds, proceed southeast on the main road, staying on the northeast side of Hawkins Creek.

7.2 km (4.5 mi)
Turn right through a clearing to reach Canuck Creek campground #4 in 200 meters. It has 4 tables at well-spaced campsites beside the creek.

Goat River

A scenic waterfall is just downstream. For more campgrounds, proceed southeast on the main road.

9 km (5.6 mi)
Reach America Creek campground #3, on the right. It has 5 tables near the creek. For one more small campground, proceed east the main road.

20 km (12.4 mi)
Reach Cold Creek campground #2. It has 2 tables.

For MONROE LAKE, now follow the directions below

0 km (0 mi)
Starting southwest on paved Monroe Lake Road, departing Hwy 3.
Bear right in 700 meters.

2.3 km (1.4 mi)
Reach a junction. Turn right, staying on pavement, to reach Monroe Lake campground in about 1 km (0.6 mi). Straight on unpaved Lamb Creek road reaches Mineral Lake day-use area in 1.5 km (0.9 mi).

MONROE LAKE CAMPGROUND #7
Overnight / Easy / Free
Elev: 1067 m (3500 ft) / Lake: 51.5 ha
5 tables, gravel boat launch
Accessible by small motorhomes and trailers

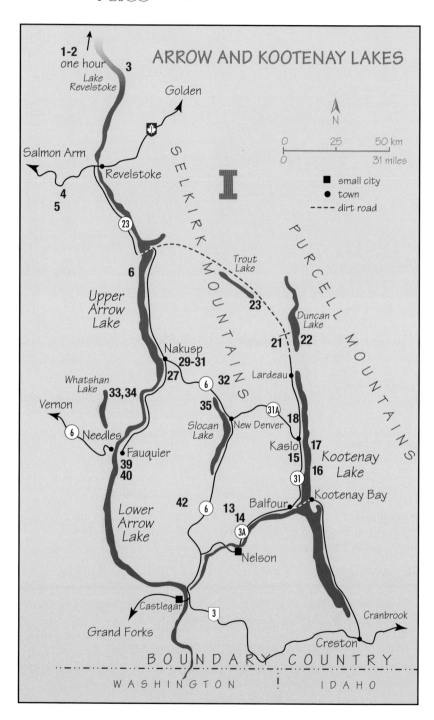

ARROW AND KOOTENAY LAKES

1-2
one hour
3
Lake
Revelstoke

Golden

Salmon Arm

Revelstoke

23

6

Upper
Arrow
Lake

4
5

Trout
Lake

23

Duncan
Lake

21   22

Nakusp
29-31

27   32   Lardeau

Whatshan
Lake   33,34

35

31A

18

Vernon

6   Needles

Fauquier

39
40

Slocan
Lake   New Denver

Kaslo   17

15   16

31

Kootenay
Lake

Lower
Arrow
Lake

42   6   13   Balfour

14

3A

Kootenay Bay

Nelson

Castlegar

Grand Forks

3

Cranbrook

Creston

B O U N D A R Y   C O U N T R Y

WASHINGTON   IDAHO

SELKIRK MOUNTAINS

PURCELL MOUNTAINS

N

0   25   50 km
0   31 miles

■ small city
● town
- - - dirt road

I: Arrow and Kootenay Lakes

At Garland Bay campground, fees apply daily from May 1 through October 31.

1	Pitt Creek	FREE
2	Potlatch Creek	FREE
3	Carnes Creek	$
4	Frog Falls	FREE
5	Wap Lake	FREE
6	Eagle Bay	FREE
13	Sasquatch Lake	FREE
14	Six-Mile Lakes	FREE
15	Fletcher Falls	FREE
16	Pebble Beach	FREE
17	Garland Bay	$
18	Milford Lake	FREE
21	Howser Glayco	FREE
22	Glacier Creek	FREE
23	Gerrard	FREE
27	Box Lake	FREE
29	Wilson Lake West	FREE
30	Wilson Lake East	FREE
31	Little Wilson Lake	FREE
32	Beaver Lake	FREE
33	Stevens Creek	FREE
34	Richy	FREE
35	Wragge Beach	$
39	Taite Creek	FREE
40	Octopus Creek	FREE
42	Little Slocan Lakes	FREE

Arrow and Kootenay Lakes

Kootenay Lake and the Purcell Mountains, from Kaslo

Like beads of sweat on straining, bulging muscles, water trickles down from the Kootenay mountain summits. Rivulets gather speed and volume, cascading into the region's inland fiords—great veins of water so deep, cold and clean that lakeshore residents pump it up to their homes and drink it unfiltered.

Upper and Lower Arrow lakes are actually a single reservoir dammed near Castlegar. It stretches 230 km (143 mi) to Revelstoke. Just north of town, the dams and reservoirs resume, with Lake Revelstoke and **Kinbasket Lake** created in the image of a taffy pull. Their combined length is 346 km (215 mi). **Kootenay Lake** is 110 km (68 mi) long, 2 to 6 km (1.2 to 3.7 mi) wide, with an additional 30-km (18.6-mi) tentacle reaching to Nelson. Small only by local comparison are 40-km (25-mi) **Slocan Lake** and 44-km (27.3-mi) **Duncan Lake**. Free campgrounds on the shores of these oceanic bodies and other lesser lakes are ideal retreats for pondering the big question: explore further, or just stay put?

On such vast liquid spaces, boating becomes travelling. But why restrict yourself to a horizontal plane? This isn't the prairie. You have another option. Up. In this part of B.C., if it's not submerged, it's vertical. Three distinct mountain ranges give the area, generally referred to as the Kootenays, a tightly pleated, accordion topography.

To the west are the gentle, rounded Monashees Mountains. The spikier Selkirks shoulder their way between the Arrow Lakes and Slocan Valley. These ranges fueled gold, silver and copper booms in the 1890s. New Denver, Silverton, Slocan, Sandon and Kaslo began as mining settlements. Farther east, the craggy Purcells separate the Kootenays from the Rocky Mountain Trench. The only way to fully appreciate this land is to ascend the peaks on foot. Read the hiking guide *Where Locals Hike in the West Kootenay*. It's described on page 536.

Kootenay towns are small. The land's skyward tilt limits population growth. Skinny lakeshores, slender valleys, and steep slopes grant livable real estate begrudgingly. Only trees flourish in great numbers here. Hospitable forests host mountainside parties, welcoming the usual gang: fir, pine, birch, spruce, larch. In a few isolated nooks, single-variety stands of cedar or hemlock spurn the festivities and refuse to socialize.

To sample the Kootenays from the road, drive or cycle the *Silver Triangle*. Start in Nelson. Follow Hwys 3A and 31 north up the west shore of Kootenay Lake to Kaslo. Turn east onto Hwy 31A and climb over the mountains to New Denver, where you can gaze across Slocan Lake to the Valhallas. Then head south on Hwy 6, through Slocan Valley, back to Hwy 3A and Nelson.

A more adventurous, north-Kootenay loop starts in Kaslo and passes several campgrounds. Drive Hwy 31 north, following the northwest shore of Kootenay Lake. Pavement ends near Duncan Lake, but the road proceeding

Relics from West Kootenay mining days

northwest is well maintained. After paralleling the northeast shore of Trout Lake, regain pavement. Curve southwest to Galena Bay, on Upper Arrow Lake. Continue south on Hwy 23, along Upper Arrow's east shore, to Nakusp. From there, a mountainous traverse southeast via Hwy 6 leads to New Denver, on Slocan Lake. Finally, turn east onto Hwy 31A and climb yet more mountains back to Kaslo.

Touring the Kootenays, you'll appreciate the shortcuts that ferries provide across the formidable lakes. But in summer, the prelude to a carefree crossing is usually a frustrating delay in a long line of vehicles waiting to board. You might have to hang out—are you sitting down?—for up to two hours.

On Kootenay Lake, a ferry shuttles between Balfour on the west shore and Kootenay Bay on the east. Departures are every 50 minutes in summer. The Balfour schedule is 6 a.m. to 12:20 a.m. The Kootenay Bay schedule is 6:50 a.m. to 1 a.m. The 9-km (5.6-mi) crossing takes 40 minutes.

On Upper Arrow Lake, a ferry links Galena Bay on the east shore with Shelter Bay on the west. Departures are every hour. The Galena Bay schedule is 5:30 a.m. to 10:30 p.m., plus 12:30 a.m. The Shelter Bay schedule is 5 a.m. to midnight. The 5-km (3-mi) crossing takes 30 minutes.

NEAR REVELSTOKE

Three campgrounds close to Trans-Canada Hwy 1 are convenient for a brief overnight stop en route to or from the West Kootenay or Rockies. Frog Falls and Wap Lake campgrounds are west of Revelstoke, south of Three Valley Gap.

FROG FALLS and WAP LAKE

If you're heading west on Hwy 1, from Revelstoke

Set your trip odometer to 0 midway across the Columbia River bridge, on the west side of Revelstoke. Proceed west on Hwy 1. At 19 km (11.8 mi) pass Three Valley Gap, at the east end of Three Valley Lake. At 21.3 km (13.3 mi) pass the rest area beside Three Valley Lake. At 21.9 km (13.6 mi) turn left (south) onto Three Valley-Mabel Lake FS road (across from a large, paved pullout) and reset your trip odometer to 0.

If you're heading northeast on Hwy 1, from Sicamous

Set your trip odometer to 0 at the junction of Hwys 1 and 97A, by the Shell and Petro Canada gas stations in Sicamous. Proceed northeast on Hwy 1. At 48.2 km (29.9 mi) cross a bridge at the northwest end of Three Valley Lake. Slow down. At 49.3 km (30.6 mi) turn right (south) onto Three Valley-Mabel Lake FS road (across from a large, paved pullout) and reset your trip odometer to 0.

For either approach above, now follow the directions below

0 km (0 mi)
Starting south on Three Valley-Mabel Lake FS road, departing Hwy 1. Ignore spurs forking right and left.

2.7 km (1.7 mi)
Proceed south on the main road.

4.4 km (2.7 mi)
Proceed southwest on the main road for Wap Lake. Turn left, just before the bridge, to quickly reach Frog Falls campground.

FROG FALLS CAMPGROUND #4
Overnight / Easy / Free
5 tables
Accessible by motorhomes and 5th-wheels

Continuing southwest on the main road, passing the turnoff to Frog Falls campground and crossing the bridged creek.

4.7 km (2.9 mi)
Proceed southwest on the main road.

11 km (6.8 mi)
Arrive at Wap Lake campground, beside the road, on the southwest shore. The main road continues south to Mabel Lake, eventually reaching Cottonwood Bay campground (page 241) on the east shore.

WAP LAKE CAMPGROUND #5
Overnight / Easy / Free
Lake: 36 ha
2 tables
Accessible by motorhomes and 5th-wheels

~

LAKE REVELSTOKE & KINBASKET LAKE

Hwy 23 glides north from Revelstoke, following the east shore of Lake Revelstoke—a 130-km (80-mi) long reservoir at 570 m (1870 ft) elevation. At its north end is 242-m (795-ft) high Mica Dam, BC Hydro's third largest power producer and North America's biggest earth-filled dam. Behind it is yet another reservoir: 216-km (134-mi) long Kinbasket Lake. It covers 41,590 hectares at 755 m (2476 ft) elevation. Beyond are the glacier-mantled Rocky Mountains. Lake Revelstoke has two campgrounds reached via paved road. Kinbasket Lake has one campground just beyond where pavement ends.

The first campground on Lake Revelstoke, **Carnes Creek**, is about a half-hour drive from Hwy 1. It's provincial-park quality. North of it is a trail ascending to an alpine ridge on Standard Peak, where the mountain-and-glacier vista is spectacular. **Pitt Creek** is the next campground on Lake Revelstoke. It's nearly an hour's drive beyond Carnes. **Potlatch Creek**, the campground on Kinbasket Lake, is near road's end, about a two-hour drive from Hwy 1.

Looking at a map, you might assume this is lonely, wild country. It's not. Most of the forest within sight has been logged intensely. Mica Dam and the paved road ensure a light but steady flow of vehicles. Something else a highway map won't show you is that the immediate topography is rather dull. You won't be admiring grand mountains along the way. The view across Kinbasket Lake is impressive, but it doesn't justify the long drive. You're a boater? Hot to explore Kinbasket Lake? Come on up. All the campgrounds have boat launches. And just beyond Potlatch, you'll find a multiseason, cement boat launch at **Sprague Bay**.

0 km (0 mi)
Starting north on Hwy 23, departing Trans-Canada Hwy 1 just east of the
Columbia River bridge in Revelstoke.

35 km (21.7 mi)
Proceed north for Kinbasket Lake. Turn left, just after crossing Carnes
Creek bridge, for Carnes Creek campground on Lake Revelstoke.

CARNES CREEK CAMPGROUND #3
Weekend / Easy / $ / May 15 – Sept 15
25 campsites with tables, boat launch
Accessible by motorhomes and 5th wheels

50 km (31 mi)
Proceed north for Kinbasket Lake. Turn right to reach Standard Peak trailhead in about 15 km (9.3 mi). The ascent is rough but passable in a 2WD
car. The trail leads about 11 km (6.8 mi) gaining 600 m (1970 ft) to a cabin in
Keystone-Standard Basin.

135 km (83.7 mi)
Proceed north for Kinbasket Lake. Turn left for Pitt Creek campground on
Lake Revelstoke.

PITT CREEK CAMPGROUND #1
Weekend / Easy / Free
6 tables, rough boat launch
Accessible by motorhomes and 5th-wheels

140 km (86.8 mi)
Proceed through the village of Mica Creek.

148 km (91.8 mi)
Pass Mica Dam. Pavement ends. Proceed on Redrock FS road.

150.5 km (93.3 mi)
Reach Potlatch Creek campground on Kinbasket Lake, on the left. Proceed
generally east, following the south shore, for Sprague Bay.

POTLATCH CREEK CAMPGROUND #2
Weekend / Easy / Free
15 well-spaced campsites with tables, boat launch
Accessible by motorhomes and 5th-wheels

Lower Arrow Lake

159 km (98.6 mi)
Turn left (northwest) for Sprague Bay.

162.8 km (101 mi)
Reach the multi-season, cement boat launch at Sprague Bay.

REVELSTOKE TO FAUQUIER

Upper and Lower Arrow Lakes are clutched in a long, narrow, steep-walled valley. The two names imply that these are individual lakes. It's actually a single, monster reservoir covering 49,128 hectares. The elevation is approximately 445 m (1460 ft). The water level fluctuates radically. As it drops, sand and cobblestone beaches grow. At its lowest, a lakeside walk can stretch into a journey. In summer, swimming is not a frigid endurance test. Despite endless undeveloped shoreline, campgrounds are few.

On Upper Arrow Lake's west shore, south of Shelter Bay ferry, **Eagle Bay** is a premier campground. A thoughtful layout and well-spaced campsites give it a provincial-park feel. It's accessible by motorhomes and 5th-wheels.

On Lower Arrow Lake's east shore, south of Fauquier, are small camp-grounds at **Taite and Octopus creeks**. Taite is off the main road, shaded by conifers, but it's not on the creek. Octopus is in the open, beside the road but also next to the boisterous creek. The up-and-down access road is 2WD-passable, but could jostle a few screws loose on a motorhome. Don't drag anything bigger than a modest trailer to Taite. The campsites at Octopus will accommodate truck-and-camper rigs, but that's about it.

Whatshan Lake is west of Lower Arrow Lake, just north of Needles. You can reach it from Hwy 6, near the Needles-Fauquier ferry (page 269), or by crossing Lower Arrow Lake on the Arrow Park ferry (page 270). Whatshan is 19 km (12 mi) long, 1.3 km (0.8 mi) wide, and covers 1733 hectares. It would be considered big if it weren't overshadowed by gigantic Lower Arrow Lake. The elevation at Whatshan is 655 m (2148 ft). There are two campgrounds—Stevens Creek and Richy—shaded by white pines at the lake's north end. Both have sand and pea-gravel beaches. Summertime water temperature is pleasant for swimming. Stevens accommodates big RVs, if you can stand the long, rattling approach. Richy is smaller and densely treed, limiting vehicle size to truck-and-camper rigs.

For EAGLE BAY, now follow the directions below

From Revelstoke, drive Hwy 23 south 50 km (31 mi), along Upper Arrow Lake's west shore, toward Shelter Bay ferry terminal. Just before the terminal, turn right (southwest) onto Shelter Bay FS road and set your trip odometer to 0. Stay on the main road following the shore. At 9.5 km (5.9 mi) turn left to reach Eagle Bay campground on Upper Arrow Lake.

EAGLE BAY CAMPGROUND #6
Weekend / Easy / Free
15 tables, 3 tent pads, pebble beach
communal fire ring, cement boat launch
Accessible by motorhomes and 5th-wheels

For TAITE and OCTOPUS CREEKS, now follow the directions below

Drive Hwy 6 to Fauquier, on the east shore of Lower Arrow Lake. It's south of Nakusp, east of Vernon. If you're crossing on the Needles-Fauquier ferry, drive 0.5 km (0.3 mi) up from the lake after disembarking. Set your trip odometer to 0 in Fauquier, at Applegrove Road.

0 km (0 mi)
Starting south on initially-paved Applegrove Road, departing Hwy 6 in Fauquier at the sign GAS AND LODGING. Pass Arrow Lake Motel. Pavement soon ends. Proceed south on Lower Fauquier Road.

Octopus Creek and Lower Arrow Lake

3 km (1.8 mi)
The road levels, following power lines.

10.1 km (6.3 mi)
Proceed south for Octopus Creek. Turn right, just before the bridge over Taite Creek, and descend on a narrow, tree-enclosed spur to reach Taite Creek campground in 0.8 km (0.5 mi).

TAITE CREEK CAMPGROUND #39
Weekend / Moderate / Free
3 tables, boat launch, beach at low water
Accessible by small motorhomes and trailers

Continuing south on the main road, now called Octopus Creek FS road, passing the turnoff to Taite Creek campground.

17.2 km (10.6 mi)
Arrive at Octopus Creek campground. One table is beside the creek, the other is within sight and sound of it.

OCTOPUS CREEK CAMPGROUND #40
Weekend / Difficult / Free
2 tables, boat launch
Too small for motorhomes and trailers

For WHATSHAN LAKE, now follow the directions below

If you're approaching from the south, near Needles

From the rest area, just above the Needles ferry terminal, drive Hwy 6 northwest 4.4 km (2.7 mi). Just before the highway switchbacks south, turn right (north) onto Whatshan Lake Road and reset your trip odometer to 0.

0 km (0 mi)
Starting north on Whatshan Lake Road.

1.6 km (1 mi)
Turn right onto Whatshan FS road, also signed WHATSHAN ACCESS ROAD-REVELSTOKE ARROW PARK.

2.5 km (1.6 mi)
Stay left. Your general direction of travel all the way to the campgrounds will be north, roughly following Whatshan Lake's east shore.

4.2 km (2.6 mi)
Whatshan Lake is visible on the left.

14.1 km (8.7 mi)
Stay left.

15.7 km (9.7 mi)
Proceed straight.

16.3 km (10.1 mi)
Cross a bridge over White Grouse Creek.

17.4 km (10.8 mi)
Proceed straight, passing Branch 5 road at the KM 30 sign.

24 km (14.9 mi)
Reach a junction. Right is signed STEVENS CREEK, REVELSTOKE, ARROW PARK. Fork left for Richy and Stevens Creek campgrounds.

24.2 km (15 mi)
Proceed north for Stevens Creek campground. Just before a culvert, turn left for Richy campground.

Arrow Park ferry, Lower Arrow Lake

RICHY CAMPGROUND #34

Destination / Difficult (due only to distance) / Free
5 tables, boat launch, dock
Too small for motorhomes and trailers

25.9 km (16.1 mi)
Turn left for Stevens Creek campground. Whatshan Peak is visible across the lake. The pinnacles along the Monashee spine are visible northwest.

STEVENS CREEK CAMPGROUND #33

Destination / Difficult (due only to distance) / Free
11 tables, boat launch, dock
Accessible by motorhomes and 5th-wheels

If you're approaching Whatshan Lake from the east, via Arrow Park ferry

Reach the Arrow Park ferry, on Lower Arrow Lake's east shore, by driving Hwy 6 about 22 km (13.6 mi) southwest from Nakusp, or about 14.3 km (8.9 mi) north from Burton. The cable ferry operates daily, on demand, 5 a.m. to 10:30 p.m. Set your trip odometer to 0 after disembarking on the west shore and turning left (east).

0 km (0 mi)
Starting east on Lower Mosquito Road. After a detour skirting a washout, resume on the main road. Follow signs for Stevens Creek and Pass.

6 km (3.7 mi)
Cross Mosquito Creek bridge and turn right onto Branch 20 road.

9 km (5.6 mi)
Reach a fork. Go left (west). Follow signs for Stevens Creek and Pass.

10.5 km (6.5 mi)
Go right and ascend on Stevens Road.

20.8 km (13 mi)
Reach a junction. Turn right onto Branch 1.

22.3 km (13.8 mi)
Turn hard left (south) onto Whatshan FS road, following the northeast shore of Whatshan Lake.

23.6 km (14.6 mi)
Turn right for Stevens Creek campground. Read page 270 for details. Proceed straight (south) for Richy campground.

25.3 km (15.7 mi)
Just after a culvert, turn right for Richy campground. Read page 270 for details.

NAKUSP TO NEW DENVER

Hwy 6 cuts through the Selkirk Mountains. It links Nakusp, on Upper Arrow Lake, with New Denver, on Slocan Lake. From Nakusp it climbs southeast through a pastoral, suspended valley, soon passing small **Box Lake.**

Shaded in afternoon, Box Lake campground offers asylum from summer sun. The cool hemlock-and-spruce forest shelters baby's breath and luxuriant ferns. Vehicle noise from across the lake occasionally punctures the otherwise secluded atmosphere.

Near Box Lake is the turnoff to deep, narrow, steep-sided **Wilson Lake.** Though small—4.5 km (2.8 mi) long, covering 140 hectares—it has two campgrounds. The elevation is 970 m (3180 ft). The west-shore campground is way too small for anything bigger than a truck-and-camper rig. The east-shore campground is the most scenic, but the access road traverses the rocky bluffs south of the lake. It's a rough 7 km (4.3 mi), passable in a 2WD car or even a small motorhome if you drive slowly, but a more rugged vehicle is preferable.

The backroad to Wilson Lake continues east. It passes campgrounds at **Little Wilson Lake** and tiny **Beaver Lake.** It also accesses a short trail to Wilson Creek Falls. Then it heads south to intersect Hwy 6 at Slocan Lake, just north of New Denver. Driving this backroad in reverse, starting near New Denver, is a long, inefficient way to reach Wilson Lake. Go that way only if you want to explore. The short approach to Wilson Lake is from Hwy 6 near Box Lake.

Near the north end of Slocan Lake, is the turnoff to the amazingly lovely and very popular **Wragge Beach,** on the lake's west shore. The campground has a white, pebbly, almost sandy beach. (See photo on back cover.) The water is clear and deep. The looming Selkirk Mountains surround you. A beautiful hemlock-and-cedar forest adds to the magic. The access road is good but passes through a regrowing area of scrawny trees. You might be surprised to drive in all this way, and still hear distant road noise across the lake. It quiets down after 10 p.m.

If you're heading southeast on Hwy 6, from Nakusp

0 km (0 mi)
Starting southeast on Hwy 6, from the junction with Hwy 23 at Nakusp.

6.6 km (4.1 mi)
Proceed southeast on Hwy 6 for Slocan Lake and New Denver. Turn left (east) onto Wilson Lake Road and reset your trip odometer to 0 for the short approach to the Wilson Lakes campgrounds. Directions continue on page 275.

7.7 km (4.8 mi)
Box Lake is visible on the right.

10.3 km (6.4 mi)
Proceed southeast on Hwy 6 for Slocan Lake and New Denver. Turn right (west) and descend (doubling back northwest) to reach Box Lake campground on the southwest shore in 1.9 km (1.2 mi).

BOX LAKE CAMPGROUND #27
Overnight / Easy / Free
Elev: 305 m (1000 ft) / Lake: 71 ha
7 tables, dock, creeklet
Inaccessible by motorhomes and trailers

Picnic in New Denver, beside Slocan Lake

Continuing southeast on Hwy 6, passing the turnoff to Box Lake campground.

19 km (11.8 mi)
Pass the southeast end of Summit Lake. Goat Range peaks in the Selkirk Range are visible northeast.

32 km (19.8 mi)
Just before you reach the north end of Slocan Lake, look for Bonanza Road on your right. Turn southwest onto it for Wragge Beach campground on Slocan Lake's northwest shore. Directions continue at the bottom of page 274.

41.4 km (25.7 mi)
Proceed southeast on Hwy 6 for New Denver. Turn left (northeast) onto East Wilson Creek FS road (just after Rosebery Provincial Park and Wilson Creek bridge) and reset your trip odometer to 0 for **Wilson Creek Falls,** Beaver Lake campground, and the long approach to the Wilson lakes campgrounds. Directions continue at the bottom of page 277.

47 km (29.1 mi)
Reach the junction of Hwys 6 and 31A at the Petro Canada gas station in New Denver, on the northeast shore of Slocan Lake.

If you're heading northwest on Hwy 6, from New Denver

0 km (0 mi)
Starting northwest on Hwy 6 from the junction with Hwy 31A at the Petro Canada gas station in New Denver.

5.6 km (3.5 mi)
Proceed northwest on Hwy 6 for Nakusp and Upper Arrow Lake. Turn right (northeast) onto East Wilson Creek FS road (just before Wilson Creek bridge and Rosebery Provincial Park) and reset your trip odometer to 0 for **Wilson Creek Falls,** Beaver Lake campground, and the long approach to the Wilson lakes campgrounds. Directions continue at the bottom of page 277.

15 km (9.4 mi)
Just past the north end of Slocan Lake, look for Bonanza Road on your left. Turn southwest onto it for Wragge Beach campground on Slocan Lake's northwest shore. Directions continue at the bottom of this page.

28 km (17.4 mi)
Pass the southeast end of Summit Lake.

36.7 km (22.8 mi)
Proceed northwest on Hwy 6 for Nakusp and Upper Arrow Lake. Turn left and descend to reach Box Lake campground on the southwest shore in 1.9 km (1.2 mi). Read page 272 for details.

39.3 km (24.4 mi)
The northwest end of Box Lake is visible on the left.

40.4 km (25 mi)
Proceed northwest on Hwy 6 for Nakusp and Upper Arrow Lake. Turn right (east) onto Wilson Lake Road and reset your trip odometer to 0 for the short approach to the Wilson Lakes campgrounds. Directions continue on page 275.

47 km (29.1 mi)
Reach the junction of Hwys 6 and 23 in Nakusp, on the east shore of Upper Arrow Lake.

For WRAGGE BEACH, now follow the directions below

0 km (0 mi)
At the turnoff from Hwy 6 onto Bonanza Road.

1 km (0.6 mi)
After the bridge, the road turns to gravel. Go right on Shannon Creek FS Road. The left road is paved, probably to private homes.

3.2 km (2 mi)
Stay right on the main road at the junction.

3.9 km (2.4 mi)
Go left (straight) on the main road at the junction. On the left is a brown sign WRAGGE BEACH ROAD.

5 km (3.1 mi)
Cross a creek. At the next junction continues straight (left). The road going uphill to the right is closed.

6.5 km (4 mi)
Go straight (left) at the junction. A sign high on a tree points the way to Wragge Beach.

8.7 km (5.4 mi)
Go straight where a fork makes a sharp turn back to the left.

9.7 km (6 mi)
After you cross a creek, the road steepens.

10.5 km (6.5 mi)
Arrive at Wragge Beach.

WRAGGE BEACH CAMPGROUND #35
Destination / Moderate / $ / June 1 – early Sept
5 tables on the lakeshore, 3 tables in the trees, day-use area
5 walk-in tent sites with tables in the trees just off the beach

For the short approach to WILSON LAKE,
now follow the directions below

0 km (0 mi)
Starting east on Wilson Lake Road, departing Hwy 6. The ascent follows Wensley Creek upstream and passes a sawmill.

3.2 km (2 mi)
Fork right.

4.5 km (2.8 mi)
Reach the high point on the ascent to Wilson Lake's west end.

5.3 km (3.3 mi)
Go right at the junction.

6.6 km (4.1 mi)
Reach a junction. Turn left and reset your trip odometer to 0 for tiny Wilson Lake West campground. Go right on Wilson Creek FS road for Wilson Lake East, Little Wilson Lake and Beaver Lake campgrounds, and to continue the long, backroad drive to Hwy 6 and Slocan Lake. The next 7 km (4.3 mi) are rough where the road climbs over rocky bluffs south of Wilson Lake. A high-clearance vehicle is recommended.

0 km (0 mi)
Turning left at the 6.6-km (4.1-mi) junction, heading for Wilson Lake West campground.

0.6 km (0.4 mi)
Fork right for the final, steep, rough descent on a narrow spur.

1 km (0.6 mi)
Arrive at tiny Wilson Lake West campground. It's a sliver of land between the shore and the base of a cliff.

WILSON LAKE WEST CAMPGROUND #29
Weekend / Moderate / Free
1 table, fishing float
Inaccessible by motorhomes and trailers

Continuing generally east on Wilson Creek FS road from the 6.6-km (4.1-mi) junction, passing the turnoff to Wilson Lake West campground. Stay on the main road, ignoring several right spurs. Before the final steep descent, Wilson Lake East campground is visible below.

14 km (8.7 mi)
Reach Wilson Lake East campground, just after a bridged creek crossing. The campsites ring a large clearing beside the road.

WILSON LAKE EAST CAMPGROUND #30
Weekend / Moderate / Free
4 tables, gravel beach, boat launch
Accessible by small motorhomes and trailers

Continuing east on Wilson Creek FS road, passing Wilson Lake East campground.

17 km (10.5 mi)
Proceed southeast on Wilson Creek FS road for Beaver Lake campground, and to continue the long, backroad drive to Hwy 6 and Slocan Lake. Turn

right onto a rough spur to reach Little Wilson Lake campground in 0.8 km (0.5 mi). It's open, grassy, near the base of 2350-m (7710-ft) Mount Ferrie.

LITTLE WILSON LAKE CAMPGROUND #31
Weekend / Difficult / Free
Elev: 900 m (2950 ft) / Lake: 27 ha
3 tables, boat launch
Accessible by small motorhomes and trailers

Continuing southeast on Wilson Creek FS road, passing the turnoff to Little Wilson Lake campground.

28 km (17.4 mi)
Proceed southeast on Wilson Creek FS road to continue the long, backroad drive to Hwy 6 and Slocan Lake. Turn right to reach forested Beaver Lake campground in 0.4 km (0.25 mi). It's backed by the 2300-m (7545-ft) peaks of the Goat Range.

BEAVER LAKE CAMPGROUND #32
Weekend / Difficult / Free
Elev: 884 m (2900 ft) / Lake: 12 ha
7 tables, level tent sites
Accessible by small motorhomes and trailers

36.5 km (22.6 mi)
Reach a junction just after crossing a bridge over Wilson Creek. Proceed right (south) for Hwy 6 and Slocan Lake. Left (northeast) is a steep, rough, but 2WD-passable spur leading 0.7 km (0.4 mi) to **Wilson Creek Falls** trailhead. It's a 1.5-km (0.9-mi) walk to the falls. See photo on next page.

43 km (26.7 mi)
Bear right.

48 km (29.8 mi)
Intersect Hwy 6 near Rosebery Provincial Park and the northeast shore of Slocan Lake. Turn right (northwest) for Nakusp. Turn left (southeast) to reach New Denver in 5.6 km (3.5 mi).

For the long approach to WILSON LAKE, now follow the directions below

0 km (0 mi)
Starting northeast on East Wilson Creek Road, departing Hwy 6 near Rosebery Provincial Park and the northeast shore of Slocan Lake.

Wilson Falls

5 km (3 mi)
Bear left.

11.5 km (7.1 mi)
Reach a junction just before a bridge over Wilson Creek. Proceed left (north) on Wilson Creek FS road for campgrounds at Beaver Lake and the Wilson lakes, and to continue the long, backroad drive to Hwy 6 near Nakusp. Right (northeast) is a steep, rough, but 2WD-passable spur leading 0.7 km (0.4 mi) to **Wilson Creek Falls** trailhead. It's a 1.5-km (0.9-mi) walk to the falls.

20 km (12.4 mi)
Proceed northwest on Wilson Creek FS road for campgrounds at the Wilson lakes, and to continue the long, backroad drive to Hwy 6 near Nakusp. Turn left to reach forested Beaver Lake campground in 0.4 km (0.25 mi). Read page 277 for details.

31 km (19.2 mi)
Proceed northwest on Wilson Creek FS road for campgrounds at Wilson Lake, and to reach Hwy 6 near Nakusp. Turn left onto a rough spur to reach Little Wilson Lake campground in 0.8 km (0.5 mi). Read page 277 for details.

34 km (21.1 mi)
Reach Wilson Lake East campground, just before a bridged creek crossing. Read page 276 for details. Continue generally west on Wilson Creek FS road for Wilson Lake West campground, and to reach Hwy 6 near Nakusp. The next 7 km (4.3 mi) are rough where the road climbs over rocky bluffs south of Wilson Lake. A high-clearance vehicle is recommended. Stay on the main road, ignoring several left spurs.

41.4 km (25.7 mi)
Bear left on Wilson Creek FS road to reach Hwy 6 near Nakusp. Turn right and reset your trip odometer to 0 for tiny Wilson Lake West campground. Directions continue on page 276.

42.7 km (26.5 mi)
Bear left.

46.1 km (28.6 mi)
Bear left.

48 km (29.8 mi)
Intersect Hwy 6. Turn left (southeast) for Slocan Lake and New Denver. Turn right (northwest) to reach Nakusp in 6.5 km (4 mi).

NEW DENVER TO BALFOUR

The few campgrounds in this section of the Kootenays are well off pavement, but all are accessible by small motorhomes and trailers. More important, all are near trailheads and serve as basecamps for hikers intrigued by Valhalla and Kokanee Glacier provincial parks. For details about the trails, read the hiking guidebook *Where Locals Hike in the West Kootenay*.

Southwest of Slocan Lake is a campground at Little Slocan Lakes. It has well-spaced campsites in a birch-and-conifer forest beside a shallow lake. In the nearby Valhallas, the trails to Drinnon Pass and Gimli Ridge are superb. Reach Little Slocan Lakes by turning off Hwy 6 at the village of Slocan (described below), or farther south at Passmore (bottom of page 283).

Southeast of Slocan Lake are two campgrounds: Sasquatch Lake and Six-Mile Lakes. Hikers will find Sasquatch (from Hwy 6, page 285) convenient to Kokanee Park's Lemon Creek trailhead. Six-Mile can also be reached from Lemon Creek, but another approach (from Hwy 3A, page 286) makes it the closest free campground to Nelson. From town, it's a 25-minute drive to Six-Mile. Half the distance is on a rocky road with narrow steep sections.

If you're heading south on Hwy 6, from New Denver

0 km (0 mi)
Starting south on Hwy 6, from the junction with Hwy 31A, at the Petro Canada gas station in New Denver, on the northeast shore of Slocan Lake.

4.5 km (2.8 mi)
Proceed south through the village of Silverton, on Slocan Lake.

31.5 km (19.5 mi)
Pass a sign announcing the turn for Drinnon Pass, which is also the north approach to Little Slocan Lakes.

32.5 km (20.2 mi)
Proceed south on Hwy 6 to reach Hwy 3A at Playmor Junction. Turn right (west) onto Gravel Pit Road and reset your trip odometer to 0 for the north approach to Little Slocan Lakes campground. Directions continue on page 283. This is also the south entrance to Slocan village.

38.5 km (23.9 mi)
Proceed south on Hwy 6 to reach Hwy 3A at Playmor Junction. Turn left (east) onto Kennedy Road (just after crossing the Lemon Creek bridge) and reset your trip odometer to 0 for Sasquatch and Six-Mile lakes campgrounds. Directions continue on page 285. This is also the signed access to Kokanee Glacier Provincial Park via Lemon Creek.

Little Slocan Lake campground

62.7 km (38.9 mi)
Proceed south on Hwy 6 to reach Hwy 3A at Playmor Junction. Turn right (northwest) onto Passmore Upper Road (across from a power station) and reset your trip odometer to 0 for the south approach to Little Slocan Lakes campground. Directions continue at the bottom of page 283.

78 km (48.4 mi)
Intersect Hwy 3A at Playmor Junction. Turn right (south) for Castlegar. Turn left (northeast) for Nelson and Kootenay Lake.

If you're heading north on Hwy 6, from Hwy 3A

0 km (0 mi)
Starting west on Hwy 6, from Hwy 3A at Playmor Junction, between Castlegar and Nelson.

15.4 km (9.5 mi)
Proceed north on Hwy 6 for New Denver. Turn left (northwest) onto Passmore Upper Road (across from a power station) and reset your trip odometer to 0 for the south approach to Little Slocan Lakes campground. Directions continue at the bottom of page 283.

39.5 km (24.5 mi)
Proceed north on Hwy 6 for New Denver. Turn right (east) onto Kennedy Road (just before the Lemon Creek bridge) and reset your trip odometer to

Silverton and Slocan Lake, from Idaho Peak

0 for Sasquatch and Six-Mile lakes campgrounds. Directions continue on page 285. This is also the signed access to Kokanee Glacier Provincial Park via Lemon Creek.

45.5 km (28.2 mi)
Proceed north on Hwy 6 for New Denver. Turn left (west) onto Gravel Pit Road and reset your trip odometer to 0 for the north approach to Little Slocan Lakes campground. Directions continue on page 283. This is also the south entrance to Slocan village, and the signed acccess to Valhalla Provincial Park's Drinnon Pass trailhead.

**For the north approach to LITTLE SLOCAN LAKES,
now follow the directions below**

0 km (0 mi)
Starting west on Gravel Pit Road, departing Hwy 6. Proceed straight and cross the Slocan River bridge.

0.8 km (0.5 mi)
Stay left on Slocan West Road.

1.2 km (0.7 mi)
Cross a bridge over Gwillim Creek.

2.3 km (1.4 mi)
Go right on Little Slocan FS road.

13.2 km (8.1 mi)
Bear left (southwest) for Little Slocan Lakes campground. Turn right onto Bannock Burn FS road for **Mulvey Basin (Gimli Ridge) trailhead** in the Valhallas.

20.3 km (12.6 mi)
Bear left (south) for Little Slocan Lakes campground. Turn right onto Hoder Creek FS road for Drinnon Pass (Gwillim Lakes) trailhead in the Valhallas.

20.5 km (12.7 mi)
Turn left and descend to reach Little Slocan Lakes campground in 200 meters. A loop road accesses the campsites.

LITTLE SLOCAN LAKES CAMPGROUND #42
Destination / Moderate / Free
Elev: 640 m (2100 ft) / Lake: 1.3 km (0.8 mi) long
6 well-spaced tables, boat launch
Accessible by small motorhomes and trailers

**For the south approach to LITTLE SLOCAN LAKES,
now follow the directions below**

0 km (0 mi)
Starting (northwest) on Passmore Upper Road, departing Hwy 6.

0.3 km (0.2 mi)
Cross a bridge over the Slocan River. Go left to follow the north bank of Little Slocan River upstream, gradually curving north.

3.3 km (2 mi)
Pavement ends.

3.7 km (2.3 mi)
Bear left on Little Slocan FS road.

5.3 km (3.3 mi)
Bear right.

7.5 km (4.7 mi)
Proceed straight on the main road.

9 km (5.6 mi)
Stay right.

13.3 km (8.2 mi)
Proceed straight where Koch Creek FS road forks left.

16.1 km (10 mi) and 23 km (14.3 mi)
Proceed straight.

24.3 km (15.1 mi)
The first of the Little Slocan Lakes is visible on the right.

25 km (15.5 mi)
Proceed straight (northeast) for the Valhalla trailheads or Slocan Lake. Turn right and descend to reach Little Slocan Lakes campground in 200 meters. Read page 283 for details.

25.2 km (15.6 mi)
Proceed straight (northeast) for Mulvey Basin (Gimli Ridge) trailhead and Slocan Lake. Turn left onto Hoder Creek FS road for Drinnon Pass (Gwillim Lakes) trailhead in the Valhallas.

32.3 km (20 mi)
Proceed straight (northeast) for Slocan Lake. Turn left onto Bannock Burn FS road for Mulvey Basin (Gimli Ridge) trailhead in the Valhallas.

43.2 km (26.8 mi)
Bear left.

44.3 km (27.5 mi)
Cross a bridge over Gwillim Creek.

44.7 km (27.7 mi)
Go right and cross the Slocan River bridge.

45.5 km (28.2 mi)
Intersect Hwy 6 beside the village of Slocan, at the south end of Slocan Lake. Turn left (north) for New Denver. Turn right (south) to reach Hwy 3A at Playmor Junction.

For SASQUATCH and SIX-MILE LAKES via Hwy 6, now follow the directions below

0 km (0 mi)
Starting east on Kennedy Road, departing Hwy 6. It soon becomes Lemon Creek FS road. Follow signs for Kokanee Glacier Park.

4.7 km (2.9 mi)
Bear right and ascend on the main road.

5.7 km (3.5 mi)
Stay left, still ascending steeply.

7.9 km (4.9 mi) and 9.2 km (5.7 mi)
Bear left.

10 km (6.2 mi)
Go right.

11.6 km (7.2 mi)
Go left.

14.5 km (9 mi)
Reach a junction. Turn left (north) to reach Kokanee Glacier Park's **Lemon Creek trailhead** in 2.3 km (1.4 mi). Turn right (southeast) onto Six-Mile Road for campgrounds at Sasquatch and Six-Mile Lakes, and to reach Hwy 3A at Kootenay Lake.

14.9 km (9.2 mi)
Reach Sasquatch Lake campground. Proceed straight (southeast) for Six-Mile Lakes campground, and to reach Hwy 3A.

The tiny lake and campground are beside the road. Warm water allows comfortable swimming in summer. Huckleberry picking is fruitful here in season.

SASQUATCH LAKE CAMPGROUND #13
Overnight / Moderate / Free
Elev: 1024 m (3360 ft)
1 table, 2 campsites
Accessible by small motorhomes and trailers

Continuing southeast on the main road, passing Sasquatch Lake.

18 km (11.2 mi)
Reach Six-Mile Lakes campground. Read page 287 for details. Proceed straight (southeast) to reach Hwy 3A at Kootenay Lake. The next 3 km (1.9 mi) are rough but passable in a 2WD car.

21 km (13 mi)
Fork left.

31 km (19.2 mi)
Intersect Hwy 3A beside Kootenay Lake's West Arm. Turn left for the Balfour ferry terminal and Kaslo. Turn right for Nelson.

~

For SIX-MILE and SASQUATCH LAKES via Hwy 3A, now follow the directions below

If you're heading northeast on Hwy 3A, from Nelson

Leaving Nelson, set your trip odometer to 0 on the northwest side of the orange bridge spanning Kootenay Lake's West Arm. Drive Hwy 3A northeast 7.9 km (4.9 mi) then turn left (north) onto Six-Mile Road (just before the blue sign for Duhamel and Willow Bay motels) and reset your trip odometer to 0.

If you're heading west on Hwy 3A, from Balfour

Leaving the Balfour ferry terminal, turn left (west) on Hwy 3A and set your trip odometer to 0. At 22 km (13.6 mi) pass the motel and store at Duhamel and slow down. At 22.4 km (13.9 mi) turn right (north) onto Six-Mile Road and reset your trip odometer to 0.

For either approach above, now follow the directions below

0 km (0 mi)
Starting north on Six-Mile Road, departing Hwy 3A.

1.5 km (0.9 mi)
Pavement ends. The road is narrow and rocky as it ascends switchbacks to gain the upper valley.

10 km (6.2 mi)
Fork right. The next 3 km (1.9 mi) are rough but passable in a 2WD car.

13 km (8.1 mi)
Reach Six-Mile Lakes campground. Proceed straight (northwest) for Sasquatch Lake campground.

Pebble Beach campground, Kootenay Lake

Two campsites are next to the road but 10 feet above it. Three more are farther back. A 3-km (1.9 mi) trail rounds the west side of the lakes. It starts south of the campsites, heads northwest, and ends just past the farthest lake.

SIX-MILE LAKES CAMPGROUND #14
Overnight / Moderate / Free
Elev: 1100 m (3608 ft) / Lakes: 2 to 7 ha
4 tables, level tent sites, nature trail
Accessible by small motorhomes and trailers

Continuing northwest on Six-Mile Road, passing Six-Mile Lakes campground.

16 km (9.9 mi)
Reach Sasquatch Lake campground. Read page 285 for details. Proceed straight (northwest) for Hwy 6, or Kokanee Glacier Park's Lemon Creek trailhead.

16.4 km (10.2 mi)
Intersect Lemon Creek FS road. Turn left (west) to reach Hwy 6 in 14.5 km (9 mi). Turn right (north) to reach Kokanee Glacier Park's Lemon Creek trailhead in 2.3 km (1.4 mi).

KOOTENAY LAKE EAST SHORE

On the entire east shore of immense Kootenay Lake, the FS maintains just one campground. It occupies a small, cobblestone crescent beach at Garland Bay. At night, the lights of Kaslo, across the lake, add romantic sparkle to this backcountry setting. What Garland often lacks are vacant campsites. It's usually full on summer weekends. Also, there are no hiking trails of significant length nearby. From the Kootenay Bay ferry terminal, Garland's about a 45-minute drive. The entry road descends steeply, so while small motorhomes and trailers can squeeze in, they need muscle to get out.

GARLAND BAY

If you're heading north on Hwy 3A, from Creston

From the junction with Hwy 3 at the north end of Creston, drive Hwy 3A north. At 79 km (49 mi) proceed through the village of Crawford Bay. At 83.2 km (51.6 mi), where left descends to the Kootenay Bay ferry terminal, turn right (north) onto Riondel Road and reset your trip odometer to 0.

If you're disembarking the ferry at Kootenay Bay

From Balfour (between Nelson and Kaslo, on Kootenay Lake's west shore), take the ferry to the east shore. After disembarking at Kootenay Bay, drive Hwy 3A uphill 1.1 km (0.7 mi). Turn left (north) onto Riondel Road and reset your trip odometer to 0.

For either approach above, now follow the directions below

0 km (0 mi)
Starting north on Riondel Road, departing Hwy 3A.

8.9 km (5.5 mi)
Curve left (west) into the village of Riondel.

9.1 km (5.6 mi)
Turn right (north) onto Eastman Avenue, following signs for Riondel campground.

9.8 km (6.1 mi)
Pass Riondel Beach and campground on the left. Proceed straight (north) on Riondel North Road.

Kootenay Lake

13 km (8.1 mi)
Cross Tam O'Shanter Creek bridge. Pavement ends. Proceed straight (north) on Powder Creek FS road.

15.7 km (9.7 mi)
Reach trailhead parking on the left for Pebble Beach campground #16. A 2-km (1.2-mi) trail descends to tent sites above the beach.

16.3 km (10.1 mi)
Proceed straight (north) on the main road where Loki South FS road ascends right. Soon pass a waterfall in a gorge on the right.

Garland Bay campground on Kootenay Lake

18.5 km (11.5 mi)
Proceed straight (north) on the main road, passing a right fork.

21.9 km (13.6 mi)
Pass the KM 9 sign and a private road descending left.

22.2 km (13.8 mi)
After crossing Bernard Creek bridge, turn left and descend to reach Garland Bay campground in 300 meters.

GARLAND BAY CAMPGROUND #17
Destination / Moderate / $ / May 1 - Oct 31
Elev: 532 m (1745 ft)
Lake: 110 km (68 mi) long, 3 km (1.9 mi) wide here, 42,174 ha
20 tables, boat launch, wharf, sandy beach
Accessible by small motorhomes and trailers

NEAR KASLO

In a province-wide beauty pageant for small towns, Kaslo might take the tiara. Among its many attributes are historic brick buildings. Victorian homes. A downtown with old-world charm. A lovely bay on Kootenay Lake's west shore. And a Purcell or Selkirk mountain view every time you lift your eyes (photo on page 29). Of no consequence to the judges of our fictitious contest, but noteworthy here, are two nearby free campgrounds.

Fletcher Falls is a pipsqueak campground in a premier setting. It's shoehorned between the mouth of a creek gorge and the shore of Kootenay Lake. Three groups of campers, a couple day-use visitors, and Fletcher is maxed out. If you can stand the unavoidably social atmosphere, after peeking at the falls you'll enjoy the grand lake-and-mountain view, the broad beach, and the soothing shoosh of the creek. The entry road, just seven minutes south of Kaslo, is SRN—steep, rough and narrow—with overhanging tree branches. Try it only in a high-clearance, low-profile vehicle. Big rigs are verboten.

About 10 minutes north of Kaslo, you can turn west to begin the 855-m (2800-ft) ascent to **Milford Lake**. The road is passable in a 2WD car, but the steep grades and tight turns will stymie a motorhome or trailer. What you'll find up there is a small campground on a tiny lake, fringed by big timber, in a logged, subalpine bowl. It does not compare to the magnificence of Kootenay Lake. So consider paying to camp at one of the beautiful provincial parks nearby on the great lake: Lost Ledge or Davis Creek. Both are reasonably priced. Directions are on page 293. Or continue driving about 40 minutes farther north to the spacious, scenic, free campgrounds on Duncan Lake (page 292).

For FLETCHER FALLS, now follow the directions below

From the **Balfour ferry** terminal, drive Hwy 31 north 27 km (16.7 mi) along Kootenay Lake's west shore. Or, from the Mohawk gas station in **Kaslo** (at the "A" Avenue and 4th Street intersection with a flashing traffic light) drive Hwy 31 south 9.2 km (5.7 mi). **From either approach**, turn east (toward Kootenay Lake), departing Hwy 31. It's only 0.7 km (0.4 mi) to the campground, but it's a rough, narrow, steep descent. Though passable in a 2WD car, it's wise to scout the road first. Or just park at the road and walk down. Day-use sites with tables are across the bridge from the tiny campground.

FLETCHER FALLS CAMPGROUND #15
Destination / Easy / Free
Elev: 532 m (1745 ft)
Lake: 110 km (68 mi) long, 3.5 km (2.2 mi) wide here, 42,174 ha
3 campsites with tables, 2 day-use tables, cobblestone beach
Inaccessible by motorhomes and trailers

For MILFORD LAKE, now follow the directions below

From Hwy 31A in Kaslo (at the "A" Avenue and North Marine Drive intersection, just west of and uphill from downtown) drive Hwy 31 north 9 km (5.6 mi). Turn left (northwest) onto Milford Lake Road and ascend numerous switchbacks to reach Milford Lake campground in about 18 km (11.2 mi).

MILFORD LAKE CAMPGROUND #18
Overnight / Moderate / Free
Elev: 1457 m (4780 ft)
2 tables, 3 campsites
Inaccessible by motorhomes and trailers

DUNCAN LAKE

The tight valley that holds Kootenay Lake in a vice-grip continues north. The upper reaches are filled by Duncan Lake—a 44-km (27.3-mi) long reservoir that, on the map, appears to be wiggling in the mountains' firm grasp.

Duncan has two provincial-park quality, RV-accessible campgrounds near its south end: Glacier Creek on the east shore, Howser Glayco on the west shore. Bear in mind that "shore" is an impermanent feature here. In spring and fall, the water level plummets, exposing a muddy, stump-studded bottom. In summer, Duncan is full-pool gorgeous.

Glacier Creek campground is a fee-free regional park. It's shaded in a mixed forest of evergreens, aspen and birch, on a small point. Several campsites are near the high-water line. The swimming area, created by a log breakwater, has floating platforms.

Howser Glayco has two parts: Howser campground and Glayco Beach day-use area. Howser's campsites are in the trees above a thin strip of sandy beach laden with drift logs. Tenters will be grateful for individual tent sites in a separate, walk-in camping area. Four Squatters Glacier is visible north. Mt. Lavina is southeast, across the lake. The sandy beach at nearby Glayco is broader and has better sun exposure. The swimming area, created by a log breakwater, has a floating platform.

Both Glacier Creek and Howser Glayco are excellent basecamps for hikers. Several nearby trails are among B.C.'s best. MacBeth Icefield, Monica Meadows, Jumbo Pass, Meadow Mountain, and Silvercup Ridge are a few of the premier alpine destinations nearby. An exciting early-season option is Fry Creek Canyon, south of Johnsons Landing, above the northeast shore of Kootenay Lake. For details, read the hiking guide *Where Locals Hike in the West Kootenay*. It's described on page 536.

Duncan Lake, from Howser campground

Approaching Duncan Lake from Galena Bay on Upper Arrow Lake? Read page 297 for directions.

If you're heading north on Hwy 31, from Kaslo

0 km (0 mi)
Starting north on Hwy 31, from Hwy 31A in Kaslo (at the "A" Avenue and North Marine Drive intersection, just west of and uphill from downtown).

9 km (5.6 mi)
Proceed straight (north) on Hwy 31 for Duncan Lake. Left (northwest) on Milford Lake Road leads about 18 km (11.2 mi) to Milford Lake campground. Read page 292 for details.

23.4 km (14.5 mi)
Pass Kootenay Lake's Lost Ledge Provincial Park on the right.

28.2 km (17.5 mi)
Pass Kootenay Lake's Davis Creek Provincial Park on the right.

28.4 km (17.6 mi)
Reach the village of Lardeau, near the north end of Kootenay Lake. Curve left, pass 5th Street, and proceed north on Hwy 31.

34.5 km (21.4 mi)
Reach a junction. Proceed straight (northwest) on Hwy 31 for Howser Glayco campground on Duncan Lake's west shore. Turn right (east) onto Argenta Road (signed for Purcell Mountains and Fry Canyon) and reset your trip odometer to 0 for Glacier Creek campground on Duncan Lake's east shore.

0 km (0 mi)
Starting east on Argenta Road, departing Hwy 31.

0.5 km (0.3 mi)
Cross the Lardeau River. Pavement ends.

1.2 km (0.75 mi)
Reach a junction. Proceed straight (north) for Glacier Creek campground. Right leads south through Argenta to Fry Creek Canyon trailhead.

1.4 km (0.9 mi)
Cross the Duncan River bridge.

11.5 km (7.1 mi)
Turn left (west) to reach Glacier Creek campground in 0.4 km (0.25 mi). Proceed straight (north) another 0.5 km (0.3 mi), then fork right onto Glacier Creek FS road to access several trailheads in the Purcell Mountains.

GLACIER CREEK CAMPGROUND #22
Destination / Easy / Free
Elev: 577 m (1893 ft)
Lake: 44 km (27.3 mi) long, 1.8 km (1.1 mi) wide, 7200 ha
24 well-spaced tables, boat launch, 3 swimming platforms
Accessible by motorhomes and 5th-wheels

Continuing northwest on Hwy 31, passing the turnoff to Glacier Creek campground.

38 km (23.6 mi)
MacBeth Icefield's twin waterfalls are visible northeast.

41.1 km (25.5 mi)
Proceed on pavement, curving left, following the sign for Gerrard and Shelter Bay ferry.

42 km (26 mi)
Pavement ends.

Duncan Lake, from Glacier Creek campground

46.8 km (29 mi)
Cross the Lardeau River bridge. Pass several houses.

48.1 km (29.8 mi)
Proceed straight (northwest) on Hwy 31 for Trout Lake. Turn right (east) onto Howser Station Road and reset your trip odometer to 0 for Howser campground.

> **0 km (0 mi)**
> Starting east on Howser Station Road, departing Hwy 31.
>
> **1.2 km (0.7 mi)**
> Proceed through the community of Howser.
>
> **1.9 km (1.2 mi)**
> Reach a junction. Proceed left for Howser campground. For Glayco Beach day-use area, go right 300 meters, then left another 100 meters.
>
> **2.2 km (1.4 mi)**
> Reach a cement boat launch on the right. Proceed left to enter Howser campground in 100 meters.

2.6 km (1.6 mi)
Reach a parking area on the right for walk-in tent sites. They're beneath wind-sheltering trees, about a meter above the lakeshore. The campground road loops back to the entrance.

HOWSER-GLAYCO CAMPGROUND #21
Destination / Easy / Free
Elev: 577 m (1893 ft)
Lake: 44 km (27.3 mi) long, 1.6 km (1 mi) wide here, 7200 ha
5 well-spaced campsites with tables,
4 walk-in tent sites with tables
Accessible by motorhomes and 5th-wheels

Continuing northwest on Hwy 31, passing the turnoff to Howser Glayco campground.

82.4 km (51.1 mi)
Reach the south end of Trout Lake. Turn left onto a spur, then right in 100 meters to enter Gerrard campground. Bear right and cross a bridge over Lardeau River to proceed northwest along the lake.

Gerrard campground is part of Goat Range Provincial Park, which protects a remote chunk of the Selkirk Mountains rising abruptly to the east. The campsites are in an abandoned apple orchard, surrounded by lush cedar forest. Grizzly bears forage here, so be extremely wary.

GERRARD CAMPGROUND #23
Weekend / Difficult (due only to distance) / Free
Elev: 715 m (2345 ft) / Lake: 24.5 km (15 mi) long, 2792 ha
5 well-spaced campsites, 4 tables
Accessible by motorhomes and 5th-wheels

Continuing northwest on Hwy 31, passing the turnoff to Gerrard campground. The road becomes narrower and rougher as it winds above the northeast shore of Trout Lake.

110 km (68.2 mi)
Reach the village of Trout Lake, at the lake's northwest end. It's another 28.5 km (17.7 mi)—half of it paved—to Galena Bay ferry terminal on Upper Arrow Lake.

If you're heading to Duncan Lake,
from Galena Bay on Upper Arrow Lake

0 km (0 mi)
Starting south on Hwy 23 from Galena Bay ferry terminal. Ascend briefly then turn left (northeast) onto Hwy 31 where Hwy 23 proceeds south to Nakusp.

28.5 km (17.7 mi)
Reach the village of Trout Lake, on the lake's northwest end.

56 km (34.7 mi)
After crossing a bridge over Lardeau River, at the southeast end of Trout Lake, proceed southeast on Hwy 31 for Duncan Lake, Kootenay Lake and Kaslo. Turn right to quickly reach Gerrard campground. Read page 296 for details.

90.3 km (56 mi)
Reach a junction. Proceed south on Hwy 31 for Glacier Creek campground on Duncan Lake, or to reach Kootenay Lake and Kaslo. Turn left and reset your trip odometer to 0 for Howser Glayco campground on Duncan Lake. Directions continue on page 295.

104 km (64.5 mi)
Reach a junction. Proceed south on Hwy 31 for Kootenay Lake and Kaslo. Turn left and reset your trip odometer to 0 for Glacier Creek campground on Duncan Lake. Directions continue on page 294.

129.5 km (80.3 mi)
Proceed south on Hwy 31 for Kaslo. Right (northwest) on Milford Lake Road leads about 18 km (11.2 mi) to Milford Lake campground. Read page 292 for details.

138.5 km (86 mi)
Reach a junction with Hwy 31A in Kaslo. Turn right (west) for New Denver. Hwy 31 descends left (east) into downtown, then continues south along Kootenay Lake's west shore to the Balfour ferry terminal. From there, Hwy 3A leads southwest to Nelson.

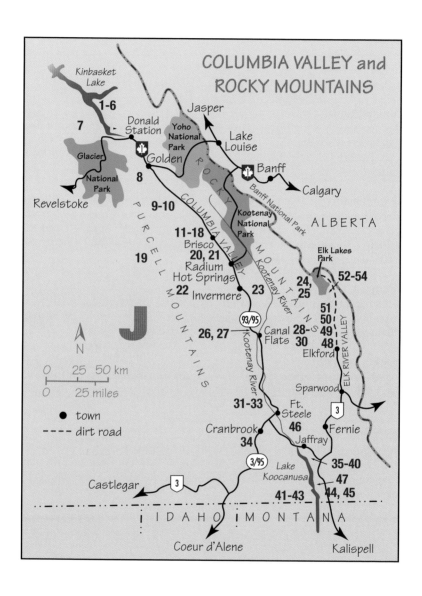

COLUMBIA VALLEY and ROCKY MOUNTAINS

Kinbasket Lake

1-6

7

Donald Station

Yoho National Park

Jasper

Lake Louise

Glacier National Park

Golden

8

Banff

Calgary

Revelstoke

9-10

COLUMBIA VALLEY

Kootenay National Park

ALBERTA

11-18

Brisco

20, 21

Elk Lakes Park

52-54

19

Radium Hot Springs

22 Invermere

23

Kootenay River

24, 25

51
50
49
48

PURCELL MOUNTAINS

N

0   25 50 km
0   25 miles

● town
---- dirt road

26, 27

Kootenay River

93/95

Canal Flats

28-30

Elkford

ROCKY MOUNTAINS

ELK RIVER VALLEY

Sparwood

31-33

Ft. Steele

46

3

Cranbrook

34

Jaffray

Fernie

3/95

Lake Koocanusa

35-40

47

Castlegar

3

41-43

44, 45

IDAHO   MONTANA

Coeur d'Alene

Kalispell

J: Columbia Valley and Rocky Mountains

At the fee campgrounds, charges apply weekends only, from April 30 through June 17. From mid-June through early September, fees apply daily. Fees start mid-May at Tie Lake and North Star Lake (weekends only).

1	Waitabit Creek	FREE	28	White R-East Fork	FREE
2	Bluewater Creek	FREE	29	White River-Graves	FREE
3	Blackwater Lake	FREE	30	Munroe Lake	FREE
4	Help Lake	FREE	31	Tamarack Lake	FREE
5	Esplanade Bay	FREE	32	Johnson Lake	FREE
6	Bush Arm	FREE	33	Larchwood Lake	FREE
7	Susan Lake	FREE	34	Palmer Bar	FREE
8	Cedar Lake	FREE	35	Kikomun Creek	FREE
9	Bittern Lake	FREE	36	Rock Creek	FREE
10	Mitten Lake	$	38	North Star Lake	$
11	Twin Lakes	FREE	39	Wapiti Lake	FREE
12	Dunbar Lake	FREE	40	Tie Lake	$
13	Botts Lake	FREE	41	Englishman Creek	$
14	Cub Lake	FREE	42	Gold Creek	FREE
15	Jade Lake	FREE	43	Gold Bay	$
16	Cleland Lake	FREE	44	Loon Lake	$
17	Topaz Lake	FREE	45	Edwards Lake	FREE
18	Cartwright Lake	FREE	46	Horseshoe Lake	FREE
19	Bugaboo-Septet	FREE	47	Dorr	$
20	Leadqueen Lake	FREE	48	Krivensky Farm	FREE
21	Hall Lake	FREE	49	Blue Lake	FREE
22	Stockdale Creek	FREE	50	Aldridge Creek	FREE
23	Horseshoe Rapids	FREE	51	Weary Creek	FREE
24	Fenwick Creek	FREE	52	Riverside	FREE
25	Palliser-Albert	FREE	53	Tobermory Creek	FREE
26	Findlay Creek	FREE	54	Upper Elk River	FREE
27	Whitetail Lake	$			

Columbia Valley and Rocky Mountains

Columbia River, at Bluewater Creek campground

At the foot of the Canadian Rockies is a heap of adjectives. They were fresh and vivid once. Now they're dull clichés, worn out in countless attempts to express the beauty of this singular mountain range. You have to experience for yourself what all those words fail to convey. The campgrounds described here will serve you on the journey.

The heart of this chapter is the Columbia Valley. It's part of the **Rocky Mountain Trench**—a 1,600-km (922-mi) long depression just west of and parallel to the Rockies. Mid-valley, between Golden and Invermere, the term *trench* seems especially apt. The Purcells tower to the east, the Rockies to the west.

The valley's natural artery is the **Columbia River.** Extensive wetlands created by the broad river make the valley an important flyway for migratory birds. The valley's man-made artery is Hwy 93/95. It transports windshield tourists in migratory numbers. Many of the five million people who visit the Rockies each year drive this highway nonstop. Once inside the famous national parks, they're confronted with CAMPGROUND FULL signs. Yet just outside the parks, some MOT campgrounds are never full. And several in the Purcells are near trails leading to national-park quality scenery.

At either end of the Columbia Valley, the Rocky Mountain Trench broadens. The scenic intensity wanes. North of Golden are MOT campgrounds near an octopus tentacle of **Kinbasket Lake.** South of Invermere, where it's sunnier and drier, you'll find many more campgrounds in gentle foothills carpeted with grassland and sprinkled with open forests of pine and fir.

NORTH OF GOLDEN

North of Golden, where the Trans-Canada turns west toward Glacier National Park, two MOT campgrounds are conveniently close to the highway. Waitabit Creek campground is large, well maintained, but next to a busy logging road. Bluewater Creek campground is small, more isolated, on the fast-flowing Columbia River, which helps muffle the sound of nearby passing trains.

A few tiny campgrounds along Bush River FS road (the main logging haul route) are acceptable at night, but they're miserable places to hang out during the day. Industrial traffic is lighter near Susan Lake campground.

Farther north, the combined efforts of the Blackwater Range (east) and the Esplanade Range (west) fail to muster any scenic oomph. Voracious logging has further humiliated these lowly mountains. The land looks exhausted.

Beyond is Kinbasket Lake, a Columbia River reservoir created by Mica Dam. It's huge: 216 km (134 mi) long, covering 41,590 hectares. The elevation is 755 m (2476 ft). The water level fluctuates wildly, but mid-June to September it should be high. The lake's visual appeal rises and falls with the water. Esplanade Bay campground is on a bluff, with a commanding view over Kinbasket Lake's Columbia Reach. Icy peaks are visible in the distance.

If you're heading north on Hwy 1, from Golden

From Golden, drive Trans-Canada Hwy 1 north 26 km (16.1 mi). Shortly before crossing the Columbia River bridge, turn right (north) onto Donald Road and reset your trip odometer to 0.

If you're heading east on Hwy 1, from Glacier National Park

From the north edge of Glacier National Park, descend on Trans-Canada Hwy 1 northeast into the Columbia River Valley. Kinbasket Lake's Columbia Reach is visible left (north). Eventually cross the Columbia River bridge. Just 300 meters beyond, cross a large bridge over the railway at Donald Station. About 500 meters farther, turn left (north) onto Donald Road and set your trip odometer to 0.

For either approach above, now follow the directions below

0 km (0 mi)
Starting north on Donald Road.

0.7 km (0.4 mi)
Reach a 3-way junction. Follow the dirt road in the middle. Left enters the mill. Right is paved.

1.3 km (0.8 mi)
Proceed straight and descend. Cross a bridge over Waitabit Creek.

2 km (1.2 mi)
Proceed straight (north) for more campgrounds. Turn left to enter Waitabit Creek campground in 100 meters. It's just below the main road.

WAITABIT CREEK CAMPGROUND #1
Weekend / Easy / Free
12 well-spaced tables, more campsites, level tent sites
Accessible by small motorhomes and trailers

Continuing north on the main road, passing the turnoff to Waitabit Creek campground.

4.1 km (2.5 mi)
Proceed straight (north) for more campgrounds. Turn left (west) to reach Bluewater Creek campground in 2 km (1.2 mi); beware of the damaged bridge ahead. The campsites are on the Columbia River.

BLUEWATER CREEK CAMPGROUND #2
Weekend / Easy / Free
2 tables, more campsites
Accessible by small motorhomes and trailers

Continuing north on the main road, passing the turnoff to Bluewater Creek campground.

7.6 km (4.7 mi)
Pass clearcuts.

12 km (7.4 mi)
Proceed straight (north) on the main road where Bush-Bluewater FS road forks right.

13 km (8 mi)
Proceed straight (north) on the main road for more campgrounds. Turn left (west) onto Susan Lake FS road and reset your trip odometer to 0 for Susan Lake campground.

> **0 km (0 mi)**
> Starting west on Susan Lake FS road.
>
> **5 km (3 mi)**
> Bear left on the main road.
>
> **6 km (3.7 mi)**
> Turn right to quickly reach Susan Lake campground

SUSAN LAKE CAMPGROUND #7
Weekend / Moderate / Free
Elev: 1524 m (5000 ft) / Lake: 45 ha
3 tables, day-use area for boat-trailer parking
Accessible by small motorhomes and trailers

Continuing north on the main road, passing the turnoff to Susan Lake campground.

24.3 km (15.1 mi)
Reach Blackwater Lake campground. It's just off the main road, on a creek, surrounded by clearcuts. A few young trees provide no shade.

BLACKWATER LAKE CAMPGROUND #3
Weekend / Moderate / Free
Elev: 970 m (3182 ft) / Lake: 14.5 ha
4 tables, wheelchair-accessible fishing ramp and toilet
Accessible by small motorhomes and trailers

29.6 km (18.4 mi)
Proceed straight (north) on the main road for more campgrounds. Turn left (west) to quickly reach Help Lake campground. Beware of the ditch ahead. The lake is tiny, but the grassy campground shaded by cedars is pleasant.

HELP LAKE CAMPGROUND #4
Weekend / Moderate / Free
2 tables, cartop boat launch
Accessible by small motorhomes and trailers

Continuing north on the main road, passing the turnoff to Help Lake campground.

35 km (21.7 mi)
Pass the Giant Cedars interpretive trail on the left. It has one table for day-use.

39 km (24.2 mi)
Proceed straight (north) on the main road for more campgrounds. Turn left (west), at the bottom of a big hill, to reach Esplanade Bay campground in about 6.5 km (4 mi). After crossing a bridge over Succor Creek, descend numerous switchbacks. Go left at the FS sign, then left again to arrive.

ESPLANADE BAY CAMPGROUND #5
Weekend / Difficult (due only to distance) / Free
12 tables, multi-season boat launch
Accessible by small motorhomes and trailers

Continuing north on the main road, passing the turnoff to Esplanade Bay campground.

44.3 km (27.5 mi)
Go right at the junction.

49.3 km (30.5 mi)
Proceed southeast, then east on the main road for remote campgrounds. Turn left for Bush Arm campground.

BUSH ARM CAMPGROUND #6
Weekend / Difficult (due only to distance) / Free
4 tables, multi-season boat launch
Accessible by small motorhomes and trailers

~~

NEAR GOLDEN

The small but agreeable campground at tiny Cedar Lake is a fifteen-minute drive west of Golden. It has a sandy beach and a shallow area where kids can play. The campsites are well-spaced in trees. This is also a popular day-use area. For more seclusion, tuck you tent under one arm, your sleeping bag under the other, and walk 1 km (0.6 mi) to the tenters-only camping area.

CEDAR LAKE

If you're heading east or west on Hwy 1

From Trans-Canada Hwy 1, take the exit into Golden. After looping off the overpass, turn left. Turn left again onto 7th Street North (signed for White-tooth Ski Area) and set your trip odometer to 0.

If you're heading north on Hwy 95, from Radium

After entering Golden's business district, cross the Columbia River bridge. Just beyond, reach a Petro Canada gas station where 9th and 10th Avenues intersect. Proceed north on 10th Avenue another 0.4 km (0.25 mi). Turn left onto 7th Street North (signed for Whitetooth Ski Area) and set your trip odometer to 0.

For either approach above, now follow the directions below

0 km (0 mi)
Starting on 7th Street North. In 400 meters curve right (north) and follow the Columbia River.

1.5 km (0.9 mi)
Cross railroad tracks.

1.8 km (1.1 mi)
Proceed on Dogtooth FS road.

2.1 km (1.3 mi)
Curve left, still on pavement. In 100 meters cross the bridge to the Columbia River's west bank.

2.7 km (1.7 mi)
Go left onto Dogtooth Canyon FS road. Pavement ends.

4.8 km (3 mi)
Stay right on the main road.

5.8 km (3.6 mi)
Stay left on the main road.

9 km (5.6 mi)
Go left at the T-junction. Right leads to the ski area.

10.4 km (6.4 mi)
Proceed straight, passing a left spur road.

10.7 km (6.6 mi)
Go left, then immediately fork right. This stretch can be very muddy.

11 km (6.8 mi)
Arrive at Cedar Lake campground. The boat launch is left (electric motors only). Campsites are 200 meters to the right.

CEDAR LAKE CAMPGROUND #8
Weekend / Moderate / Free
Elev: 1036 m (3400 ft) / Lake: 5 ha
3 tables, 4 campsites, walk-in tent sites
sandy beach, boat launch
Too small for motorhomes and trailers

GOLDEN TO RADIUM HOT SPRINGS

The MOT campgrounds in this stretch of the Columbia Valley are all west of Hwy 95.

Mitten Lake (page 309) is the largest in the area. It also has the biggest campground and best mountain view. It's about a 15-minute drive from the village of Parson. On a blazing hot summer day, it's worth the trip just to go swimming. The water temperature is pleasant. Access is easy for small motorhomes and trailers.

About a 1-hour drive from Brisco are the famous Bugaboo Spires, in the Purcell Mountains. The granite monoliths shoot skyward, thousands of feet above the surrounding glaciers. Just outside **Bugaboo Provincial Park** is Bugaboo-Septet campground (page 311). It has an excellent view of the celebrated spires. Several hiking trails are nearby; all lead to tremendous vantage points. Hike to Conrad Kain Hut, or Cobalt Lake. Big RVs can survive the long access road to the Bugaboos, but the campground is too small for them.

Cobalt Lake, Bugaboo Provincial Park

On the benchland between Brisco and the Bugaboos, the outstanding campground is at easily-accessible **Cartwright Lake.** Though the view is east to the Rockies, hikers basecamping here will head west to the Bugaboos, Templeton Lake, or Septet Pass (up Frances Creek FS road). Of the two Cartwright camping areas, the north shore offers more privacy than the west shore. Both accommodate small motorhomes and trailers.

Near Cartwright are a dozen other campgrounds on smaller (6- to 43-hectare) **benchland lakes** in mature pine and fir forest. Cleland Lake has a view of the Rockies. Teal-coloured Dunbar Lake has a view of the Purcells. Shallow, reedy Hall Lake has wheelchair-accessible facilities including a dock and observation trail. Big RVs will encounter difficulties at, or en route to, most of these tiny campgrounds. The directions on page 315 will guide you through the rat's nest of narrow, sometimes very muddy roads. Suggestion: If you get confused during your benchland wanderings, follow the frequently signed Bugaboo-Cartwright or Westside roads north to intersect Bugaboo Creek FS road, then turn right (east) to reach Hwy 93.

Yet another hikers' haven is Stockdale Creek. The campground is virtually viewless, but nearby trails more than compensate. **Lake of the Hanging Glacier**—a 2.5-km (1.6-mi) long glacier-fed lake beneath dramatic cliffs—is blow-your-mind beautiful. The 16-km (9.9-mi) roundtrip hike gains

710 m (2330 ft). The trail up Farnham Creek to Commander Glacier is another exciting option. Stockdale Creek campground is too small for motorhomes and trailers.

If you're heading southeast on Hwy 95, from Golden

0 km (0 mi)
Starting southeast on Hwy 95, from 9th Street (the last traffic light) in Golden.

1.2 km (0.7 mi)
Cross the long bridge next to the railroad yard.

34 km (21.1 mi)
Pass the general store and post office in Parson.

35.7 km (22.1 mi)
Proceed southeast on Hwy 95 for Radium Hot Springs. Turn right (west) onto Spillamacheen FS road for Mitten Lake campground. Directions continue on page 309.

77 km (47.7 mi)
Proceed southeast on Hwy 95 for Radium Hot Springs. Turn right (west) onto Brisco Road for Bugaboo-Septet campground and benchland lakes campgrounds including Cartwright Lake. Directions continue on page 311. The turn is signed for Bugaboo Glacier Provincial Park.

105 km (65.1 mi)
Reach the junction of Hwys 95 and 93 in Radium Hot Springs. Turn right (west) onto Forsters Landing Road for Stockdale Creek campground. Directions continue on page 320. Turn left (northeast) onto Hwy 93 for Kootenay National Park. Proceed south on Hwy 93/95 for Invermere and Cranbrook.

If you're heading northwest on Hwy 95, from Radium Hot Springs

0 km (0 mi)
Starting northwest on Hwy 95 from the junction with Hwy 93 in Radium Hot Springs. For Stockdale Creek campground, go west at this junction onto Forsters Landing Road. Directions continue on page 320.

28 km (17.4 mi)
Proceed northwest on Hwy 95 for Golden. Turn left (west) onto Brisco Road for Bugaboo-Septet campground and benchland lakes campgrounds including Cartwright Lake. Directions continue on page 311. The turn is signed for Bugaboo Glacier Provincial Park.

Mitten Lake

69.3 km (43 mi)
Proceed northwest on Hwy 95 for Golden. Turn left (west) onto Spilla-macheen FS road for Mitten Lake campground. Directions continue below.

71 km (44 mi)
Pass the general store and post office in Parson.

105 km (65 mi)
Reach 9th Street (the last traffic light) in Golden. Proceed north through town to intersect Trans-Canada Hwy 1.

For MITTEN LAKE, now follow the directions below

0 km (0 mi)
Starting west on Spillamacheen FS road, departing Hwy 95. Cross railroad tracks, then several bridges over the Columbia River and wetlands.

1.6 km (1 mi)
Proceed straight on the main road. Soon begin ascending.

Brisco store, on Hwy 95

3.5 km (2.2 mi)
Curve left where Aspen Road is right.

4.2 km (2.6 mi)
Proceed straight on the main road.

5.5 km (3.4 mi)
Bear right.

6.2 km (3.8 mi)
Bear left.

7.1 km (4.4 mi)
Turn left onto Mitten Lake Road.

7.3 km (4.5 mi)
Fork left immediately after the yellow KM 7 sign.

9.6 km (6 mi) and 10 km (6.2 mi)
Bear left, passing right spurs.

11.3 km (7 mi)
Bear right.

15.2 km (9.4 mi)
Reach a junction. Go left for Mitten Lake campground. Turn right to reach Bittern Lake campground #9 (tiny lake, dock, 1 table) in 0.8 km (0.5 mi). It's too small for motorhomes and trailers.

18 km (11.2 mi)
Mitten Lake and the Purcell Mountains are visible.

18.5 km (11.4 mi)
Reach the first Mitten Lake campsite, beside the road.

18.9 km (11.7 mi)
Bear right and descend.

19.5 km (12.1 mi)
Arrive at Mitten Lake's main camping area.

MITTEN LAKE CAMPGROUND #10
Weekend / Moderate / $ / mid-May to mid-Sept
Elev: 996 m (3267 ft) / Lake: 1.4 km (0.8 mi) long, 60 ha
25 campsites, most with tables, boat launch, dock
Accessible by small motorhomes and trailers

**For CARTWRIGHT LAKE and BUGABOO-SEPTET,
now follow the directions below**

Bugaboo area trailheads and campgrounds are infamous for car-eating porcupines. Seriously. Under cover of darkness, these nocturnal varmints munch tires, hoses and fan belts. Their voracious appetite for rubber could leave you stranded. Thwart the porcs by wrapping chicken wire around your vehicle and securing it with rocks and pieces of wood. Moth balls liberally scattered under and around a vehicle are also rumoured to keep the rascals away.

0 km (0 mi)
Starting west on Brisco Road, departing Hwy 95. Proceed toward the mill.

0.5 km (0.3 mi)
Turn right (north) along the railroad tracks. Soon curve west again and cross two bridged channels of the Columbia River.

3.5 km (2.2 mi)
Reach a junction. Turn right, following the sign BUGABOO 45 KM.

5 km (3 mi)
Reach a junction and trail info sign. Go left, ascending steeply.

6.4 km (4 mi)
Go right on Bugaboo Creek FS road. You've completed most of the ascent from the valley floor. The road improves.

7 km (4.3 mi)
Reach a junction. Proceed right on the better road for Cartwright Lake and Bugaboo-Septet campgrounds. Turn left onto Brisco West - Westside Road and reset your trip odometer to 0 for campgrounds at several small bench-land lakes. Directions continue on page 315.

7.1 km (4.4 mi)
Proceed on the middle fork: Bugaboo Creek FS road.

8.5 km (5.3 mi) and 9.6 km (6 mi)
Stay straight on the main road.

18.6 km (11.5 mi)
Proceed right (west) for Bugaboo-Septet campground. Directions continue on page 314. Turn left (south) onto Bugaboo-Cartwright FS road and reset your trip odometer to 0 for Cartwright Lake campgrounds.

0 km (0 mi)
Starting south on Bugaboo-Cartwright FS road, heading for Cartwright Lake.

1.4 km (0.9 mi) and 3 km (1.9 mi)
Stay straight (southeast) on the main road.

4.4 km (2.7 mi)
Proceed straight (southeast) through the intersection (passing the KM 16 sign) for Cartwright Lake. Right leads to Templeton Lake trailhead.

5.3 km (3.3 mi)
Proceed straight (southeast) on the main road for Cartwright Lake's west campground. Turn left (east) and descend to reach Cartwright Lake's north campground in 0.9 km (0.5 mi). One table is near the entry. Reach six more in the next 300 meters.

CARTWRIGHT LAKE NORTH CAMPGROUND #18a
Weekend / Moderate / Free
Elev: 1190 m (3903 ft) / Lake: 1 km (0.6 mi) long, 43 ha
7 tables, dock, boat launch
Accessible by small motorhomes and trailers

Cartwright Lake

Continuing southeast on the main road, passing the turnoff to Cartwright Lake's north campground.

5.6 km (3.5 mi)
Proceed straight (southeast) on the main road.

6.3 km (3.9 mi)
Turn left (east) and descend to reach Cartwright Lake's west campground in 300 meters. Four campsites are on the shore. Two secluded campsites are behind the main area.

CARTWRIGHT LAKE WEST CAMPGROUND #18b
Weekend / Moderate / Free
12 tables, dock, boat launch
Accessible by small motorhomes and trailers

Continuing west on Bugaboo Creek FS road from the 18.6-km (11.5-mi) junction, passing the turnoff to Cartwright Lake campgrounds.

20.9 km (13 mi)
Cross a bridged creek.

21.2 km (13.1 mi)
Proceed straight.

23.4 km (14.5 mi)
Bear left.

23.8 km (14.8 mi)
Stay left, along the creek.

40.2 km (24.9 mi)
Reach Bugaboo Falls overlook.

43.3 km (26.8 mi)
Reach a junction. Proceed left (south) for Bugaboo-Septet campground. Right (west) leads to the Conrad Kain Hut and Cobalt Lake trailheads.

44 km (27.3 mi)
Reach a junction. For Bugaboo-Septet campground, turn left (east) and cross the bridge over Bugaboo Creek. Bugaboo Creek FS road continues right (south), soon passing a lodge en route to Bugaboo Pass trailhead.

44.1 km (27.35 mi)
Reach a fork just beyond the bridge. Turn left (north) for Bugaboo-Septet campground. Right (south) leads to Chalice Creek trailhead.

44.3 km (27.5 mi)
Turn left to reach Bugaboo-Septet campground in 100 meters.

The generator from the nearby lodge is audible, but Bugaboo Creek does its best to compete. The campsites are just above the creek. The ridge to the east blocks early morning sunlight.

BUGABOO-SEPTET CAMPGROUND #19
Destination / Difficult (due only to distance) / Free
Elev: 1500 m (4920 ft)
4 tables / Inaccessible by motorhomes and trailers

Cleland Lake

For BENCHLAND LAKES, now follow the directions below

0 km (0 mi)
Starting south on Brisco West - Westside Road, departing Bugaboo Creek
FS road at the 7-km (4.3-mi) junction. Bear left in 100 meters. At 200 meters
cross a bridged creek.

0.6 km (0.4 mi)
Bear left on Brisco West - Westside Road for Twin and Dunbar lakes. Directions
continue on page 316. Turn right onto Cleland Lake FS road and reset your
trip odometer to 0 for Cleland Lake.

0 km (0 mi)
Starting on Cleland Lake FS road.

1.8 km (1.1 mi) and 2.2 km (1.4 mi)
Bear left and ascend.

2.5 km (1.6 mi)
Proceed straight for Cleland Lake. Left is a steep, rough, narrow road to
Cub Lake campground #14. The lake and campground are tiny.

2.6 km (1.6 mi)
Bear left.

2.8 km (1.7 mi)
Reach a junction at Cleland Lake. Go right or left for Cleland Lake campsites. The rough road left continues to Jade Lake campground.

CLELAND LAKE CAMPGROUND #16
Weekend / Moderate / Free
Elev: 1158 m (3798 ft) / Lake: 24 ha
3 tables, 2 docks / Accessible by small motorhomes and trailers

3.8 km (2.4 mi)
Reach Jade Lake campground #15. The lake and campground are tiny.

Continuing left on Brisco West - Westside Road from the 0.6-km (0.4-mi) junction, heading for Twin and Dunbar lakes.

1 km (0.6 mi)
Bear right.

1.1 km (0.7 mi)
Bear left.

1.7 km (4.3 mi)
Bear right.

3.5 km (2.2 mi)
Bear left.

6.1 km (3.8 mi)
Reach a junction and sign BRISCO WEST. Go left.

6.3 km (3.9 mi)
Cross a bridged creek.

6.4 km (4 mi)
Proceed straight (south) for more benchland lakes campgrounds. Right is a narrow, rough, two-track road (small, sturdy vehicles only) leading to Botts Lake campground.

In about 0.3 km (0.2 mi) reach a possible campsite in a grassy, level clearing beside the creek. At 0.4 km (0.25 mi) reach a viewless campsite with a table, backed by a sandy bank. At 0.5 km (0.3 mi) arrive at a table on the shore of tiny, reedy Botts Lake.

BOTTS LAKE CAMPGROUND #13
BOTTS LAKE CAMPGROUND #13
Overnight / Difficult / Free
2 tables / Inaccessible by motorhomes and trailers

Continuing south on the main road, passing the turnoff to Botts Lake campground.

7.8 km (4.8 mi)
Proceed straight (south) for more benchland lakes campgrounds. Right is a narrow, two-track road leading about 40 meters to a one-table campsite on tiny Twin Lakes. It has a mountain view. A weir on the nearby creek creates water music.

8.2 km (5.1 mi)
Bear right.

8.6 km (5.3 mi)
Reach a junction. Proceed straight (southwest) on Westside Road for Hall Lake campground. Turn right (northwest) and reset your trip odometer to 0 for campgrounds at Twin and Dunbar lakes.

0 km (0 mi)
Starting northwest, departing Westside Road. In 200 meters reach Twin Lakes campground beside the road, in ugly trees, at the grim end of the tiny lake. Two campsites are on a bench above the shore, another is across the road.

TWIN LAKES CAMPGROUND #11
Overnight / Difficult / Free
3 tables / Inaccessible by motorhomes and trailers

0.9 km (0.5 mi)
Proceed straight and continue ascending.

2 km (1.2 mi)
Arrive at Dunbar Lake campground. It has a mountain view. The campsites are in trees, along the lake, beside the road. There are cabins nearby.

DUNBAR LAKE CAMPGROUND #12
Overnight / Difficult / Free
4 tables
Inaccessible by motorhomes and trailers

Continuing southwest on Westside Road from the 8.6-km (5.3-mi) junction, heading for Hall Lake.

9.4 km (5.8 mi)
Proceed southeast on Westside Road for Hall Lake. Turn right (west) onto a rough, narrow road, go over a steep hill, then turn left (south) to quickly reach Halfway Lake campground. The lake and campground are tiny.

11.1 km (6.9 mi)
Reach a junction. Turn right (west) onto Frances Creek FS road for Cartwright Lake, and to rejoin Bugaboo Creek FS road. Proceed left (southeast) on Westside Road and reset your trip odometer to 0 for Hall Lake.

0 km (0 mi)
Continuing left (southeast) on Westside Road, heading for Hall Lake.

0.7 km (0.4 mi)
Cross a big cement bridge.

2.8 km (1.7 mi)
Turn left (east) onto a spur road for Hall Lake.

3.4 km (2.1 mi)
Arrive at Hall Lake campground.

HALL LAKE CAMPGROUND #21
Overnight / Difficult (due only to distance) / Free
3 tables, wheelchair-accessible facilities, dock, observation trail
Accessible by small motorhomes and trailers

Continuing right (west) on Frances Creek FS road from the 11.1-km (6.9-mi) junction, heading for Cartwright Lake and Bugaboo Creek FS road.

13 km (8.1 mi)
Reach a junction. Proceed straight (northwest) on Bugaboo-Cartwright FS road for Cartwright Lake and Bugaboo Creek FS road. Frances Creek FS road continues left (west). It eventually reaches several trailheads, but in just 100 meters a right spur leads 0.6 km (0.4 mi) to Leadqueen Lake campground #20. It's a single campsite at a reedy widening of a creek, with a mountain view. It's useful for hikers heading to McLean Lake, Tiger Pass or Septet Pass.

14.3 km (8.9 mi)
Bear left.

14.5 km (9 mi)
Pass a KM 45 sign.

15 km (9.3 mi)
Proceed straight (northwest) on the main road.

17.2 km (10.7 mi)
Bear right on the main, upper road.

18.9 km (11.7 mi)
Cross a bridged creek. Proceed straight (northwest) on the main road, passing a minor fork.

20.9 km (13 mi)
Proceed straight (northwest) on the main road to intersect Bugaboo Creek FS road. Turn right (east) to reach Cartwright Lake's west campground in 300 meters. Read page 313 for details.

21.6 km (13.4 mi)
Proceed straight (northwest) on the main road.

21.9 km (13.6 mi)
Proceed straight (northwest) on the main road to intersect Bugaboo Creek FS road. Turn right (east) to reach Cartwright Lake's north campground in 0.9 km (0.5 mi). Read page 312 for details.

22.8 km (14.1 mi)
Proceed straight (northwest) through the intersection (passing the KM 16 sign) to intersect Bugaboo Creek FS road. Left leads to Templeton Lake trailhead.

24.2 km (15 mi)
Proceed straight (northwest) on the main road where Bugaboo-Lily FS road forks left.

25.8 km (16 mi)
Proceed straight (north) passing a left fork and the KM 13 sign.

27.2 km (16.9 mi)
Intersect Bugaboo Creek FS road. Turn left (west) for Bugaboo-Septet campground and Bugaboo Provincial Park. Directions continue on page 314, from the 18.6-km (11.5-mi) point. Turn right (east) and reset your trip odometer to 0 for Hwy 95 at Brisco.

0 km (0 mi)
Starting east on Bugaboo Creek FS road, from the junction with Bugaboo-Cartwright FS road, heading for Hwy 95.

9 km (5.6 mi) and 10.1 km (6.3 mi)
Bear left on the main road.

11.5 km (7.1 mi)
Proceed straight on the main road and start descending. Pass Westside Road on the right.

11.6 km (7.2 mi)
Stay left.

12.2 km (7.6 mi)
Bear left and continue descending. Slow down as the road narrows and curves sharply.

13.6 km (8.4 mi)
Bear right.

15.1 km (9.4 mi)
Bear left and cross bridged channels of the Columbia River.

18.6 km (11.5 mi)
After skirting the mill, intersect Hwy 95 at Brisco.

For STOCKDALE CREEK, now follow the directions below

From the junction of Hwys 93 & 95 in Radium Hot Springs, drive west onto Forsters Landing Road. In 1.4 km (0.9 mi) reach a junction just before the Slocan Group mill. Set your trip odometer to 0 here, so it will be in sync with the KM signs. Horsethief Creek FS road is passable in a 2WD car, but slow down near 41 km (25 mi) where deep waterbars (ditches) cross the road.

0 km (0 mi)
Starting left (west) on Horsethief Creek FS road. Soon cross railroad tracks, then a bridge over the Columbia River.

2.9 km (1.8 mi)
Reach a junction. Stay left on the main road. Steamboat Mountain Road (signed for Red Rock) forks right (north). Ignore all forks until the next major junction.

7 km (4.3 mi)
Proceed straight on the main road, passing a right fork.

Lake of the Hanging Glacier

9.2 km (5.7 mi)
Reach the KM 9 sign and a major junction with Westside Road. Proceed straight (southwest) on Horsethief Creek FS road, signed for Hanging Glacier. Left leads southeast to Invermere.

13.5 km (8.4 mi)
Go left.

21.5 km (13.3 mi)
Reach the valley bottom, where the road follows Horsethief Creek.

23.2 km (14.4 mi)
Curve left and cross a bridge to the south side of Horsethief Creek.

36 km (22.3 mi)
Bear right where a left (south) fork ascends the McDonald Creek drainage.

39.5 km (24.5 mi)
Proceed southwest on the main road for Lake of the Hanging Glacier trailhead. Turn right, just before the KM 39 sign, to enter Stockdale Creek campground.

STOCKDALE CREEK CAMPGROUND #22
Weekend / Difficult (due only to distance) / Free
Elev: 1300 m (4265 ft)
2 tables, 3 campsites
Accessible by small motorhomes and trailers

~~

41 km (25.4 mi)
The road deteriorates. Slow down. Beware of water bars.

50 km (31 mi)
The road is rough and narrow

50.2 km (31.1 mi)
Arrive at Lake of the Hanging Glacier trailhead.

~~

SOUTH OF KOOTENAY NATIONAL PARK

Twenty minutes of uncommonly smooth, easy, off-pavement driving is all it takes to reach secluded Horseshoe Rapids campground on the raging **Kootenay River,** just south of Kootenay Park. But the small campground is frequented by rafters, kayakers and canoeists. Be glad if you find a vacant campsite. Class II and III rapids make this an ideal river for multi-day canoe trips.

Willing to drive 45 minutes on backroads? Southeast of Horseshoe Rapids, closer to the spine of the **Rockies,** Palliser-Albert is a premier campground at the confluence of the clear, cold Palliser and Albert rivers. It's on the way to Height of the Rockies Provincial Park, so it's handy for hikers.

Horseshoe Rapids and Palliser-Albert are outstanding campgrounds in beautiful settings. But if you're a hiker, camping at either of them should be a supplement to, not a substitute for, time spent in the Rocky Mountain national parks. It's worth paying to camp in the heart of this resplendent mountain range. And hiking there is a must. Read the guidebook *Don't Waste Your Time in the Canadian Rockies*. It's described on page 534.

If you're heading south on Hwy 93, in Kootenay National Park

From McLeod Meadows campground near the south end of Kootenay National Park, drive Hwy 93 south 8 km (5 mi). Before the highway starts ascending, turn left (southeast) onto Settlers Road and reset your trip odometer to 0.

Kootenay River, from Horseshoe Rapids campground

If you're heading northeast on Hwy 93, from Radium Hot Springs

From Kootenay National Park's south-entrance toll booth at Radium Hot Springs, drive Hwy 93 northeast 19 km (11.8 mi). At the bottom of the hill, turn right (southeast) onto Settlers Road and reset your trip odometer to 0.

For either approach above, now follow the directions below

0 km (0 mi)
Starting southeast on Settlers Road, departing Hwy 93.

11.8 km (7.3 mi)
Cross Kootenay National Park's south boundary.

12.5 km (7.8 mi)
Reach a junction. Turn left (east) onto Kootenay-Palliser Road and reset your trip odometer to 0 for Palliser-Albert campground. Directions continue on page 324. Bear right and proceed south on Kootenay-Settlers Road for Horseshoe Rapids campground.

18 km (11 mi)
Pass an aspen grove and meadows.

19.2 km (11.9 mi)
Pass a left spur to a possible overnight pullout in a meadow.

19.5 km (12.1 mi)
Just after a culvert, turn left and descend on a small, rough road to reach Horseshoe Rapids campground in 0.8 km (0.5 mi). The turn is just before Bear Creek road forks right.

HORSESHOE RAPIDS CAMPGROUND #23
Destination / Moderate / Free
Elev: 1050 m (3445 ft)
2 tables, level tent site on the point
Inaccessible by motorhomes and trailers

Turning left (east) at the 12.5-km (7.8-mi) junction, passing the turnoff to Horseshoe Rapids campground. Reset your trip odometer to 0.

0 km (0 mi)
Starting east on Kootenay-Palliser Road, heading for Palliser-Albert campground. Stay left on the main road in 100 meters. Soon cross a bridge over the Kootenay River.

2.2 km (1.4 mi)
Turn right (south) where Cross River FS road forks left.

24.5 km (15.2 mi)
Cross the bridge to the south side of Palliser River and reach a junction. Right (south) leads 7 km (4.3 mi) to Fenwick Creek campground #24 just northeast of Fenwick Falls. Turn left (northeast) on Palliser-Albert FS road for Palliser-Albert campground. Heading east, stay on the main road, ignoring spurs.

28 km (17.4 mi)
Reach a junction near the 40 KM sign. Turn left (north) onto Albert River FS road for Palliser-Albert campground. Proceed straight (east) on Palliser FS road to view Palliser Falls canyon, near the KM 47 sign.

30 km (18.6 mi)
Reach Palliser-Albert campground on the left, just west of the rivers' confluence. Well-spaced campsites are on level terraces in the open pine forest.

Rocky Mountain valley

PALLISER-ALBERT CAMPGROUND #25
Weekend / Difficult (due only to distance) / Free
4 tables, 7 campsites, large spaces for RVs
Accessible by small motorhomes and trailers

FAIRMONT HOT SPRINGS TO KIMBERLEY

This is the south end of the Columbia Valley. The scenery is less compelling here than farther north where the Rockies rise steeper and the valley is narrower. But knowing a little about the area gives it some intrigue.

The easily overlooked hamlet of Canal Flats, for example, is the site of a fascinating phenomenon. It's on a narrow (2-km / 1.2-mi) strip of land separating Columbia Lake (headwaters of the north-bound Columbia River), from the south-bound Kootenay River. Now fast-forward your attention downstream. Each of the rivers, having wandered about 300 km (186 mi) in opposite directions, meet again and get married at Castlegar. Sharing the same name—Columbia River—they go on to achieve greatness as the fourth longest river in North America. The happy ending to this story takes place in Portland, Oregon, where the Columbia flows peacefully into the Pacific Ocean.

Just south of Canal Flats, the White River FS road leads east past Whiteswan Lake Provincial Park to small campgrounds beside the river's East Fork.

Despite such vast volumes of liquid, this is dry country, and the campgrounds are located on insignificant bodies of water. The Purcells, to the west, catch most of the moisture before it can reach the Columbia Valley. When clouds pass overhead, they're often running on empty. Expect sunshine. In summer, it gets hot enough here to make you wonder if this is really Canada.

As for specific campgrounds, Findlay Creek is a nondescript place to spend the night not far from Hwy 93/95. **Whitetail Lake** is weekend worthy, if you can tolerate the rough access road. Whitetail is popular because of its adequate size and fishing reputation. Both Findlay and Whitetail are suitable for small RVs.

Several campgrounds at small lakes near Skookumchuck are close to Hwy 93/95. Consider them for a brief overnighter. **Tamarack** and **Larchwood lakes** are pretty. Tamarack has the better mountain view but a twisty access road—tedious in a car, enjoyable on a mountain bike. Both campgrounds accommodate small RVs.

If you're heading south on Hwy 93/95, from Fairmont Hot Springs

0 km (0 mi)
Starting south on Hwy 93/95 from the Fairmont Hot Springs entry sign.

20.5 km (12.7 mi)
Turn right (west) at the sign BLUE LAKE FOREST CENTRE and reset your trip odometer to 0 for Findlay Creek and Whitetail Lake campgrounds. Directions continue on page 328.

25.5 km (15.8 mi)
Cross the Kootenay River bridge at Canal Flats.

30 km (18.5 mi)
For White River campgrounds, turn left (east) off Hwy 93/95 at the Whiteswan Provincial Park turnoff, onto White River Forest Service Road. Directions continue on page 329.

48.5 km (30.1 mi)
Turn right (west) and reset your trip odometer to 0 for Johnson Lake campground. Directions continue on page 331.

54.2 km (33.6 mi)
Cross the Kootenay River bridge just south of Skookumchuck.

55.3 km (34.3 mi)
Turn right (west) onto Farstad Way (toward the pulp mill) and reset your trip odometer to 0 for campgrounds at Tamarack and Larchwood lakes. Directions continue on page 331.

66.7 km (41.4 mi)
Reach the junction of Hwys 93/95 and 95A, near Wasa, northeast of Kimberley.

If you're heading north on Hwy 93/95, from near Kimberley

0 km (0 mi)
Starting north on Hwy 93/95, from the junction with Hwy 95A, near Wasa, northeast of Kimberley.

11.4 km (7.1 mi)
Turn left (west) onto Farstad Way (toward the pulp mill) and reset your trip odometer to 0 for campgrounds at Tamarack and Larchwood lakes. Directions continue on page 331.

12.5 km (7.8 mi)
Cross the Kootenay River bridge just south of Skookumchuck.

18.2 km (11.3 mi)
Turn left (west) and reset your trip odometer to 0 for Johnson Lake campground. Directions continue on page 331.

36.7 km (22.8 mi)
For White River campgrounds, turn right (east) off Hwy 93/95 at the Whiteswan Provincial Park turnoff, onto White River Forest Service Road. Directions continue on page 329.

41.2 km (25.5 mi)
Cross the Kootenay River bridge at Canal Flats.

46.2 km (28.6 mi)
Turn left (west) at the sign BLUE LAKE FOREST CENTRE and reset your trip odometer to 0 for Findlay Creek and Whitetail Lake campgrounds. Directions continue on page 238.

66.7 km (41.4 mi)
Reach the Fairmont Hot Springs entry sign.

For FINDLAY CREEK and WHITETAIL LAKE,
now follow the directions below

0 km (0 mi)
Starting (west) at the sign BLUE LAKE FOREST CENTRE, departing Hwy 93/95.

0.8 km (0.5 mi)
Pavement ends. Proceed south on Findlay Creek FS road.

2.2 km (1.4 mi)
Proceed straight, passing a left fork.

4.8 km (3 mi)
From the pullout on the left, a short trail leads to Findlay Falls.

5.7 km (3.5 mi)
Proceed straight (generally west) where Skookumchuck FS road forks left.

11.4 km (7.1 mi)
Reach a junction. Proceed straight (west) for Whitetail Lake. Turn left (south) and reset your trip odometer to 0 for Findlay Creek.

0 km (0 mi)
Starting south, heading for Findlay Creek.

0.4 km (0.2 mi)
The campground is visible across the creek.

1.9 km (1.2 mi)
After crossing the bridge, turn left (east) onto a small, rough road.

3.4 km (2.1 mi)
Arrive at Findlay Creek campground.

FINDLAY CREEK CAMPGROUND #26
Overnight / Moderate / Free
2 tables
Accessible by small motorhomes and trailers

~

Continuing west on Findlay Creek FS road, passing the turnoff to Findlay Creek campground.

13 km (8.1 mi)
Turn right (northwest).

Watch for moose feeding during morning or early evening.

24 km (14.9 mi)
Near the north end of Whitetail Lake, fork right and curve south to reach the campground in about 1.6 km (1 mi). Proceed another 1 km (0.6) to reach four more campsites with tables.

WHITETAIL LAKE CAMPGROUND #27
Weekend / Moderate / $
Elev: 1066 m (3495 ft) / Lake: 3.8 km (2.4 mi) long, 157.5 ha
24 tables, boat launch
Accessible by small motorhomes and trailers

For WHITE RIVER campgrounds, now follow the directions below

0 km (0 mi)
Initially heading southeast on White River Forest Service Road, soon curve north to head east for a long time.

10.5 km (6.5 mi)
Continue straight through a large intersection.

17.5 km (10.9 mi)
Reach parking for **Lussier Hotsprings,** near the west boundary of Whiteswan Provincial Park. The springs are accessed by a short hike down to the Lussier River. No liquor, dogs, or nudity are permitted at the springs. Haul out your trash.

21 km (13 mi)
Pass Alces Lake to the north. Continue straight on Whiteswan FS road, where a road goes right (southwest). Continue staying on the main road until just past the 32-km (19.8-mi) sign. Small **Alces Lake** is a good place to look for moose feeding during morning or early evening. A hiking trail from the north side of Alces Lake goes for 8 km (5 mi) to the northwest end of Whiteswan Lake at the road for Home Basin campground.

25 km (15.5 mi)
Pass along the south side of the west end of Whiteswan Lake. It's good for trophy rainbow-trout. The park's White River campground is open year-round, and has a fee May 9 – Sept 30.

28 km (17.4 mi)
Pass the park's Inlet Creek campground at the northeast end of Whiteswan Lake.

32.5 km (20.2 mi)
Immediately after crossing a bridge, reach a T-junction. Turn right onto White River Road.

43.7 km (27.1 mi)
At a Y-junction, bear right (east) at the fork of North White and Middle White roads. It might also be signed for Munroe Lake.

45 km (28 mi)
Go left (northeast) onto the Middle Fork FS Road for the White River camp-sites. For Munroe Lake, turn right on East White FS road and continue about 18 km (11.2 mi). There's an intimate campsite at small Munroe Lake campground #30, set against the mountains.

Continuing left (northeast) from the junction, on Middle Fork FS road.

In less than 100 meters, follow the narrow road left, leading down to White River campground. The last 100 meters is not suitable for trailers. A second site is adjacent. Situated at the confluence of the East and Middle forks of the White River, these two sites are a pleasant, streamside setting for hikers, kayakers, and anglers. It's popular with hunters in fall, but is lightly used in summer.

WHITE RIVER-GRAVES CREEK RECREATION SITE #29
Weekend / Moderate (due to distance) / Free
5 tables, 3 fire pits
Inaccessible by motorhomes, 5th-wheels, and shorter trailers

~

WHITE RIVER EAST FORK RECREATION SITE #28
Weekend / Moderate (due to distance) / Free
several sites in meadow
Accessible by motorhomes and shorter trailers

The Middle Fork FS road continues northeast to the trailhead at 68 km (42.2 mi)
for Height of the Rockies Park. That end of the valley was burned in the massive
2003 fire.

~

For JOHNSON LAKE, now follow the directions below

About 50 meters off Hwy 93/95, the access road forks. Turn left to reach the
south camping area in 0.5 km (0.3 mi). Go right 0.8 km (0.5 mi) then turn
sharply left to reach the north camping area, on the reedy end of the lake, in
another 100 meters.

JOHNSON LAKE CAMPGROUND #32
Overnight / Easy / Free
Elev: 854 m (2800 ft) / Lake: 13.5 ha
4 tables / Accessible by small motorhomes and trailers

~

For TAMARACK and LARCHWOOD LAKES,
now follow the directions below

0 km (0 mi)
Starting (west) on initially-paved Farstad Way, departing Hwy 93/95.

2 km (1.2 mi)
Turn left onto Torrent Road.

2.6 km (1.6 mi)
Bear right on the main road and cross railroad tracks.

3 km (1.8 mi)
Re-cross the creek and railroad tracks. Pavement ends.

4.6 km (2.9 mi)
Reach a junction. Turn left (southwest) for Tamarack Lake. Turn right (north) and reset your trip odometer to 0 for Larchwood Lake.

0 km (0 mi)
Starting north, heading for Larchwood Lake.

3.4 km (2.1 mi)
Bear left, ascending on the main road.

4.4 km (2.7 mi)
Arrive at Larchwood Lake campground. The lake is 200 meters beyond.

LARCHWOOD LAKE CAMPGROUND #33
Weekend / Easy / Free
Elev: 854 m (2800 ft) / Lake: 15.5 ha
3 well-spaced tables / Accessible by small motorhomes and trailers

~

Continuing southwest at the 4.6-km (2.9-mi) junction, passing the turnoff to Larchwood Lake.

4.9 km (3 mi)
Bear left.

7.4 km (4.6 mi)
Fork right.

8.4 km (5.2 mi)
Arrive at Tamarack Lake campground.

TAMARACK LAKE CAMPGROUND #31
Weekend / Easy / Free
Elev: 883 m (2895 ft) / Lake: 32 ha
2 tables, 3 campsites, dock
Accessible by small motorhomes and trailers

~

Horseshoe Lake and the Rocky Mountains

NEAR CRANBROOK AND FT. STEELE

Tiny Palmer Bar Lake is a convenient place to camp near Cranbrook. It's about a 15-minute drive southwest of town. Though small, the campground is accessible by motorhomes and 5th-wheels.

Southeast of historic Fort Steele, the Rockies leap skyward, giving a lazy camper plenty to look at from the comfort of a folding chair at destination-rated Horseshoe Lake campground. A more energetic camper can work-off a pasta lunch by mountain biking the dirt roads ringing the lake. Truly motivated campers can hike a rigorous trail into the Steeples. The trailhead is about 2 km (1.2 mi) south of the lake. Horseshoe Lake accommodates small motorhomes and trailers.

PALMER BAR LAKE

If you're heading southwest on Hwy 3/95 from Cranbrook

0 km (0 mi)
Starting southwest on Hwy 3/95, from the Tourist Info office across from Jim Smith Road, at the southwest end of Cranbrook.

10 km (6.2 mi)
Turn right onto Moyie River Road.

14 km (8.7 mi)
Bear right.

20 km (12.4 mi)
Arrive at Palmer Bar Lake campground.

PALMER BAR CAMPGROUND #32
Weekend / Easy / Free
4 tables, cartop boat launch
Accessible by motorhomes and 5th-wheels

~

HORSESHOE LAKE

If you're heading south or north, on Hwy 93/95

Just 1 km (0.6 mi) north of Fort Steele, turn east onto Wardner—Ft. Steele Road, signed for Norbury Lake Provincial Park. Follow it southeast another 11.5 km (7.1 mi), then turn left (north) at the sign for Horseshoe Lake.

If you're heading northwest on Hwy 3/93, from Jaffray

From Jaffray-Baynes Lake Road in Jaffray, drive Hwy 3/93 northwest 11 km (6.8 mi). Just before the Kootenay River bridge, turn right onto Wardner—Ft. Steele Road, signed for Norbury Lake Provincial Park. Reset your trip odometer to 0. At 15 km (9.3 mi) pass the park entrance. At 19 km (11.8 mi) turn right (north) at the sign for Horseshoe Lake.

For either approach above, now follow the directions below

In 300 meters, reach a fork. Campsites are 0.5 km (0.3 mi) in either direction. Right follows the east side of Horseshoe Lake. Left follows the west shore, where the mountain view is better. If you go left, bear left on the upper road, avoiding the sometimes flooded lower road. The lake is ringed by aspen-and-pine forest.

HORSESHOE LAKE CAMPGROUND #46
Destination / Easy / Free
Elev: 854 m (2800 ft) / Lake: 12 ha
12 tables / Accessible by small motorhomes and trailers

~

JAFFRAY TO ELKO

Looking at a B.C. road map, nobody notices Jaffray (southeast of Cranbrook) and Elko (south of Fernie). Most people aren't even aware of these hamlets when driving right through them on Hwy 3/93. Yet they're significant landmarks for campers. In the gently rolling grassland and open forests between Jaffray and Elko, you'll find several MOT campgrounds. Others are farther south, near and on Lake Koocanusa. The scenery is easily shrugged off. But the sun is a reliable fixture in the frequently blue sky. And the campgrounds are peaceful, good for a few days of down-time. Settle in. Ease off the mental accelerator. Nap in the shade. Play music under the trees. Chase your kids through a meadow. Cool off in the creeks and lakes.

Lake Koocanusa is a 110-km (68-mi) long reservoir created by Libby Dam on the Kootenay River in Montana. It averages 1 km (0.6 mi) wide. About half the lake is in Canada. The name was contrived—a combination of Kootenay, Canada, and USA. You won't be taking many photos of this artificial, mundane lake, but Kooc offers a lot of shoreline for boaters to explore. Bear in mind that the water level fluctuates.

WAPITI LAKE

If you're heading southeast on Hwy 3/93, from near Cranbrook

Just northeast of Cranbrook, Hwys 3/95, 93/95, and 3/93 converge. From the junction, drive Hwy 3/93 southeast 26 km (16 mi) to the Kootenay River bridge, just past Wardner. Reset your trip odometer to 0 on the bridge, proceed southeast 5.6 km (3.5 mi), then turn right (south) onto paved Rosicky Road. Reset your trip odometer to 0.

If you're heading northwest on Hwy 3/93, from Jaffray

From Jaffray-Baynes Lake Road in Jaffray, drive Hwy 3/93 northwest 6 km (3.7 mi). Turn left (south) onto paved Rosicky Road and reset your trip odometer to 0.

For either approach above, now follow the directions below

0 km (0 mi)
Starting south on paved Rosicky Road, departing Hwy 3/93.

0.4 km (0.2 mi)
Turn sharply left at the ranch, onto unpaved Shelbourne Road.

1.5 km (0.9 mi)
Turn right at the signpost.

1.6 km (1 mi)
Stay left and continue descending.

Wapiti Lake

2.2 km (1.4 mi)
Reach Wapiti Lake.

2.8 km (1.7 mi)
Arrive at Wapiti Lake campground on the southeast shore.

WAPITI LAKE CAMPGROUND #39
Weekend / Easy / Free
Elev: 777 m (2550 ft) / Lake: 4 ha
5 tables / Accessible by small motorhomes and trailers

MOST JAFFRAY - ELKO CAMPGROUNDS

If you're heading southeast on Hwy 3/93 from Jaffray

0 km (0 mi)
Starting southeast on Hwy 3/93 from Jaffray-Baynes Lake Road in Jaffray.
For North Star Lake campground, or the campgrounds near and on Lake
Koocanusa's west shore, go south at this junction onto Jaffray-Baynes Lake
Road. Directions continue on page 338.

200 meters
Turn left (north) onto Tie Lake Road and reset your trip odometer to 0 for Tie Lake campground. Directions continue on page 341.

5.1 km (3.2 mi)
Pass the lumber mill at Galloway.

12.1 km (7.5 mi)
Turn right (west) onto Rock Lake Road and reset your trip odometer to 0 for Rock Creek campground. Directions continue on page 341.

15.6 km (9.7 mi)
Turn right (southwest) onto Kikomun-Newgate Road and reset your trip odometer to 0 for Kikomun Creek campground. Directions continue on page 338.

17.6 km (10.9 mi)
Reach Elko, where Hwys 3 and 93 split. Proceed straight (northeast) on Hwy 3 for Fernie. Turn right (south) onto Hwy 93 and reset your trip odometer to 0 for Dorr campground on Lake Koocanusa's east shore, and campgrounds at Loon and Edwards lakes. Directions continue on page 342.

If you're heading northwest on Hwy 3/93 from Elko

0 km (0 mi)
Starting northwest on Hwy 3/93 from Elko, where Hwys 3 and 93 converge. For Dorr campground on Lake Koocanusa's east shore, and campgrounds at Loon and Edwards lakes, go south at this junction onto Hwy 93. Directions continue on page 342.

2 km (1.2 mi)
Turn left (southwest) onto Kikomun-Newgate Road and reset your trip odometer to 0 for Kikomun Creek campground, or the campgrounds near and on Lake Koocanusa's west shore. Directions continue on page 338.

5.5 km (3.4 mi)
Turn left (west) onto Rock Lake Road and reset your trip odometer to 0 for Rock Creek campground. Directions continue on page 341.

12.5 km (7.8 mi)
Pass the lumber mill at Galloway.

17.4 km (10.8 mi)
Turn right (north) onto Tie Lake Road and reset your trip odometer to 0 for Tie Lake campground. Directions continue on page 341.

17.6 km (10.9 mi)
Reach Jaffray. Turn left (south) onto Jaffray-Baynes Lake Road and reset

your trip odometer to 0 for North Star Lake campground. Directions continue below.

24.5 km (15.2 mi)
Proceed straight (northwest) on Hwy 3/93 for Cranbrook. Turn left (south) onto paved Rosicky Road and reset your trip odometer to 0 for Wapiti Lake campground. Directions continue on page 335.

∼

For NORTH STAR LAKE and LAKE KOOCANUSA'S WEST SHORE, now follow the directions below

0 km (0 mi)
Starting south on Jaffray-Baynes Lake Road, departing Hwy 3/93 in Jaffray.

4.7 km (2.9 mi)
Proceed straight (south) for Lake Koocanusa. Turn left (east) to reach North Star Lake campground in 1.8 km (1.1 mi).

NORTH STAR LAKE CAMPGROUND #38
Weekend / Easy / $ / mid-May to early Sept
Elev: 847 m (2780 ft) / Lake: 25 ha
9 campsites with tables / Accessible by small motorhomes and trailers

∼

Continuing south on the main road, passing the turnoff to North Star Lake campground.

16 km (9.9 mi)
Reach a 4-way junction at the northeast edge of Kikomun Creek Provincial Park. Turn right (west) onto Newgate Road and reset your trip odometer to 0 for campgrounds near and on Lake Koocanusa's west shore.

For KIKOMUN CREEK and LAKE KOOCANUSA'S WEST SHORE, now follow the directions below

0 km (0 mi)
Starting southwest on Kikomun-Newgate Rd, departing Hwy 3/93.

5 km (3 mi)
Proceed straight (southwest) for Lake Koocanusa. Turn right, then bear left at the next two forks, to reach Kikomun Creek campground in 2 km (1.2 mi).

Low-tech, intra-camper communication system

KIKOMUN CREEK CAMPGROUND #35
Weekend / Easy / Free
5 well-spaced tables
Accessible by small motorhomes and trailers

Continuing southwest on Kikomun-Newgate Road, passing the turnoff to Kikomun Creek campground.

7.2 km (4.5 mi)
Reach a 4-way junction at the northeast edge of Kikomun Creek Provincial Park. Proceed straight (west) onto Newgate Road and reset your trip odometer to 0 for campgrounds near and on Lake Koocanusa's west shore; directions continue below.

**Starting west on Newgate Road, from the junction
at the northeast edge of Kikomun Creek Provincial Park,
heading for Lake Koocanusa's west shore**

0 km (0 mi)
Starting west on Newgate Road, heading for campgrounds near and on
Lake Koocanusa's west shore. Soon cross the bridge spanning Lake
Koocanusa.

5.6 km (3.5 mi)
Turn left (south), generally following Lake Koocanusa's west shore.

18.6 km (11.5 mi)
Proceed generally south on the main road for Gold Creek and Gold Bay
campgrounds. Turn left to reach Englishman Creek campground on Lake
Koocanusa in 1 km (0.6 mi).

ENGLISHMAN CREEK CAMPGROUND #41
Weekend / Easy / $ / mid-May to early Sept
30 tables, 42 campsites, boat launch
Accessible by motorhomes and 5th-wheels

*Continuing south on the main road, passing the turnoff to Englishman Creek
campground.*

26.6 km (16.5 mi)
Reach Gold Creek campground beside the road.

GOLD CREEK CAMPGROUND #42
Weekend / Easy / Free
2 tables / Accessible by motorhomes and 5th-wheels

31.6 km (19.6 mi)
Turn left onto a rough road to reach Gold Bay campground on Lake
Koocanusa in 1 km (0.6 mi).

GOLD BAY CAMPGROUND #43
Weekend / Easy / $ / mid-May to early Sept
25 sites with tables / boat launch
Accessible by motorhomes and 5th-wheels

For TIE LAKE, now follow the directions below

0 km (0 mi)
Starting north on Tie Lake Road, departing Hwy 3/93.

2.7 km (1.7 mi)
Reach a junction. Go right to quickly reach Tie Lake campground on the southeast shore. The road circles the lake.

TIE LAKE CAMPGROUND #40
Weekend / Easy / $ / mid-May to early Sept
Elev: 850 m (2790 ft) / Lake: 134 ha
10 campsites with tables, gravel boat launch, day-use area
Accessible by motorhomes and 5th-wheels

For ROCK CREEK, now follow the directions below

0 km (0 mi)
Starting west on Rock Lake Road, departing Hwy 3/93. The surface is good gravel. Ignore signs for Rock Lake Camp. It's not the campground we want.

1.6 km (1 mi)
Bear left onto a narrow, rough road, where the main road curves right.

3.7 km (2.3 mi)
Reach a 4-way junction and turn right. Soon pass through beautiful meadows.

4.2 km (2.6 mi)
Proceed straight. Pass left and right forks. Descend through forest.

4.6 km (2.9 mi)
Turn left onto a spur to arrive at Rock Creek campground in 100 meters. It's in a forest-fringed meadow beside the languorous creek.

ROCK CREEK CAMPGROUND #36
Weekend / Easy / Free
3 campsites
Inaccessible by motorhomes and 5th-wheels

For LAKE KOOCANUSA'S EAST SHORE and LOON & EDWARDS LAKES,
now follow the directions below

0 km (0 mi)
Starting south on Hwy 93, from the junction of Hwys 3 and 93 at Elko.

13 km (8.1 mi)
Cross a bridge over Elk River.

16 km (9.9 mi)
Proceed straight (southeast) on Hwy 93 for campgrounds at Loon and Edwards lakes. Turn right (southwest) onto Dorr Road and reset your trip odometer to 0 for Dorr campground on Lake Koocanusa.

> **0 km (0 mi)**
> Starting southwest on Dorr Road, departing Hwy 93.

> **7.7 km (4.8 mi)**
> Turn right (west).

> **11.2 km (6.9 mi)**
> Arrive at Dorr campground on Lake Koocanusa.

DORR CAMPGROUND #47

Weekend / Easy / $ / April 30 to early Sept
nearly 60 campsites, gravel boat launch
Accessible by motorhomes and 5th-wheels

Continuing southeast on Hwy 93, passing the turnoff to Dorr campground.

24 km (14.9 mi)
Reach the community of Grasmere. Turn right (west) onto Schoolhouse Road and reset your trip odometer to 0 for campgrounds at Loon and Edwards lakes.

> **0 km (0 mi)**
> Starting west on Schoolhouse Road, departing Hwy 93.

> **0.4 km (0.2 mi)**
> Turn left (south) onto Edwards Lake Road for Edwards Lake campground. Turn right (north) onto Loon Lake Road to reach Loon Lake campground at 2 km (1.2 mi). Partially-treed campsites are on the south and west shores.

Volunteer backroad maintenance

LOON LAKE CAMPGROUND #44
Weekend / Easy / $ / April 30 to early Sept
Elev: 802 m (2630 ft) / Lake: 45 ha
40 campsites with tables, gravel boat launch
Accessible by motorhomes and 5th-wheels

Continuing left (south) at the 0.4-km (0.2-mi) junction, passing the turnoff to Loon Lake campground.

0.9 km (0.6 mi)
Reach a junction. Make a tight hairpin turn right. Bear left on this road until the lake is visible.

3.4 km (2.1 mi)
Arrive at small Edwards Lake. The first camping area has three tables. Proceed 0.5 km (0.3 mi) along the shore for two more tables.

EDWARDS LAKE CAMPGROUND #45
Weekend / Easy / Free
Elev: 802 m (2630 ft) / Lake: 42.5 ha
5 tables, boat launch / Accessible by motorhomes and 5th-wheels

Elk Lakes Provincial Park, premier hiking country

ELK VALLEY

In the far lower-right-hand corner of B.C., on Hwy 3, is the town of Sparwood. Directly north of Sparwood is Elkford. And north of Elkford is a string of free campgrounds up Elk River Valley, en route to Elk Lakes Provincial Park. The road is good, the setting is beautiful, the campgrounds are pleasant, and the trail into the park is very rewarding. Allow a full day for the roundtrip hike to Upper Elk Lake, where Rocky Mountain peaks and alpine slopes are visible. Upper Petain Basin is a splendid two-day backpack trip.

Early explorers often saw herds of 100 elk here, hence the name. The valley is also home to mule and white-tail deer, bighorn sheep, mountain goats, and bears—blacks and grizzlies. Read *B.C. Stands for Bear Country* (page 33). Follow all the recommended precautions. And unless you're a hunter, clear out of here on September 1. This big, tranquil valley suddenly seems very small and scary when hunting season begins.

The Elk Valley road is usually snowfree by mid-June and is maintained through September.

If you're heading east or west on Hwy 3, in the southeast corner of B.C.

Drive Hwy 3 to Sparwood. It's 29 km (18 mi) northeast of Fernie, or 18 km (11.2 mi) northwest of the Alberta border. In Sparwood, turn north onto Hwy 43 and follow it 33 km (20.5 mi) to Elkford, where pavement ends. Set your trip odometer to 0.

0 km (0 mi)
Starting north on Elk Lakes FS road, from Elkford.

10.5 km (6.5 mi)
Reach Krivensky Farm campground #48 on the right. It has 5 tables in a field near the Elk River.

20.8 km (12.9 mi)
Reach Blue Lake campground #49 on the left. It has 3 tables on the tiny lake.

39 km (24.2 mi)
Reach Aldridge Creek campground #50 on the right. It has 2 tables beside the Elk River.

46.3 km (28.7 mi)
Soon after crossing a bridge to the east side of Elk River, reach Weary Creek campground #51 on the left, beside the road. It has 1 table on the river. Just beyond, the FS road intersects Kananaskis Power Line Road. Bear left and proceed north.

58 km (36 mi)
Reach Riverside campground #52 on the left. It has 2 tables between the road and the river.

63.5 km (39.4 mi)
Reach Tobermory Creek campground #53 on the left. It has 4 tables in open forest. The FS maintains a cabin here for public use. It has 4 bunks and a woodstove. It's available first come, first served.

64.5 km (40 mi)
Reach Upper Elk River campground #54 on the left. It has 3 tables beside the Elk River, and a view of meadows and mountainside avalanche chutes.

69 km (42.8 mi)
Reach Elk Lakes trailhead at road's end. An easy, 20-minute walk on a level trail leads to tent sites in Elk Lakes Provincial Park.

CENTRAL BRITISH COLUMBIA
from Trans-Canada Hwy 1, north past Hwy 16

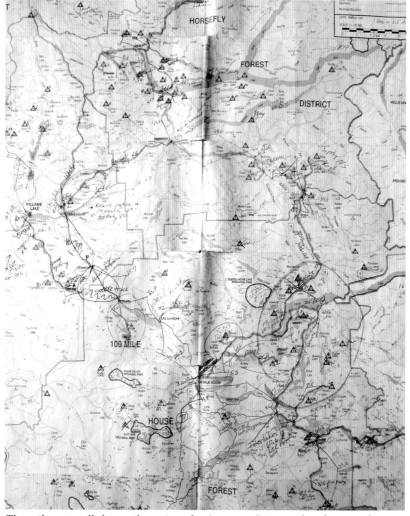

The authors travelled more than 16,000 km (10,000 mi) to complete the research for this book.

Taltzen Lake, near Smithers

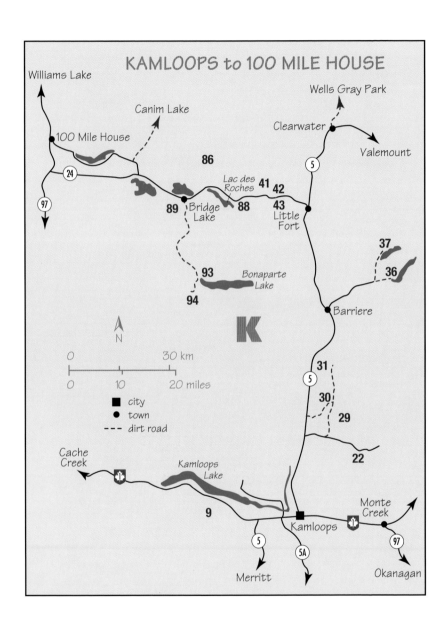

KAMLOOPS to 100 MILE HOUSE

Williams Lake

Canim Lake

Wells Gray Park

Clearwater

Valemount

100 Mile House

86

Lac des Roches 41 42

89 88 43 Little Fort

Bridge Lake

37

36

93 Bonaparte Lake

94

Barriere

N

0   30 km

0   10   20 miles

31

30

29

■ city
● town
- - - dirt road

22

Cache Creek

Kamloops Lake

9

Monte Creek

Kamloops

5

5A

97

Merritt

Okanagan

K: Kamloops to 100 Mile House

At the fee campgrounds, charges apply May 15 to September 30.

9	Duffy Lake	$
22	Heffley Lake	$
29	Community Lake	$
30	Sullivan Lake	$ weekends only
31	Badger Lake	$ weekends only
36	East Barriere Lake	$
37	Vermelin Creek	FREE
41	Deer Lake	FREE
42	Goose Lake	FREE
43	Latremouille Lake	FREE
86	Needa Lake	FREE
88	Phinetta Lake	FREE
89	Crystal Lake	FREE
93	Bonaparte Lake	FREE
94	Hammer Lake	FREE

Paintbrush

Kamloops to 100 Mile House

Find your own secluded hideaway.

WEST OF KAMLOOPS

Duffy Lake campground is no place for family frolic. It's just a clearing plastered with cow pies. But it's close enough to Kamloops that it's worth knowing about in case you need a place to sleep. A 10-minute drive on Hwy 1, then 15 minutes off pavement will get you there. Convenience is

Duffy's only asset. Though big RVs will find adequate room, the backroad is bumpy enough to loosen a few screws. It gets muddy too, so avoid it after heavy rain.

If you're heading west on Hwy 1, from Kamloops

0 km (0 mi)
Starting west on Trans-Canada Hwy 1, from the junction with Hwy 5A at Kamloops.

6.5 km (4 mi)
Stay in the far right lane on Hwys 1/97 where Hwy 5 bears left.

14.5 km (9 mi)
Pass the gas station at Cherry Creek.

23.5 km (14.6 mi)
Turn left onto Greenstone Mtn. Road (signed for Dominic Lake Resort) and reset your trip odometer to 0.

If you're heading east on Hwy 1, from Savona

0 km (0 mi)
Starting east on Trans-Canada Hwy 1, from Savona.

24 km (14.9 mi)
Pass Rodeo Drive and the green highway sign stating the distance to Kamloops (22 km).

27.5 km (17.1 mi)
Turn right onto Greenstone Mtn. Road (signed for Dominic Lake Resort) and reset your trip odometer to 0.

For either approach above, now follow the directions below

0 km (0 mi)
Starting on Greenstone Mtn. Road.

2.4 km (1.5 mi)
Go right. Proceed through a burned area.

9.7 km (6 mi)
Turn left and ascend steeply.

12.3 km (7.6 mi)
Turn right.

13.5 km (8.4 mi)
Arrive at Duffy Lake campground. The best campsite is 300 meters farther, on a grassy knoll overlooking the lake.

DUFFY LAKE CAMPGROUND #9

Weekend / Moderate / $ / May 15 – Sept 30
Elev: 1158 m (3800 ft) / Lake: 24 ha
6 tables, 30 campsites
Accessible by motorhomes and 5th-wheels

NORTH OF KAMLOOPS

Camp at some of the lakes north of Kamloops and you'll enjoy a bonus: a lovely drive on smooth, gently meandering roads. Heffley, Community, Sullivan and Badger lakes are particularly worth steering your wheels toward. The mixed forest en route includes studly ponderosa pines and burly Douglas firs and is occasionally broken by verdant grassland. In spring, the birch and aspen leaves are crisp, lime green. In fall, they're electric gold.

Heffley Lake (below) is just 20 minutes from Hwy 5, and a total of 45 minutes from Kamloops. Access is entirely paved. But the campground is small, the road busy, the area rife with cabins and country homes. Don't expect solitude or wilderness. It's simply a handy, comfortable place for a night's sleep.

As for **Community, Sullivan and Badger lakes** (page 354), none is a garden of earthly delights. They're just small lakes, with ordinary campgrounds, in scenically mediocre settings. Community is the least attractive. Sullivan Lake is across the road from the campground. Badger is on a treeless slope, so bring your own shade. Sullivan and Badger accommodate monster RVs. Big rigs should avoid Community. Oblivious cows—lovable despite their mental and physical lethargy—often loiter on the roads, so drive warily.

The two **Barriere lakes** (page 356) are farther north, closer to Little Fort than to Kamloops. East Barriere Lake campground, though well designed, is virtually treeless. You'll have no privacy from fellow campers or from the homes a short distance away. **Vermelin Creek** campground is just a modest gravel beach on beautiful North Barriere Lake. Claim part of it for yourself, and you'll be a happy camper. Both lakes are accessible by motorhomes and 5th-wheels, but Vermelin Creek campground is too small for them.

HEFFLEY LAKE

If you're heading north on Hwy 5, from Hwy 1 at Kamloops

In 24.2 km (15 mi) turn right (east) onto paved Old Hwy 25, signed for Sun Peaks Resort. Set your trip odometer to 0.

Heffley Lake

If you're heading south on Hwy 5, from Hwy 24 at Little Fort

In 69.5 km (43.1 mi) turn left (east) onto paved Old Hwy 25, signed for Sun Peaks Resort. Set your trip odometer to 0.

For either approach, now follow the directions below

0 km (0 mi)
Starting east on paved Old Hwy 25, signed for Sun Peaks Resort. In 0.2 km (0.1 mi), bear left at Heffley Creek store.

8.1 km (5 mi)
Proceed straight for Heffley Lake. Turn left (north) onto Sullivan Lake Road for Community, Sullivan or Badger lakes campgrounds. Read further directions on page 354.

18 km (11.2 mi)
Pass Golden Horn Road, signed for Hitch and Reel Resort. Slow down after the long, cement, roadside barrier.

19 km (11.8 mi)
Pass the second access to Embleton Mtn. trail on the left. Just 50 meters beyond, turn right and descend for Heffley Lake campground.

In 40 meters reach a fork. The middle road leads to one campsite. Right leads in 100 meters to the main campground. The lake is not visible there. The small road between the first and third tables leads to a secluded, treed campsite without a table but overlooking the lake. Bear right, past the campsites, to reach a day-use area in 150 meters. It has tables on the shore.

HEFFLEY LAKE CAMPGROUND #22
Overnight / Easy / $ / May 15 - Sept 30
Elev: 948 m (3110 ft) / Lake: 4.5 km (2.8 mi) long, 172 ha
11 tables, 30 campsites in a grassy clearing ringed by tall trees
Accessible by motorhomes and 5th-wheels

COMMUNITY, SULLIVAN AND BADGER LAKES

0 km (0 mi)
Starting north on Sullivan Lake Road, from the 8.1-km (5-mi) junction on Old Hwy 25. Ascend through a small, upper valley.

9 km (5.6 mi)
Reach a junction. Turn right (east) for Community Lake. Proceed straight (north) for Sullivan or Badger lakes.

0 km (0 mi)
Starting east on Community Lake FS road. Rain can make this steep ascent dangerously muddy.

3.3 km (2 mi)
Reach a 3-way junction. Take the middle fork signed for Community Lake. Tall trees are on the left, a clearcut is on the right.

4.2 km (2.6 mi)
Bear right.

5.9 km (3.7 mi)
Go left at the 3-way junction.

6.1 km (3.8 mi)
Arrive at Community Lake campground.

COMMUNITY LAKE CAMPGROUND #29
Weekend / Moderate / $ / May 15 to Sept 30, except Tues & Wed
Elev: 1372 m (4500 ft) / Lake: 1.5 km (0.9 mi) long, 36 ha
2 tables, boat launch, dock
Accessible by small motorhomes and trailers

Continuing north on Sullivan Lake Road, from the 9-km (5.6-mi) junction, passing the turnoff to Community Lake campground.

11.5 km (7.1 mi)
Proceed straight where a road forks right.

11.7 km (7.3 mi)
Reach a signed junction. Bear right for Sullivan and Badger lakes. Left descends to Hwy 5.

12.5 km (7.8 mi)
Proceed straight.

13.9 km (8.6 mi)
Turn right at the fork.

14.1 km (8.7 mi)
Turn left for Sullivan Lake campground. The lake is on the right. The access road rejoins the main road in 0.4 km (0.25 mi).

SULLIVAN LAKE CAMPGROUND #30
Weekend / Moderate / $ / weekends, May 15 to Sept 30
Elev: 1148 m (3765 ft) / Lake: 2 km (1.2 mi) long, 87 ha
4 tables (3 grouped, 1 separate)
Accessible by motorhomes and 5th-wheels

Continuing north on Sullivan Lake Road, passing Sullivan Lake campground.

14.9 km (9.2 mi)
Pass Knouff Lake Resort.

17 km (10.5 mi)
Pass a small lake.

20 km (12.4 mi)
Proceed straight through the 4-way junction.

21 km (13 mi)
Badger Lake is visible.

21.5 km (13.3 mi)
Fork left on Badger Creek FS road.

22.3 km (13.8 mi)
Reach a sign PUBLIC ACCESS. Fork left on either of two roads.

22.7 km (14.1 mi)
Arrive at Badger Lake campground. A loop road accesses the campsites.

BADGER LAKE CAMPGROUND #31

Weekend / Moderate / $ / weekends, May 15 to Sept 30
Elev: 1082 m (3542 ft) / Lake: 2.3 km (1.4 mi) long, 53 ha
15 tables, good boat launch, no shade
Accessible by motorhomes and 5th-wheels

Departing Badger Lake, instead of returning the way you came, consider this short-cut to Hwy 5. With a mountain bike, and someone willing to drive your vehicle, you can bike down this road and enjoy a thrilling descent.

0 km (0 mi)
Starting west from the 11.7-km (7.3-mi) junction just south of Sullivan Lake.

7 km (4.3 mi)
Curve right on the main road after a major descent.

8 km (5 mi)
Stay left and continue descending.

12 km (7.4 mi)
Intersect Hwy 5. Turn left (south) for Kamloops. Turn right (north) for Barriere, Little Fort or Clearwater.

EAST AND NORTH BARRIERE LAKES

If you're heading north on Hwy 5, from Hwy 1 at Kamloops

In 63.7 km (39.5 mi) angle right off Hwy 5. Go through the *Welcome to Barriere* portal. About 2 km (1.2 mi) farther, cross a bridge over Barriere River. Just 300 m (328 yd) beyond, across from the secondary school, turn right (northeast) onto the paved road signed for N. Barriere Lake Resort (33 km). Set your trip odometer to 0.

If you're heading south on Hwy 5, from Hwy 24 at Little Fort

In 29 km (18 mi) turn left (east) onto Barriere Town Road, signed for Barriere and Dunn lakes. Reach a junction near the secondary school in 1.2 km (0.7 mi). Set your trip odometer to 0 and proceed straight (northeast).

For either approach above, now follow the directions below

0 km (0 mi)
Starting northeast from the junction near the secondary school in Barriere.

Pitch your tent on the beach at Vermelin Creek campground on North Barriere Lake.

1.9 km (1.2 mi)
Bear right.

16.6 km (10.3 mi)
Cross a bridge over Barriere River.

17.4 km (10.8 mi)
Reach a junction. There's a public phone here. Pavement ends. Set your trip odometer to 0 before going either way. Proceed straight (northeast) for East Barriere Lake campground. Turn left (north) for Vermelin Creek campground on North Barriere Lake and read the directions on page 358.

0 km (0 mi)
Proceeding straight (northeast) from the 17.4-km (10.8-mi) junction, heading for East Barriere Lake.

0.5 km (0.3 mi)
Stay on the main road.

3.1 km (1.9 mi)
Bear left at the fork.

5.5 km (3.4 mi)
The road ends at the entrance to East Barriere Lake campground. It's well designed, with level campsites on a 400-meter loop. But it lacks forest cover and seems naked and exposed. Also, directly across the narrow west end of the lake are luxurious homes with huge windows. You might feel you're being watched. And you might watch them.

EAST BARRIERE LAKE CAMPGROUND #36
Weekend / Easy / $ / May 1 to Sept 10
Elev: 640 m (2100 ft) / Lake: 12 km (7.4 mi) long, 1000 ha
12 tables, 20 campsites
Accessible by motorhomes and 5th-wheels

0 km (0 mi)
Starting north from the 17.4-km (10.8-mi) junction, heading for Vermelin Creek campground on North Barriere Lake.

4.5 km (2.8 mi)
Cross a bridge over Barriere River.

7.9 km (4.9 mi) and 8.9 km (5.5 mi)
Proceed straight on the main road.

10.4 km (6.4 mi)
Cross a bridge over Harper Creek. Just after, bear right at the junction.

13.1 km (8.1 mi)
Pass a boat launch on the right.

15.1 km (9.4 mi)
Turn right to enter Vermelin Creek campground. It's just after a yellow 15 KM sign, near a small peninsula in the lake.

This is simply a gravel beach that you can drive onto. There's one individual campsite next to the road as you enter. Otherwise camp in the open on the beach. It would be crowded with three vehicles, but tolerable if everyone was quiet and considerate. The lakeshore is undeveloped. The forested, hilly setting is beautiful.

VERMELIN CREEK CAMPGROUND #37
Weekend / Easy / Free
Elev: 610 m (2000 ft) / Lake: 7 km (4.3 mi) long, 497 ha
3 campsites without tables
Inaccessible by motorhomes and 5th-wheels

WEST ON HWY 24

Publicizing Hwy 24 would be easy. An advertising agency could forego the standard ploy of exaggeration and simply tell the truth. They could call it the *Aspenland Skyway*. Nobody would question the name's veracity.

This sleek ribbon of pavement links Hwy 5, at Little Fort, with Hwy 97, just south of 100 Mile House. It climbs modest mountains known for temperate weather and consistently blue skies. Then it careens through the range at about 1200 m (3935 ft) elevation, where aspen trees thrive. Their trunks are wedding-dress white. Their leaves are lime in spring, gold in fall. They lighten and brighten the forest. Add the occasional roadside lake, and traffic-free driving, and the result is a delightful, stress-relieving experience behind the wheel.

South of the Bridge Lake community are campgrounds on Bonaparte and Hammer lakes. Unless you're an angler or a boater, Bonaparte is hardly worth the necessary 45-minute drive from Hwy 24. Bonaparte is a big lake, but the campground is mediocre. It allows you no privacy and no view because it's just a clearing entirely framed by trees. Hammer is a fine lake with a pleasant, medium-size campground set in tall trees near the shore. Check it out if you're likely to stay a couple nights.

Your stop-and-plop options include very convenient campgrounds at Latremouille, Phinetta and Crystal lakes. Phinetta is idyllic. Crystal is also appealing. Latremouille is closest to pavement, but even it should be quiet, because Hwy 24 is lightly travelled, especially at night.

If you're heading west on Hwy 24, from Hwy 5 in Little Fort

0 km (0 mi)
Starting west on Hwy 24 from Little Fort.

16.6 km (10.3 mi)
Turn left for Latremouille Lake campground. Descend to reach the campground in 300 meters. The first loop on the right has 6 tables, 7 campsites. The left loop has 1 table and 3 sites near the lake. The highway is just above, but it's not busy, so noise might not be a problem for you.

LATREMOUILLE LAKE CAMPGROUND #43

Weekend / Easy / Free
Elev: 1190 m (3903 ft) / Lake: 2.7 km (1.7 mi) long, 75 ha
7 tables, 10 campsites
Accessible by motorhomes and 5th-wheels

Continuing west on Hwy 24, passing the turnoff to Latremouille Lake campground.

17 km (10.5 mi)
Pass a big pullout with a bearproof garbage bin.

18.8 km (11.7 mi)
Turn right to reach Goose Lake campground in 200 meters.

GOOSE LAKE CAMPGROUND #42
Overnight / Easy / Free
3 tables, many more campsites, rough boat launch
Accessible by motorhomes and 5th-wheels

Continuing west on Hwy 24, passing the turnoff to Goose Lake campground.

19.8 km (12.3 mi)
Turn right (north) onto Taweel FS road for Deer Lake campground. Proceed north on the main road for about 5 km (3.1 mi). Watch for the access on the right. The campground is spacious, the lake is small.

DEER LAKE CAMPGROUND #41
Weekend / Easy / Free
Elev: 1402 m (4600 ft) / 1 km (0.6 mi) long, 33 ha
8 tables, rough boat launch
Inaccessible by large motorhomes and 5th-wheels

Continuing west on Hwy 24, passing the turnoff to Deer Lake campground.

22 km (13.6 mi)
Reach 1311-m (4300-ft) McDonald Summit.

30.2 km (18.7 mi)
Phinetta Lake is visible.

30.7 km (19 mi)
Turn left (south) onto Opax Road for Phinetta Lake campground.

> **0 km (0 mi)**
> Starting south on Opax Road.

> **0.2 km (0.1 mi)**
> Turn left at the Opax Mountain Cafe.

Though it's beside Hwy 24, Phinetta Lake campground is idyllic.

0.4 km (0.25 mi)
Proceed straight.

0.6 km (0.4 mi)
Turn right to enter the campground. At the fork, right leads 100 meters to a secluded campsite with a table. Left leads to 2 well-spaced tables by the lake. Big rigs can turn around 300 meters beyond the campground.

PHINETTA LAKE CAMPGROUND #88
Weekend / Easy / Free
Elev: 1128 m (3700 ft) / Lake: 0.8 km (0.5 mi) long, 23 ha
3 tables
Accessible by motorhomes and 5th-wheels

Continuing west on Hwy 24, passing the turnoff to Phinetta Lake campground.

34.4 km (21.3 mi)
Pass the turnoff to Eagle Island Resort.

40.4 km (25 mi)
Pass a rest area on the left, overlooking Lac des Roches. RVs can probably still stop here for dinner and a night's sleep.

49.4 km (30.6 mi)
Pass Cottonwood Bay Road on the right. It leads north to Bridge Lake Provincial Park. Soon after, a blue sign announces the left turn for Green Lake and the community of Bridge Lake.

50.2 km (31.1 mi)
Turn left (south) onto Bridge Lake Business Route (the community's east access) for Crystal, Bonaparte, or Hammer lakes. In 1.1 km (0.7 mi) reach the junction at Bridge Lake store and set your trip odometer to 0.

Or, proceeding west on Hwy 24, pass the west end of Bridge Lake Business Route at 51.8 km (32.1 mi). Set your trip odometer 0, then continue following directions on page 365.

SOUTH OF HWY 24

0 km (0 mi)
For campgrounds at Crystal, Bonaparte, or Hammer lakes, go south on N. Bonaparte Road, from the signed junction at Bridge Lake store. Proceed straight on the main road when the pavement ends in 200 meters.

1.5 km (0.9 mi)
Pass Burn Lake on the left.

2.3 km (1.4 mi)
Reach a junction. Set your trip odometer to 0 before going either way. Left leads south to Eagan, Sharpe, Bonaparte, and Hammer lakes. Proceed straight for Crystal Lake campground.

> **0 km (0 mi)**
> Proceeding straight at the 2.3-km (1.4-mi) junction.
>
> **1 km (0.6 mi)**
> Crystal Lake is visible.
>
> **1.6 km (1 mi)**
> Turn left to reach Crystal Lake campground in 100 meters. The lake is surrounded by mixed forest and low hills.

Crystal Lake

CRYSTAL LAKE CAMPGROUND #89
Weekend / Easy / Free
Elev: 1122 m (3680 ft) / Lake: 2.5 km (1.6 mi) long, 150 ha
4 tables, 6 campsites, boat launch
Accessible by small motorhomes and trailers

0 km (0 mi)
Starting south on Eagan Lake Road, from the 2.3-km (1.4-mi) junction. Alert drivers can safely motor at 80 kph (50 mph) on this wide, well-maintained thoroughfare.

8.6 km (5.3 mi)
Bear right.

12.6 km (7.8 mi)
Proceed straight on the main road where Eagan Crescent rejoins it. Pass a ranch.

14.7 km (9.1 mi)
Pass a barn and the turnoff to Eagan Lake Resort.

15.4 km (9.5 mi)
Reach a junction. Turn left for Bonaparte Lake.

21.5 km (13.3 mi)
Bear right.

22.6 km (14 mi)
Cross a little bridge and bear right.

23.4 km (14.5 mi), 25 km (15.5 mi) and 26.3 km (16.3 mi)
Bear right.

26.7 km (16.6 mi)
Reach a fork. Set your trip odometer to 0 before going either way. Bear left for Bonaparte Lake. Turn right (south) for Hammer Lake.

> **0 km (0 mi)**
> Bearing left at the 26.7-km (16.6-mi) fork.

> **0.4 km (0.25 mi)**
> Proceed straight and descend to reach Bonaparte Lake campground in 100 meters. It's just a big forest-enclosed clearing with no view.

BONAPARTE LAKE CAMPGROUND #93
Weekend / Moderate / Free
Elev: 1170 m (3838 ft) / Lake: 18.5 km (11.5 mi) long,
3325 hectares
6 tables, good boat launch
Accessible by motorhomes and 5th-wheels

0 km (0 mi)
Starting south for Hammer Lake, from the 26.7-km (16.6-mi) junction.

1.9 km (1.2 mi)
Proceed straight past Bonaparte Lodge.

3 km (1.9 mi)
Bear right.

5.2 km (3.2 mi)
Reach a triangular junction. Go right. In 150 meters, go right again.

6 km (3.7 mi)
Reach a junction. Turn left and in 100 meters curve left again to arrive at Hammer Lake campground.

HAMMER LAKE CAMPGROUND #94
Weekend / Difficult (due only to distance) / Free
Elev: 1260 m (4133 ft) / Lake: 2.5 km (1.6 mi) long, 66 ha
9 tables on a loop, 6 lakeshore campsites, boat launch
Accessible by motorhomes and 5th-wheels

Upon returning to Bridge Lake store, bear left at the junction to reach Hwy 24 in 0.9 km (0.5 mi). Turn left to continue west. Set your trip odometer 0.

0 km (0 mi)
Resuming west on Hwy 24, from the west end of Bridge Lake Business Route.

9.5 km (5.9 mi)
Turn right (north) onto Shertenlib Road for Needa Lake campground. It's oddly located on a narrow, shallow arm of the lake, where views are nil. The shore is inhospitable. A boat is necessary to appreciate the lake.

0 km (0 mi)
Starting north on Shertenlib Road.

0.4 km (0.25 mi)
Bear left. The road is wide and fairly smooth.

1.9 km (1.2 mi) and 2.7 km (1.7 mi)
Turn left.

5.5 km (3.4 mi)
Go right and ascend Windy Mountain FS road.

7.1 km (4.4 mi)
Cross the bridge.

9.2 km (5.7 mi) and 11.3 km (7 mi)
Stay on the main road.

17.8 km (11 mi)
Turn right and reset your trip odometer to 0. At 0.3 km (0.2 mi) descend right. At 0.4 km (0.25 mi) go right again. At 1.1 km (0.7 mi) go right yet again to enter small Needa Lake campground.

NEEDA LAKE CAMPGROUND #86
Weekend / Moderate / Free
Elev: 1111 m (3645 ft) / Lake: 5 km (3.1 mi) long, 205 ha
5 tables, rough boat launch
Accessible by small motorhomes and trailers

Continuing west on Hwy 24, passing the turnoff to Needa Lake campground.

12.7 km (7.9 mi)
Pass Sheridan Lake store.

15.8 km (9.8 mi)
Reach a junction just past Interlakes store. Proceed straight (west) on Hwy 24 to reach Hwy 97. Turn right (north) onto Horse Lake FS road to access superior campgrounds in the **East Cariboo** via excellent backroads. The turn is signed for several lakes: Hathaway (14 km), Drewry (25 km), Canim (43 km), and Mahood (57 km). It's also the southwest approach to Wells Gray Provincial Park. Read page 436 for directions.

47.6 km (29.5 mi)
Intersect Hwy 97. Turn right (north) to quickly reach 100 Mile House. Turn left (south) for Clinton.

EAST ON HWY 24

0 km (0 mi)
Starting east on Hwy 24, departing Hwy 97 just south of 100 Mile House.

11.2 km (6.9 mi)
Pass the signed turnoff for Horse Lake on the left.

31.8 km (19.7 mi)
Reach a junction just before Interlakes store. Proceed straight (east) to access campgrounds along Hwy 24 en route to Hwy 5 at Little Fort. Turn left (north) onto Horse Lake FS road to access superior campgrounds in the East Cariboo region via excellent backroads. The turn is signed for several lakes: Hathaway (14 km), Drewry (25 km), Canim (43 km), and Mahood (57 km). It's also the southwest approach to Wells Gray Provincial Park. Read directions on page 436.

35 km (21.7 mi)
Pass Sheridan Lake store.

Some backroads lead to lodges and private cottages, as well as campgrounds.

38.1 km (23.6 mi)
Turn left (north) onto Shertenlib Road for Needa Lake campground. Read further directions on page 365.

47.6 km (29.5 mi)
Proceed straight (east) on Hwy 24. Or turn right (south) onto Bridge Lake Business Route (the community's west access) for campgrounds at Crystal, Bonaparte, and Hammer lakes. In 0.9 km (0.6 mi) reach the junction at Bridge Lake store, set your trip odometer to 0, and read further directions on page 362.

49.2 km (30.5 mi)
Pass the east end of Bridge Lake Business Route.

59 km (36.6 mi)
Pass a rest area on the right, overlooking Lac des Roches. RVs can stop here to cook a meal and maybe spend the night.

68.7 km (42.6 mi)
Turn right (south) onto Opax Road to quickly reach Phinetta Lake campground. Read further directions at the bottom of page 360.

Willow-herb

77.4 km (48 mi)
Reach 1311-m (4300-ft) McDonald Summit.

79.6 km (49.4 mi)
Turn left (north) onto Taweel FS road for Deer Lake campground. Read further directions on page 360.

80.6 km (50 mi)
Turn left to reach Goose Lake campground in 200 meters. Read page 360 for details.

82.8 km (51.3 mi)
Turn right to reach Latremouille Lake campground in 300 meters. Read page 359 for details. Continuing west on Hwy 24, soon begin a long descent into the Thompson River valley.

99.4 km (61.6 mi)
Intersect Hwy 5 in Little Fort. Turn left (north) for Clearwater. Turn right (south) for Kamloops.

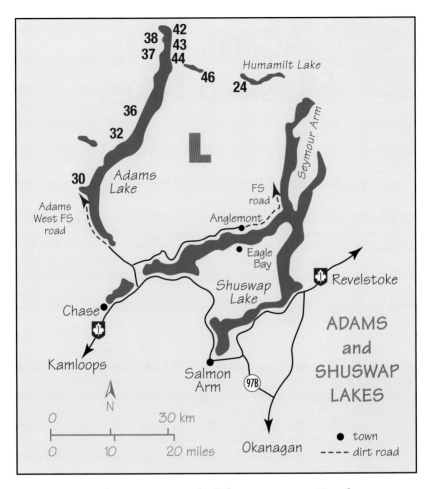

L: Adams and Shuswap Lakes

24	Humamilt Lake West	FREE	42	Tsikwustum Creek North	FREE
30	Skwaam Bay	$	43	Tsikwustum Creek South	FREE
32	Sandy Point	$	44	Momich River	FREE
36	Honeymoon Bay	$	46	Momich Lake East	FREE
37	Rocky Point	FREE			
38	Gordon Bay	FREE			

Adams and Shuswap Lakes

Adams and Shuswap lakes are equally beautiful. Both are impressively long and wide, surrounded by high, forested mountains. Yet they are very different lakes.

The shoreline of Adams is almost undeveloped. Driving around it you'll enjoy frequent lake views and encounter plenty of free campgrounds— many of them provincial-park quality. Adams Lake is 62.5 km (39 mi) long and covers 13,108 hectares. The elevation is 412 m (1,350 ft).

Shuswap Lake is a popular summer vacation destination and retirement area. It's 71 km (44 mi) long and covers 30,512 hectares. The elevation is 346 m (1,135 ft). Houseboats toodle up and down its many arms, cottages and homes ring the shore, but you won't find a single free campground here. Nevertheless, the drive along Shuswap is worthwhile. So make a loop around both lakes. Head north along the west shore of Adams Lake. Cross the low mountains via Humamilt Lake. Then go south, down the west shore of Seymour Arm and the north shore of Shuswap Lake, back to the Trans-Canada.

ADAMS LAKE WEST

If you're heading west on Trans-Canada Hwy 1, from Sorrento

From the pedestrian walkway with flashing lights, drive 9.2 km (5.7 mi), then turn left off Hwy 1 and onto an overpass. The turn is signed for North Shuswap Resort Area, Roderick Haig-Brown, and Adams Lake. Set your trip odometer to 0.

If you're heading east on Trans-Canada Hwy 1, from Kamloops

From the junction with Hwy 97, near Monte Creek, drive 27 km (16.7 mi), then turn right off Hwy 1 and onto an overpass. The turn is signed for North Shuswap Resort Area, Roderick Haig-Brown, and Adams Lake. Set your trip odometer to 0.

Premier camping on Adams Lake

For either approach above, now follow the directions below

0 km (0 mi)
Turning south off Hwy 1. Curve right to loop onto the overpass.

0.3 km (0.2 mi)
Bear right on the main road. (Turtle Valley Road forks left. It accesses Skimikin Lakes campground, described on page 203.)

0.7 km (0.4 mi)
Midway across the South Thompson River bridge.

3.9 km (2.4 mi)
Turn left on Holding Road to proceed up the west side of Adams Lake. (Right, toward Scotch Creek and Anglemont, accesses the north side of Shuswap Lake, and Seymour Arm.

12.3 km (7.6 mi)
Pass Adams Lake store.

14.7 km (9.1 mi)
Arrive at a mill and a logging company sign END OF PUBLIC ROAD. Don't be alarmed; you can continue by turning left. Set your trip odometer to 0.

0 km (0 mi)
Turning left before the mill. Ascend the paved road past the house. Pavement soon ends. Continue on the wide gravel road. Bear left through the weigh-scale area. Immediately after is a 4-way junction. Stay straight on the main road.

3.4 km (2.1 mi)
Adams Lake Provincial Park is on the right.

12.8 km (7.9 mi)
Bear right and descend on the main road.

18.7 km (11.6 mi)
Left (northwest) is a pastoral valley. Cross a bridge. This is Squam Bay (spelled Skwaam on maps).

19 km (11.8 mi)
Reach a stop sign and 4-way junction. Continue straight on Adams West FS road.

20.5 km (12.7 mi)
Turn right for Skwaam Bay campground.

> Descend from the main road. In 100 meters fork left for the easiest lake access. In 200 meters arrive at the first table, in forest above the lake. In 350 meters reach another fork. Left leads to private cottages. Turn right. Arrive at 2 tables on the lakeshore, 450 meters from the main road. The view is across the lake to beautiful Douglas fir forest on high hillsides. Several cottages are visible to the right.

SKWAAM BAY CAMPGROUND #30
Destination / Moderate / $ / mid-May to mid-Sept
3 tables, 4 campsites, pebble beach
Accessible by motorhomes and 5th-wheels

Continuing northeast on Adams West FS road, passing the turnoff to Skwaam Bay campground.

27.8 km (17.2 mi)
Continue straight. Samatosum FS road forks left. Stay on the main road paralleling the lake. Ignore, narrower logging roads and private roads.

36.8 km (22.8 mi)
Reach a junction. To continue northeast up the lake, stay left on Adams West FS road. To reach the aptly named Sandy Point campground on Adams Lake, turn right at the sign BRENNAN CREEK 2 KM.

Skwaam Bay campground on Adams Lake

In 1.4 km (0.9 mi) fork right and descend. In another 100 meters the road forks again. Left leads to the day-use area and beach. Right is the narrow road into the campground. A tiny school is nearby.

SANDY POINT CAMPGROUND #32
Destination / Moderate / $ / mid-May to mid-Sept
12 tables in a cedar grove, big sandy beach, excellent swimming
Accessible by small trailers, but not motorhomes or 5th-wheels

Continuing northeast on Adams West FS road, passing the 36.8-km (22.8-mi) junction.

49.3 km (30.6 mi)
Stay right on the main road.

50.6 km (31.4 mi)
Watch carefully for the small, obscure, right fork descending to Honeymoon Bay campground on Adams Lake. Set your trip odometer to 0 here, whether turning or continuing.

In 0.6 km (0.4 mi) reach the FS sign and another fork. Left descends to a small rocky beach. Right descends to the campground in 100 meters. The initial group of 5 tables is on the lake but fully exposed to sun, wind or rain. Proceed 0.5 km (0.3 mi) to other lake sites sheltered by trees. The first of these has a spring nearby. The fifth site is best. Despite large cutblocks visible across the lake, the setting is beautiful. RVs might be able to turn around at road's end.

HONEYMOON BAY CAMPGROUND #36
Destination / Moderate / $ / weekends mid-May to mid-Sept
11 tables, rocky lakeshore with small strips of sand
Accessible by small trailers or motorhomes, but not 5th-wheels

Continuing northeast on Adams West FS road, from the turnoff to Honeymoon Bay campground. Set your trip odometer to 0.

0 km (0 mi)
On Adams West FS road, at the turnoff to Honeymoon Bay campground.

5 km (3.1 mi)
Stay right on the main road. A small road ascends left.

15.4 km (9.5 mi)
Turn right for Rocky Point campground. (The main road pulls away from the lake. Once the lake is again visible, watch for this unsigned road on the right.)

Arrive at the first table in 200 meters. Bear right and proceed 0.4 km (0.25 mi) to reach two more tables on the point. The surrounding topography is less dramatic here than farther south on the lake. RVs have room to maneuver.

ROCKY POINT CAMPGROUND #37
Weekend / Difficult (due only to distance)
3 unsheltered tables, boat launch
Accessible by motorhomes and 5th-wheels

Continuing north on Adams West FS road, passing the turnoff to Rocky Point campground.

17.7 km (11 mi)
Stay straight on the main road to round the north end of Adams Lake. Turn right for Gordon Bay campground.

The beach at Sandy Point campground on Adams Lake

0 km (0 mi)
Turning right and descending.

0.4 km (0.25 mi)
Bear right.

0.6 km (0.4 mi)
The road divides into three. Left goes to two tables on the lake. The middle fork leads 400 meters to a large, open campsite ideal for 5th-wheels. It's across a narrow channel from an island. Right ascends 300 meters to a sandy loop with 5 tables in the trees. Honeymoon Bay and Brennan Creek campgrounds are prettier and their shorelines more spacious.

GORDON BAY CAMPGROUND #38
Weekend / Difficult (due only to distance) / Free
7 tables, boat launch
Accessible by motorhomes and 5th-wheels

Continuing north on Adams West FS road, passing the turnoff to Gordon Bay campground.

21.3 km (13.2 mi)
Reach a major junction near the north end of Adams Lake. Set your trip odometer to 0 and turn right on Adams East FS road.

ADAMS LAKE EAST

0 km (0 mi)
Heading northeast on Adams East FS road.

5.3 km (3.3 mi)
Cross a bridge over Adams River.

5.6 km (3.5 mi)
Stay straight.

7.6 km (4.7 mi)
Bear right where a left fork is signed for Gannett Lake. You're now heading south.

8.3 km (5.1 mi)
Ignore a minor right fork. Stay on the main road. Soon start descending.

10 km (6.2 mi)
Cross a small bridge over Gannett Creek, just before (north of) the KM 6 sign.

10.5 km (6.5 mi)
Cross a bridge over Michael Creek. The road is now following the east shore of Adams Lake.

11.7 km (7.3 mi)
The road veers right, toward the point.

12 km (7.4 mi)
Turn right for Tsikwustum campground, across from Michael Creek FS road. A sign welcomes the public but warns that forestry work crews have precedence. Reach the campground 150 meters from the main road. The rocky lakeshore has a few patches of sand.

TSIKWUSTUM CREEK NORTH CAMPGROUND #42
Weekend / Difficult (due only to distance) / Free
7 tables, many more campsites, good boat launch
Accessible by motorhomes and 5th-wheels

View from Gordon Bay campground on Adams Lake

Continuing south on Adams East FS road, passing the turnoff to Silviculture campground.

12.1 km (7.4 mi)
Cross a bridge.

12.4 km (7.7 mi)
The main road widens. Turn right for Tsikwustum campground.

> Descend to reach the campground in 0.5 km (0.3 mi). Right leads 100 meters to 2 separate campsites with tables. Left leads 100 meters to one table, 2 campsites, and enough room for RVs to turn around.

TSIKWUSTUM CREEK SOUTH CAMPGROUND #43
Weekend / Difficult (due only to distance) / Free
3 tables, boat launch, rocky lakeshore
Narrow, brushy access road will scratch big RVs

Continuing south on Adams East FS road, passing the turnoff to Tsikwustum campground.

12.6 km (7.8 mi)
Stay on the main road curving right.

18.7 km (11.6 mi)
Reach a major junction. Bear right and descend for Momich River campground, beyond which there are no more campgrounds on the east shore of Adams Lake. Left is Momich-Stukemapten FS road, described below. That's the way to Shuswap Lake's Seymour Arm. Set your trip odometer to 0 here if turning left.

19 km (11.8 mi)
Turn right for BC Parks' Momich River campground, which is likely still free because of the remote location.

Descend to enter the campground in 0.5 km (0.3 mi). Just before the sign, a right fork loops into the north section, passing 6 campsites (2 with tables, all in the trees, none with lake views) and reaching a cement boat launch. Stay straight at the sign to enter the main section where most campsites have lake views. Bear left for sites near the river, right for more privacy on the lake. An obnoxious generator across the river might be audible.

MOMICH RIVER CAMPGROUND #44
Destination / Difficult (due only to distance) / Free
22 tables, pebble beach, boat launch, mega-wharf
Accessible by motorhomes and 5th-wheels,
but not on north-section loop

ADAMS LAKE SOUTHEAST TO SEYMOUR ARM

Turning left (east) onto Momich-Stukemapten FS road, before the turnoff to Momich River campground. Set your trip odometer to 0.

0 km (0 mi)
Starting on Momich-Stukemapten FS road, from the 18.7-km (11.6-mi) junction on Adams East FS road.

0.5 km (0.3 mi)
Go right.

2.5 km (1.6 mi)
Small Momich Lake is on the right.

6.9 km (4.3 mi)
The road is now high on a cliffside. Visible below is Momich Lake's east end.

Momich River campground on Adams Lake

7.9 km (4.9 mi)
Go right at the fork and descend.

8.4 km (5.2 mi)
Follow a hairpin turn right.

10.1 km (6.3 mi)
Cross the bridged inlet stream. Immediately after, turn right for Momich Lake East campground. The three campsites are merely pullouts on the right side of the access road, which ends at 0.5 km (0.3 mi) in a turn-around. The forest is cool, shady, mossy. The green lake invites swimming.

MOMICH LAKE EAST CAMPGROUND #46
Weekend / Difficult (due only to distance) / Free
2 tables, 3 campsites, boat launch, sandy beach, little privacy
Accessible by small trailers, but not motorhomes or 5th-wheels

Continuing east on Momich-Stukemapten FS road, passing the turnoff to Momich Lake East campground.

10.9 km (6.8 mi)
Turn left at a fork signed for Cayenne Camp.

12.2 km (7.6 mi)
Bear left on Cayenne Creek FS road.

12.5 km (7.8 mi)
Cross a bridged creek then immediately turn left at a T-junction.

13.5 km (8.4 mi)
Pass a lake on the left.

15.4 km (9.5 mi)
Bear left at the fork.

18 km (11.2 mi)
Bear left.

20.6 km (12.8 mi)
Reach a junction just before a bridged creek. Turn left, again following a sign for Cayenne Camp.

21 km (13 mi)
Turn right at the T-junction.

26.2 km (16.2 mi)
Stay straight and soon descend.

27.5 km (17.1 mi)
Cross a bridged stream. Humamilt Lake is visible left.

28.9 km (17.9 mi)
Pass a KM 27 sign on the right. Slow down for Humamilt Lake campground.

29.5 km (18.3 mi)
Turn left for Humamilt Lake campground. Stay straight on Celista Creek FS road for Seymour Arm. Set your trip odometer to 0 here, whether turning or continuing.

Descend from the main road. Arrive at the first table in 100 meters. Proceed another 50 meters to the other 6 campsites scattered in a forest of cedar, fir and birch, near the southwest end of the lake.

Humamilt Lake campsite

HUMAMILT LAKE CAMPGROUND #24
Destination / Difficult (due only to distance) / Free
Elev: 580 m (1902 ft) / Lake: 12 km (7.5 mi) long, 438 ha
7 tables, boat launch, exceptionally beautiful forest and lake
Inaccessible by motorhomes and trailers

Continuing east on Celista Creek FS road, from the turnoff to Humamilt Lake campground. Set your trip odometer to 0.

0 km (0 mi)
Continuing east on Celista Creek FS road. **0.9 km (0.5 mi)**, stay straight, along the south side of Humamilt Lake.

5.5 km (3.4 mi)
Stay left.

11.5 km (7.1 mi)
Pass Humamilt Lake East campground. It has 2 tables and an outhouse, but it's just an overnight pullout between the road and the marshy east end of the lake. During the day, the dust and noise of passing vehicles is annoying.

12.2 km (7.6 mi)
Bear left on the main road.

14 km (8.7 mi)
Face a road looping toward you. Go left on the broader, main road.

14.9 km (9.2 mi)
Cross a bridge over Celista Creek and reach a T-junction. Turn right (south).
Along the creek to your right is an ancient forest of cedar and hemlock—
a rare delight in this heavily logged land.

18.8 km (11.7 mi)
Stay straight on the main road.

21.7 km (13.4 mi)
Arrive at a well-signed **major junction** beside a mill, near the north end of
Shuswap Lake's Seymour Arm. Set your trip odometer to 0. Turn left (east)
on Celista-Seymour FS road (also signed for Seymour Arm) to quickly
reach Nellie Lake campground. Continue straight (south) on Celista Creek
FS road and later Ross-Ruckell FS road to reach Trans-Canada Hwy 1.

0 km (0 mi)
On Celista FS road, heading south to follow the west side of Seymour Arm.

1 km (0.6 mi)
The signed access road for Albas Provincial Park is on the left. The lakeside campground is several kilometers below the main road.

1.1 km (0.7 mi)
Bear left.

2.6 km (1.6 mi)
Stay straight.

3.1 km (1.9 mi)
Go right at this major junction and ascend on Ross-Ruckell FS road.
Shuswap Lake's enormous Seymour Arm is visible left, far below.

7.1 km (4.4 mi)
Stay straight on the main road, then cross a bridged creek.

11.2 km (6.9 mi) to 28.1 km (17.4 mi)
Stay straight on the main road.

30.8 km (19.1 mi)
The road is rough now and very close to the lakeshore.

32.3 km (20 mi)
Pavement begins. Pass a luxurious log home on the left.

41.3 km (25.6 mi)
Stay straight, along the lake.

63 km (39.1 mi)
Curve right.

65.3 km (40.5 mi)
Cross a bridge over Scotch Creek.

66 km (41 mi)
Bear left. Scotch Creek FS road forks right (north).

76 km (47.1 mi)
Midway across the Adams River bridge.

76.6 km (47.5 mi)
Holding Road forks right, accessing the west side of Adams Lake. Proceed straight (south).

79.8 km (49.5 mi)
Midway across the South Thompson River bridge. Continue onto the highway overpass and loop left.

80.6 km (50 mi)
Intersect Trans-Canada Hwy 1. Salmon Arm is right (east), Kamloops is left (west).

Ancient cedar and hemlock, a rare delight in this heavily-logged land

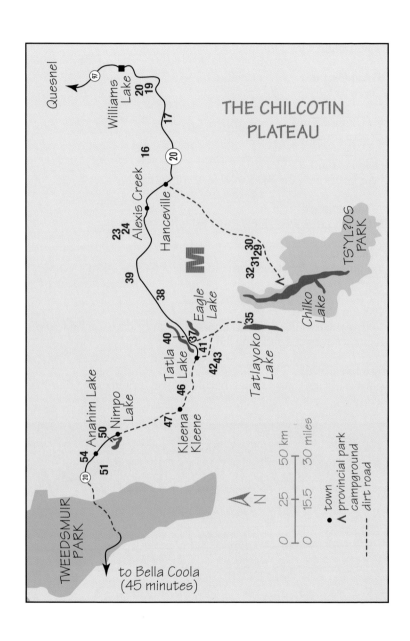

THE CHILCOTIN PLATEAU

Quesnel

97

Williams Lake

20
19

17

THE CHILCOTIN PLATEAU

Alexis Creek 16

20

Hanceville

23
24

39

38

M

Eagle Lake

32 31 29
30

TS'YL?OS PARK

Chilko Lake

Tatla Lake 40
37
41
42 43

35

Tatlayoko Lake

Anahim Lake

Nimpo Lake

47

46

Kleena Kleene

54
50
51

20

TWEEDSMUIR PARK

to Bella Coola
(45 minutes)

50 km
30 miles

N

• town
∧ provincial park
  campground
----- dirt road

0   25   50 km
0   15.5 30 miles

M: The Chilcotin Plateau

At the fee campgrounds, charges apply May 15 to September 30. But at Tatla Lake fees apply through October 15.

1	McCall Flats	FREE	37	Eagle Lake	FREE
16	Raven Lake	FREE	38	Pyper Lake	FREE
17	Becher Pond	FREE	39	Puntzi Lake	FREE
19	McIntyre Lake	FREE	40	Tatla Lake	$
20	Till Lake	FREE	41	Pinto Lake	FREE
23	Two Lakes	FREE	42	Sapeye Lake	$
24	Alexis Lakes	FREE	43	Horn Lake	$
29	Big Lake	$	46	One Eye Lake	FREE
30	Davidson Bridge	FREE	47	Clearwater Lake	FREE
31	Vedan Lake	FREE	50	Dean River (Fish Trap)	FREE
32	Chaunigan Lake	FREE	51	Kappan Lake	FREE
35	Tatlayoko Lake	FREE	54	Little Anahim Lake	FREE

B.C. stands for Big Catch.

The Chilcotin Plateau

The Coast Mountains rise beyond Chilko Lake's west shore. In the foreground is a Russell fence, common through the Chilcotin.

Hunkered in the middle of central B.C. is the city of Williams Lake. Wedged into a narrow fiord that splits the Coast Range is the town of Bella Coola. Linking them is Hwy 20. It's 456 km (283 mi) long. A third of the distance is dirt—an often dusty, occasionally muddy reminder that this province is vast. So vast that paving all the main arteries isn't feasible, and that maybe what the initials really stand for is Big Country.

Hwy 20 traverses lonely terrain: the Chilcotin Plateau, virtually a big country unto itself. Driving west, you'll swoop into the Fraser River canyon, then climb onto the plateau. Until the rapid descent through mountainous **Tweedsmuir Provincial Park** to the Pacific Ocean, the highway bobs and weaves over hilly expanses of grass broken by forests of aspen and lodgepole pine. This is premier ranch land, where the vistas test the limits of your eyesight.

Across the plateau, as in other B.C. ranch lands such as Telkwa Valley outside Smithers, you'll see drift fences. They keep cattle from drifting—off the ranch, onto the road, into trouble. There are many styles of drift fence. The most artistic is the Russell fence. Like old covered bridges, Russell fences are certifiably quaint. They beg to be photographed.

Contrary to this grand setting, Chilcotin campgrounds tend to be small. But west of Williams Lake, no cities clog Hwy 20. The dots on the map are just hamlets. So there's no population pressure on these small campgrounds. Crowds don't seem to be a problem. At the campgrounds near Hwy 20, expect company. Those a day's journey from the highway just might be vacant when you arrive. Rub your lucky charm.

Concerned about too much solitude? Picturing yourself waiting hours for a saviour after your vehicle breaks down? The Chilcotin isn't that lonely. Actually, the Chilcotin is, but the roads aren't. That's because the traffic is not dispersed; it's confined to a relatively minimal network of roads. Traffic on Hwy 20 is light but steady. Huge ranches sprawl across the Chilcotin, keeping most backroads in regular use. There's always the occasional logging truck. And in big country like this, people tend to be open and trusting. They habitually offer help if it appears needed.

But you are hereby warned: watch your fuel gauge. Gas stations are rare as vegetarians out here. You can count on filling up in the communities of Alexis Creek, Tatla Lake, Nimpo Lake, and Anahim Lake (largest settlement in the West Chilcotin). Mega Fuels is the dominant gas station on Hwy 20. Most stations are open until 8 p.m. in summer. It's critical that you have plenty of gas and other necessities before driving southwest to **Ts'yl?os Park** and Chilko Lake.

Now, about that dust and mud. Dust is simply annoying. Mud can be dangerous. Surprised by a quagmire, your vehicle can swerve off the road no matter how quick or deft your are at the wheel. After a long, hard rain, slow down and stay alert. Shift into 4WD if you have it. With only 2WD be extra cautious, even on flat straight-aways. Any backroad or campground access road can get laundry-chute slick. Hwy 20 can have surprisingly long stretches of deep mud, particularly south of Nimpo Lake. The highway is unpaved (dirt and/or gravel) from Tatla Lake northwest to just south of Nimpo Lake, and from near Anahim Lake to the bottom of the Big Hill. Though the Big Hill is ski-run steep, its all-weather gravel surface offers better traction than the rest of unpaved Hwy 20, so you don't have to avoid it after encountering mud elsewhere.

Before travelling the Chilcotin Plateau, visit **www.bcparks.ca** to print out helpful maps of Ts'yl?os and Tweedsmuir provincial parks. The website also has campground and activity information, as well as links to wilderness outfitters and charter transport services (planes and boats).

WEST ON HWY 20, FROM WILLIAMS LAKE

0 km (0 mi)
In Williams Lake, at the junction of Hwys 97 and 20. (It's a major intersection with traffic lights, near the rodeo grounds. You'll encounter no more traffic lights until Bella Coola.) Head southwest onto Hwy 20, soon ascending steeply.

2.6 km (1.6 mi)
Turn left (southeast) for campgrounds on Chimney Lake Road. Read page 415 for further directions.

25 km (15.5 mi)
Midway across the Fraser River canyon bridge.

34 km (21.1 mi)
For campgrounds at McIntyre and Till lakes, turn right at the sign MELDRUM CREEK 31. (You're out of the canyon now, on the plateau.)

0 km (0 mi)
Starting north on Meldrum Creek FS road.

0.6 km (0.4 mi)
Reach McIntyre Lake campground, on the right, beside a shrinking, marshy lake ringed by meadow and trees.

MCINTYRE LAKE CAMPGROUND #19
Overnight / Easy / Free
Elev: 930 m (3050 ft) / Lake: 16.4 ha
4 tables at well-spaced campsites
Accessible by motorhomes and 5th-wheels

Heavy rain slows travel on a Chilcotin backroad.

Continuing north on Meldrum Creek FS road, passing McIntyre Lake campground.

3.8 km (2.4 mi)
Stay straight on the main road. Proceed through vast meadows and forested, rolling hills.

13.5 km (8.4 mi)
Turn left for Till Lake campground.

15.4 km (9.5 mi)
Go left at the 3-way junction.

16.3 km (10.1 mi)
Pass Till Lake's first campsite, on the right.

16.8 km (10.4 mi)
Reach Till Lake's last, best campsite. It has a large grassy area.

TILL LAKE CAMPGROUND #20
Weekend / Moderate / Free
Elev: 869 m (2850 ft) / Lake: 2.5 km (1.6 mi) long, 102.5 ha
10 tables, more campsites
Accessible by motorhomes and 5th-wheels

Continuing west on Hwy 20, passing the turnoff to McIntyre and Till lakes campgrounds.

47.7 km (29.6 mi)
Pass the one-honk hamlet of Riske Creek. (Big Creek Ecological Reserve, Farwell Canyon, and Gang Ranch are south of here.)

69.3 km (43 mi)
Turn right onto Alex Graham FS road for Raven Lake campground. Set your trip odometer to 0.

0 km (0 mi)
Starting north on well-graded Alex Graham FS road.

13 km (8.1 mi)
Stay straight on the main road.

15.8 km (9.8 mi)
Turn right (just before the KM 16 sign) to enter Raven Lake campground. It's less appealing than Till Lake.

RAVEN LAKE CAMPGROUND #16
Overnight / Moderate / Free
Elev: 1252 m (4107 ft) / Lake: approx 45 ha
12 tables
Accessible by small motorhomes and trailers

Continuing west on Hwy 20, passing the turnoff to Raven Lake campground.

83.6 km (51.8 mi)
Pass Hanceville Rest Area.

91.8 km (56.9 mi)
Reach Lee's Corner, in Hanceville. Set your trip odometer to 0 whether turning or continuing. Turn left (south) for Chilko Lake and Ts'yl?os Provincial Park. The road is signed for Konni Lake (94 km), Taseko Lake (105 km), and Nemiah Valley (105 km).

Lee's Corner at Hanceville is where you turn south for Chilko Lake.

TS'YL?OS PROVINCIAL PARK

The following directions will guide you deep into the Chilcotin, through hilly grassland and forests of aspen and pine, to Ts'yl?os Park and 80-km (50-mi) long **Chilko Lake**. Nearing Nemiah Valley, your attention will be drawn toward the highest peak in the **Chilcotin Range**: 3066-m (10,056-ft) Mt. Tatlow, known as Ts'yl?os Mtn. to the people of the Tsilhquot'in Nation.

A sweeping view of a watery, icy wilderness is your reward for completing the drive to Chilko Lake. On sunny days it appears to be filled with turquoise paint, because of suspended glacial sediment. Guarding the lake and dialing up the scenic drama are the brawny, glacier-studded Coast Mountains. Chilko is the largest natural, high-elevation lake in North America, and an important spawning ground for Chinook and Sockeye salmon.

Because it's within a provincial park, Nu Chugh Beniz campground on Chilko Lake's east side is not free. But it's cheap because it's remote. Plan to stay there if you drive in the 120 km (72 mi). It requires about five hours for the round-trip. Several campsites are on the shore. Most have tremendous views. Develop a deeper rapport with this awesome place by walking over the bluff north of the campground, to a small, rocky point.

Consider breaking up the journey at any of several free campgrounds. The first one is about two-thirds of the way to Ts'yl?os Park, at Davidson Bridge. The next is just beyond, at Big Lake. Another is at Vedan Lake—not far off the main road. It has a view of Mt. Tatlow and is often windy enough to excite boardsailors.

The road to Ts'yl?os Park is all-weather gravel, fairly wide and reasonably smooth—most of the way. It narrows and deteriorates (rutted dirt or mud) just west of Konni Lake, in Nemiah Valley. Unless it's muddy, even this last stretch is usually passable in a low-clearance 2WD car. Just drive the final 4.4 km (2.7 mi) to Chilko Lake slowly and cautiously, to avoid bottoming-out. Small motorhomes and trailers can probably make it to the 26.3-km (16.3-mi) junction beyond the Vedan Lake turnoff. The Coast Mountain view is spectacular there, though Chilko Lake is not yet visible. Big-rig pilots should scout the final 4.4 km (2.7 mi) on foot. If you can't drive it, don't turn back; it's an enjoyable walk.

Want to hike in the cold, hard, unforgiving but beautiful mountains west of Chilko Lake? Be aware: this is prime bear habitat. Take all the necessary precautions for blacks and grizzlies.

HANCEVILLE TO CHILKO LAKE

0 km (0 mi)
At Lee's Corner, in Hanceville, starting on the road south, heading for Konni Lake, Nemiah Valley, Chilko Lake and Ts'yl?os Provincial Park.

5.6 km (3.5 mi)
Turn left.

8.8 km (5.6 mi)
Turn right.

21.8 km (13.5 mi)
Go left at the T-junction.

71.2 km (44.1 mi)
Stay right where Road 4500 forks left.

72 km (44.6 mi)
Stay left.

78.4 km (48.6 mi)
Reach Davidson Bridge campground, on the right, just before the bridge over Taseko River. (Left is a signed 4WD road leading about 18 km / 11 mi to Fish Lake campground.)

The Chilcotin is fishing country.

DAVIDSON BRIDGE CAMPGROUND #30
Weekend / Difficult (due only to distance) / Free
3 well-spaced campsites between the road and the river
Accessible by motorhomes and 5th-wheels

83 km (51.5 mi)
Reach Big Lake campground Site #29, on the right. The campground has
2 sites with views southwest to Mt. Tatlow. The 97-hectare lake is at 1326 m
(4350 ft).

89.6 km (55.5 mi)
After descending part way into the valley, reach a signed **junction**. Set your
trip odometer to 0 whether turning or continuing. Turn right for Vedan and
Chaunigan lakes campgrounds. Continue on the main road for Konni Lake,
Nemiah Valley, Chilko Lake and Ts'yl?os Provincial Park.

0 km (0 mi)
Starting northwest on Vedan-Elkins Lake FS road.

Looking south to Mt. Tatlow, from Vedan Lake

8.2 km (5.1 mi)
After crossing a stream between two lakes, reach a sign before a drift fence and house on the right. Proceed straight (south) for Vedan Lake. (Right ascends steeply to Chaunigan Lake campground #32, on the mesa above you, at 1494 m / 4900 ft. The road is steep and narrow, not recommended for big RVs. The campground has a pebble beach on the 440-hectare lake. Nearby is an airstrip.)

8.6 km (5.3 mi)
Stay straight.

9.1 km (5.6 mi)
Arrive at Vedan Lake campground, in a stand of pine and aspen. Mt. Tatlow is visible south.

VEDAN LAKE CAMPGROUND #31
Weekend / Difficult (due only to distance) / Free
Elev: 1220 m (4002 ft) / Lake: 5 km (3 mi) long, 303 ha
3 tables, gravel boat launch
Inaccessible by large motorhomes and 5th-wheels

Continuing southwest on Nemiah Valley Road, passing the turnoff to Vedan Lake campground. Set your trip odometer to 0.

0 km (0 mi)
Resuming the descent into Nemiah Valley.

7 km (4.2 mi)
Reach the east end of Konni Lake and Nemiah Valley.

14.5 km (9 mi)
Stay left at the fork.

26.3 km (16.3 mi)
Reach a signed junction. Go left for Ts'yl?os Park and Chilko Lake. When dry, the road beyond is usually passable in a 2WD car. The final 4.4 km (2.7 mi) to the lake is narrow and deeply rutted. It can be seriously muddy when wet.

29.6 km (18.4 mi)
Go right.

30.7 km (19 mi)
Fork left to arrive in 100 meters at Nu Chugh Beniz campground in Ts'yl?os Provincial Park, on the east shore of 18,447-hectare Chilko Lake, at 1172 m (3844 ft).

NU CHUGH BENIZ CAMPGROUND
Destination / Difficult / $ / June 15 – Sept 30
Elev: 1172 m (3844 ft) / Lake: 80 km (50 mi) long, 18,447 ha
12 campsites with tables, one is a pull through, 4 tent pads
Inaccessible by motorhomes and 5th-wheels

WEST ON HWY 20, FROM HANCEVILLE

0 km (0 mi)
At Lee's Corner, in Hanceville. Continuing west on Hwy 20, the scenery improves. Mountains are visible on the horizon.

22.2 km (13.8 mi)
Reach Alexis Creek store and gas station.

32.9 km (20.4 mi)
Turn right (northwest) for Alexis Lakes campground—not recommended for 2WD if the road's muddy.

At 2.4 km (1.5 mi) from the main road, fork right for a gentler ascent. The road proceeds northwest, staying above and just west of Alexis Creek. At 27 km (16.7 mi) arrive at the south end of narrow Alexis Lake. The campground is on the east side.

ALEXIS LAKES CAMPGROUND #24
Weekend / Moderate / Free
Elev: 1038 m (3405 ft) / Lake: 5 km (3 mi) long, 91.5 ha
several well-spaced campsites in a sandy, pine forest
Inaccessible by motorhomes and 5th-wheels

Follow the main road north another 1.6 km (1 mi) up the west side of Alexis Lake to reach Two Lake campground #23. The campground and the lake are small.

~

Continuing west on Hwy 20, passing the turnoff to Alexis Lakes campground.

55.8 km (34.6 mi)
Cross a bridge over the Chilcotin River.

77.4 km (48 mi)
Pass a gas station in Redstone.

83.8 km (52 mi)
Reach Chilanko Forks (barely noticeable), where various signs urge you to visit Puntzi Lake. Set your trip odometer to 0 whether turning or continuing. Turn right for Puntzi Lake campground—not recommended for big RVs.

0 km (0 mi)
Starting north on gravel Puntzi Lake road.

4.4 km (2.7 mi)
Go left at the fork. Proceed through an ugly, diseased, lodgepole-pine forest.

6.5 km (4 mi)
Turn right after passing a couple resorts. This final approach is steep and narrow. Arrive at the lakeside campground in 300 meters.

PUNTZI LAKE CAMPGROUND #39
Weekend / Moderate / Free
Elev: 955 m (3132 ft) / Lake: 9 km (5.6 mi) long, 1688 ha
5 well-spaced campsites, rough boat launch
Inaccessible by motorhomes and trailers

~

Calypso orchids

Resuming southwest on Hwy 20, from the turnoff to Puntzi Lake campground. Set your trip odometer to 0.

0 km (0 mi)
At Chilanko Forks.

9.4 km (5.8 mi)
Turn left for Pyper Lake campground.

0 km (0 mi)
Starting south on Chipman Road.

2.9 km (1.8 mi)
Go right at the fork.

3.4 km (2.1 mi)
Arrive at Pyper Lake.

PYPER LAKE CAMPGROUND #38
Overnight / Easy / Free
Elev: 981 m (3218 ft) / Lake: 3.5 km (2.2 mi) long, 172 ha
2 tables at a small lakeside meadow
Accessible by motorhomes and 5th-wheels

Continuing southwest on Hwy 20, passing the turnoff to Pyper Lake campground.

37.2 km (23 mi)
Pass a rest area at a small lake on the southeast side of the highway.

39 km (24.2 mi)
Turn right (north) for Tatla Lake campground.

Low-clearance 2WD cars might struggle on this potholed access if it's muddy. Reach a fork 0.5 km (0.3 mi) off the main road. Right leads to campsites, left to the boat launch. RV pilots should scout the narrow, final 100 meters to the campsites; if impassable, park near the boat launch. The campground is on a meadowy, aspen-sprinkled hillside overlooking the long, narrow lake.

TATLA LAKE CAMPGROUND #40
Overnight / Easy / $ / May 15 to Oct 15
Elev: 910 m (2985 ft) / Lake: 30 km (18.6 mi) long, 1720 ha
2 tables, 3 campsites
Accessible by small motorhomes and trailers

Continuing southwest on Hwy 20, passing the turnoff to Tatla Lake campground.

39.7 km (24.6 mi)
Turn left (southeast), following directions on page 400, to quickly reach large Eagle Lake campground or to proceed farther south to the destination campground at Tatlayoko Lake. Set your trip odometer to 0 whether continuing on Hwy 20 or turning.

Continuing southwest on Hwy 20, passing the turnoff to Eagle and Tatlayoko lakes campgrounds. Set your trip odometer to 0.

0 km (0 mi)
On Hwy 20, where Eagle Lake Road forks southeast.

2.1 km (1.3 mi)
Turn left (south) for Pinto Lake campground. Parallel the highway. Arrive

Tatlayoko Lake campground

at the campground in 1.4 km (0.9 mi). Big mountains are visible south. Proceed west to reach the highway in 0.3 km (0.2 mi).

PINTO LAKE CAMPGROUND #41
Overnight / Easy / Free
Elev: 910 m (2985 ft) / Lake: 9.5 ha
3 tables beside the small lake
Accessible by motorhomes and 5th-wheels

3.8 km (2.4 mi)
Pass Pinto Lake's west access on the left.

8.5 km (5.3 mi)
The highway curves. Pass prominent signs for Chilko Lake (south).

9.9 km (6.1 mi)
Reach the general store in the town of Tatla Lake. Set your trip odometer to 0. Hwy 20 proceeds northwest; for directions continue reading on page 403.

SOUTH OF HWY 20, TO TATLAYOKO LAKE

Though overshadowed by Chilko Lake, strikingly beautiful Tatlayoko Lake is another wonder of the Chilcotin. At its north end, 45 minutes south of Hwy 20, is a large, provincial-park-quality, free campground. The sites are sheltered in a grand Douglas fir forest—a welcome change from the more common, unimpressive forests of lodgepole pine. Directly across the lake are the spectacular, snow-clutching Niut mountains.

The Niuts also create an exceptionally scenic backdrop for smaller Horn Lake, just 25 minutes south of Hwy 20. Like Tatlayoko, this spacious campground lives up to the setting. It's rated *Destination*. It has a nightly fee.

The campgrounds at Tatlayoko and Horn lakes are inaccessible by motorhomes and 5th-wheels. But big rigs can easily glide into the sprawling campground at Eagle Lake, a mere six minutes south of Hwy 20. Rarely do campgrounds this convenient earn a *Weekend* rating. Eagle does, thanks to its pastoral, park-like atmosphere.

0 km (0 mi)
Starting southeast on Eagle Lake Road (39.7 km / 24.6 mi southwest of Chilanko Forks), departing Hwy 20.

4.3 km (2.7 mi)
Continue straight.

5 km (3 mi)
Turn left (east) to enter Eagle Lake West campground, in a large clearing.

EAGLE LAKE CAMPGROUND #37
Weekend / Easy / Free
Elev: 1060 m (3477 ft) / Lake: 10 km (6.2 mi) long, 1185 ha
2 tables, many more campsites
Accessible by motorhomes and 5th-wheels

Continuing south on Eagle Lake Road, passing Eagle Lake campground.

13.2 km (8.2 mi)
Proceed through a ranch.

16.2 km (10 mi)
Reach a T-junction with a bigger road. Turn left (south) for Tatlayoko lakes. (Right leads northwest 12.4 km / 7.7 mi to a junction where you can turn left for Horn and Sapeye lakes, or right to reach the town of Tatla Lake on Hwy 20 in another 4.3 km / 2.7 mi. For directions continue reading on page 401.)

20 km (12.4 mi)
Bear right (south) for Tatlayoko Lake.

22 km (13.6 mi) and 33 km (20.5 mi)
Pass through ranches.

34.6 km (21.5 mi)
Bear right at the fork.

35.2 km (21.8 mi)
Reach Tatlayoko Lake.

36.1 km (22.4 mi)
Turn right to enter Tatlayoko Lake campground. It extends south along the lake, where one of the sites is on a scenic viewpoint. The Niut mountains are directly across the lake. The road proceeds south, staying above the lake. It drops to the shore and ends in about 15 km (9.3 mi).

TATLAYOKO LAKE CAMPGROUND #35
Destination / Difficult (due only to distance) / Free
Elev: 827 m (2713 ft) / Lake: 23 km (14 mi) long, 3928 ha
8 tables, 10 campsites
Inaccessible by motorhomes and 5th-wheels

Heading northwest from the 16.2-km (10-mi) T-junction on Eagle Lake Road (page 400). Set your trip odometer to 0.

0 km (0 mi)
Starting on Tatla Lake Road, heading northwest. (This is the shortest route between Tatlayoko Lake and the town of Tatla Lake. It also accesses Horn and Sapeye lakes.)

12.4 km (7.7 mi)
Reach a 3-way junction. Set your trip odometer to 0 again. Turn left for Horn and Sapeye Lakes. Right leads north 4.3 km (2.7 mi) to the town of Tatla Lake on Hwy 20.

> **0 km (0 mi)**
> Starting on Westbranch Road, heading southwest to Horn and Sapeye lakes.

> **10 km (6.2 mi)**
> Horn Lake and the Niut Range are visible south.

Horn Lake campground

11.5 km (7.1 mi)
Turn right for homely Sapeye Lake campground. Bear left (south) for the superior campground at Horn Lake.

0 km (0 mi)
Starting on the spur road to Sapeye Lake campground. Mud could prohibit 2WD cars.

0.4 km (0.25 mi)
Turn right.

1.2 km (0.7 mi)
Turn left.

1.7 km (1 mi)
Arrive at the campground, above the lake.

SAPEYE LAKE CAMPGROUND #42

Overnight / Easy / $ / May 15 – Sept 30
Elev: 887 m (2910 ft) / Lake: 5 km (3 mi) long, 290 ha
5 campsites in a confined area
Inaccessible by motorhomes and 5th-wheels

Continuing south on Westbranch Road, passing the turnoff to Sapeye Lake campground.

13 km (8.1 mi)
Turn left to enter Horn Lake campground. The well-separated campsites even have gravel parking pads. The Niut mountains are visible south.

HORN LAKE CAMPGROUND #43
Destination / Easy / $ / May 15 – Sept 30
Elev: 915 m (3000 ft) / Lake: 4 km (2.5 mi) long, 190 ha
14 tables, good boat launch, provincial-park quality
Inaccessible by motorhomes and 5th-wheels

NORTHWEST ON HWY 20, FROM TATLA LAKE

0 km (0 mi)
At the general store in the town of Tatla Lake. Set your trip odometer to 0. Pavement soon ends as you head northwest on Hwy 20.

26.2 km (16.2 mi)
Turn right for One Eye Lake campground.

> Drive 200 meters in on Holm Road. Then turn right. This spur road is narrow and rough but passable in 2WD when dry. At 1.2 km (0.7 mi) watch for a granddaddy pothole just before arriving at the campground.

ONE EYE LAKE CAMPGROUND #46
Weekend / Easy / Free
Elev: 907 m (2975 ft) / 5 km (3 mi) long, 483 ha
3 tables, 4 campsites, boat launch
Inaccessible by motorhomes and 5th-wheels

Continuing northwest on Hwy 20, passing the turnoff to One Eye Lake campground.

32 km (19.8 mi)
Cross the bridge over Kleena Kleene River, in the otherwise barely noticeable hamlet of Kleena Kleene.

37.3 km (23.1 mi)
Turn left for Clearwater Lake campground. If muddy, the narrow access road will challenge 2WD cars.

Descend from the highway to reach the small campground in 0.4 km (0.25 mi). The treed lakeshore limits views of distant mountains.

CLEARWATER LAKE CAMPGROUND #47
Weekend / Easy / Free
Elev: 960 m (3150 ft) / Lake: 3 km (1.8 mi), 210 ha
2 tables in a grassy clearing, rough boat launch
Inaccessible by large motorhomes and 5th-wheels

Continuing northwest on Hwy 20, passing the turnoff to Clearwater Lake campground.

67 km (41.5 mi)
Pavement resumes.

78 km (48.4 mi)
Reach Nimpo Lake store and gas station. Set your trip odometer to 0.

0 km (0 mi)
At Nimpo Lake store and gas station, heading northwest on Hwy 20.

4.8 km (3 mi)
Turn left for Fish Trap campground on Dean River. It's just 50 meters off the highway.

FISH TRAP CAMPGROUND #50
Overnight / Easy / Free
Elev: 1117 m (3664 ft)
3 tables, 5 campsites, rough boat launch
Accessible by motorhomes and 5th-wheels

Continuing northwest on Hwy 20, passing the turnoff to Fish Trap campground.

20 km (12.4 mi)
Reach the village of Anahim Lake. (Anahim Street leads to the store and gas station.)

21.1 km (13.1 mi)
Turn left for Kappan Lake campground.

0 km (0 mi)
Starting southwest on Kappan Mtn. FS road.

5 km (3 mi)
Proceed straight through the intersection.

9.6 km (6 mi)
Turn right for the final, steep descent to the lake.

11.3 km (7 mi)
Arrive at the campground on the lake's southeast end.

KAPPAN LAKE CAMPGROUND #51
Overnight / Easy / Free
Elev: 1113 m (3650 ft) / Lake: 7 km (4.3 mi) long, 350 ha
6 tables, no privacy, sandy beach, good boat launch
Inaccessible by large motorhomes and 5th-wheels

Continuing northwest on Hwy 20, passing the turnoff to Kappan Lake campground.

23.7 km (14.7 mi)
Turn right for Little Anahim Lake campground. It's just 30 meters off the highway but minimal nighttime traffic should grant you uninterrupted sleep.

LITTLE ANAHIM LAKE CAMPGROUND #54
Overnight / Easy / Free
Elev: 1083 m (3552 ft) / Lake: 3.5 km (2.2 mi) long, 165 ha
5 campsites, no tables, boat launch
Accessible by motorhomes and 5th-wheels

Continuing northwest on Hwy 20, passing the turnoff to Little Anahim Lake campground. Pavement soon ends.

56 km (34.8 mi)
Enter Tweedsmuir Provincial Park. Set your trip odometer to 0. The highway soon tops 1524-m (5000-ft) Heckman Pass.

TWEEDSMUIR TO BELLA COOLA

The Chilcotin Plateau ends near Tweedsmuir Provincial Park's east boundary. You're entering the **Coast Mountains** here. But instead of climbing over them, the road descends through them. Pavement is finally halted by the sea at Bella Coola, on the tail of a fiord long ago gouged by a glacier.

This section of Hwy 20 is a marvel. Wrested from sheer cliffs, it allows vehicles to safely travel what would otherwise be the exclusive domain of mountain goats and eagles. Acrophobic passengers: blindfold yourself, or risk a catatonic reaction. Called the **Big Hill,** it rapidly drops 1244 m (4015 ft) between Heckman Pass and Atnarko Valley. The government refused to build the road, saying it was too costly and would serve too few people. So the locals built it themselves, finishing the task in 1953. It's Bella Coola's only land link to the rest of the planet.

Approaching Bella Coola, gazing up at the sheer valley walls, California's Yosemite National Park comes to mind. Hikers will be goggle-eyed. Sadly, not many trails pierce this lush, vertical world. The few in Tweedsmuir Park are well worth hoofing. A dayhike in the **Rainbow Range** reveals why the name is apt. Peaks averaging 2500 m (8200 ft) sport an array of Florentine colours: purple, rouge, mustard. Backpacking in the Rainbows is also possible, but an even better option is trekking into the alpine highlands above **Hunlen Falls.** Allow 3 to 4 days for the 58-km (36-mi) roundtrip. Hunlen tumbles 366 m (1200 ft), making it one of Canada's longest freefall cascades: 260 m (853 ft).

The area's greatest deficiency, however, isn't trailheads. It's free campgrounds. There's only one (McCall Flats) in the 197-km (122-mi) stretch between Little Anahim Lake and Bella Coola. At least it's conveniently located near Tweedsmuir's west boundary. Too bad it's in a graveyard of giant cedar stumps. Your other options are the two pay-campgrounds in the Park.

0 km (0 mi)
At Tweedsmuir Park's east boundary, heading west.

6.3 km (3.9 mi)
Pass the Rainbow Range trailhead on the right.

7 km (4.2 mi) Begin descending the Big Hill. Atnarko Valley is 1244 m (4015 ft) below but only 19.2 km (11.9 mi) distant.

26.2 km (16.2 mi)
Pavement resumes here in Atnarko Valley. You've completed the Big Hill descent. A 4WD road on the left leads to Hunlen Falls trailhead. (The falls trail is steep, regaining most of the elevation you just lost on the Big Hill.) Young Creek picnic area is also on the left.

28 km (17.4 mi)
Pass Tweedsmuir Park Headquarters on the left. It's staffed only part-time, but maps are always available at the kiosk.

44 km (27.3 mi)
Pass the provincial park Fisheries Pool campground, where you can watch salmon spawning.

52 km (32.2 mi)
Proceed on Hwy 20 for Bella Coola. Turn left for McCall Flats campground.

> **0 km (0 mi)**
> Starting south on the spur road, departing Hwy 20.
>
> **0.7 km (0.4 mi)**
> Cross a bridge and turn right.
>
> **2.2 km (1.4 mi)**
> Go right.
>
> **2.8 km (1.7 mi)**
> Arrive at McCall Flats campground on Bella Coola River.

MCCALL FLATS CAMPGROUND #1
Destination / Easy / Free
5 tables, bearproof garbage cans
Accessible by small motorhomes and trailers

Continuing west on Hwy 20, passing the turnoff to McCall Flats campground.

54 km (33.5 mi)
Pass Burnt Bridge picnic area on the left. Park here to hike the MacKenzie trail, a loop affording views south of 2677-m (8780-ft) Stupendous Mountain.

54.3 km (33.7 mi)
Cross the bridge over Burnt Creek—west boundary of Tweedsmuir Park.

64.8 km (40.2 mi)
Pass the Summer trail parking area on the right.

69.3 km (43 mi)
Cross the bridge over Bella Coola River.

86 km (53.3 mi)
Reach the community of Hagensborg. The original settlers were Norwegian descendants from Minnesota who felt at home in this fiord.

104 km (64.5 mi)
Arrive in Bella Coola.

SOUTHEAST ON HWY 20, FROM TWEEDSMUIR

0 km (0 mi)
At the Rainbow Range trailhead, heading east on Hwy 20.

6.3 km (3.9 mi)
Cross Tweedsmuir Park's east boundary.

38.6 km (23.9 mi)
Soon after pavement resumes, turn left for Little Anahim Lake campground. Just 30 meters off the highway, it's accessible by motorhomes and 5th-wheels. It has 5 campsites but no tables.

41.2 km (25.5 mi)
Turn right (southwest) for Kappan Lake campground. Read further directions on page 405.

42.3 km (26.2 mi)
Reach the village of Anahim Lake. (Anahim Street leads to the store and gas station.)

57.4 km (35.6 mi)
Turn right for Fish Trap campground on Dean River. Just 50 meters off the highway, it's accessible by motorhomes and 5th-wheels. It has 5 campsites.

62.2 km (38.6 mi)
Reach Nimpo Lake store and gas station. Set your trip odometer to 0 before continuing southeast on Hwy 20.

SOUTHEAST ON HWY 20, FROM NIMPO LAKE

0 km (0 mi)
At Nimpo Lake store and gas station, heading southeast on Hwy 20.

11.3 km (7 mi)
Pavement ends.

40.8 km (25.3 mi)
Turn right for Clearwater Lake campground. Read further directions on page 404.

Backroad near Bella Coola River

46 km (28.6 mi)
Cross the bridge over Kleena Kleene River.

51.7 km (32.1 mi)
Turn left for One Eye Lake campground. Read further directions on page 403.

78 km (48.4 mi)
Soon after pavement resumes, reach the general store in the town of Tatla Lake. Set your trip odometer to 0 before continuing northeast on Hwy 20.

NORTHEAST ON HWY 20, FROM TATLA LAKE

0 km (0 mi)
At the general store in the town of Tatla Lake, heading northeast on Hwy 20.

1.4 km (0.9 mi)
The highway curves. Prominent signs direct you to Chilko Lake, but before committing to this approach consider the more scenic vantage reached via Nemiah Valley from Hanceville (page 392). To reach provincial-park quality Horn Lake campground, turn right (south) here; in 4.3 km (2.7 mi) bear right on Westbranch Road. Read further directions on page 401.

6.1 km (3.8 mi)
Turn right for Pinto Lake campground. Just 0.3 km (0.2 mi) from the highway, it's accessible by motorhomes and 5th-wheels. It has 3 campsites.

7.8 km (4.8 mi)
Pass Pinto Lake's east access on the right.

9.9 km (6.1 mi)
Turn right (southeast) to quickly reach large Eagle Lake campground or to proceed farther south to the provincial-park quality Tatlayoko Lake campground. Read page 400 for further directions.

10.6 km (6.6 mi)
Turn left (north) for Tatla Lake campground. Read page 398 for further directions.

40.2 km (24.9 mi)
Turn right (south) for Pyper Lake campground. Read page 397 for further directions.

49.6 km (30.8 mi)
Reach Chilanko Forks. Turn left (north) for Puntzi Lake campground. Read page 396 for further directions.

56 km (34.7 mi)
Pass a gas station in Redstone.

77.6 km (48.1 mi)
Cross a bridge over the Chilcotin River.

111.2 km (68.9 mi)
Reach Alexis Creek store and gas station.

133.4 km (82.7 mi)
Reach Lee's Corner, in Hanceville. Set your trip odometer to 0 whether turning or continuing. Turn right (south) for Chilko Lake and Ts'yl?os Provincial Park. Read page 392 for further directions. Continue east on Hwy 20 to reach Williams Lake in 92.5 km (57.4 mi).

EAST ON HWY 20, FROM HANCEVILLE

0 km (0 mi)
At Lee's Corner, in Hanceville, heading east on Hwy 20.

7.8 km (4.8 mi)
Pass Hanceville Rest Area.

22.5 km (14 mi)
Turn left (north) for Raven Lake campground. Read page 390 for further directions.

58.5 km (36.3 mi)
Turn left (north) for McIntyre and Till Lakes campgrounds. Read page 388 for further directions. Continuing east, Hwy 20 soon descends off the Chilcotin Plateau, into the Fraser River canyon.

67.5 km (41.9 mi)
Midway across the Fraser River canyon bridge.

90 km (55.8 mi)
Turn right (southeast) for campgrounds on Chimney Lake Road. Read page 415 for further directions.

92.6 km (57.4 mi)
Arrive in Williams Lake, at the junction of Hwys 20 and 97.

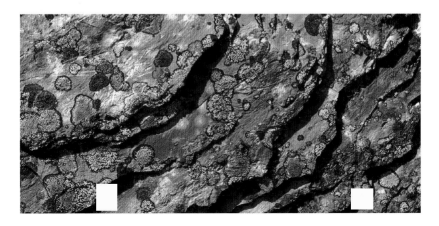

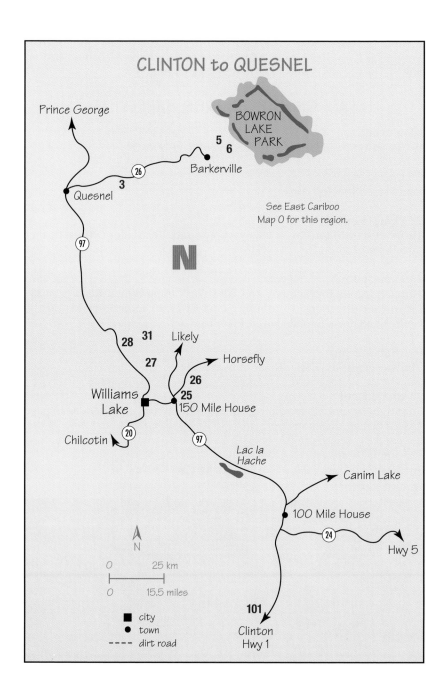

CLINTON to QUESNEL

BOWRON LAKE PARK

Prince George

5 6

26 Barkerville

3

Quesnel

See East Cariboo
Map 0 for this region.

97

N

28 31 Likely

27 Horsefly

26

25

Williams Lake

150 Mile House

20

Chilcotin

97

Lac la Hache

Canim Lake

100 Mile House

24

Hwy 5

N

0   25 km

0   15.5 miles

■ city
● town
---- dirt road

101

Clinton
Hwy 1

N: Clinton to Quesnel

At the fee campgrounds, charges apply May 12 to October 15.

3	Lightning Creek	FREE	26	Dewar Lake	FREE
5	Atan Lake	FREE	27	Forest lake	FREE
6	Chisel Lake	FREE	28	Blue Lake West	FREE
21	Brunson Lake	FREE	31	Tyee Lake	FREE
22	Felker Lake	$	78	Greeny Lake	FREE
23	Chimney Lake North	$	79	Lower Lake	FREE
24	Chimney Lake Centre	$	101	Beaverdam Lake	FREE
25	Dugan Lake	FREE	107	Helena Lake	FREE

Barkerville

Clinton to Quesnel

Picturesque access road leading to Brunson Lake campground, southeast of Williams Lake

SOUTHEAST OF WILLIAMS LAKE

The paved Chimney Lake Road links a rural bedroom community with the city of Williams Lake. It runs the length of a lovely, shallow valley. The pastoral scenery comprises meadows, marshes, lakes, forests, a meandering stream, and substantial country homes. You'll find several easy-to-reach free campgrounds here. They're even handy when travelling north or south on Hwy 97, because you can access Chimney Lake Road from Enterprise. Read pages 421-22 for directions.

Enough people live along Chimney Lake Road that passing cars are frequently audible from the campgrounds. On weekdays, commuters start whizzing by at 6:30 a.m. They continue until 11:30 p.m. The quietest and prettiest campground is at small Brunson Lake. Felker and Chimney lakes are larger, and the campgrounds closer to the road. At Chimney Lake, the proximity of houses and the road create the feeling that you're camping in a city park. It's also popular with waterskiers.

CHIMNEY LAKE ROAD

0 km (0 mi)
In Williams Lake, at the junction of Hwys 97 and 20. (It's a major intersection with traffic lights, near the rodeo grounds.) Head southwest onto Hwy 20, soon ascending steeply.

2.6 km (1.6 mi)
Near the top of the hill, turn left (southeast) onto Chimney Lake Road. You'll continue climbing, then descend steeply.

10.5 km (6.5 mi)
Turn left.

15 km (9.3 mi)
Turn right for Brunson Lake campground.

Reach the first campsite 0.5 km (0.3 mi) off the pavement. The campground is on an open, grassy, lightly-treed promontory overlooking the small but picturesque lake. The shore is mostly forested. The resident loons seem to be unusually loud. Their robust calls echo among the surrounding low hills. Expect an onslaught of mosquitoes in June and July.

BRUNSON LAKE CAMPGROUND #21
Weekend / Easy / Free
Elev: 808 m (2650 ft) / Lake: 53 ha
1 table, 4 well-spaced campsites
Accessible by small motorhomes and trailers

Continuing southeast on Chimney Lake Road, passing the turnoff to Brunson Lake campground.

25.4 km (15.7 mi)
The north end of Felker Lake and nearby houses are visible.

28 km (17.4 mi)
Turn right to enter Felker Lake campground. It's on the shore, beside a meadow.

FELKER LAKE CAMPGROUND #22
Weekend / Easy / $ / May 12 – Oct 15
Elev: 876 m (2873 ft) / 2.7 km (1.7 mi) long, 200 ha
10 tables, rough boat launch
Accessible by motorhomes and 5th-wheels

Continuing southeast on Chimney Lake Road, passing the turnoff to Felker Lake campground.

29.7 km (18.4 mi)
Turn right for Chimney Lake North campground. It's 100 meters off the pavement, near houses at the northwest end of the lake.

CHIMNEY LAKE NORTH CAMPGROUND #23
Weekend / Easy / $ / May 12 – Oct 15
Elev: 883 m (2896 ft) / Lake: 6 km (3.7 mi) long, 430 ha
4 tables, good gravel boat launch
Accessible by motorhomes and 5th-wheels

Continuing southeast on Chimney Lake Road, passing the turnoff to Chimney Lake North campground.

30.1 km (18.7 mi)
Turn right for Chimney Lake Centre campground, the largest on Chimney Lake. It's in a wide meadow peppered with trees. Shade is minimal. The shallow water is comfortably warm in summer.

CHIMNEY LAKE CENTRE CAMPGROUND #24
Weekend / Easy / $ / May 12 – Oct 15
Elev: 883 m (2896 ft) / Lake: 6 km (3.7 mi) long, 430 ha
25 campsites, many with tables, rough boat launch
Accessible by motorhomes and 5th-wheels

Continuing southeast on Chimney Lake Road, passing the turnoff to Chimney Lake Centre campground, heading for Hwy 97.

35.4 km (21.9 mi)
Pavement ends.

40.7 km (25.2 mi)
Turn left at the 3-way junction.

Chimney Lake

47.8 km (29.6 mi)
Stay right, on the main road.

49.9 km (30.9 mi)
Cross railroad tracks.

50.7 km (31.4 mi)
Reach Hwy 97 at Enterprise. Turn left (northwest) for Williams Lake. Turn right (southeast) for Lac la Hache.

150 MILE HOUSE TO 100 MILE HOUSE

Several campgrounds are easily reached off Hwy 97 between 150 Mile House and 100 Mile House. All are at small or medium-sized lakes and are sufficiently pleasant for a weekend stay. But with little topography to speak of, the scenery is unexciting. So most of these campgrounds are best appreciated by travellers in need of a convenient one-night refuge.

The campgrounds on Chimney Lake, as well as those on Dugan, Helena and Greeny lakes, are accessible by motorhomes and 5th-wheels. Dugan Lake (page 459) is very close to 150 Mile House, and not far from Williams Lake.

Lower Lake is an option if you must stay near 100 Mile House, but others are closer to Hwy 97. Try Greeny Lake, northeast of Lac la Hache. It's a bit more convenient and a lot more attractive. It's also bigger, so you're more likely to find a vacant site.

Howard Lake is about 50 minutes from Hwy 97, but the route is straight-forward and the campground is rated *Destination*.

If you're heading southeast on Hwy 97, from 150 Mile House

0 km (0 mi)
On Hwy 97 in 150 Mile House, at Mega Fuels gas station in 150 Centre.

19.3 km (12 mi)
For campgrounds on Chimney Lake Road (which continues northwest to Williams Lake) turn right onto initially paved Enterprise Road. Read further directions on page 421.

32 km (19.8 mi)
Pass a pullout with a litter barrel.

35 km (21.7 mi)
For Helena Lake campground, turn right (southwest) onto Wright Station Road, just before a sign welcoming you to Lac la Hache.

0 km (0 mi)
Starting on Wright Station Road (paved for 1 km, then good gravel).

100 meters
Cross a bridge and railroad tracks, then go left.

5.1 km (3.2 mi)
Turn left.

8.1 km (5.1 mi)
Turn right at the T-junction.

12 km (7.4 mi)
Arrive at Helena Lake campground. Don't follow the road left away from the lake; it departs the area. The lake is visible from most campsites.

HELENA LAKE CAMPGROUND #107
Weekend / Easy / Free
Elev: 960 m (3150 ft) / Lake: 4.5 km (2.8 mi) long, 238 ha
4 tables, 10 campsites
Accessible by motorhomes and 5th-wheels

Helena Lake

Continuing southeast on Hwy 97, passing the turnoff to Helena Lake campground.

37.5 km (23.3 mi)
Pass the turnoff to Lac la Hache Provincial Park.

51.4 km (31.9 mi)
For Greeny Lake campground, turn left (northeast) by the general store in the town of Lac la Hache, at the sign for Timothy Lake.

0 km (0 mi)
Starting northeast on paved Timothy Lake Road.

7.2 km (4.5 mi)
Turn right at the junction and continue on gravel.

11.5 km (7.1 mi)
Turn right at the lodgepole fence to enter Greeny Lake campground. Most campsites are in the open, along the shore. Those at the end are in the trees.

GREENY LAKE CAMPGROUND #78
Weekend / Easy / Free
Elev: 937 m (3073 ft) / 2.6 km (1.6 mi) long, 72.5 ha
12 tables at a reedy-edged, narrow lake
Accessible by motorhomes and 5th-wheels

~

Continuing southeast on Hwy 97, passing the turnoff to Greeny Lake campground.

75 km (46.5 mi)
For Lower Lake campground, Canim Lake, and Howard Lake campground (rated *Destination*) turn left (east) across from Exeter Truck Route, at the north edge of 100 Mile House. Read further directions on page 422.

77.6 km (48.1 mi)
Arrive in 100 Mile House, at the centre of town, between the Petro Canada gas station (left) and the Forest Service District Office (right).

If you're heading north on Hwy 97, from 100 Mile House

0 km (0 mi)
On Hwy 97 in the centre of 100 Mile House, between the Petro Canada gas station (right) and the Forest Service District Office (left).

2.6 km (1.6 mi)
For Lower Lake campground, Canim Lake, and Howard Lake campground (rated *Destination*) turn right (east) across from Exeter Truck Route, at the north edge of 100 Mile House. Read further directions on page 422.

26.2 km (16.2 mi)
For Greeny Lake campground, turn right (northeast) by the general store in the town of Lac la Hache, at the sign for Timothy Lake. Read further directions on page 419.

42.6 km (26.4 mi)
For Helena Lake campground, turn left (southwest) onto Wright Station Road, just past the northwest end of Lac la Hache (the lake itself). Read further directions on page 418.

58.3 km (36.1 mi)
Proceed northwest on Hwy 97 to reach 150 Mile House. For campgrounds on Chimney Lake Road, which continues northwest to Williams Lake, turn left onto Enterprise Road and set your trip odometer to 0. Read below the next entry.

Greeny Lake

77.6 km (48.1 mi)
Arrive in 150 Mile House, at Mega Fuels gas station in 150 Centre. Proceed west on Hwy 97 for Williams Lake. Continue north for Likely, Horsefly, and campgrounds near Quesnel Lake. Read page 458 for further directions. Just ten minutes north of 150 Mile House is Dugan Lake campground. Directions are on page 459.

Turning off Hwy 97, heading southwest to Chimney Lake Road campgrounds.

0 km (0 mi)
Starting southwest on Enterprise Road.

0.8 km (0.5 mi)
Cross railroad tracks. Pavement ends. Proceed on Chimney Lake FS road.

2.9 km (1.8 mi)
Stay left on the main road.

10 km (6.2 mi)
Turn right (west) at the 3-way junction.

14.5 km (9 mi)
The south end of Chimney Lake is visible.

15.3 km (9.5 mi)
Pavement begins.

20.6 km (12.8 mi)
Turn left for Chimney Lake Centre campground. Read page 416 for description.

21 km (13 mi)
Turn left for Chimney Lake North campground. Read page 416 for description.

22.7 km (14.1 mi)
Turn left for Felker Lake campground. Read page 416 for description.

35.7 km (22.1 mi)
Turn left for Brunson Lake campground. Read page 415 for description.

40 km (24.8 mi)
Turn right and ascend steeply for Williams Lake.

48 km (29.8 mi)
Turn right onto Hwy 20 to descend to Williams Lake.

50.6 km (31.4 mi)
Arrive in Williams Lake, at the junction of Hwys 20 and 97.

LOWER, CANIM, AND HOWARD LAKES

There are various ways to reach Canim Lake. The shortest route, and the only one that's paved, starts just north of 100 Mile House. It's described below. Canim is a significant, beautiful lake, so it's unfortunate there are no free campgrounds on its shore. You will, however, find several nearby. Of special note is Howard Lake, rated *Destination*. It's located above and just south of Canim Lake.

0 km (0 mi)
Starting east on Canim Lake Road. It departs Hwy 97 across from Exeter Truck Route, 2.6 km (1.6 mi) north of the Forest Service District Office in 100 Mile House.

8 km (5 mi)
Proceed through the village of Edwards Lake.

15.3 km (9.5 mi)
Turn right for Drewry Lake West campground. See photo on page 437.

Camp in the open or snuggled into trees at Howard Lake.

In about 1 km (0.6 mi) bear right. FS directional signs should guide you the remaining 19 km to the lake's southwest end. The rough, winding road gets very muddy when wet.

DREWRY LAKE WEST CAMPGROUND #80
Weekend / Difficult / Free
Elev: 1067 m (3500 ft) / Lake: 5 km (3 mi) long, 577 ha
6 campsites with tables, boat launch
Inaccessible by motorhomes and 5th-wheels

Continuing northeast on Canim Lake Road, passing the turnoff to Drewry Lake West campground.

18 km (11.2 mi)
Turn left (west) onto Archie Meadow Road for Lower Lake campground.

0 km (0 mi)
Starting west on Archie Meadow Road.

3 km (1.9 mi)
Turn right.

4.2 km (2.6 mi)
Arrive at Lower Lake campground #79—a small grassy clearing beside the road, just above the tiny lake. It's accessible by small motorhomes and trailers.

Continuing northeast on Canim Lake Road, passing the turnoff to Lower Lake campground.

29 km (18 mi)
Reach a junction. Proceed left (northeast) on Canim Lake Road for campgrounds north of Canim Lake. Read further directions on page 438. Bear right (east) onto Canim Lake South Road for Howard Lake campground. Set your trip odometer to 0.

0 km (0 mi)
Starting east on Canim Lake South Road. This is at the junction of Canim Lake Road and Canim Lake South Road, near the west end of Canim Lake, about 29 km (18 mi) northeast of Hwy 97 and 100 Mile House.

9.4 km (5.8 mi)
Turn right and ascend for Howard Lake campground. See photo on page 423.

The road soon levels and widens but remains bumpy. In 3.8 km (2.4 mi) reach the first campsites—one on the left, another on the lakeshore. The main campground is 200 meters farther, in a large clearing. Secluded lakeshore sites are slightly beyond.

HOWARD LAKE CAMPGROUND #81
Destination / Easy / Free
Elev: 937 m (3073 ft) / Lake: 3.8 km (2.4 mi) long, 175 ha
20 campsites with tables, good boat launch
Accessible by motorhomes and 5th-wheels

Continuing north on Canim Lake South Road, passing the turnoff to Howard Lake campground.

25 km (15.5 mi)
Reach a junction with Mahood Lake FS road. Turn left (northeast) for Mahood Lake. Bear right (south) to reach Hwy 24 in about 43 km (27 mi). En route to Hwy 24, stay right on the main road at all junctions.

Beaverdam Lake campground

NORTH TO 100 MILE HOUSE

North of Clinton, you'll notice a transition: from dry, rolling, sagebrush country, to flater, cooler forests and grasslands. The lone free campground between Clinton and 100 Mile House is at shallow Beaverdam Lake. The distant scenery includes the southern Chilcotin Mtns. Specifically, you can see 2270-m (7445-ft) Mt. Kerr in Marble Range Provincial Park. Beaverdam's gorgeous lakeside meadow and the showy blue skies that often prevail might lull you into a relaxing stay—if the mosquitoes have abated. Heading south? Stop here for a peaceful interlude prior to forging into combat on Hwy 1.

BEAVERDAM LAKE

If you're heading south on Hwy 97, from 100 Mile House

Drive south to 70 Mile House and the southern access to Green Lake. From this junction, continue nearly another 15 km (9.3 mi), then turn right (northwest) onto Meadow Lake Road. Set your trip odometer to 0.

If you're heading north on Hwy 97, from Clinton

Drive 17 km (10.5 mi) north, then turn left (northwest) onto Meadow Lake Road. (It's 1.5 km / 0.9 mi north of the turnoff to Chasm Provincial Park.) Set your trip odometer to 0.

For either approach above, now follow the directions below

0 km (0 mi)
Starting northwest on Meadow Lake Road, signed for Gang Ranch and Alkali. Proceed through vast meadowlands.

10.4 km (6.4 mi)
Turn left to enter Beaverdam campground. Be prepared for mosquitoes at this shallow, reedy lake. See photo on previous page.

BEAVERDAM CAMPGROUND #101
Weekend / Easy / Free
Elev: 1110 m (3640 ft) / Lake: 1.4 km wide and long, 143 ha
3 tables, many more campsites
Accessible by motorhomes and 5th-wheels

WILLIAMS LAKE TO QUESNEL

Three handy campgrounds ensure you'll find a home for the night near Hwy 97 between Williams Lake and Quesnel. Forest Lake (11.2 km / 6.9 mi off the highway) has beautiful trees and a meadow. Tyee Lake (16.7 km / 10.4 mi off the highway) has a large clearing but isn't special. Blue Lake West (2.7 km / 1.7 mi off the highway) feels like it's in a mountain setting. All are accessible by motorhomes and 5th-wheels.

If you're heading north on Hwy 97, from Williams Lake

0 km (0 mi)
In Williams Lake, at the junction of Hwys 97 and 20. (It's a major intersection with traffic lights, near the rodeo grounds.) Proceed north on Hwy 97. Set your trip odometer to 0.

25 km (15.6 mi)
For campgrounds at Forest and Tyee lakes, turn right (northeast) onto Lynes Creek FS road. Reset your trip odometer to 0. Read further directions on page 427.

33.2 km (20.6 mi)
For Blue Lake West campground, turn right (northeast) onto Blue Lake Road. Reset your trip odometer to 0. Read further directions on page 428.

44 km (27.3 mi)
Pass McCleese Lake store and gas station.

If you're heading south on Hwy 97 from Quesnel

From the south end of Quesnel, by Maple Park Mall, drive south 69.5 km (43.1 mi) to a rest area at the north end of McCleese Lake. Reset your trip odometer to 0.

0 km (0 mi)
Starting from the rest area at McCleese Lake.

11.7 km (7.2 mi)
For Blue Lake West campground, turn left (northeast) onto Blue Lake Road. Reset your trip odometer to 0. Read further directions on page 428.

19.8 km (12.3 mi)
For campgrounds at Forest and Tyee lakes, turn left (northeast) onto Lynes Creek FS road. Directions continue below.

For FOREST AND TYEE LAKES, now follow the directions below

0 km (0 mi)
Starting northeast on Lynes Creek FS road. Begin ascending.

0.4 km (0.25 mi)
Pavement ends.

8.1 km (5 mi)
Reach a junction. For Tyee Lake, bear left and proceed north, ignoring minor right forks into private land. For more attractive Forest Lake, turn right (southeast).

0 km (0 mi)
Turning right (southeast) at the 8.1-km (5-mi) junction, heading for Forest Lake.

2 km (1.2 mi)
Turn right at the junction.

3.1 km (1.9 mi)
Arrive at Forest Lake campground. The lake is reedy-edged. There's a meadow on the shore and beautiful trees nearby.

FOREST LAKE CAMPGROUND #27
Weekend / Easy
Elev: approx. 900 m (2950 ft) / Lake: 2 km (1.2 mi) long, 98 ha
1 table, 6 well-spaced campsites
Accessible by motorhomes and 5th-wheels

Forest Lake

Continuing north on Lynes Creek FS road, passing the turnoff to Forest Lake campground.

16.2 km (10 mi)
Fork left and descend gradually.

16.7 km (10.4 mi)
Bear left to enter Tyee Lake campground. Many campsites are bunched together in a large clearing. The last campsite is a bit higher, with a lakeshore table and secluded level tentsite.

TYEE LAKE CAMPGROUND #31

Weekend / Easy / Free
Elev: 915 m (3000 ft) / Lake: 7 km (4.3 mi) long, 408 ha
8 tables, boat launch
Accessible by motorhomes and 5th-wheels

For BLUE LAKE WEST, now follow the directions below

0 km (0 mi)
Starting northeast on Blue Lake Road.

0.2 km (0.1 mi)
Bear left and ascend steeply.

2.7 km (1.7 mi)
Turn right to reach Blue Lake West campground in 0.4 km (0.25 mi).

The lake is small, narrow, steep-sided. Unlike most pastoral, plateau lakes, the setting here feels mountainous. Half the campsites are on the shore, the rest have lakeviews. One is on a bench 15 meters above the lake. There's no boat launch, but with a canoe or kayak you can camp on an island.

BLUE LAKE WEST CAMPGROUND #28
Weekend / Easy / Free
Elev: 820 m (2690 ft) / Lake: 34 ha
6 tables, 9 campsites
Accessible by motorhomes and 5th-wheels

NEAR BARKERVILLE

The best free campground in this area is closer to Quesnel than to Barkerville. It's just off Hwy 26, beside Lightning Creek. The campgrounds at Atan and Chisel lakes are northeast, closer to Barkerville. Each has only two campsites, and are frequently used by people embarking on the nearby Bowron Lake canoe route. You're equally apt to enjoy quiet and privacy at Lightning Creek.

Plan on spending a day at Barkerville. It's an impeccably restored gold-rush town where actors in period costume carry on as if it were 1860. Without stepping out of character, they even interact with visitors. The result is often hilarious, as well as educational. In its prime, Barkerville appeared destined to become a major city. But when the gold rush died, so did the town. It was empty and silent for 75 years. Restoration began in 1958. Today, you'll see more than 40 buildings that look exactly as they did in the 1800s. Many of the original businesses—including the bakery, restaurants, general store, blacksmith, printer, and photographer—are operating and open to the public. You can visit Barkerville any day of the year. Visit **www.bcparks.ca** for more information.

Heading east from the junction of Hwys 97 and 26

0 km (0 mi)
Starting east on Hwy 26, departing Hwy 97 just north of Quesnel. It's about 5.2 km (3.2 mi) north of where Carson Avenue and Front Street intersect along the river. Hwy 26 is signed for Wells (74 km / 46 mi) and Barkerville (81 km / 50 mi).

26 km (16.1 mi)
Pass the historic site at Cottonwood.

32.5 km (20.2 mi)
Turn right, onto Swift River FS road, for Lightning Creek campground.

In 200 meters, just before a bridge, turn left to enter the campground. Pass campsites right and left to reach a large, secluded site at road's end in about 400 meters. Spurs fork right to gravel sites on the creek. Aspen brighten the pretty forest.

LIGHTNING CREEK CAMPGROUND #3
Overnight / Easy / Free
7 tables, 10 campsites
Accessible by motorhomes and 5th-wheels

Continuing east on Hwy 26, passing the turnoff to Lightning Creek campground.

75.5 km (46.8 mi)
Pass the RCMP office on the northeast edge of Wells.

81 km (50.2 mi)
For Barkerville, proceed a few minutes farther south. For Atan and Chisel lakes campgrounds, turn left (northeast) onto Bowron Lake Road, signed for Bowron Lakes Provincial Park (28 km). The precise location of this turn might vary slightly due to an extensive mining operation, but it should still be obvious. Set your trip odometer to 0.

0 km (0 mi)
Starting northeast on Bowron Lake Road. The mining operation near this turn might vary the following distances slightly.

0.6 km (0.4 mi)
Bear left at the sign for Bowron Park.

4 km (2.5 mi)
Pass the Yellowhawk Trail parking area on the right.

7 km (4.2 mi)
Pass the Jubilee Trail parking area on the right.

16.7 km (10.4 mi)
Reach a major fork. Turn right on 2900 FS road (smaller, worse), signed for Atan and Chisel lakes.

17.4 km (10.8 mi)
Fork left at an old cabin. Slow down as the road starts descending.

20.7 km (12.8 mi)
Cross a bridged creek.

21.3 km (13.2 mi)
Follow the middle road. The right fork was decommissioned.

23.3 km (14.4 mi)
Turn left to reach Atan Lake campground in 100 meters.

ATAN LAKE CAMPGROUND #5
Overnight / Moderate / Free
Elev: 1030 m (3378 ft) / Lake: 1 km (0.6 mi) long, 29 ha
1 table, 2 campsites, gravel boat launch
Inaccessible by motorhomes and trailers

Continuing on the main road, passing the turnoff to Atan Lake campground.

25.6 km (15.9 mi)
Turn left for Chisel Lake campground. Descend on a good, stony road to reach the lake in 300 meters. A private cabin is visible across the water. The blunt, forested mountains of Bowron Lakes Park are beyond.

CHISEL LAKE CAMPGROUND #6
Overnight / Moderate / Free
Elev: 1030 m (3378 ft) / Lake: 1 km (0.6 mi) long, 32 ha
2 tables, 3 campsites, gravel boat launch
Accessible by small motorhomes and trailers

Alpine forget-me-nots

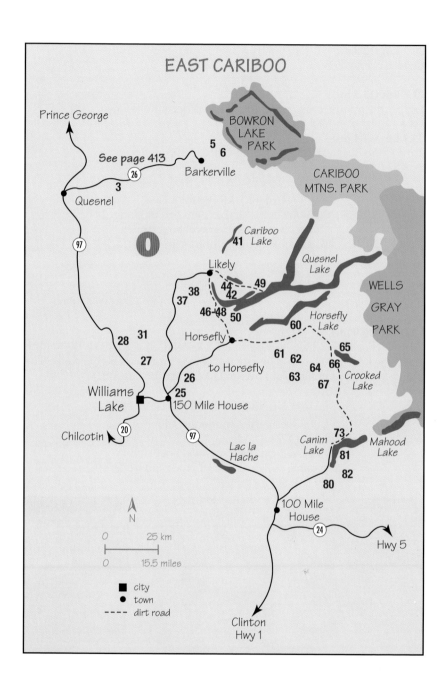

EAST CARIBOO

Prince George

See page 413

26

3

Quesnel

97

Barkerville

5
6

BOWRON
LAKE
PARK

CARIBOO
MTNS. PARK

Cariboo
Lake

41

Likely

Quesnel
Lake

WELLS

38
37

44
42

49

46-48 50

28   31

27

26

25

Horsefly

to Horsefly

60

61   62

63

GRAY

PARK

Horsefly
Lake

65

64 66

67

Crooked
Lake

Williams
Lake

150 Mile House

20

Chilcotin

97

Lac la
Hache

73

Canim
Lake

81

82

80

Mahood
Lake

100 Mile
House

24

Hwy 5

N

0   25 km

0   15.5 miles

■ city
● town
--- dirt road

Clinton
Hwy 1

O: East Cariboo

25	Dugan Lake	FREE	50	Squaw Flats	FREE
26	Dewar Lake	FREE	51	Horsefly Bay	FREE
27	Forest Lake	FREE	60	Prairie Creek	FREE
28	Blue Lake West	FREE	61	Horsefly River	FREE
31	Tyee Lake	FREE	62	McKinley Lake	FREE
37	Jacobie Lake	FREE	63	Tisdall Lake	FREE
38	Bootjack Lake	FREE	64	Elbow Lake	FREE
41	Ladies Creek	FREE	65	Crooked Lake North	FREE
42	Winkley Creek	FREE	66	Crooked Lake South	FREE
44	Spanish Lake	FREE	67	Bosk Lake	FREE
46	Polley Lake	FREE	73	Christmas Lake	FREE
47	Raft Creek	FREE	80	Drewry Lake West	FREE
48	Mitchell Bay	FREE	81	Howard Lake	FREE
49	Abbott Creek	FREE	82	Drewry Lake East	FREE

Elk

East Cariboo

BETWEEN HWY 24 AND CANIM LAKE

Well-maintained gravel roads at consistently low elevation allow easy travel to the sensuously long lakes between Hwy 24 and Canim Lake. And the area supports a healthy mix of deciduous and coniferous trees. Add those two facts to reach an obvious conclusion: leaf peepers should come here to enjoy an autumn drive. Vibrant reds, oranges, yellows and golds woven into the green forest fabric are dazzling. For the deluxe tour, depart Hwy 24 at the Interlakes Store just north of Sheridan Lake. Go north, past Hathaway and Drewry lakes, to Canim Lake. Pavement resumes near the southwest end of Canim Lake. Loop back to 100 Mile House and Hwy 97 via Forest Grove.

If you're heading west on Hwy 24, from Little Fort

At the junction of Hwys 5 and 24 in Little Fort, set your trip odometer to 0 as you head west on Hwy 24. Proceed 67.6 km (42 mi) to the signed junction at Interlakes Store, just north of Sheridan Lake. Reset your trip odometer to 0.

If you're heading north on Hwy 97, from Clinton

About 9.4 km (5.8 mi) before 100 Mile House, turn right (east) onto Hwy 24. Set your trip odometer to 0 and proceed 29.4 km (18.2 mi) east to the signed junction at Interlakes Store, just north of Sheridan Lake. Reset your trip odometer to 0.

If you're heading southeast on Hwy 97, from Williams Lake

About 9.4 km (5.8 mi) south of 100 Mile House, turn left (east) onto Hwy 24. Set your trip odometer to 0 and proceed 29.4 km (18.2 mi) east to the signed junction at Interlakes Store, just north of Sheridan Lake. Reset your trip odometer to 0.

Witness a fall-colour extravaganza on East Cariboo backroads, where aspen and birch thrive among the conifers.

For all approaches above, now follow the directions below

0 km (0 mi)
Starting north on Horse Lake FS road, departing Hwy 24 at Interlakes Store. The junction is signed for several lakes: Hathaway (14 km), Drewry (25 km), Canim (43 km), and Mahood (57 km). This is also the southwest approach to Wells Gray Provincial Park.

4.6 km (2.9 mi)
Reach a 3-way junction. Follow the paved middle fork: Mahood Lake Road, the southwest approach to Wells Gray Park.

9.3 km (5.8 mi)
Proceed straight for Hathaway Lake. Pavement soon ends.

14.4 km (8.9 mi)
Pass Hathaway Resort, where there's a public phone.

17.1 km (10.6 mi)
Reach a spacious, treed, one-vehicle campsite on the right. It's attractive, beside 5-km (3-mi) long Hathaway Lake, but the nearby road can be busy, especially on summer weekends. A sign labels this a Dispersed-Use Site and threatens closure or development if campers don't keep it clean.

17.9 km (11.1 mi)
Pass the north end of Hathaway Lake.

21.2 km (13.1 mi)
Pass Drewry Lake Ranch.

24.6 km (15.3 mi)
Bear left where Bowers-Decka FS road forks right.

25.4 km (15.7 mi)
Bear left where Bowers Lake FS road forks right.

26 km (16.1 mi)
Reach Drewry Lake East campground on the left. It's set in mixed forest between the road and the lake.

DREWRY LAKE EAST CAMPGROUND #82
Weekend / Difficult (due only to distance) / Free
Elev: 1067 m (3500 ft) / Lake: 5 km (3 mi) long, 577 ha
4 tables, 6 campsites, boat launch
Accessible by small motorhomes, but not 5th-wheels

Late September at Drewry Lake

26.3 km (16.3 mi)
Pass Drewry Lake boat launch. Proceed north on the main road for Canim or Mahood lakes.

33 km (20.5 mi)
Stay straight.

39 km (24.2 mi)
Bear left and descend.

42.6 km (26.4 mi)
Reach a junction. Right leads northeast to Mahood Lake and Wells Gray Park. Turn left (northwest) onto Canim Lake South Road to reach 25-km (15.5-mi) long Canim Lake and return to pavement. It passes homes and cabins and grants only occasional views of the lake. Canim has no free campgrounds, but Howard Lake is nearby.

58.2 km (36.1 mi)
Fork sharply left, off Canim Lake South Road, for Howard Lake campground.

The road ascends, soon levels and widens, but remains bumpy. Reach the first campsites (one on the left, another on the lakeshore) in 3.8 km (2.4 mi). The main campground is 200 meters farther, in a large clearing. Secluded lakeshore sites are slightly beyond.

HOWARD LAKE CAMPGROUND #81
Destination / Difficult (due only to distance) / Free
Elev: 937 m (3073 ft) / Lake: 4 km (2.5 mi) long, 175 ha
20 campsites with tables, good boat launch
Accessible by motorhomes and 5th-wheels

Continuing southwest on Canim Lake South Road, passing the turnoff to Howard Lake campground.

61.8 km (38.3 mi)
Pavement resumes.

67.6 km (42 mi)
Reach a junction. Left leads 30 km (18.6 mi) southwest to 100 Mile House. For details read page 424 directions in reverse starting at the 29-km (18-mi) point. Right (northeast) follows Canim Lake's west shore, then proceeds on excellent backroads through the East Cariboo to Crooked Lake and eventually Horsefly and Quesnel lakes. Set your trip odometer to 0 and read the directions below.

CANIM LAKE TO HORSEFLY

The deeper you explore the East Cariboo, the more rewarding your journey. The mixed forest here can be quite scenic. In early summer, multiple shades of green are an inspirational sight. In fall, various hues of amber rustle overhead as you go. And the main Hendrix Creek road north of Canim Lake allows fast, easy travel, just like the road between Canim Lake and Hwy 24.

Here's a grand East Cariboo loop: from Sheridan Lake on Hwy 24, drive north to 25-km (15.5-mi) long Canim Lake, swing around its west shore, head north on Hendrix Creek Road to Crooked Lake, then west to Horsefly, and finally southwest to 150 Mile House, where you can follow Hwy 97 southeast back to Hwy 24. Allow two days of continuous driving, or 4 to 5 days if you linger at a few lakes. Lacking the obvious presence of aspen and birch, the road from Bosk Lake west to Horsefly is less enjoyable than roads farther south. Nevertheless, the ultimate East Cariboo week would include the drive from Horsefly north to Quesnel Lake, Likely, and Spanish Lake, following directions on page 445.

Horsefly FS District deserves appreciation. Their campgrounds are superbly organized and maintained. They've made the district a special resource for campers. Many of the lakes have inviting gravel beaches allowing you to easily dive in for a brisk swim. For the optimal view of the Cariboo Mountains, check out Crooked Lake South and Elbow Lake campgrounds.

0 km (0 mi)
Starting northeast on paved Canim Lake Road, from the 67.6-km (41.9-mi) junction on Canim Lake South Road, near the southwest end of Canim Lake.

8 km (5 mi)
Pass Canim Beach Provincial Park on the right.

12.6 km (7.8 mi)
Pavement ends.

17.6 km (10.9 mi)
Proceed straight on the main road, heading for Hendrix Lake.

19.1 km (11.8 mi)
Turn right and descend to reach Christmas Lake campground in 150 meters.

CHRISTMAS LAKE CAMPGROUND #73
Overnight / Difficult (due only to distance) / Free
Elev: 915 m (3000 ft) / Lake: 32 ha
1 table, room for only 1 vehicle
Accessible by small motorhomes and trailers

Continuing northeast on the main road, passing the turnoff to Christmas Lake campground.

30.3 km (18.8 mi)
Bear left and ascend on the main road paralleling Hendrix Creek.

46.8 km (29 mi)
Bear right on the main road.

51.2 km (31.7 mi)
Bear left on the main road.

53 km (32.9 mi)
Proceed straight on the main road.

54.9 km (34 mi)
Bear right, still heading for Crooked Lake.

55.5 km (34.4 mi)
Bosk Lake is visible through trees on the left.

57.6 km (35.7 mi)
For Crooked Lake, stay right on the road signed for Eureka Peak Lodge. For Bosk Lake campground, turn left just before crossing a bridged creek. It's 200 meters off the main road in a large clearing.

BOSK LAKE CAMPGROUND #67
Weekend / Difficult (due only to distance) / Free
Elev: 994 m (3260 ft) / Lake: 6 km (3.7 mi) long, 500 ha
4 tables, sandy beach, bearproof garbage bin
Accessible by motorhomes and 5th-wheels

Continuing northeast on the main road, passing the turnoff to Bosk Lake campground.

57.9 km (35.9 mi)
After crossing the bridged creek, proceed straight. Hendrix-Gotchen FS road forks right.

60.1 km (37.3 mi)
Bear right.

65.2 km (40.4 mi)
Reach a junction. Set your trip odometer to 0 before going either way. Proceed straight (north) for Crooked Lake—worth a look even if you don't camp there. It's a beautiful lake beneath the Cariboo Mountains, near 2426-m (7957-ft) Eureka Peak. Turn left onto Black Creek-Bosk Lake FS road (following directions on page 442) to head northwest toward Elbow, Tisdall and McKinley lakes, as well as Horsefly.

0 km (0 mi)
Proceeding north for Crooked Lake, from the 65.2-km (40.4-mi) junction.

1.4 km (0.9 mi)
Pass small Cruiser Lake on the left.

5.1 km (3.2 mi)
Stay left.

Crooked Lake

6.7 km (4.2 mi)
Bear right and descend.

7.4 km (4.6 mi)
Reach Crooked Lake South campground on the right. Views of the mountains and the lake are much better here than at the north campground.

CROOKED LAKE SOUTH CAMPGROUND #66
Destination / Difficult (due only to distance) / Free
Elev: 933 m (3060 ft) / Lake: 10.5 km (6.5 mi) long, 1092 ha
3 well-spaced tables, sandy beach, bearproof garbage bin
Accessible by motorhomes and 5th-wheels

Continuing north, passing the turnoff to Crooked Lake south campground.

9 km (5.5 mi)
Cross a bridged creek. Just beyond, go right at the junction.

9.7 km (6 mi)
Reach Crooked Lake North campground on the right. It's a large clearing tucked into a cove with no beach. The lake appears smaller here.

CROOKED LAKE NORTH CAMPGROUND #65
Destination / Difficult (due only to distance) / Free
Elev: 933 m (3060 ft) / Lake: 10.5 km (6.5 mi) long, 1092 ha
4 tables, many more campsites, rough boat launch,
bearproof garbage bin
Accessible by motorhomes and 5th-wheels

0 km (0 mi)
Starting on Black Creek-Bosk Lake FS road, from the 65.2-km (40.4-mi) junction (page 440), heading northwest toward Elbow, Tisdall and McKinley lakes, as well as Horsefly. The road is narrow but generally smooth.

3.7 km (2.3 mi)
Bear left.

3.9 km (2.4 mi)
Proceed straight. Grass is growing in mid-road. Slow down to avoid a few potholes. Elbow Lake is soon visible.

7.2 km (4.5 mi)
Proceed straight along the lake. The road gets rougher.

9.3 km (5.8 mi)
Turn right for Elbow Lake campground. A 300-meter loop accesses the campsites, most of which have views of the lake and mountains.

ELBOW LAKE CAMPGROUND #64
Destination / Difficult (due only to distance) / Free
Elev: 908 m (2978 ft) / Lake: 4 km (2.5 mi) long, 338 ha
5 tables, more campsites, gravel beach
Accessible by motorhomes and 5th-wheels

Continuing generally west on Black Creek-Bosk Lake FS road, passing the turnoff to Elbow Lake campground.

11.2 km (6.9 mi)
Stay right. In 100 meters cross a bridged creek.

12.1 km (7.5 mi)
Bear left.

17 km (10.5 mi)
Go right at the triangular junction.

18.5 km (11.5 mi)
Reach another triangular junction and set your trip odometer to 0. Left leads southwest to Tisdall Lake campground. Right (northwest) continues to McKinley Lake and Horsefly.

0 km (0 mi)
Turning left for Tisdall Lake campground, from the 18.5-km (11.5-mi) junction on Black Creek-Bosk Lake FS road.

2.2 km (1.4 mi)
Turn right.

3.4 km (2.1 mi)
Arrive at Tisdall Lake campground. The campsites are well spaced. Several have lakeviews. The mountains are less impressive here than at Crooked or Elbow lakes.

TISDALL LAKE CAMPGROUND #63

Destination / Difficult (due only to distance) / Free
Elev: 960 m (3150 ft) / Lake: 5.5 km (3.4 mi) long, 490 ha
11 tables, good boat launch, bearproof garbage bin
Accessible by motorhomes and 5th-wheels

Continuing northwest on Black Creek-Bosk Lake FS road, from the 18.5-km (11.5-mi) junction and turnoff to Tisdall Lake campground. Set your trip odometer to 0.

0 km (0 mi)
Continuing northwest on Black Creek-Bosk Lake FS road, heading for McKinley Lake and Horsefly.

1.6 km (1 mi) and 5.3 km (3.3 mi)
Proceed straight on the main road.

6.7 km (4.2 mi)
Turn right for McKinley Lake campground.

Drive through an aspen grove. At 1.8 km (1.1 mi) bear right where the left fork is signed for private cottages. Reach the campground at 2.2 km (1.4 mi). It's beautiful, at the lake's narrow west end, near the outlet stream. The campsites are well-spaced, near the shore, backed by trees. A water temperature control structure keeps the water favourably cool for salmon. In late August or September you'll see Sockeye salmon spawning here. You'll also see eagles converging to feed on the dead fish.

MCKINLEY LAKE CAMPGROUND #62
Weekend / Moderate (from Horsefly) / Free
Elev: 863 m (2830 ft) / Lake: 7.5 km (4.7 mi) long, 514 ha
5 tables, good boat launch, bearproof garbage bin
Accessible by small motorhomes and trailers

Continuing west on Black Creek-Bosk Lake FS road, passing the turnoff to McKinley Lake campground.

10.7 km (6.6 mi)
Turn right to reach Horsefly River campground in 100 meters. It's accessible by RVs, but only tiny ones can squeeze in or turn around. By late September, the stench of rotting salmon carcasses is intense here.

HORSEFLY RIVER CAMPGROUND #61
Overnight / Moderate (from Horsefly) / Free
2 tables in a tiny clearing
Too small for motorhomes and 5th-wheels

Continuing west on Black Creek-Bosk Lake FS road, passing the turnoff to Horsefly River campground.

12.2 km (7.6 mi)
Proceed straight on the main road.

12.3 km (7.6 mi)
Reach a major junction. Bear left (west) to reach the town of Horsefly in 28 km (17.4 mi). (For Horsefly Lake turn right / northeast. At the major junction, turn left / north. Near the south shore, fork left for Prairie Creek campground #60. It's a tiny campground about midway on the 45-km / 28-mi long lake.)

27.7 km (17.2 mi) and 29.7 km (18.4 mi)
Stay straight on the main road.

39.3 km (24.4 mi)
Pavement resumes.

40.2 km (24.9 mi)
Reach a junction. The Horsefly Forest District office is on the right. Proceed street to reach the town of Horsefly.

Marvel at the grandeur of Quesnel Lake from Mitchell Bay campground.

40.6 km (25.2 mi)
Cross a single-lane bridge over the Horsefly River and arrive in the town of
Horsefly, near Clarke's General store on paved Horsefly Road. A green
sign states distances to various points. Left leads 53 km (32.9 mi) southwest
to Hwy 97. Right leads 22 km (13.6 mi) north to Quesnel Lake, and 25 km
(15.5 mi) to Mitchell Bay. Also turn right to drive northeast 11 km (6.8 mi) to
the southwest end of Horsefly Lake. Black Creek is 29 km (18 mi) east,
behind you. To continue, set your trip odometer to 0 and follow the directions
on the next page.

HORSEFLY TO LIKELY

The forest is noticeably lusher north of Horsefly compared to farther south
in Cariboo country. You'll even see a few big cedar trees here. That, plus the
sheer size of **Quesnel Lake,** lends the region a coastal atmosphere.
It's refreshing.

This is also where you'll find B.C.'s highest concentration of provincial-
park-quality free campgrounds. Mitchell Bay and Raft Creek are outstanding examples. They earn *Destination* ratings because they have striking
mountain scenery and are on tremendous Quesnel Lake. It's among the
biggest bodies of water in the province. From the northwest end, it measures

80 km (50 mi) to the tip of the north arm, and 104 km (64 mi) to the tip of the east arm. Boaters must be wary of the powerful winds that sometimes whip the lake into dangerously oceanic conditions. From the safety of the shore, however, these storms can be wildly entertaining.

You can quickly reach Horsefly via paved road. It's a mere 30-minute drive from 150 Mile House (page 458). But backroad nomads will want to journey from Hwy 24 near Sheridan Lake, all the way north to Horsefly, keeping their tires on dirt nearly the entire way. Prominent landmarks on this route are Canim Lake, and Hendrix and Black Creeks. Directions start on page 434.

0 km (0 mi)
At the junction in Horsefly, by Clarke's General Store, where a large blue sign marking the road east to Crooked Lake states LODGING, CAMPING.

If you arrived here via Black Creek FS road, turn right (north) onto paved Horsefly Road. If you arrived here via paved Horsefly Road, stay on the main road. **From either approach**, follow the main road as it curves left (north) between the school and the Cornerhouse Place Stores.

0.8 km (0.5 mi)
The road bends right.

1.2 km (0.7 mi)
Pavement ends.

2.4 km (1.5 mi)
Bear right at a sign for Mitchell Bay.

5.3 km (3.3 mi)
Proceed straight. This winding road gets rough, but the hard dirt-and-gravel surface provides traction even when wet. A comfortable speed is about 50 kph (30 mph). Watch for livestock.

10.7 km (6.6 mi)
Bear right. The Horsefly River is along here.

13.4 km (8.3 mi)
Cross a small bridge and reach a tiny campground above a noisy riffle.

SQUAW FLATS CAMPGROUND #50
Overnight / Moderate / Free
2 tables, bearproof garbage bin
Accessible by motorhomes and small trailers

Squaw Flats campground on Horsefly River

Continuing on the main road, passing Squaw Flats campground. Soon ascend high above the river and attain broad views.

16.7 km (10.4 mi)
Bear right at the fork and descend.

19.4 km (12 mi)
Reach a junction. Turn left (northwest) for Mitchell Bay or Raft Creek campgrounds on Quesnel Lake.

21.1 km (13.1 mi)
Stay left.

21.6 km (13.4 mi)
Bear left and proceed on Horsefly-Likely FS road. Mitchell Bay Landing is right.

24.1 km (15 mi)
Turn right and descend to reach Mitchell Bay campground in 150 meters.

This provincial-park quality campground is in a grassy clearing, surrounded by birch trees, just 4 meters above the lakeshore. The campsites are well-spaced but within view of each other.

MITCHELL BAY CAMPGROUND #48
Destination / Moderate / Free
Elev: 728 m (2388 ft) / Quesnel Lake: 27,013 ha
5 tables, rock and gravel beach, boat launch
Accessible by small motorhomes and trailers

Continuing northwest on Horsefly-Likely FS road, passing the turnoff to Mitchell Bay campground.

28.1 km (17.4 mi)
Giant cottonwoods line the road ahead.

29.8 km (18.5 mi)
Turn right for Raft Creek campground.

In 50 meters reach two tables in a clearing on the right. At 100 meters is another secluded campsite. The last site, the one best-suited for big RVs, is 300 meters from the main road. It's on the beach and has 3 tables. Just beyond is a large turnaround.

RAFT CREEK CAMPGROUND #47
Destination / Moderate / Free
Elev: 728 m (2388 ft) / Quesnel Lake: 27,013 ha
7 tables, a few secluded campsites, good boat launch
Accessible by motorhomes and 5th-wheels

Continuing northwest on Horsefly-Likely FS road, passing the turnoff to Raft Creek campground.

31.2 km (19.3 mi)
Go right for Likely. Left is Moorehead-Gavin Lake FS road.

33 km (20.5 mi)
Reach an **exceptional viewpoint** on the right. There's a table and outhouse on the left. You can survey a tremendous expanse of Quesnel Lake, about 200 m (656 ft) below you. Prominent above the north shore is (1570-m (5150-ft) Spanish Mtn. Farther northeast is 2057-m (6747-ft) Mt. Brew.

35.7 km (22.1 mi)
Bear right for Likely. Just beyond is a yellow KM 14 sign.

47.7 km (29.6 mi)
Intersect the paved Likely Road. Turn right to quickly reach the town of

Raft Creek campground, Quesnel Lake

Likely, where Quesnel River departs the northwest end of Quesnel Lake. Left leads 81.6 km (50.6 mi) south to 150 Mile House and Hwy 97. Read directions on page 456.

50.1 km (31.1 mi)
Cross the long bridge over Quesnel River where it departs the northwest end of Quesnel Lake. The town of Likely is just beyond. The bridge offers exciting entertainment—salmon watching—from August through early October. For campgrounds beyond Likely, set your trip odometer to 0 midway across the bridge and continue reading directions on page 450.

LIKELY TO HORSEFLY

Two of Cariboo country's premier campgrounds—Raft Creek and Mitchell Bay—are on the west shore of hugely impressive Quesnel Lake. They're easily reached within a 30-minute drive of Likely, en route to Horsefly.

0 km (0 mi)
In Likely, midway across the Quesnel River bridge, heading west on paved Likely Road.

2.4 km (1.5 mi)
Turn left onto Horsefly-Likely FS road.

14.4 km (8.9 mi)
Bear left and proceed south for Raft Creek and Mitchell Bay campgrounds.

17.2 km (10.7 mi)
Reach an **exceptional viewpoint** of Quesnel Lake. You can survey a tremendous expanse of Quesnel Lake, about 200 m (656 ft) below you. Prominent above the north shore is 1570-m (5150-ft) Spanish Mtn. Farther northeast is 2057-m (6747-ft) Mt. Brew.

18.9 km (11.7 mi)
Go left. Right is Moorehead-Gavin Lake FS road.

20.3 km (12.6 mi)
Turn left for Raft Creek campground. Read page 448 for details and a photo.

26 km (16.1 mi)
Turn left and descend to reach Mitchell Bay campground in 150 meters. This provincial-park quality campground is in a grassy clearing, surrounded by birch trees, just 4 meters above the lakeshore. The campsites are well-spaced but within view of each other.

MITCHELL BAY CAMPGROUND #48
Destination / Moderate / Free
Elev: 728 m (2388 ft) / Quesnel Lake: 27,013 ha
5 tables, rock and gravel beach, boat launch
Accessible by small motorhomes and trailers

Continuing generally south, it's another 24.1 km (15 mi) to Horsefly. Stay on the main road, bearing right at major junctions.

BEYOND LIKELY

You're about to hit the motherlode. Three out of the four free campgrounds beyond Likely are rated Destination. Take your pick from this campers' bonanza.

(1) Winkley Creek is 20.7 km (12.8 mi) southeast, on 104-km (64.5-mi) long Quesnel Lake. It has a large gravel beach. The campsites are in the open. It's lovely when the sky is blue and the temperature mild. But keep in mind the potential exposure to rain, wind or blazing sun. Motorhomes and 5th-wheels should have no trouble getting here.

Quesnel Lake

(2) Spanish Lake is 14.3 km (8.9 mi) east-southeast. The campsites are wonderfully secluded, more so than those at most provincial parks. The gorgeously forested setting rivals any campground in this book. Mountains rise 1000 m (3280 ft) above the 8-km (5-mi) long lake. As for access, the final 0.7 km (0.4 mi) is steep and narrow. Small motorhomes and trailers can make it, but only with good brakes and plenty of torque.

(3) Abbott Creek is 30.6 km (19 mi) east-southeast, on Quesnel Lake. The mountains appear less dramatic here than at Spanish Lake, but it's still an exceptional campground. The sandy beach is divine. This is just about the lake's widest point. The far shore is 3.5 km (2.2 mi) distant. The immensity of it is a compelling sight. If you can stand the paint-shaker effect on the last 3 km (2 mi), Abbott is accessible by motorhomes and 5th-wheels. This final approach is also steep, so big RVs need lots of torque to power out.

(4) Ladies Creek is 36 km (22.3 mi) northeast, on 9.5-km (6-mi) long Cariboo Lake. It looks remote on the map, but the wide, gravel road is generally smooth, allowing you to average 80 kph (50 mph). So it's easily accessible by motorhomes and 5th-wheels. Despite visible clearcuts, the lake has a wild atmosphere. So does the campground, framed by tall, thick-girthed hemlock and spruce. The large sandy beach seems luxurious in such a setting. Music, provided by the namesake creek, is audible. You might also hear a creek tumbling to the lake's far shore.

(1) Winkley Creek

0 km (0 mi)
In Likely, on the northeast side of the Quesnel River bridge. Just beyond, proceed straight (east) on Keithley Creek Road.

0.5 km (0.3 mi)
Proceed straight. The road ascending left leads to Quesnel Forks campground.

1.5 km (0.9 mi)
Reach a fork. Both ways are paved. Turn right (southeast) for Winkley Creek campground on Quesnel Lake. Left leads to campgrounds at Spanish Lake, Abbott Creek (Quesnel Lake), and Ladies Creek (Cariboo Lake).

5.6 km (3.5 mi)
Pass Cedar Point Park on the right.

6.4 km (4 mi)
Stay left at the fork and ascend. Pavement ends.

9.4 km (5.8 mi)
Proceed straight. The road levels.

16 km (9.9 mi)
Go right at the fork. It's signed for Winkley Creek.

18.1 km (11.2 mi)
Go right at the fork and continue descending.

20.4 km (12.6 mi)
Turn right.

20.7 km (12.8 mi)
Arrive at Winkley Creek campground.

WINKLEY CREEK CAMPGROUND #42
Destination / Moderate / Free
Elev: 728 m (2388 ft) / Lake: 1.2 km (0.7 mi) wide here
9 well-spaced tables, bearproof garbage bin, good boat launch
Accessible by motorhomes and 5th-wheels

(2) Spanish Lake

0 km (0 mi)
In Likely, on the northeast side of the Quesnel River bridge. Just beyond, proceed straight (east) on Keithley Creek Road.

0.5 km (0.3 mi)
Proceed straight. The road ascending left leads to Quesnel Forks campground.

1.5 km (0.9 mi)
Reach a fork. Both ways are paved. Turn left for campgrounds at Spanish Lake, Abbott Creek (Quesnel Lake), and Ladies Creek (Cariboo Lake). Right leads southeast to Winkley Creek campground on Quesnel Lake.

2.3 km (1.4 mi)
Pavement ends.

2.7 km (1.7 mi)
Reach a fork near a well-preserved rustic cabin. For Spanish Lake and Abbott Creek, turn right and ascend steeply on the road signed for Tasse Lake. Left leads northeast to Ladies Creek.

3.6 km (2.2 mi)
The steep ascent ends.

7.5 km (4.7 mi)
Proceed straight (southeast) on the main road.

13.6 km (8.4 mi)
Turn left to reach Spanish Lake campground in 0.7 km (0.4 mi). (See photo on page 455.) RVs must be capable of negotiating steep terrain. Secluded campsites are on the point. One is on a small cove.

SPANISH LAKE CAMPGROUND #44
Destination / Moderate / Free
Elev: 937 m (3073 ft) / Lake: 8 km (5 mi) long, 448 ha
6 tables, bearproof garbage bin, good boat launch
Accessible by small motorhomes and trailers

(3) Abbott Creek on Quesnel Lake

Follow directions to the Spanish Lake turnoff at 13.6 km (8.4 mi) and continue straight (southeast) on the main road.

19.2 km (11.9 mi)
Bear left on the main road.

20.7 km (12.8 mi)
Go right at the fork and ascend.

24.5 km (15.2 mi)
Go right and descend. Attain a view east into the Cariboo Mountains of Wells Grey Park.

25.1 km (15.6 mi)
Proceed straight and descend.

27.6 km (17.1 mi)
Go left and descend steeply on a rougher road.

29.2 km (18.1 mi)
Go right. Left is signed for Shoals Bay Rd.

30.2 km (18.7 mi)
The final descent is very steep.

30.6 km (19 mi)
Arrive at Abbott Creek campground on Quesnel Lake's north shore.

ABBOTT CREEK CAMPGROUND #49
Destination / Difficult / Free
Elev: 728 m (2388 ft) / Lake: 3.5 km (2.2 mi) wide here
6 spacious campsites with tables
Accessible by motorhomes and 5th wheels

(4) Ladies Creek on Cariboo Lake

0 km (0 mi)
In Likely, on the northeast side of the Quesnel River bridge. Just beyond, proceed straight (east) on Keithley Creek Road.

0.5 km (0.3 mi)
Proceed straight.

Spanish Lake

1.5 km (0.9 mi)
Reach a fork. Both ways are paved. Turn left for campgrounds at Ladies Creek (Cariboo Lake), Spanish Lake, and Abbott Creek (Quesnel Lake). Right leads southeast to Winkley Creek campground on Quesnel Lake.

2.7 km (1.7 mi)
Reach a fork near a well-preserved rustic cabin. Bear left (north) on the flat road for Ladies Creek. The road ascending steeply right (signed for Tasse Lake) leads to Spanish Lake and Abbott Creek.

8 km (5 mi) and 8.1 km (5.1 mi)
Proceed straight on the main road.

9 km (5.6 mi)
Follow the main road through a big, sweeping curve left.

10.8 km (6.7 mi)
Cross a large, high bridge over the Cariboo River.

11.2 km (6.9 mi)
Bear right on the main road.

16.8 km (10.4 mi)
Proceed straight on the main road. Kangaroo Creek FS road forks left.

22.7 km (14.1 mi)
Go right. The road is rougher now, with potholes.

23.5 km (14.6 mi)
Cross a bridge over the broad, wild Cariboo River.

23.7 km (14.7 mi)
Turn left at the T-junction.

26.8 km (16.6 mi) and 29.2 km (18.1 mi)
Proceed straight on the main road.

36 km (22.3 mi)
Turn left and descend to reach Ladies Creek campground on Cariboo Lake in 100 meters.

LADIES CREEK CAMPGROUND #41

Destination / Difficult (due only to distance) / Free
Elev: 812 m (2663 ft) / Lake: 9.5 km (6 mi) long, 1010 ha
6 spacious campsites with tables, gravel boat launch
Accessible by motorhomes and 5th-wheels

LIKELY TO 150 MILE HOUSE

0 km (0 mi)
In Likely, midway across the Quesnel River bridge, heading west on paved Likely Road.

2.4 km (1.5 mi)
Proceed straight (west) on paved Likely Road. Left is Horsefly-Likely FS road. It leads south to campgrounds at Polley Lake and on the west shore of Quesnel Lake. Directions continue on page 449.

9.3 km (5.8 mi)
Bear left on Likely Road.

13.8 km (8.6 mi)
Turn left for Bootjack Lake campground.

> **0 km (0 mi)**
> Starting south on Bootjack Lake FS road.

Ladies Creek campground

0.2 km (0.1 mi)
Stay straight on the main road.

0.5 km (0.3 mi) and 0.8 km (0.5 mi)
Bear right on the main road.

1.3 km (0.8 mi)
Morehead Lake is visible on the right.

6.8 km (4.2 mi)
Bear left on the main road.

8.8 km (5.5 mi)
Go right at the junction.

9.1 km (5.6 mi)
Arrive at Bootjack Lake campground. The area is treed. The brushy shore has no beach. Low, forested hills provide mediocre scenery. The campgrounds at Spanish Lake, and Raft Creek on Quesnel Lake, are superior.

BOOTJACK LAKE CAMPGROUND #38
Weekend / Easy / Free
Elev: 985 m (3231 ft) / Lake: 4.5 km (2.8 mi) long, 251 ha
6 tables, 3 more campsites, gravel boat launch, dock
Accessible by motorhomes and 5th-wheels

Continuing southwest on Likely Road, passing the turnoff to Bootjack Lake campground.

30.3 km (18.8 mi)
Pass Morehead-Gavin FS road on the left. It heads east, reaching the small campground at Gavin Lake campground #36, next to the Forest Education Centre, in about 6.7 km (4.2 mi). The lake is 2.6 km (1.6 mi) long.

34.8 km (21.6 mi)
Pass Beaver Valley FS road on the left. It leads southeast about 40 km (24.8 mi) to Horsefly.

48.3 km (30 mi)
Pass Big Lake store.

79.5 km (49.3 mi)
Proceed straight (south) to intersect Hwy 97 at 150 Mile House. Turn left onto Horsefly Road and follow directions on page 459 (from 4.5 km / 2.8 mi) for campgrounds at Dugan or Dewar lakes, or to reach Horsefly in 48 km (29.8 mi). Dugan Lake is only 5 minutes away.

84 km (52 mi)
Intersect Hwy 97 at 150 Mile House. Williams Lake is right (west). Left leads south to Lac la Hache and 100 Mile House.

150 MILE HOUSE TO HORSEFLY

Access to Quesnel Lake from Hwy 97 is fast and easy via Horsefly Road. It starts just north of 150 Mile House. Within 10 minutes it passes campgrounds at Dugan and Dewar lakes. Neither is special, but both are convenient. Dugan is open, Dewar is treed. Passing cars and trains are sometimes audible at both. Horsefly Road ends at, you guessed it, the town of Horsefly. Pavement ends there too. But it's not far north to Quesnel Lake. Follow directions on page 445. You'll find two provincial-park-quality campgrounds on the west shore: Mitchell Bay and Raft Creek. From there, it's a short drive up the lake's northwest arm to Likely, beyond which there are four more campgrounds rated *Destination*.

Quesnel River, near Likely

0 km (0 mi)
Starting north on Likely Road, departing Hwy 97 at 150 Mile House.

4.5 km (2.8 mi)
Turn right (northeast) onto Horsefly Road, at the big white sign for Resort Lakes.

7.3 km (4.5 mi)
For Dugan Lake campground, turn right onto Dugan Lake Road.

In 0.4 km (0.2 mi) curve right, passing a home on the left, to enter the campground. The best sites are just beyond, between the trees and the lake. Tenters will find plenty of level grass. Road noise is audible.

DUGAN LAKE CAMPGROUND #25
Overnight / Easy / Free
Elev: 930 m (3050 ft) / Lake: 1.2 km long and wide, 94 ha
6 campsites, several tables around a pasture, boat launch
Accessible by motorhomes and 5th-wheels

Continuing northeast on Horsefly Road, passing the turnoff to Dugan Lake camp-ground.

12.8 km (7.9 mi)
For Dewar Lake campground, turn right onto Spokin Lake Road.

In 300 meters, turn right onto a spur road. A huge sign here warns about thin ice in winter. Reach the lake in another 50 meters.

DEWAR LAKE CAMPGROUND #26
Overnight / Easy / Free
Elev: 990 m (3247 ft) / Lake: 1.2 km (0.7 mi) long, 43 ha
4 tables, Accessible by motorhomes and 5th-wheels

Continuing northeast on Horsefly Road, passing the turnoff to Dewar Lake camp-ground.

52.5 km (32.6 mi)
Arrive in Horsefly. For Crooked Lake, continue reading the East of Horsefly directions below. For Mitchell Bay and Raft Creek campgrounds on Quesnel Lake, read the Horsefly to Likely directions on page 445.

EAST OF HORSEFLY

The section **Canim Lake to Horsefly** (page 438) covers in detail the area from Canim Lake, north to Crooked Lake, then generally west to Horsefly. But if you're going the opposite way—heading east from Horsefly— the following directions will guide you as far as the two *Destination*-rated campgrounds at Crooked Lake.

0 km (0 mi)
In Horsefly, near Clarke's General store, starting east on Black Creek FS road. It's signed for Crooked Lake. There's also a big blue sign LODGING, CAMPING. Set your trip odometer to 0 and immediately cross a single-lane bridge over the Horsefly River.

0.4 km (0.25 mi)
Bear right and pass the Horsefly Forest District office. Pavement ends within a kilometer.

11 km (6.8 mi) and 13.1 km (8.1 mi)
Stay straight on the main road.

28.4 km (17.6 mi)
Reach a major junction. Go right (east).

Dugan Lake is a handy campground near 150 Mile House.

28.5 km (17.7 mi)
Proceed straight on the main road.

29 km (18 mi)
Cross a long bridge over the Horsefly River.

34 km (21.1 mi)
Turn left for McKinley Lake campground. Read further directions on page 443.

35.4 km (21.9 mi) and 39.1 km (24.2 mi)
Proceed straight on the main road.

40.7 km (25.2 mi)
Reach a triangular junction. Right leads southwest to Tisdall Lake campground. Read further directions on page 443. Continue left (southeast) for Elbow and Crooked lakes.

42.3 km (26.2 mi)
Bear left at the triangular junction.

47.2 km (29.3 mi)
Stay right.

48 km (29.8 mi)
Cross a bridged creek, then stay left.

50 km (31 mi)
Turn left for Elbow Lake campground. Read page 442 for details.

52.1 km (32.3 mi)
Proceed straight along the lake.

55.3 km (34.3 mi)
Proceed straight.

55.5 km (34.4 mi)
Bear right.

59.2 km (36.7 mi)
Reach a junction. Set your trip odometer to 0 before going either way. Turn left (north) for the two Crooked Lake campgrounds. Right is Hendrix Creek FS road. It quickly passes Bosk Lake campground on the right, then continues south. Pavement resumes along the west shore of Canim Lake. Reach the junction of Canim Lake Road and Canim Lake South Road, near the lake's southwest end, in 65.2 km (40.4 mi). From there, it's 32 km (20 mi) southwest to 100 Mile House and Hwy 97.

0 km (0 mi)
Proceeding north for Crooked Lake, from the 59.2-km (36.7-mi) junction.

1.4 km (0.9 mi)
Pass small Cruiser Lake on the left.

5.1 km (3.2 mi)
Stay left.

6.7 km (4.2 mi)
Bear right and descend.

7.4 km (4.6 mi)
Reach Crooked Lake South campground on the right. Read page 441 for details.

9 km (5.5 mi)
Cross a bridged creek. Just beyond, go right at the junction.

9.7 km (6 mi)
Reach Crooked Lake North campground on the right. Read page 442 for details.

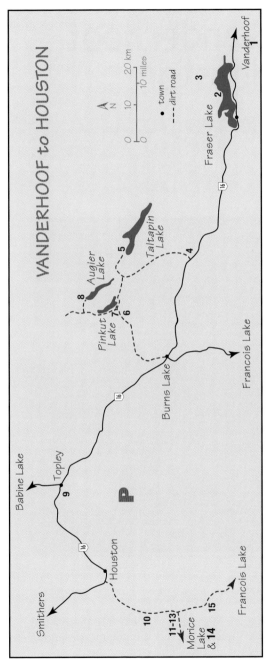

P: Vanderhoof to Houston

1	Hogsback Lake	FREE
2	Peterson's Beach mid-May to mid-Sept	$
3	Ormond Lake	FREE
4	Co-op Lake	FREE
5	Taltapin Lake	FREE
6	Division Lake	FREE
7	Pinkut Lake	FREE
8	Augier Lake	FREE
9	Sunset Lake	FREE
10	Aspen	FREE
11	Owen Flats A	FREE
12	Owen Flats B	FREE
13	Lamprey Creek	FREE
14	Morice Lake	FREE
15	Owen Lake	FREE

Lupine

Hwy 16: Vanderhoof to Houston

Hogsback Lake

PRINCE GEORGE TO FRASER LAKE

Between Prince George and the town of Fraser Lake, Hwy 16 pierces the geographic heart of the province: Vanderhoof. But it's still an uneventful drive. So even if you're not ready to pitch the tent, veer off the pavement and check out Hogsback Lake campground. Mere minutes from the highway, it has a relaxing, park-like atmosphere. The lake is pretty, adorned with lily pads, ringed by Douglas fir. And the water is warm; dive in and refresh yourself. If you want to string up the tarp and establish a home in the outdoors for a few days, you'll probably want a bigger lake, grander surroundings, and a more spacious campground than Hogsback Lake. Follow the directions to Augier Lake (page 472), northeast of Burns Lake.

No other campground in this book draws crowds like Peterson's Beach, on the north shore of Fraser Lake. All summer, especially weekends and holidays, the scene here is precisely what free camping should enable you to avoid: raucous crowds, whining jet skis, roaring water-ski boats, blasting stereos, screaming brats. If you're very sociable, this provincial-park quality campground has advantages: easy access to a long, lovely beach; warm water, ideal for swimming; a shallow area for kids to play in. But even if you prefer bears to people, Peterson's is convenient to Hwy 16 and might be worth trying in spring or fall when a crowd is less likely. You can always push on north to Ormond Lake, ringed by high hills. The shore is brushy, unattractive for swimming and sunning, but Ormond can be vacant when Peterson's is throbbing with humanity.

HOGSBACK LAKE

If you're heading west on Hwy 16, from Prince George

Set your trip odometer to 0 at the junction of Hwys 97 and 16 in Prince George and head southwest on Hwy 16. For Hogsback Lake, drive to 82.4 km (51.1 mi), then turn left (south) onto Mapes Road. Reset your trip odometer to 0.

If you're heading east on Hwy 16, from Vanderhoof

Near the top of a rise, at Vanderhoof's east end, set your trip odometer to 0 as you pass the tan Forest Service building. Drive 14.3 km (8.9 mi), then turn right (south) onto Mapes Road. Reset your trip odometer to 0.

Now follow the directions below

0 km (0 mi)
Starting south on Mapes Road.

10.1 km (6.3 mi)
Reach a T-junction. Turn left onto Blackwater Road.

11.9 km (7.4 mi)
Turn right onto Hogback Lake Road, then immediately fork left.

13 km (8.1 mi)
Continue straight through the intersection.

13.6 km (8.4 mi)
Go left at the sign.

13.8 km (8.6 mi)
Arrive at Hogsback Lake. A clearing at the boat launch has two tables and is
the only place big RVs should attempt to park. The road left rises then
drops to two lakeshore campsites. Right leads to two sites above a lily-
padded cove.

HOGSBACK LAKE CAMPGROUND #1
Weekend / Easy / Free
Elev: 730 m (2395 ft) / Lake: 1 km (0.6 mi) long, 45 ha
6 tables, boat launch, historic hiking trail
Inaccessible by large motorhomes and trailers

PETERSON'S BEACH, ON FRASER LAKE

If you're heading west on Hwy 16, from Vanderhoof

From the junction of Hwys 16 and 27 (the Fort St. James turnoff) just west of
Vanderhoof, drive Hwy 16 west 34.5 km (21.4 mi), then turn right (north)
toward Nautley. This turnoff is 2.2 km (1.4 mi) west of the Nechako River
bridge. Set your trip odometer to 0.

If you're heading east on Hwy 16, from the town of Fraser Lake

From the Visitor Info Centre (located next to Fraser Lake Recreation Centre,
on the east side of town), drive Hwy 16 east 16.8 km (10.4 mi), then turn left
(north) toward Nautley. Set your trip odometer to 0.

For either approach above, now follow the directions below

Pass Beaumont Provincial Park. In 3.6 km (2.2 mi), cross the bridge over
Nautley River—the shortest river in B.C. Proceed through the village
of Nautley. At 4.3 km (2.7 mi) reach a junction where pavement ends.
Turn right onto Sutherland FS road to reach Ormond Lake. For directions
continue reading at the bottom of page 467. Turn left onto Stella Road East
to reach Peterson's Beach. Set your trip odometer to 0 before turning either
way.

Turning left (west) onto Stella Road East, from Nautley village.

0 km (0 mi)
Starting on Stella Road East, heading west to Peterson's Beach on Fraser
Lake.

10.7 km (6.6 mi)
Turn left at the large signboard for Peterson's Beach.

Peterson's Beach campground

The gated entry is open 7 a.m. to 10 p.m. ATVs are prohibited. Quiet hours are 11 p.m. to 7 a.m. Many campsites are close together. A few along the lake are divided by trees and have their own pebble beach. Opposite the campground entrance is the signed Ormond Creek trail. It leads 13.2 km (8.2 mi) north to Ormond Lake. A short way up you'll achieve lake views.

PETERSON'S BEACH CAMPGROUND #2
Weekend / Easy / $ / mid-May to mid-Sept
Elev: 670 m (2198 ft) / Lake: 18.5 km (11.5 mi) long, 5385 ha
25 tables, excellent swimming beach
good boat launch, hiking trail
very popular, often crowded, provincial-park quality
Accessible by motorhomes and 5th-wheels

Turning right (northeast) onto Sutherland FS road, from Nautley village.

0 km (0 mi)
Starting on Sutherland FS road, heading initially northeast to Ormond Lake.

2.1 km (1.3 mi)
Turn left (northwest) at the signed junction. Dog Creek Road forks right.

15 km (9.3 mi)
Turn left at the signed junction, onto Sutherland-Oona FS road.

15.9 km (9.6 mi)
Turn left and descend 100 meters to Ormond Lake campground. It's set in forest with a few aspen. A treed bowl back from the lake shelters a spacious campsite with 2 tables—ideal for a large group.

ORMOND LAKE CAMPGROUND #3
Weekend / Moderate / Free
Elev: 838 m (2750 ft) / Lake: 4 km (2.5 mi) long, 317 ha
11 tables, several secluded campsites, 2 good boat launches
Accessible by motorhomes and 5th-wheels

NORTHEAST OF BURNS LAKE

A network of good roads allows easy travel to a cluster of sizable lakes and their attendant campgrounds northeast of the town of Burns Lake.

Augier Lake is the area's most picturesque. Its campground is also the best. Though smaller than gigantic Babine or Francois lakes, at about 10 km (6.2 mi) long Augier is no bird bath. And in comparison, its setting has enough topographical relief to be dramatic. Forested hills rise 274 m (900 ft) above the shore. You can admire them from a pebble beach. The direct route to Augier—north on Old Babine Road from the town of Burns Lake—is described on page 472.

For a weekend stay, also consider **Taltapin or Division lakes.** Boaters prefer Taltapin because it's bigger. Division is a mere pond but has a more attractive campground.

Simply need a place to crash for the night? Co-op Lake is convenient, east of town, just a few minutes north of Hwy 16.

If you're heading west on Hwy 16, from Vanderhoof

0 km (0 mi)
At the BC Hydro building (right) and community museum (left) in Vanderhoof, heading west on Hwy 16.

62.2 km (38.6 mi)
In the town of Fraser Lake, Francois Lake Road goes left (southwest).

82.6 km (51.2 mi)
Pass a sign welcoming you to Lakes Resort District.

102 km (63.2 mi)
Pass a pullout with a garbage can, on the left. Slow down. A few kilometers farther is the first turnoff for campgrounds to the north.

106.5 km (66 mi)
Turn right (north) onto Augier FS road for Co-op or Taltapin Lakes. For Division, Pinkut and Augier lakes, continue northwest on Hwy 16 to the town of Burns Lake. Read further directions on page 472. Set your trip odometer to 0 whether turning or continuing.

Turning right (north) off Hwy 20, onto Augier FS road, 106.4 km (66 mi) west of Vanderhoof. Set your trip odometer to 0.

0 km (0 mi)
Starting north on Augier FS road.

2.2 km (1.4 mi)
Turn right for Co-op Lake campground. It's 300 meters off the main road.

CO-OP LAKE CAMPGROUND #4
Overnight / Easy / Free
Elev: 900 m (2952 ft) / Lake: 34 ha
5 tables around a big clearing
Accessible by motorhomes and 5th-wheels

Continuing north on Augier FS road, passing the turnoff to Co-op Lake campground.

4.8 km (3 mi)
Stay straight on the main road.

24 km (14.9 mi)
Reach a major junction. Turn right for Taltapin Lake. Continue left for Pinkut and Augier lakes.

0 km (0 mi)
Turning right, starting northeast on Augier-Taltapin FS road, heading for Taltapin Lake.

1.9 km (1.2 mi)
Cross a small bridge, then fork right.

5 km (3 mi)
Go right at the fork.

6.1 km (3.8 mi) and 7.1 km (4.4 mi)
Bear left.

8.2 km (5.1 mi)
Arrive at Taltapin Lake campground. Right leads 50 meters to 4 tables. Left leads 0.4 km (0.25 mi) to seven tables. A clearcut mars the view. Other lakes in the area are more appealing.

TALTAPIN LAKE CAMPGROUND #5
Weekend / Difficult (due only to distance) / Free
Elev: 884 m (2900 ft) / Lake: 16 km (10 mi) long, 2105 ha
5 tables around a big clearing
Accessible by motorhomes and 5th-wheels

Continuing left (northwest) on Augier FS road, passing the turnoff to Taltapin Lake campground.

34.2 km (21.2 mi)
Reach a major intersection. **Turn sharply right** to enter Pinkut Lake campground in 0.5 km (0.3 mi). **Turn left** to quickly arrive at Division Lake campground or proceed southwest to Hwy 16 and the town of Burns Lake. **Continue straight** (north) on Augier Main FS road for Augier Lake campground (read further directions at the top of page 473).

PINKUT LAKE CAMPGROUND #7
Weekend / Difficult (due only to distance) / Free
Elev: 930 m (3050 ft) / Lake: 7.5 km (4.7 mi) long, 586 ha
5 tables, good boat launch
Accessible by motorhomes and 5th-wheels

Turning left (southwest) onto Old Babine Road, from the 34.2-km (21.2-mi) junction on Augier FS road. Set your trip odometer to 0.

0 km (0 mi)
Starting southwest on Old Babine Road, heading for Division Lake and Hwy 16.

Pinkut Lake

2.2 km (1.4 mi)
Turn left for Division Lake campground. It's 200 meters off the main road.

DIVISION LAKE CAMPGROUND #6
Weekend / Difficult (due only to distance) / Free
Elev: 975 m (3200 ft) / Lake: 25 ha
3 tables, 4 campsites
Accessible by motorhomes and 5th-wheels

~

Continuing southwest on Old Babine Road, passing the turnoff to Division Lake campground.

17.5 km (10.9 mi)
Reach Hwy 16, at the town of Burns Lake, across from Lakes District Secondary School.

~

Camp in a grove of quaking aspen at Sunset Lake.

For the direct route to Augier Lake

0 km (0 mi)
Starting north on Old Babine Road, from Hwy 16 in the town of Burns Lake, across from Lake District Secondary School. Set your trip odometer to 0.

15.3 km (9.5 mi)
Turn right for small Division Lake campground, 200 meters off the main road.

17.5 km (10.9 mi)
Reach a major intersection. Proceed straight through, then go right 0.5 km (0.3 mi) to enter Pinkut Lake campground, described on page 470. Continue left (north) onto Augier Main FS road for Augier Lake campground. Right is Augier FS road (good gravel), which you can follow southeast 34.2 km (21.2 mi) back to Hwy 16 by keeping right at main junctions.

Continuing left (north) onto Augier Main FS road, from the 17.5-km (10.9-mi) intersection on Old Babine Road, passing the turnoff to Pinkut Lake campground, heading for Augier Lake campground.

28.5 km (17.7 mi)
Turn right (east) onto Augier-Campsite FS road, near the KM 47 sign.

33.5 km (20.8 mi)
Arrive at Augier Lake campground, on the northeast shore.

AUGIER LAKE CAMPGROUND #8
Weekend / Difficult (due only to distance) / Free
910 m (2985 ft) / Lake: 10 km (6.2 mi) long, 906 ha
15 tables, pebble beach, good boat launch
Accessible by motorhomes and 5th-wheels

BURNS LAKE TO HOUSTON

Sunset Lake campground near Hwy 16 is handy if you're buzzing through the area. The soothing lake is ringed by low hills, and adorned with quaking aspen and sun-licking, lime grass. And it's just 5.3 km (3.3 mi) from the highway.

If you're heading northeast on Hwy 16, from Houston

From midway across the Bulkley River bridge, on the northeast side of Houston, drive 29.2 km (18.1 mi) to the hamlet of Topley. Set your trip odometer to 0. Turn right (south) onto Sunset Road.

If you're heading northwest on Hwy 16, from the town of Burns Lake

Drive 36 km (22.3 mi) to where the paved Broman Lake Frontage Road parallels the highway. Set your trip odometer to 0. Continue 14 km (8.7 mi) northwest on Hwy 16 to the hamlet of Topley. Turn left (south) onto Sunset Road.

For either approach, now follow the directions below

0 km (0 mi)
Turning south onto Sunset Road.

0.4 km (0.25 mi)
Cross railroad tracks and bear right on pavement.

2 km (1.2 mi)
Pavement ends. Continue straight.

4 km (2.5 mi)
Turn right onto Rondeau Road.

5.3 km (3.3 mi)
Turn right for Sunset Lake campground. Proceed straight, past the sign, through the barbed-wire fence. Turn left for the day-use area, right for campsites. Expect to hear cows bellowing across the small lake. If it's breezy, the rustle of quaking aspen will improve the concert.

SUNSET LAKE CAMPGROUND #9
Weekend / Easy / Free
Elev: 866 m (2840 ft) / Lake: 2.5 km (1.6 mi) long, 125.5 ha
6 tables, 5 campsites, good boat launch, dock
Accessible by motorhomes and 5th-wheels

MORICE RIVER & OWEN LAKE

Big, beautiful, weekend-worthy campgrounds await you south of Houston. Several smaller ones allow pleasant overnight stops on deeper forays. **Aspen** is just 18 km (11 mi) from Hwy 16. **Owen Lake** is farther (40 km / 25 mi) but worth it; the drive is easy, on a broad, well-maintained road. Both are provincial-park quality, and Owen is rated *Destination*.

If you're heading west on Hwy 16, through Houston

From the sign WELCOME TO HOUSTON just east of town, drive 7 km (4.3 mi) through the business district to the west side of town. Turn left (south) at the large signs described below. Set your trip odometer to 0.

If you're heading southeast on Hwy 16, from Smithers

Drive almost to Houston. Immediately after the railroad overpass just west of town, turn right (south) at the large signs described below. Set your trip odometer to 0.

For either approach above, now follow the directions below

0 km (0 mi)
Turning south on the prominently-signed paved road. You'll see a large, brown, wood sign with white letters NORTHWOOD - HOUSTON DIVISION. Small road signs point south FRANCOIS LK 64, MORICE LAKE 82, OWEN LAKE 40.

1.5 km (0.9 mi)
Pass the mill. Pavement ends. You're now on well-maintained Morice River FS road.

Aspen campground, on Morice River, is provincial-park quality.

17.8 km (11 mi)
Turn right for Aspen campground.

Arrive at the campground in 0.4 km (0.25 mi). It's lovely, beside broad, fast-flowing, quiet Morice River. An accommodating layout enables large RVs to park and turn around in an initial spacious clearing. Beyond are individual campsites separated by fir, spruce, aspen, and berry bushes.

ASPEN CAMPGROUND #10
Weekend / Easy / Free
8 sites with tables, exceptionally well-designed campground
Accessible by motorhomes and 5th-wheels

Continuing south on Morice River FS road, passing the turnoff to Aspen campground.

27.8 km (17.2 mi)
Reach a signed junction. Set your trip odometer to 0. Right soon reaches the Owen Flats campgrounds then proceeds southwest about 55 km (34 mi) to Morice Lake campground. Left leads in 15 minutes to Owen Lake campground, described on page 478.

Turning right (west) at the 27.8-km (17.2-mi) junction on Morice River FS road. Set your trip odometer to 0.

0 km (0 mi)
Turning right (west), still on Morice River FS road.

0.7 km (0.4 mi)
Cross a bridge. Immediately after, on the right, is the first of three roadside tables comprising Owen Flats "A" campground. The other tables are at 0.8 km (0.5 mi) and 0.9 km (0.6 mi).

OWEN FLATS "A" CAMPGROUND #11
Overnight / Moderate / Free
3 tables between the road and Morice River
Accessible by small motorhomes and trailers

Continuing west on Morice River FS road, passing Owen Flats "A" campground.

1.9 km (1.2 mi)
Stay straight where Chisholm FS road forks right, near the KM 29 sign.

2.3 km (1.4 mi)
Turn right for Owen Flats "B" campground.

Small motorhomes and trailers can make it, although your paint job might suffer. In 200 meters fork left. Arrive in another 150 meters. The narrow road loops back to the entrance. The campsites offer limited views. Across the Morice River is a stand of dead trees. Aspen campground is better.

OWEN FLATS "B" CAMPGROUND #12
Weekend / Moderate / Free
8 riverbank tables, room for only 4 vehicles
Accessible by small motorhomes and trailers

Continuing west on Morice River FS road, passing the turnoff to Owen Flats "B" campground.

3 km (1.9 mi)
Stay straight.

14.7 km (9.1 mi)
Bear right, continuing level on the main road. Pimpernel FS road ascends left.

Inviting expanse of grass at Owen Lake campground

17 km (10.5 mi)
Turn right (just before the bridge) for Lamprey Creek campground.

In 150 meters arrive at the campground, on the confluence of Morice River and Lamprey Creek. Trees block views of water from the campsites.

LAMPREY CREEK CAMPGROUND #13
Weekend / Moderate / Free
3 tables, comfortably spaced campsites
Accessible by small motorhomes and trailers

Continuing west on Morice River FS road, passing the turnoff to Lamprey Creek campground.

17.2 km (10.7 mi)
Reach a major junction. Right is Morice West FS road; there are no more campgrounds that way. Turn left to continue southwest on Morice River FS road. In about 38 km (23.6 mi) it ends at the northeast corner of impressively large and scenic Morice Lake.

55.2 km (34.2 mi)
Arrive at Morice Lake campground.

MORICE LAKE CAMPGROUND #14

Destination / Difficult (due only to distance) / Free
Elev: 797 m (2615 ft) / Lake: 40.5 km (25 mi) long, 9708 ha
18 tables, boat launch, glacier views, provincial-park quality
Accessible by motorhomes and 5th wheels

Turning left (southeast) at the 27.8-km (17.2-mi) junction (page 475) on Morice River FS road. Set your trip odometer to 0.

0 km (0 mi)
Starting on Morice-Owen FS road, heading southeast toward Francois and Ootsa lakes.

12.6 km (7.8 mi)
Turn right for Owen Lake campground. In 300 meters arrive at the campground—a big, open, very inviting grassy area scattered with tables. Owen Creek is nearby. The only secluded campsite is right of the dock. You'll find a little privacy farther west, away from the lake. All sites have views. Logging trucks are audible, but the road is obscured. A 10-km (6.2-mi) trail ascends to treeline on 2124-m (6967-ft) Nadina Mountain, visible west. For permission to hike, ask at Nadina Mountain Lodge, 1.5 km (0.9 mi) down the road.

OWEN LAKE CAMPGROUND #15

Destination / Moderate / Free
Elev: 762 m (2500 ft) / Lake: 7.5 km (4.7 mi) long, 296 ha
14 tables, dock, good boat launch, provincial-park quality
Accessible by motorhomes and 5th-wheels

A revitalizing plunge, after a long, hot, backcountry drive

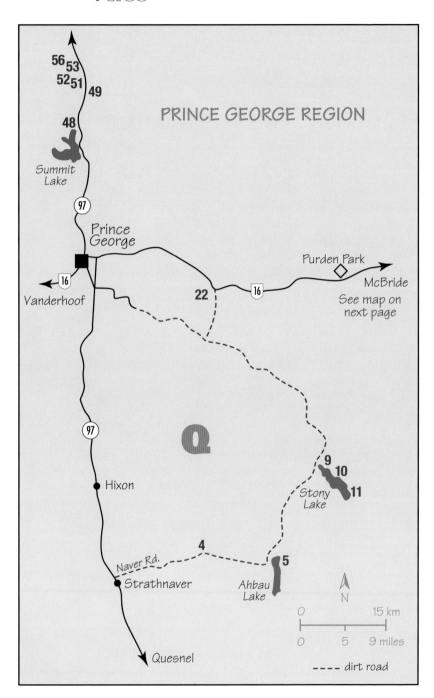

Q: Prince George Region

At the fee campgrounds, charges apply June 15 to September 30.

1	LaSalle Lakes	FREE
4	Naver Creek	FREE
5	Ahbau Lake	FREE
6	Holmes (Beaver) River	FREE
9	Stony Lake West	FREE
10	Stony Lake North	FREE
11	Stony Lake East	FREE
12	Yellowjacket Creek	$
13	Canoe Reach Marina	$
14	Horse Creek	$
22	Willow North	FREE
48	Summit Lake	FREE
49	Crystal Lake	FREE
51	100 Road Bridge	FREE
52	Dominion Lake	FREE
56	Davie Lake South	FREE

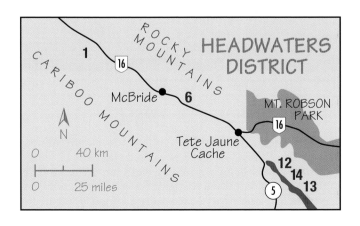

Prince George Region

Camping above Blackwater River, Prince George region

HWY 97 NORTH OF PRINCE GEORGE

Northbound travellers will find several handy campgrounds within an hour of leaving Prince George. The ragged shoreline of Summit Lake is pretty. Summer sunsets are a soothing sight here. The campground is comfortably spacious, with two distinct sections. A potential drawback, however, is noise. The nearby city occasionally regurgitates urban dissonance in the form of headbanging partiers. Vandalism has also been a problem.

So don't be surprised if a camping fee is instituted at Summit Lake, to help pay for a guard and maintenance. This would ensure a good experience for everyone.

Crystal Lake campground, 69 km (43 mi) north of Prince George, is as attractive as it is convenient. The well-spaced campsites are in a variety of forested settings including lakeshore, secluded niche, and atop a small knoll.

0 km (0 mi)
In Prince George, at the junction of Hwys 97 and 16, heading north on Hwy 97.

28 km (17.4 mi)
Cross the Salmon River bridge (blue metal).

50.4 km (31.2 mi) and 54.5 km (33.8 mi)
Ignore Summit Lake Road turnoffs on the left. They don't access the campground.

56 km (34.7 mi)
Turn left onto Tallus Road for Summit Lake campground.

> **0 km (0 mi)**
> Starting west on Tallus Road.
>
> **0.9 km (0.5 mi)**
> Turn right onto Caine Creek FS road.
>
> **1.8 km (1.1 mi)**
> The lake is visible. Turn left to enter the cleared section of the campground. Continue right to enter the treed section.
>
> **2 km (1.2 mi)**
> Arrive at the cleared section of Summit Lake campground.

SUMMIT LAKE CAMPGROUND #48a
Weekend / Easy / Free
Elev: 706 m (2315 ft)
Lake: 7 km (4.3 mi) long, 5.6 km (3.5 mi) wide, 314 ha
11 tables, more campsites
Accessible by motorhomes and 5th-wheels

Continuing to the treed section of the campground, from the 1.8-km (1.1-mi) junction on the access road.

In another 0.6 km (0.4 mi), reach the entrance. Turn left to arrive in 350 meters. This section feels more intimate because trees border the lakeshore and shelter the large grassy clearing.

SUMMIT LAKE CAMPGROUND #48b
Weekend / Easy / Free
7 tables, more campsites
Accessible by motorhomes and 5th-wheels

Continuing north on Hwy 97, passing the turnoff to Summit Lake campground.

69 km (42.8 mi)
Turn right for Crystal Lake campground.

0 km (0 mi)
Starting east on a broad, rocky road. In 0.5 km (0.3 mi), bear left.

0.8 km (0.5 mi)
Cross an oil pipeline swath.

2.3 km (1.4 mi)
Pass the first entrance.

2.4 km (1.5 mi)
Reach the main entrance to Crystal Lake campground. It's a small lake in the hills, ringed by lodgepole pine forest. Many spacious campsites are scattered around it. Don't drive or camp on the mossy, grassy groundcover, or it will soon be gone. You'll find plenty of bare ground to pitch your tent or park your vehicle on.

CRYSTAL LAKE CAMPGROUND #49
Weekend / Easy / Free
Elev: 724 m (2375 ft) / Lake: 36 ha
20 tables, rough boat launch
Accessible by motorhomes and 5th-wheels

Continuing north on Hwy 97, passing the turnoff to Crystal Lake campground.

70.3 km (43.6 mi)
Turn left onto Davie Lake FS road for two nearby campgrounds.

0 km (0 mi)
Starting west on Davie Lake FS road.

North of Prince George

1.3 km (0.8 mi)
A spur road descends to a lone campsite on the Crooked River.

1.7 km (1.1 mi)
Turn right to enter 100 Road Bridge campground. The Crooked River is
clear and slow-moving here. The bottom is rocky, the bank reedy. It's
ideal for canoeing.

100 ROAD BRIDGE CAMPGROUND #51
Overnight / Easy / Free
3 tables, 4 riverside campsites
Accessible by motorhomes and 5th-wheels

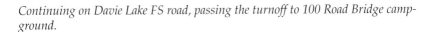

*Continuing on Davie Lake FS road, passing the turnoff to 100 Road Bridge camp-
ground.*

4.4 km (2.7 mi)
Turn left to enter Dominion Lake campground in 200 meters. It's on a treed
bench, so reaching the shore or seeing the lake is awkward. Other campgrounds in the area are superior.

DOMINION LAKE CAMPGROUND #52
Overnight / Easy / Free
Elev: 700 m (2296 ft) / Lake: 1.6 km (1 mi) long, 67 ha
2 tables, 4 campsites
Inaccessible by motorhomes and 5th-wheels

Continuing north on Hwy 97, passing the turnoff to 100 Road Bridge and Dominion Lake campgrounds.

76 km (47 mi)
Pass the turnoff to Crooked River Provincial Park.

77.6 km (48.1 mi)
Pass Grizzly Avenue in the community of Bear Lake. You can buy gas and food here.

78.6 km (48.7 mi)
Turn left for Davie Lake South campground. Big RVs will find the access rough but passable.

Drive 3.2 km (2 mi) off the highway. Fork left and descend to arrive in another 200 meters. There's a large grassy clearing. The campground is surrounded by bushy trees.

DAVIE LAKE SOUTH CAMPGROUND #56
Overnight / Easy
Elev: 683 m (2240 ft) / Lake: 6.5 km (4 mi) long, 938 ha
6 tables, good boat launch
Accessible by motorhomes and 5th-wheels

AHBAU & STONY LAKES, SOUTHEAST OF PRINCE GEORGE

Stony and Ahbau are beautiful, healthy-sized lakes graced with large campgrounds. Stony's campsites are mostly in the open, Ahbau's are treed. Stony has an especially wild, remote atmosphere despite visible clearcuts across the lake. On the way to these lakes, Naver Creek site is useful for an overnight stay. It's 19.5 km (12 mi) off Hwy 97, via an easy backroad.

If you're heading south on Hwy 97, from Prince George

0 km (0 mi)
In Prince George, at the junction of Hwys 16 and 97, starting south on

Ahbau Lake

Hwy 97 (signed for Airport and Vancouver). Set your trip odometer to 0. Follow signs for Quesnel.

60 km (37.2 mi)
Cross a bridge in the community of Hixon.

77.1 km (47.8 mi)
For Ahbau and Stony lakes, turn left (east) onto Naver FS road. Continue reading directions on page 488.

If you're heading north on Hwy 97, from Quesnel

0 km (0 mi)
Set your trip odometer to 0 at the sign ENTERING PRINCE GEORGE FOREST SERVICE DISTRICT. Watch for it on your right, after descending a long hill, about 29 km (18 mi) north of Quesnel.

12.8 km (7.9 mi)
Pass Dunkley Lumber Mill on the right (indicated as Strathnaver on maps).

14.4 km (8.9 mi)
For Ahbau and Stony lakes, turn right (east) onto Naver FS road. Continue reading directions on page 488.

91.5 km (56.7 mi)
Reach the junction of Hwys 97 and 16, in Prince George.

For either approach, now follow the directions above

0 km (0 mi)
Turning east onto Naver FS road, from Hwy 97.

4.2 km (2.6 mi)
Stay straight.

19.3 km (12 mi)
Reach a major three-way junction. Bear right for Ahbau and Stony lakes. Turn left for Naver Creek campground.

> **0 km (0 mi)**
> Turning left (north) on Naver FS road.

> **0.3 km (0.2 mi)**
> Just after the bridge arrive at Naver Creek campground. Turn right or left for campsites. Right is beside the creek. Left is away from the creek but has more shade and useful old cement foundations.

NAVER CREEK CAMPGROUND #4
Overnight / Easy / Free
4 tables, very convenient to Hwy 97
Accessible by motorhomes and 5th-wheels

Continuing southeast on Naver-Ahbau FS road, passing the turnoff to Naver Creek campground.

36 km (22.3 mi)
Cross the Ahbau Creek bridge.

36.4 km (22.6 mi)
Reach a signed junction. Set your trip odometer to 0 before turning either way. Bear left (north) for Stony Lake. Turn right (south) for provincial-park quality Ahbau Lake campground.

> **0 km (0 mi)**
> Starting on FS road 1000, heading south to Ahbau Lake.

> **2.7 km (1.7 mi)**
> Go right.

3.1 km (1.9 mi)
Reach a fork. Enter the campground either way. Right leads 300 meters
to 6 campsites with flat space for tents, plus a secluded site at the end.
A connector road linking the forks has 7 sites, 2 with tables. Along the
lakeshore are 7 tables; another 3 are across the road. All sites are treed,
most are level. The treed shore allows little room to play or relax.

AHBAU LAKE CAMPGROUND #5
Destination / Moderate / Free
Elev: 900 m (2952 ft) / Lake: 8.7 km (5.4 mi) long, 813 ha
24 well-spaced campsites, 15 tables, cement boat launch
Accessible by motorhomes and 5th-wheels

Continuing north from the 36.4-km (22.6-mi) junction on Naver-Ahbau FS road,
passing the turnoff to Ahbau Lake campground.

0 km (0 mi)
On Naver-Ahbau FS road, at the turnoff to Ahbau Lake, heading north for
Stony Lake.

2.5 km (1.6 mi)
Stay straight.

3.3 km (2 mi)
Turn left for Hay Lake campground.

> Descend from the main road to reach Hay Lake campground in about
> 75 meters. You'll find just one table at this beautiful, individual camp-
> site. It's accessible by motorhomes and 5th-wheels, but only if unoccu-
> pied; walk in and check before driving.

7.5 km (4.6 mi)
It's possible to launch a boat here at the north end of Lodi Lake.

14.5 km (9 mi)
Stay straight for Stony Lake.

17.2 km (10.7 mi)
Stay left on the main road.

18.8 km (11.7 mi)
Curve right.

22.2 km (13.8 mi)
Reach a junction with Willow FS road. Go right (southeast) on Willow FS
road to scenic campgrounds on Stony Lake's northeast shore.

26.7 km (16.6 mi)
Turn right for Stony Lake West campground.

In 50 meters reach the campground—a large, flat open area. It's excellent for swimming, sunning, or just enjoying the scenery. A campsite on the rocky beach is the only one with a lake view.

STONY LAKE WEST CAMPGROUND #9
Weekend / Difficult (due only to distance) / Free
Elev: 992 m (3254 ft) / Lake: 8.7 km (5.4 mi) long, 876.5 ha
2 tables, 4 campsites, good boat launch
Accessible by motorhomes and 5th-wheels

Continuing southeast on Willow FS road, passing the turnoff to Stony Lake West campground.

27.7 km (17.2 mi)
A narrow road forks right, leading 0.5 km (0.3 mi) to an unofficial campsite accessible by small motorhomes and trailers. It's a big, open clearing on the lake, with room for two vehicles. You'll find no outhouse or tables.

30.2 km (18.7 mi)
Turn right for Stony Lake North campground.

Arrive at the campground in 0.4 km (0.25 mi). A grassy perimeter and distinctly-separate campsites create a spacious feeling. Views are of surrounding forested hills. The large, gravel beach is ideal for swimming and sunning. Canoeists can explore the lake's islands.

STONY LAKE NORTH CAMPGROUND #10
Destination / Difficult (due only to distance) / Free
Elev: 992 m (3254 ft) / Lake: 8.7 km (5.4 mi) long, 876.5 ha
3 tables, boat launch
Accessible by motorhomes and 5th-wheels

Continuing southeast on Willow FS road, passing the turnoff to Stony Lake North campground.

34 km (21.1 mi)
Bear right.

34.6 km (21.5 mi)
Turn right to enter Stony Lake East campground in just 200 meters.

Stony Lake East campground

STONY LAKE EAST CAMPGROUND #11

Destination / Difficult (due only to the distance) / Free
Elev: 992 m (3254 ft) / Lake: 8.7 km (5.4 mi) long, 876.5 ha
2 tables on an open, gravel beach, good views, boat launch
Accessible by motorhomes and 5th-wheels

PRINCE GEORGE TO MCBRIDE VIA HWY 16

Want to camp along Hwy 16 between Prince George and Mt. Robson Provincial Park? You have three choices. None will disappoint, because all are well maintained, in enjoyable settings, mere minutes from pavement.

Willow North is near P.G. It's small, on the Willow River, with a sufficient buffer from the highway so you won't hear vehicles whooshing past. LaSalle Lake, northwest of McBride, is more inviting, but traffic is audible. Beaver River, southeast of McBride, is a model campground offering a rare combination of peace, beauty and convenience.

East of Purden Lake, it's as if the hills of the Interior Plateau finally begin to mature. No longer soft, innocent adolescents, they puff out their chests, flex their muscles, and swagger like aspiring young mountains. Where Hwy 16 bends southeast through the valley, the Rockies rear up to your left, the Cariboos to your right. Upon reaching McBride, you're surrounded by peaks. Trailhead turnoffs are signed along the way.

If you're heading east on Hwy 16, from Prince George

0 km (0 mi)
In Prince George, at the junction of Hwys 97 and 16.

12.6 km (7.8 mi)
Pass the turnoff for Giscome and Upper Fraser River.

29 km (18 mi)
Turn left (north) and descend to reach a secluded rest area in about 150 meters. It's treed, beside the Willow River. A sign states you must limit your stay to 8 hours. Fires and tents are prohibited.

29.2 km (18.1 mi)
Cross the Willow River bridge.

30.5 km (18.9 mi)
Pass a pullout with garbage cans. Just after, turn right (south) for Willow North campground.

> **0 km (0 mi)**
> Starting south on Willow North FS road.
>
> **0.2 m (0.1 mi)**
> Fork right and descend.
>
> **0.7 km (0.4 mi)**
> Pass a tent pad and fire ring on the left.
>
> **0.8 km (0.5 mi)**
> Arrive at Willow North campground. It's a large, flat, gravel area on the Willow River. The small river rapids enhance the atmosphere. Highway traffic is not audible.

WILLOW NORTH CAMPGROUND #22

Overnight / Easy / Free
3 tables, 1 tent pad
Inaccessible by large motorhomes and 5th-wheels

Continuing east on Hwy 16, passing the turnoff to Willow North campground.

LaSalle Lake

50.8 km (31.5 mi)
Pass **Bowron Rest Area** on the left.

53.5 km (33.2 mi)
Pass the turnoff to Purden Lake Provincial Park.

156 km (96.7 mi)
Pass the signed turnoff for Crescent Spur. Slow down for the next campground.

158.7 km (98.4 mi)
Turn right for LaSalle Lake campground. The turn is immediately north of where the southeast-bound lanes merge. The campground is just 0.4 km (0.25 mi) off the highway, so traffic is audible.

LASALLE LAKE CAMPGROUND #1
Overnight / Easy / Free
Elev: 880 m (2886 ft) / Lake: 11 ha
9 tables, a couple secluded sites, dock, grassy perimeter
Accessible by motorhomes and 5th-wheels

Beaver River

Continuing southeast on Hwy 16, passing the turnoff to LaSalle Lake campground.

165 km (102.3 mi)
Pass a rest area just before the Goat River bridge.

205.5 km (127.4 mi)
Enter McBride. Pass the Headwaters Forest District office on the left.

If you're heading northwest on Hwy 16, from McBride

0 km (0 mi)
On the northwest edge of McBride, at the Headwaters Forest District office.

40.5 km (25.1 mi)
Pass a rest area just after the Goat River bridge.

46.8 km (29 mi)
Turn left for LaSalle Lake campground. Read the previous page for details.

49.5 km (30.7 mi)
Pass the signed turnoff for Crescent Spur.

154.8 km (96 mi)
Pass Bowron Rest Area on the right.

175 km (108.6 mi)
Turn left (south) for Willow North campground. Read further directions on page 492, from the 30.5-km point.

176.5 km (109.4 mi)
Turn right (north) and descend to reach a secluded rest area in about 150 meters. It's treed, beside the Willow River. A sign states you must limit your stay to 8 hours. Fires and tents are prohibited.

193 km (119.6 mi)
Pass the turnoff for Giscome and Upper Fraser River.

205.5 km (127.5 mi)
Arrive in Prince George at the junction of Hwys 97 and 16.

SOUTHEAST OF MCBRIDE

Near the Rockies, guarded by muscular mountains, is the tidy little town of McBride. It's small enough and has sufficient charm that it adds to, rather than detracts from, the beauty of Robson Valley. A short drive east of McBride is Beaver River campground, which has the rare distinction of being convenient (just off Hwy 16), scenic (on a pretty bend of the river), and well kept (the FS office is in the nearby town). Southeast of McBride are campgrounds—described below—on Kinbasket Lake, where the topography is so grand that first-time visitors point, exclaim, and stare. It makes you wonder if Mt. Robson Park's west boundary is too far east.

If you're heading southeast on Hwy 16, from McBride

0 km (0 mi)
Just outside McBride, midway across the Fraser River bridge. Before the bridge, pass a highway sign ALBERTA BORDER 145, JASPER 171. (Soon after the bridge, pass a left-turn sign for a hiking trail on 2270-m / 7446-ft McBride Peak. The trailhead is reached via Rainbow Road, which is rough, narrow, extremely steep, and on the edge of a near-vertical slope. There are no warning signs, but it's dangerous. Only experienced off-roaders piloting small, powerful 4WD vehicles should attempt it.)

9.8 km (6.1 mi)
Midway across the Holmes River bridge.

10 km (6.2 mi)
Turn left (east) onto Holmes River FS road for the Beaver River campground. Set your trip odometer to 0.

If you're heading northwest on Hwy 16, from Tete Jaune Cache

From the junction of Hwys 5 and 16 at Tete Jaune Cache, drive Hwy 16 northwest 52.7 km (32.7 mi). Turn right (east) onto Holmes River FS road, just before the bridge. (It's 11.3 km / 7 mi past Baker Creek Rest Area, and 11 km / 6.8 mi before McBride.) Set your trip odometer to 0.

For either approach above, now follow the directions below

In 300 meters pass a rockslide and cross a cattle guard. Proceed along the southeast side of the river. At 1.1 km (0.7 mi) turn left through a big, brown, gated fence to arrive at the campground. A short trail leads downstream to Beaver Falls.

BEAVER RIVER CAMPGROUND #6
Weekend / Easy / Free
6 riverside tables, some sites in trees, audible river
Accessible by motorhomes and 5th-wheels

KINBASKET LAKE

Wedged between the Columbia Mountains on the west and the Rocky Mountains on the east is Kinbasket Lake. It's 210 km (130 mi) long and sits at 755 m (2475 ft) elevation. The campgrounds described below are on Canoe Reach, the lake's north arm. Just 20 km (12.4 mi) of off-pavement driving can earn you a secluded campsite with spectacular scenery. Views are across the turquoise water to 2653-m (8700-ft) Mt. Thompson and other burly peaks coated with lush vegetation and draped with glaciers. The lakeshore is rocky and the water frigid, so don't plan on swimming. If you're hauling a boat, check out the excellent facilities at Canoe Reach Marina campground. That's also where you can most easily maneuver a large RV.

If you're heading south on Hwy 5, from Tete Jaune Cache

From midway across the Fraser River bridge, at the junction of Hwys 16 and 5, drive south 19.8 km (12.3 mi) to the Visitor Information Centre (on the left) in Valemount. Continue south 3.3 km (2 mi) to a large sign SLOCAN FOREST PRODUCTS LTD. Turn left (east) here, onto Cedarside Road, also signed for Kinbasket Lake. Set your trip odometer to 0.

If you're heading north on Hwy 5, toward Valemount

A couple kilometers before Valemount's business district, look for a large sign SLOCAN FOREST PRODUCTS LTD. Turn right (east) here, onto Cedarside Road, also signed for Kinbasket Lake. Set your trip odometer to 0.

Kinbasket Lake

For either approach above, now follow the directions below

0 km (0 mi)
Turning east off Hwy 5, toward Slocan Forest Products. Immediately turn left (staying on pavement) toward the weigh scales. Do not go straight on the dirt road into the mill.

2.6 km (1.6 mi)
Cross railroad tracks and Canoe Road. Proceed straight onto the dirt road.

10.1 km (6.3 mi)
Reach a junction. Go straight onto Canoe East FS road. Kinbasket Lake is visible in 2 km (1.2 mi). Right at the junction follows the lake's west shore.

22.8 km (14.1 mi)
Turn right for Yellowjacket Creek campground. Descend from the main road. In 300 meters the road forks at a sign. Go right then straight to arrive at a rocky beach in 150 meters. Left leads 150 meters to campsites—the nicest on Canoe Reach. Trees provide shelter from wind and sun.

YELLOWJACKET CREEK CAMPGROUND #12
Destination / Moderate / $ / June 15 – Sept 30
4 tables secluded in trees, 2 more campsites, rocky beach
Accessible by small motorhomes and trailers, but not 5th-wheels

Continuing south on Canoe East FS road, passing the turnoff to Yellowjacket Creek campground.

23 km (14.3 mi)
Cross a bridge over a creek.

23.3 km (14.4 mi)
Bear right at the fork.

25.9 km (16.1 mi)
Cross bridged Horse Creek.

26 km (16.2 mi)
Turn right for Horse Creek campground. Descend from the main road. In 50 meters fork either way to treed campsites. Some near the lakeshore have views.

HORSE CREEK CAMPGROUND #14
Destination / Moderate / $ / June 15 – Sept 30
3 tables, 6 more campsites, rocky beach
Accessible by small motorhomes and trailers, but not 5th-wheels

Continuing south on Canoe East FS road, passing the turnoff to Horse Creek campground.

26.4 km (16.4 mi)
Turn right for Canoe Reach Marina campground, beyond which there are no more campgrounds on the east shore of Kinbasket Lake. Descend from the main road. In 0.5 km (0.3 mi) arrive at the campground: a large, open, level, gravel lot.

CANOE REACH MARINA CAMPGROUND #13
Destination / Moderate / $ / June 15 – Sept 30
7 tables, cooking shelter, sandy playpen for kids
breakwater, cement boat ramp, mooring dock
Accessible by motorhomes and 5th-wheels

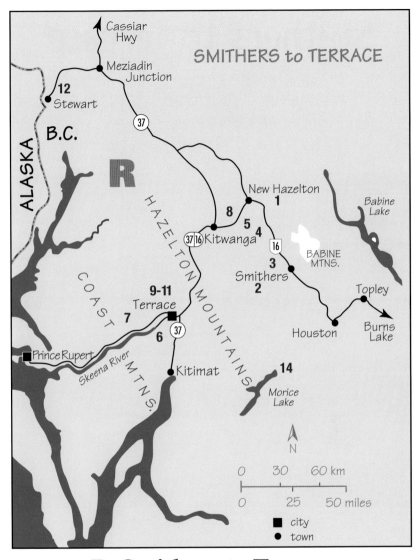

SMITHERS to TERRACE

R: Smithers to Terrace

1	Suskwa River	FREE	7	Exstew River	FREE
2	Dennis Lake	FREE	8	Keynton (Bell) Lake	FREE
3	Twin Falls	FREE	9	Pine Lakes	FREE
4	Taltzen Lake	FREE	10	Red Sand Lake	FREE
5	Kitseguecla Lake	FREE	11	Hart Farm	FREE
6	Lakelse River	FREE	12	Clements Lake	FREE

Smithers to Terrace

Excellent unofficial campsite on the Bulkley River, when it's not in flood

NEAR SMITHERS

Ask any young, mountain-minded athlete, "What are the primo towns in B.C.?" The shortlist is sure to include Smithers. It faces the Babine Mountains across the Bulkley Valley, while sitting comfortably with its back against the Hudson Bay Range. So, if you're a hiker or mountain biker, this isn't just a place to camp while travelling through. The Smithers area deserves an entire week of your precious vacation time.

Smithers has several free campgrounds within 30 or 45 minutes' drive: (1) Dennis Lake is 29.5 km (18.3 mi) west; (2) Twin Falls is 9.3 km (5.8 mi) northwest; (3) Taltzen and Kitsequecla lakes are 38 km (23.6 mi) northwest.

Crater Lake, on the slopes of Hudson Bay Mtn, is an enjoyable hike for families.

(1) Dennis Lake (page 502) is rated Destination, largely because of excellent hiking opportunities nearby. For non-hikers, it's a long drive for just a brief overnight stay. The potholed access road can get very muddy. And the campground is too small for motorhomes and trailers. But the scenery includes Hudson Bay Mountain, where you'll find one of the area's premier trails. Drive to the ski area, park at road's end, then ascend past the cabins to pick up the trail gently rising through meadows to Crater Lake. Scramblers can push on to the summit. The Silvern Creek trail is also close to Dennis Lake.

(2) Twin Falls (page 503) is primarily a trailhead and day-use area. The cascades plunging 150 m (492 ft) from Kathlyn Glacier on Hudson Bay Mountain are a tremendous sight. Experienced hikers can climb the steep route up Glacier Gulch. It follows a boulder-shattering meltwater torrent to the glacier toe. The unofficial campground is tiny and the parking lot busy, so don't plan on more than one night here. But the campsites are beneath huge cedars, within earshot of the falls, the setting is spectacular, and the hiking superb. For those reasons, Twin Falls is rated Destination.

(3a and 3b) Taltzen and Kitsequecla lakes (page 504) are beautiful. The ever-encroaching flora is remarkably lush. Cedars crowd the shorelines. Healthy Devil's club seems to float in mid-air (touch it for a painful explanation of its name). Across the lakes, distant mountains enhance the wild atmosphere. Both campgrounds are rated Weekend.

After an energetic exploration of the Bulkley Valley, you'll probably want to suds your duds, yourself, and your vehicle. In Smithers, check out Wash The Works, a spacious laundromat with clean public showers and a multi-bay car wash. It's between Queen and Manitoba streets, on Glacier Frontage Road, which parallels Hwy 16.

(1) DENNIS LAKE

0 km (0 mi)
Starting on King Street (one street southeast of Main), heading southwest from Hwy 16 in Smithers. Set your trip odometer to 0.

0.7 km (0.4 mi)
Turn left onto Railway Avenue, following ski-area signs.

2.5 km (1.6 mi)
Cross railroad tracks.

4.7 km (2.9 mi)
Pavement ends.

6.2 km (3.8 mi)
Stay straight, continuing uphill.

7.4 km (4.6 mi)
Bear right.

11.3 km (7 mi)
Stay straight on the main road, passing the turnoff to the cross-country ski area.

16 km (10 mi)
Turn left for Dennis Lake campground. Right leads to the ski area, where the Crater Lake / Hudson Bay Mountain trail begins.

19.3 km (12 mi)
Stay straight.

21.8 km (13.5 mi)
Bear left on McDonell Lake FS road.

24.1 km (14.9 mi)
Cross a bridged creekbed.

26 km (16.1 mi)
Turn right for Silvern Lakes trailhead.

26.9 km (16.7 mi)
Cross the Silvern Creek bridge.

29.5 km (18.3 mi)
Turn left for Dennis Lake campground. It's 0.8 km (0.5 km) off the main road. The rough, descending spur is passable in a 2WD car.

DENNIS LAKE CAMPGROUND #2
Destination / Moderate / Free
2 tables, 4 tent pads, good boat launch.
Inaccessible by motorhomes and trailers

(2) TWIN FALLS

0 km (0 mi)
At the junction of Hwy 16 and Toronto Street, in Smithers, heading northwest on Hwy 16. (There's a Taco Bell and KFC at this junction, as well as the last traffic lights before leaving town.) Set your trip odometer to 0.

2.8 km (1.7 mi)
Bear left at the Y-junction onto Lake Kathlyn Road. Immediately after, stay on the main road where Proctor forks left.

4.2 km (2.6 mi)
Ascend left on unsigned Kathlyn Road, toward the mountains. Beach Road continues straight. (Already you can see Kathlyn Glacier. The trail ascends just left of it.)

5.1 km (3.2 mi)
Go left on Glacier Gulch Road.

6.8 km (4.2 mi)
Stay straight on pavement and keep ascending. Davidson Road (dirt) forks right.

6.9 km (4.3 mi)
Pavement ends. Proceed straight on the better dirt road.

9.3 km (5.8 mi)
Arrive at Twin Falls day-use area and unofficial campground.

TWIN FALLS CAMPGROUND #3
Destination / Easy / Free
2 tables, Glacier Gulch hiking trail
Accessible by small motorhomes and trailers

(3a) TALTZEN LAKE

If you're heading northwest on Hwy 16, from Smithers

0 km (0 mi)
At the junction of Hwy 16 and Toronto Street, in Smithers. (There's a Taco Bell and KFC at this junction, as well as the last traffic lights before leaving town.) Set your trip odometer to 0.

21.5 km (13.3 mi)
Cross Trout Creek bridge.

23.6 km (14.6 mi)
Turn left (west) onto Kitsequecla Road. Reset your trip odometer to 0.

If you're heading southeast on Hwy 16, from Moricetown

0 km (0 mi)
At the paved Moricetown Canyon overlook—worth stopping to see. Set your trip odometer to 0.

5.8 km (3.6 mi)
Pass the north end of Kitsequecla Road.

7.3 km (4.5 mi)
Turn right (west) onto the south end of Kitsequecla Road. Reset your trip odometer to 0.

For either approach above, now follow the directions below

0 km (0 mi)
Starting on Kitsequecla Road.

0.7 km (0.4 mi)
Turn left onto Kitsequecla Lake Road.

9.6 km (6 mi)
Stay right on the main road.

13.7 km (8.5 mi)
Stay left on the main road.

Twin Falls

14 km (8.7 mi)
Pass Taltzen Lake.

14.4 km (8.9 mi)
Turn left and descend to reach Taltzen Lake campground in 200 meters. The lake is tiny but beautiful. See photo on page 347.

TALTZEN LAKE CAMPGROUND #4
Weekend / Easy / Free
Elev: 700 m (2296 ft) / Lake: 10.6 ha
4 tables
Inaccessible by large motorhomes and trailers

(3b) KITSEQUECLA LAKE

Follow directions to Taltzen Lake, but instead of descending left, turn right onto the ascending spur road. Set your trip odometer to 0.

0 km 0 mi
Starting northwest on the spur road directly across from the Taltzen Lake turnoff. Ascend through lush forest on this narrow, rough road.

2.7 km (1.7 mi)
Turn left for Kitsequecla Lake campground. (Rocky Ridge Chalets are right.) The final 450 meters descend a rutted, narrow road. If dry, it's passable in a 2WD car. The mountain setting is scenic, but you'll find only 2 drive-in campsites. The other 2 are walk-in tents sites, 20 meters from road's end.

KITSEQUECLA LAKE CAMPGROUND #5
Weekend / Moderate (due to rough access) / Free
Elev: 732 m (2400 ft) / Lake: 1.7 km (1.1 mi) long, 70.6 ha
4 tables, rough boat launch, dock
Inaccessible by motorhomes and trailers

NEAR NEW HAZELTON

Suskwa River and Keynton Lake campgrounds, both near New Hazelton, are small, well maintained, secluded, and in pretty settings. They're not spectacular, but even this is an advantage: they don't attract and hold crowds. If either is vacant when you arrive, you're assured of a lovely, soothing night in the bush. Free-camping in B.C. occasionally gets better than this, but not often.

Suskwa River campground is on a grassy riverbank clearing, deep in a forested river valley, east of New Hazelton, near the Babine Range. A few giant cottonwood trees add a touch of grandeur. Summers are less buggy here than at most lakes. Though accessible by motorhomes and 5th-wheels, Suskwa is too small to comfortably accommodate them.

Kitsequecla Lake

Also called Bell Lake, Keynton Lake is just big enough to be worth launching a canoe on. A few campsites are in a clearing on the shore. The view is north to the Kispiox Range. Keynton is accessible by small motorhomes and trailers, but you'll need a strong engine for the steep ascents. The smooth, scenic access road is west of New Hazelton, along the Skeena River.

SUSKWA RIVER

If you're heading northwest on Hwy 16 from Smithers, drive Hwy 16 to the paved Moricetown Canyon overlook (worth stopping to see). Continue 25 km (15.5 mi). Be ready to turn right.

If you're heading northeast on Hwy 16, from its junction with Hwy 37, drive through New Hazelton. Shortly beyond, set your trip odometer to 0 as you start descending near the turnoff for Ross Lake Provincial Park. Continue 8.5 km (5.3 mi) southeast. Be ready to turn left.

For either approach, turn north onto Suskwa FS road. It's near the crest of a hill, just southeast of a cement guardrail. Reset your trip odometer to 0.

For SUSKWA RIVER, now follow the directions below

0 km (0 mi)
Starting on Suskwa FS road, heading north from Hwy 16.

1.7 km (1.1 mi)
Immediately after crossing the Bulkley River bridge, stay straight (northeast) for Suskwa River campground. A spur forks right here, leading 200 meters to an excellent unofficial campsite on the river—accessible by small motorhomes and trailers.

4.5 km (2.8 mi)
Continue straight at the junction. There's a public phone here.

5.2 km (3.2 mi) and 6.1 km (3.8 mi)
Stay straight on the main road.

14.8 km (9.2 mi)
Cross the Suskwa River bridge. Just past the bridge, turn left onto Itzul West FS road.

15.5 km (9.6 mi)
Pass a small unofficial campsite on the left, beside the river.

17 km (10.5 mi)
Turn left for Suskwa River campground, before the main road ascends steeply around a slope. Arrive in 1.1 km (0.7 mi).

SUSKWA RIVER CAMPGROUND #1

Weekend / Moderate / Free
4 tables on a grassy riverbank clearing
Too small for motorhomes and 5th-wheels

~

KEYNTON LAKE

Drive Hwy 16 northwest from Smithers to New Hazelton. Turn right (north) off Hwy 16. Set your trip odometer to 0.

0 km (0 mi)
Turning north off Hwy 16, heading to Old Hazelton.

6 km (3.7 mi)
At the junction by the store and gas station in Old Hazelton, turn right onto Kispiox Valley Road.

Suskwa River campground

11.1 km (6.9 mi)
Cross the Kispiox River bridge and bear left.

11.9 km (8.4 mi)
Turn left onto the dirt road, initially ascending steeply.

19.6 km (12.2 mi)
Bear left on the main road—generally level to 15 km (9.3 mi). Roche de Boule is soon visible southwest.

26 km (16.1 mi)
Pass towering cottonwoods.

28.6 km (17.7 mi)
Cross a small bridge, then turn right and ascend.

> If you enjoyed the drive in, on your way out, you could go right at this junction. The road leads southwest through the hills to intersect Hwy 37 just north of Kitwanga. The distance to pavement is about the same as retracing your approach.

30.2 km (18.7 mi)
Go right at the fork.

31.1 km (19.3 mi)
Turn left and ascend steeply.

31.6 km (19.6 mi)
Reach the first site at Keynton Lake campground. The lake is just ahead.

KEYNTON LAKE CAMPGROUND #8
Weekend / Moderate / Free
Elev: 396 m (1300 ft) / Lake: 1.5 km (0.9 mi) long, 60 ha
6 tables in lakeshore clearing, 2 secluded campsites
dock, good boat launch
Accessible by small motorhomes and trailers

NEAR TERRACE

Terrace is a camper-friendly city. Five nearby campgrounds range from good to excellent: (1) Exstew River, 37 km (23 mi) west, on the way to Prince Rupert. Even big RVs can settle in here. (2) Lakelse River, 18.2 km (11.3 mi) southwest. The secluded sites are in a magnificent grove of giant cedars and spruce. But don't try to squeeze your Winnebago between them. (3) Pine Lakes, 11.6 km (7.2 mi) north. This is a good basecamp for hikers. A trail circles the lakes, and Sleeping Beauty Mtn trailhead is close. (4) Red Sand Lake, 26.6 km (16.5 mi) north. Perhaps the best MOT campground in central B.C. It's spacious, laid out like a provincial park, has plenty of lakeshore sites and ample room for titanic RVs. The long, sandy beach is ideal for swimming, Frisbee tossing, or novel reading. But Red Sand Lake is no secret. It's extremely popular. (5) Hart Farm, 27.6 km (17.1 mi) north, at the south end of Kitsumkalum (Kalum) Lake. The lake is way bigger than Red Sand, but the campground is much smaller and more intimate.

(1) EXSTEW RIVER

If you're heading northeast on Hwy 16, from Prince Rupert

In about 101 km (62.6 mi), look for the Exstew River bridge. Midway across, set your trip odometer to 0. In another 0.6 km (0.4 mi), turn left (northwest) onto Exstew River road (unsigned). Reset your trip odometer to 0. (If you reach a railroad overpass, you're too far.)

If you're heading southwest on Hwy 16, from Terrace

0 km (0 mi)
Midway across the Kitsumkalum (Kalum) River bridge, just past the sawmill and Canadian Tire store, on the west edge of Terrace.

One of the Seven Sisters, from Hwy 16, northeast of Terrace

20.2 km (12.5 mi)
Pass the turnoff for Shames Mtn. Ski Area on the right.

27.6 km (17.1 mi)
Cross a railroad overpass.

31 km (19.2 mi)
Turn right (northwest) onto Exstew River road (unsigned). It's just after a yellow sign warning of logging trucks. Reset your trip odometer to 0.

For either approach above, now follow the directions below

0 km (0 mi)
Starting on Exstew River road (unsigned), heading northwest from Hwy 16. Immediately cross railroad tracks.

5.8 km (3.6 mi)
Stay straight on the main road.

6.2 km (3.8 mi)
Turn left for Exstew River campground.

EXSTEW RIVER CAMPGROUND #7
Weekend / Easy (unless high water impedes access) / Free
Usually closed May long-weekend and the week prior
8 tables, more campsites
Accessible by motorhomes and 5th-wheels

~

(2) LAKELSE RIVER

From downtown Terrace, follow Lakelse Road across the Skeena River via the old, wood bridge (parallel to the railroad bridge). Just beyond the bridge, turn right (south) onto Queensway Drive. Go under the newer Hwy 16 bridge and set your trip odometer to 0.

From Hwy 16, heading west into Terrace, turn left (south) onto Queensway Drive just after the junction with Hwy 37 (Lakelse Road, leading south to Kitimat). Set your trip odometer to 0.

From Hwy 16, heading east through Terrace, cross two bridges over the Skeena River. After the second bridge, turn left (north) at the junction of Hwy 16 and Hwy 37 (Lakelse Road, leading south to Kitimat). Just before the old bridge over the Skeena, turn sharply left (south) onto Queensway Drive. Go under the newer Hwy 16 bridge and set your trip odometer to 0.

0 km (0 mi)
Starting on Queensway Drive, heading south, initially following the Skeena River.

5.2 km (3.2 mi)
Turn right onto Old Remo Road.

6.4 km (4 mi)
Bear right, staying on pavement. Cross railroad tracks.

7.3 km (4.5 mi) and 12.5 km (7.8 mi)
Stay right.

13.4 km (8.3 mi)
At the bottom of a small hill, turn left onto a rough, dirt road.

15.2 km (9.4 mi)
Stay straight.

17 km (10.5 mi)
The road is beside the Skeena River.

Cedars at Lakelse River campground

18.2 km (11.3 mi)
Turn left (before the bridge) to enter Lakelse River campground.

LAKELSE RIVER CAMPGROUND #6
Destination / Easy
10 tables, secluded sites among giant trees, provincial-park quality
Inaccessible by motorhomes and 5th-wheels

Spacious beach at Red Sand Lake

(3) PINE LAKES (4) RED SAND LAKE (5) HART FARM

0 km (0 mi)
Midway across the Kitsumkalum (Kalum) River bridge, just past the sawmill and Canadian Tire store, at the west edge of Terrace, heading west on Hwy 16.

0.3 km (0.2 mi)
Turn right (north) onto unsigned West Kalum FS road, identified by a gas station on the northwest corner. Pavement ends immediately.

6.4 km (4 mi)
Stay straight on the main road.

9 km (5.6 mi)
Stay straight for Pine Lakes, Red Sand Lake and Hart Farm campgrounds. (Left leads about 9.6 km / 6 mi to **Sleeping Beauty Mtn trailhead**. If you don't have 4WD for the final 1 km / 0.6 mi of road, you'll have to walk it. The trail ends at subalpine meadows and lakes in 2.5 km / 1.6 mi, but experienced hikers can continue up to alpine ridges.)

Head-high elderberry bushes flourish along roadsides in the Kispiox Range.

11.6 km (7.2 mi)
Stay straight for Red Sand Lake and Hart Farm campgrounds. Turn left for Pine Lakes campground.

> Pine Lakes campground comprises two small camping areas, each with a couple tables. Reach the first area in about 200 meters, on the right. The second is 0.6 km (0.4 mi) farther. There's only one Pine Lake, but the shore is serpentine, so there appears to be a couple lakes. A 6-km (3.7-mi) trail circles the lake.

PINE LAKES CAMPGROUND #9
Weekend / Easy / Free
Elev: 213 m (700 ft) / Lake: 27.5 ha
5 tables, hiking trail
Inaccessible by motorhomes and trailers

Continuing northwest on West Kalum FS road, passing the turnoff to Pine Lakes campground.

15.7 km (9.7 mi), 21.5 km (13.3 mi) and 24.7 km (15.3 mi)
Bear right at these forks.

26.6 km (16.5 mi)
Stay straight for Hart Farm campground. Turn right to reach provincial-park quality Red Sand Lake campground in 1 km (0.6 mi).

> The sandy lake is unique in this region. The mountain views are stirring. Most campsites are near the shore. Short, easy hiking trails begin here.

RED SAND LAKE CAMPGROUND #10
Destination / Easy / Free
Elev: 37 m (121 ft) / Lake: 38.5 ha
14 tables, 2 sites for disabled campers, cooking shelter
Accessible by motorhomes and 5th-wheels

Continuing north on West Kalum FS road, passing the turnoff to Red Sand Lake campground.

27.6 (17.1 mi)
Turn right to reach Hart Farm campground on Kitsumkalum (Kalum) Lake.

HART FARM CAMPGROUND #11
Weekend / Easy / Free
Elev: 122 m (400 ft) / Lake: 10.5 km (6.5 mi) long, 1905 ha
5 tables / Accessible by small motorhomes and trailers

HWY 37A TO STEWART

The scenery along Hwy 37A, between Meziadin Junction and Stewart, is the kind you see in coffee table books filled with extraordinary photographs. It's comparable to the Icefields Parkway through Banff and Jasper national parks. Here, 37 hanging glaciers are visible along a 60-km (37-mi) stretch of pavement. Where the water isn't frozen, it's gushing. Waterfalls plunge into this sheer-sided canyon like kids at a swimming-pool party. All manner of greenery thrives in the wet, coastal climate. Devil's club slurps up the moisture, growing taller than NBA players, sprouting leaves 45 cm (18 inches) wide.

More magnificence awaits you just beyond the quaint, fiord town of Stewart. Continue around the corner into Hyder, Alaska, then follow the road north for about 40 minutes to see the Salmon Glacier—fifth largest in the world—and mountains galore. If the weather is socked-in when you arrive, wait a day or two for the clouds to lift; the scenery is definitely worth it.

Another reason to visit Hyder is to watch grizzly bears congregate at nearby Fish Creek, where they feed on salmon. Between mid-July and

Glaciers are visible along a 60-km (37-mi) stretch of Hwy 37.

October, plan to spend several hours—7 to 10 in the morning, or 7 to 10 at night—waiting for the bears to appear. They almost always do. Observing them at close range in the wild is a unique and thrilling experience. US Forest Service rangers stand by to make sure people behave appropriately.

Its remote location and abrupt end at the sea ensure that Hwy 37A is never busy. So the overnight pullouts along the way are likely to be very quiet after dark. But use them with discretion and respect. Look for and obey any new signs prohibiting "overnight parking." Pull in late, drive away early, and leave no trace of your stay.

0 km (0 mi)
At Meziadin Junction, departing Hwy 37, heading west on Hwy 37A.

3 km (1.9 mi)
Pass an overnight pullout on the left, overlooking Meziadin Lake.

12.3 km (7.6 mi)
Cross the Surprise Creek bridge.

13 km (8.1 mi)
Pass a large overnight pullout on the left.

17 km (10.5 mi)
Turn right for an overnight pullout. It's across from three hanging glaciers.

19.2 km (11.9 mi)
Turn left for a comfortable overnight pullout beneath cottonwoods.

19.9 km (15 mi)
Cross the Little Entrance Creek bridge.

23.8 km (14.8 mi)
Proceed on Hwy 37A for Stewart. The paved road left (south) leads 0.6 km (0.4 mi) to **Bear Glacier viewpoint** and rest area. It might serve as a quiet overnight pullout.

25.4 km (15.7 mi)
Bear Glacier is visible nearby to the left.

29.7 km (18.4 mi)
Pass an overnight pullout on the left, just before the Cullen Creek bridge. A short road departs the highway, allowing you to park back in the trees. The roaring creek muffles highway noise. Terrific waterfalls are visible south.

33.6 km (20.8 mi)
Pass an overnight pullout on the right, beside a loud creek.

39.7 km (24.6 mi)
Pass a pullout with a litter barrel on the right.

44 km (27.3 mi)
Pass a round overnight pullout on the left, just before the highway swings right.

48 km (29.8 mi)
Pass a rest area.

Clements Lake

48.4 km (30 mi)
Turn left for Clements Lake campground.

> Reach a T-junction in 100 meters. Turn left, then proceed straight. Arrive at the lake 1.2 km (0.7 mi) from the highway. Impressive waterfalls are visible across the lake. There's a lone campsite about 30 meters past the first group of tables.

CLEMENTS LAKE CAMPGROUND #12
Destination / Easy / Free
Lake: 3 km (1.9 mi) long, 17 ha
4 tables grouped at the lakeshore, floating dock
Accessible by small motorhomes and trailers

Continuing southwest on Hwy 37A, passing the turnoff to Clements Lake campground.

59.6 km (37 mi)
Arrive in Stewart, on the north end of Portland Canal, next to the international border at Hyder, Alaska. Continue north of Hyder to see the Salmon Glacier.

Ministry of Tourism, Sport & the Arts
Recreation Districts

For information about campgrounds in a particular district, speak to the Recreation Officer. Instead of calling the office direct, dial Inquiry B.C. (660-2421 from within Vancouver, in Victoria 387-6121; 1-800-663-7867 from elsewhere in B.C.) Tell them the name of the office and the phone number. They'll connect you at no charge.

For on-line information about recreation regions, go to
www.tsa.gov.bc.ca/publicrec

The hours of operation for most offices are Monday through Friday, 8 a.m. to 12 noon, and 1 p.m. to 4:30 p.m.

Campbell R. / North Island District
ph: (250) 286-9422
370 S. Dogwood Street
Campbell River, BC V9W 6Y7

Cascades District
ph: (250) 378-8433
3840 Airport Road
Merritt, BC V1K 1B8

Chilliwack District
ph: (604) 702-5734
46360 Airport Road
Chilliwack, BC V2P 1A5

Columbia / Shuswap District
ph: (250) 837-7610
1761 Big Eddy Road
Revelstoke, BC V0E 3K0

Headwaters District
ph: (250) 587-6700
687 Yellowhead South, Hwy 5
Clearwater, BC V0E 1N0

Kamloops District
ph: (250) 371-4404
1265 Dalhousie Drive
Kamloops, BC V2C 5Z5

Kootenay / Boundary District
ph: (250) 365-8617
845 Columbia Avenue
Castlegar, BC V1N 1H3

Nadina / Skeena / Stikine District
ph: (250) 847-6337
3333 Tatlow Road
Smithers, BC V0J 2N0

North Coast / Kalum District
ph: (250) 638-5109
Room 200, 5220 Keith Avenue
Terrace, BC V8G 1L1

Okanagan District
ph: (250) 558-1728
2501 14th Avenue
Vernon, BC V1T 8Z1

100 Mile / Chilcotin District
ph: (250) 395-7823
300 S. Cariboo Hwy 97
100 Mile House, BC V0K 2E0

Prince George District
ph: (250) 614-7507
2000 S. Ospika Blvd.
Prince George, BC V2N 4W5

Quesnel / Central Cariboo District
ph: (250) 398-4754
200 - 640 Borland Street
Williams Lake, BC V2G 4T1

Rocky Mountain District
ph: (250) 426-1763
1902 Theatre Road
Cranbrook, BC V1C 7G1

S. Island / Sunshine Coast District
ph: (604) 485-0769
7077 Duncan Street
Powell River, BC V8A 1W1

Squamish District
ph: (604) 898-2125
42000 Loggers Lane
Squamish, BC V0N 3G0

Vanderhoof District
ph: (250) 567-6416
1522 Hwy 17 East
Vanderhoof, BC V0J 3A0

B.C. Road Map

Modestly priced B.C. road maps are available at Tourist Info Centres in towns and cities throughout the province.

If you live out-of-province, the Hello B.C. tourism office will mail you a British Columbia Road Map and Parks Guide and regional guides. Call 1-800-435-5622 from anywhere in North America, (604) 435-5622 from within Vancouver, or (250) 387-1642 from overseas.

REPORT ALL FOREST FIRES TO 1-800-663-5555

B.C. Stands for Best Camping

Camp Free in B.C. authors Kathy and Craig have free-camped all their lives. While she was still a baby in diapers, Kathy's parents took her camping most weekends. Her earliest memories are of her mother cooking dinner under a tarp draped from the back of the family's pickup while her father listened to the rain. As a boy, Craig was obsessed with fly fishing. He backpacked to remote trout streams, until he realized the joy of hiking and camping is an end in itself and all that fishing gear was just slowing him down. Together, Kathy and Craig have perfected the art of free-camping. Their camping adventures have taken them throughout North America, Europe, Patagonia, Australia and New Zealand. They've driven all kinds of vehicles to all kinds of places in all kinds of weather. It hasn't always been idyllic.

One time, they pitched their tent at midnight on the grounds of an English country manor. They were hitchhiking. Unable to afford a hotel, they had only two choices. A fenced, tussocky paddock crowded with cattle? Or the manor lawn? They knocked at the imposing door to ask permission, but nobody appeared. So they set their travel alarm for 5:30 a.m. The next morning, they packed quickly, left unseen, and walked three kilometers to Stonehenge. They watched it emerge from the fog at sunrise, before anyone else arrived.

Asleep under the stars beside a creek near Payson, Arizona, they were startled by a gang of Hell's Angels in the middle of the night. The bikers roared in, only a few feet from the Copelands' heads, but otherwise weren't a problem. Until morning. After the bikers took off, Craig discovered they'd dumped one of their buddies. He was bleeding and out cold.

Again in Europe, they were exploring the Cairngorm Mountains of northern Scotland. This time they were driving Freida—a rusty, old, Bedford Beagle they'd bought for CDN $150. As always, they wanted to camp free. A sign on a dirt road caught their eye: *Forestry Personnel Only*. They risked it, but couldn't find even a tiny pullout. So they started turning around, backed into a ditch and became hopelessly mired. "Guess this is where we say goodbye to Freida," Craig said. But before they could load their backpacks and start hiking, a forestry official drove up in his truck. After a light rebuke, he towed them out. Feeling lucky, the Copelands splurged that night and paid for a campsite at the national park.

On the Oregon side of the Columbia River Gorge is the Eagle Creek Trail, which the Copelands had just finished hiking. It was so late they decided to camp in their car at the trailhead, but later wished they hadn't. A light directly over their heads woke them up. Another hiker? A policeman? A thief? A murderer? They laid there wondering, zipped into their sleeping bags, stuffed into the back of their car, their hearts pounding with adrenalin. "He's going to break into the car," Kathy whispered. Craig roared like a bear. They saw the flashlight bob away into the night. It was probably a teenage burglar, but they didn't wait to find out. They raced onto the highway and, still dazed, approached the bridge over the Columbia. With Kathy still in her bag and Craig in his underwear, they presented an interesting site to the matron in the toll booth. They eventually fell asleep, parked on a residential street in North Bonneville, Washington.

Now you can understand why Kathy and Craig are thrilled to have lived in British Columbia, and now live nearby on the Alberta side of the Rockies. They say B.C. offers the easiest, most enjoyable, most abundant free camping of anyplace they've ever traveled.

The Authors

INDEX

Other Titles from hikingcamping.com

The following guidebooks were boot-tested and written by Kathy and Craig Copeland. Look for them in outdoor shops and bookstores. You can visit www.hikingcamping.com to read excerpts and purchase online. The website offers updates for each book, plus field reports on many of the trails and campsites.

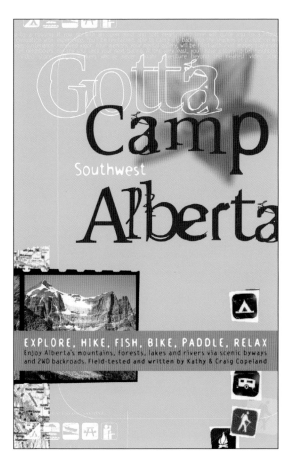

Gotta Camp Southwest Alberta

ISBN 978-0-9735099-0-8 Make your weekend or vacation adventurous and revitalizing. Enjoy Alberta's scenic byways and 2WD backroads—in your low-clearance car or your big RV. Follow precise directions to 150 idyllic campgrounds—from the foothill lakes to the Rocky Mountains. Camp in national parks, provincial parks, and recreation areas. Find retreats where the world is yours alone. Simplify life: slow down, ease up. Return home soothed by the serenity of nature. 400 pages, colour throughout. First edition, May 2007.

Don't Waste Your Time® in the Canadian Rockies
The Opinionated Hiking Guide

ISBN 0-9689419-7-4 Even in this glorious mountain realm, not all scenery is created equal. Some destinations are simply more striking, more intriguing, more inspiring than others. Now you can be certain you're choosing a rewarding hike for your weekend or vacation. This uniquely helpful, visually captivating guidebook covers Banff, Jasper, Kootenay, Yoho and Waterton Lakes national parks, plus Mt. Robson and Mt. Assiniboine provincial parks. It rates each trail Premier, Outstanding, Worthwhile, or Don't Do, explains why, then provides a comprehensive route description. 544 pages, 250 colour photos, 138 dayhikes and backpack trips, with a map for each. All-new 5th edition, updated July 2006.

Where Locals Hike in the Canadian Rockies
The Premier Trails in Kananaskis Country, near Canmore and Calgary

ISBN 9-9689419-8-2 The 55 most rewarding dayhikes and backpack trips within two hours of Calgary's international airport. All lead to alpine meadows, ridges and peaks. Though these trails are little known compared to those in the nearby Canadian Rocky Mountain national parks, the scenery is equally magnificent. Discerning trail reviews help you choose your trip. Detailed route descriptions keep you on the path. 296 pages, trail maps, full colour throughout. August 2005

WHERE LOCALS HIKE in the West Kootenay
The Premier Trails in Southeast B.C., near Nelson and Kaslo

ISBN 978-0-9689419-9-7 See the peaks, glaciers and cascades that make locals passionate about these mountains. The 50 most rewarding dayhikes and backpack trips in the Selkirk and west Purcell ranges of southeast British Columbia. Includes Valhalla, Kokanee Glacier, and Goat Range provincial parks, as well as hikes near Arrow, Slocan, and Kootenay lakes. Discerning trail reviews help you choose your trip. Detailed route descriptions keep you on the path. 272 pages, park maps, full colour throughout. Updated 2nd edition, April 2007.

Done In A Day: Whistler
The 10 Premier Hikes

ISBN 978-0-9735099-7-7 Where to invest your limited hiking time to enjoy the greatest scenic reward. Choose an easy, vigourous, or challenging hike. Start your adventure within a short drive of the village. Witness the wonder of Whistler and be back for a hot shower, great meal, and soft bed. Boot-tested, certified spectacular by the Opinionated Hikers: Kathy & Craig Copeland. Full colour throughout. 96 pages. First edition, summer 2007.

Done In A Day: Moab
The 10 Premier Hikes

ISBN 978-0-9735099-8-4 Where to invest your limited hiking time to enjoy the greatest scenic reward. Choose an easy, vigourous, or challenging hike. Start your adventure within a short drive of town. Witness the wonder of canyon country and be back for a hot shower, great meal, and soft bed. Boot-tested, certified spectacular by the Opinionated Hikers: Kathy & Craig Copeland. Full colour throughout. 96 pages. First edition, summer 2007.

Hiking from here to WOW in the North Cascades
50 Trails to the Wonder Of Wilderness

ISBN 978-0-89997-444-6 The authors hiked more than 1,400 miles through North Cascades National Park plus the surrounding wilderness areas, including Glacier Peak, Mt. Baker, and the Pasayten. They took more than 1,000 photos and hundreds of pages of field notes. Then they culled their list of favourite hikes down to 50—each selected for its power to incite awe. Their 272-page book describes where to find the cathedral forests, psychedelic meadows, spiky summits, and colossal glaciers that distinguish the American Alps. And it does so in refreshing style: honest, literate, entertaining, inspiring. Like all *WOW Guides*, this one is full-colour throughout, with a trail map for each day-hike and backpack trip. First edition, May 2007.

Hiking from here to WOW in Utah Canyon Country
110 Trails to the Wonder Of Wilderness

ISBN: 978-0-89997-452-1 The authors hiked more than 1,600 miles through Zion, Bryce, Escalante-Grand Staircase, Glen Canyon, Grand Gulch, Cedar Mesa, Canyonlands, Moab, Arches, Capitol Reef, and the San Rafael Swell. They took more than 2,000 photos and hundreds of pages of field notes. Then they culled their list of favourite hikes down to 110—each selected for its power to incite awe. Their 480-page book describes where to find the redrock cliffs, slickrock domes, soaring arches, and ancient ruins that make southern Utah unique in all the world. And it does so in refreshing style: honest, literate, entertaining, inspiring. Like all *WOW Guides*, this one is full-colour throughout, with a trail map for each dayhike and backpack trip. First edition, March 2008.